☆ ☆ ☆ ☆ ☆ ☆

GRAY FOX

ROBERT E. LEE *and the Civil War*

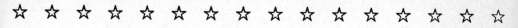

GRAY FOX

ROBERT E. LEE
and
THE CIVIL WAR

by Burke Davis

WINGS BOOKS
New York • Avenel, New Jersey

ACKNOWLEDGMENTS

Grateful acknowledgment is made to the following for permission to use copyrighted materials:

APPLETON-CENTURY-CROFTS, INC., New York, N.Y., for permission to use excerpts from A DIARY FROM DIXIE, by Mary Boykin Chesnut, Copyright, 1905, by D. APPLETON & COMPANY; from PERSONAL REMINISCENCES, by J. William Jones; and from GENERAL LEE, by Fitzhugh Lee.

DOUBLEDAY & COMPANY, INC., New York, N.Y., for permission to use extracts from RECOLLECTIONS AND LETTERS OF GENERAL ROBERT E. LEE, by Robert E. Lee, Copyright, 1904, 1924, by Doubleday & Company, Inc.

HOUGHTON MIFFLIN COMPANY, Boston, Massachusetts, for permission to use excerpts from A DIARY FROM DIXIE, by Mary Boykin Chesnut, edited by Ben A. Williams; and from Inman's SOLDIER OF THE SOUTH, Copyright, 1928.

HENRY E. HUNTINGTON LIBRARY AND ART GALLERY, San Marino, California, for permission to use passages from TO MARKIE, edited by Avery O. Craven, Copyright, 1933, by the President and Fellows of Harvard College.

CHARLES SCRIBNER'S SONS, New York, N.Y., for permission to reprint excerpts from REMINISCENCES OF THE CIVIL WAR, by John B. Gordon; and from MILITARY MEMOIRS OF A CONFEDERATE, by E. P. Alexander.

This edition is published by Wings Books, distributed by Outlet Book Company, Inc., 40 Engelhard Avenue, Avenel, New Jersey 07001 by arrangement with Holt, Rinehart and Winston.

Manufactured in the United States of America

Library of Congress Cataloging in Publication Data

Davis, Burke, 1913–
   Gray Fox: Robert E. Lee and the Civil War.

   Originally published: New York: Rinehart, 1956.
   Bibliography: p.441.
   Includes index.
   1. Lee, Robert E. (Robert Edward), 1807-1870. 2. United States—History—Civil War, 1861=1865—Campaigns and battles. 3. Generals—Confederate States of America. Army—Biography. I. Title.
E467.I.L4D3   1981   973.7'3'0924 [B]   81-3127
ISBN 0-517-34772-5   AACR2

17 16 15 14 13 12 11

CONTENTS

CONTENTS

LIST OF MAPS

FOREWORD

Robert E. Lee is one of the great tragic figures of American history, and one not well understood.

His reserve seldom permitted him to speak his inner thoughts, and almost never to reveal his emotions—but he could storm in a temper, as during The Seven Days when his plans went awry; he could mourn that he was to blame for defeat, as at Gettysburg; he could scold subordinates for the merest infraction of discipline; he could bare his soul, as on the morning of Appomattox.

But Lee was more often the gentleman-soldier of tradition, generous, forgiving, silent in the face of failure. In such a role he has seemed, as an historical figure, a hero of mythology. This book, which pretends to be nothing more than a swift, brief retelling of Lee's activities during the Civil War, is an effort to reduce the Lee of our myth to terms in which he can be understood by living Americans. The method is chiefly narrative propulsion based almost entirely on the testimony of eyewitnesses.

Richard N. Current, an able historian, author and Lincoln biographer, asked of this book: "Why *Gray Fox?* I have never thought of Lee in that way." I believe that the Lee who so incredibly drove the Federal army in the Seven Days, who split his army before superior force at Second Manassas, Antietam and Gettysburg, and courted ruin in his great stroke at Chancellorsville, was perhaps the most daring soldier of American history. Not only was he bold.

He made the most breath-taking moves out of what appeared to be military sagacity—but more often he handled his inferior force as if he could literally smell out the intent of the enemy, and he was seldom wrong.

Lee knew failure throughout the war and long before the end calmly and accurately predicted the Confederacy's fate. Yet, in the smashing climax which brought ruin, as Grant drove down upon Richmond through the Wilderness, Lee's movement of his army, confronting and checking the enemy time after time was done with such intuitive precision as to remain a military miracle to this day.

It will not require laborious study of his war against ever-superior armies in the Virginia theater to illuminate his shrewdness, courage, audacity in attack and tenacity in defense. The kindly face, fatherly beard and gentle manner have concealed too long one of the fiercest of the great captains. He left a glimpse of this when, looking down upon the slaughter of the enemy at Fredericksburg, he said, "It is well that war is so terrible—we should grow too fond of it."

Burke Davis

Cornwallis House
Guilford College, N.C.

1 "SECESSION IS NOTHING BUT REVOLUTION"
(*April 1861*)

COLONEL LEE and his guest walked out on the sixty-foot portico of Mrs. Lee's great house on the Virginia hillside to admire the view. Washington seemed quite close today, below them in the pale sunlight of early April. The city's familiar landmarks shone, as if they had been spread there as a view for Arlington:

The half-finished dome of the Capitol wore a crown of scaffolding with a raffish air; the stump of the Washington Monument rose amid acres of stone and rubble; the incomplete Treasury Building was already, they said, quarters for a regiment of cavalry; the fantastic red spires of the Smithsonian Institution bristled from a green plain.

Lee's visitor was Thomas B. Bryan, a friend from Illinois who was soon to join the growing Federal Army. He stood with the colonel beside one of the preposterously large columns copied from an Athenian temple and looked over the lawn where, not so many years before, the aging Lafayette had received his American friends on a farewell tour. Parkland and groves tumbled for half a mile to the Potomac. Water glinted beyond the trees.

The colonel was an arresting figure in plain, neat civilian dress.

He was fifty-four years old, but his five feet, eleven inches were held erect. Though he had a deceptively larger look, he weighed not quite 170 pounds. There was a subtle distortion of his physique which escaped all but the sharpest eyes: The upper body was enormous, on a scale to dwarf the narrow hips, slight legs and tiny feet. Chest and shoulders were massive, and his huge head rose from a short, thick neck.

He wore a brush of black mustache, with no beard. There were streaks of gray in his brown hair, but these were scarcely noticeable, despite his protest of thirteen years before, when he had come home from the Mexican War, that his family had stared at the furrows in his face and the white hairs in his head.[1] His complexion was highly colored. There was a quiet animation in his dark brown eyes.

Despite its rather heroic features—a large Roman nose, broad forehead and deep temples—the face was dominated by its expression of calm self-assurance; it was this, perhaps, which had so often inspired confidence in women, children, soldiers, secretaries of war, and the commanding general of the United States Army.

On this spring day only a vague sadness of face gave Lee's visitor a hint of his personal struggle through the weeks when the troubles of the country had been mounting, and the Union seemed to be dissolving.

The colonel gave no impression of wealth or expensive taste, either in his clothing or in the appearance of the manor house. This was accurate enough, for only lately he had so despaired of his low income as to give up the proper landscaping of his wife's home, and was forced to tend only small clearings about the house. It had not been long since he had confessed to his son Custis, "The necessity I daily have for money has, I fear, made me parsimonious."

Lately, too, he had revealed to a cousin a wry feeling of failure in life, of the "small progress I have made on . . . my professional and civil career." Until now, the fact was, his twenty-three years in the army had brought him no higher than the salary of $1,025 a year.

Lee and Bryan were not long on the hillside studying the sights, but there was a brief moment so striking to the visitor that it later seemed prophetic, and he could not forget it. Lee's voice dropped its tone of "almost jovial cheerfulness" to a "deep gravity."

The colonel raised one of his big hands, pointing over the water to the Capitol.

"That beautiful feature of our landscape," he said, "has ceased to charm me as it once did. I fear the mischief that is brewing there."[2]

If there was a proprietary air about his words, it was not strange.

Robert Edward Lee and the city—and the huge house, too—were much of an age. A more imaginative or self-centered man might have been aware of the kinship, whose bonds were much like those of the early history of the country itself. He was the son of Lighthorse Harry Lee, great cavalryman of the Revolution, also Washington's intimate and his funeral orator whose rhetoric seemed likely to endure: "First in war, first in peace. . ."

Robert Lee was born in the mansion Stratford Hall, not far away, in a room where, by family tradition, two signers of the Declaration of Independence had been born before him. His mother was Ann Hill Carter, of the line of old King Carter, one of the wealthiest of Virginia families. His boyhood began with his father's bankruptcy and imprisonment for debt, and had ended with his nursing his invalid mother in her fallen estate at an unpretentious house in Alexandria.

He was an honor cadet at West Point, and had gone to the war with Mexico at the elbow of General Winfield Scott, old Fuss and Feathers, whose admiration for Lee amounted almost to awe. Robert emerged from the Mexican War with a reputation as the army's most talented young officer. He had since filled every choice post to which influence and merit could guide him: He had headed the pet projects of the Engineer Corps in New York harbor, Florida,

Baltimore harbor, the Savannah water front, and had battled the Mississippi at St. Louis; he had been West Point's superintendent, had fought Indians on the border; had put down the John Brown raid with the capture of the Kansas fanatic. Until lately, he had been second in command in frontier Texas.

Men even now spoke of Scott's admiration for Lee, quoting the aging warrior: "If war comes, it would be cheap for our country to insure Lee's life for $5,000,000 a year."

Veteran officers remembered the days in Mexico, and some said that Lee's genius for handling troops had enabled Scott to win fame and his war "without coming from his tent."

In the three and a half months since the secession of South Carolina everyone seemed to turn to Lee; everlastingly, they had the same question as to his intentions. It was not surprising to him; this was a matter he had wrestled with long before, without coming to his final painful conclusion.

As long ago as 1856 he had seen the coming storm, and had written:

> Mr. Buchanan, it appears, is to be our next President. I hope he will be able to extinguish fanaticism both North and South, cultivate love for the country and Union, and restore harmony between the different sections.

He had also expressed himself on slavery at about that time:

> There are few, I believe, in this enlightened age, who will not acknowledge that slavery as an institution is a moral and political evil. . . . I think it a greater evil to the white than to the black race.

He did not, he said, think the Negroes ready for complete freedom:

> The painful discipline they are undergoing is necessary for their further instruction as a race, and I hope will prepare

them for better things. . . . Their emancipation will sooner result from the mild and melting influences of Christianity, than from the storms and tempests of controversy.

Not long after he wrote this, Lee had experienced personal distress over slavery; his wife's father, George Washington Parke Custis, died, leaving an involved estate. His will freed his slaves, who were to be given freedom when the estate was settled—within five years at longest. When time dragged on, three of the family Negroes ran away, were captured in Maryland, and sent deeper into Virginia to another plantation.

Several Northern newspapers had excoriated Lee, charging him with guile, and with cruelly whipping his slaves. Old Mr. Custis, one paper said, "had fifteen children by his slave women."

Lee's only recorded reaction was in a letter to his son Custis: "*The N. Y. Tribune* has attacked me for my treatment of your grandfather's slaves, but I shall not reply. He has left me an unpleasant legacy."[3]

In Texas, where Lee was stationed in the winter of 1860, he had clung to hope for the Union. He wrote his family that he would not permit himself to believe that the Union would be wrecked "until all ground for hope is gone." He added a note of hopelessness, however:

> . . . As far as I can judge by the papers, we are between a state of anarchy and civil war. May God avert both of the evils from us!
>
> I fear that mankind for years to come will not be sufficiently Christianized to bear the absence of restraint and force. I see that four states have declared themselves out of the Union; four more will apparently follow. . . . Then, if the border states are brought into the gulf of revolution, one half of the country will be arrayed against the other.
>
> I must try and be patient and await the end, for I can do nothing to hasten or retard it.

Lee was often called upon to declare himself in pre-war Texas, and his statements were unvarying: He stood for the Union, but could not think of making war on Virginia. One officer, R. W. Johnson, who served with Lee on the Indian frontier and was soon to become a Federal general, saw Lee as he was leaving Texas, called to Washington headquarters.

"Colonel, do you intend to go South or remain North?" Johnson asked. "I am very anxious to know just what you propose doing."

Lee replied, "I shall never bear arms against the United States —but it may be necessary for me to carry a musket in defense of my native state, Virginia, in which case I shall try to do my duty."

The Federal commander in Texas, General Twiggs, surrendered his command to state troops, in effect delivering all to the Confederacy. A sharp-eyed woman, Mrs. Caroline Darrow, told Lee the news in San Antonio, and wrote: "His lips trembling and his eyes full of tears, he exclaimed, 'Has it come so soon as this?'" At night, she overheard Lee praying in his hotel room.[4]

Lee did not waver from his course, but he seemed unable to speak or write of it without emotion. In a letter to a son, though it bore the marks of a struggle for calm, he revealed the depths of his feelings. He was by no means one with the Secessionists, but his country was Virginia:

> The South, in my opinion, has been aggrieved by the acts of the North, as you say. I . . . would defend any state if her rights were invaded.
>
> But I can anticipate no greater calamity for the country than a dissolution of the Union. It would be an accumulation of all the evils we complain of, and I am willing to sacrifice everything but honor for its preservation.
>
> I hope . . . that all constitutional means will be exhausted before there is a recourse to force. Secession is nothing but revolution. . . .
>
> It is idle to talk of secession. Anarchy would have been

established, and not a government by Washington, Hamilton, Jefferson, Madison and the other patriots of the Revolution. . . . Still, a Union that can only be maintained by swords and bayonets, and in which strife and civil war are to take the place of brotherly love and kindness, has no charm for me.

I shall mourn for my country and for the welfare and progress of mankind. If the Union is to be dissolved and the Government disrupted, I shall return to my native state and share the miseries of my people, and save in defense will draw my sword on none.[5]

And he had come home in that mood, just a few troubled days ago, having declared that he thought the world would have "one soldier less." The days had been full, and the country's tension had mounted rapidly: Twiggs had been dismissed from the army and replaced, Lincoln had been inaugurated, South Carolina had cut supplies from Fort Sumter in Charleston harbor. Near the end of March, Lee had flattering offers: A commission as a full colonel, signed by Lincoln—and a letter from L. P. Walker in Montgomery, Alabama, a lawyer, now styled Secretary of War, Confederate States of America, who offered the rank of brigadier general in the new army, ending rather insistently:

> You are requested to signify your acceptance of said appointment, and should you accept you will sign before a magistrate the oath of office herewith and forward the same, with your letter of acceptance to this office.

Many of his brother officers were acting, but Lee could not. For one thing, he was not convinced that Virginia would come to secession; there was wild talk of it everywhere, but he hoped there would be calm heads in Richmond.

Almost his first act, upon returning to Arlington in March, had been to call on General Scott. At the general's office he met an old friend, Lieutenant Colonel Erasmus Keyes, with whom he had served on West Point's Board of Visitors, and who was now secretary to Scott—a post Lee had once been offered. Keyes wrote: "Lee . . . entered my room and inquired if Lieutenant General Scott was disengaged. I stepped quickly forward, seized his hand, greeted him warmly, and said:

" 'Lee, it is reported that you concurred in Twiggs' surrender in Texas; how's that?' "

Lee's manner became one of "great seriousness."

"I am here to pay my respects to General Scott," he said. "Will you be kind enough, Colonel, to show me to his office?"

Lee was alone with the commander for two hours, and when he emerged did not tarry to talk with old army friends.

Keyes thought it a strange interview, for invariably, when Scott had an important talk, he reviewed it in detail for his military secretary. Keyes said:

"On this occasion he told me not a word, and he made no reference to the subject of his conversation with Colonel Lee. His manner that day, when we dined alone, was painfully solemn."

The secretary was positive, however, that Scott had offered to resign command of the Federal army in favor of Lee, and that Lee had declined the offer.

The house to which Lee returned literally shouted of the Union and its great early days. In every room, casually placed, were priceless relics from Mount Vernon: Portraits by famed artists of the young republic, paintings of Martha Washington and Nelly Custis; of Mrs. Lee's ancestor, Colonel Daniel Parke, who had taken Marlborough's victory message from Blenheim to Queen Anne; Washington's camp furniture, china, silver plate, punch bowls, watches—packets of his letters, including one announcing the arrival of the French fleet which had meant independence.

Robert Lee had come here courting, a penniless young aristocrat with an eye for Mary Anne Randolph Custis, one of Virginia's real heiresses, daughter of Washington's adopted son. It was almost thirty years ago; they were grandparents now, and the colonel's "Mim" was an arthritic invalid at fifty-three, looking much older than her years. She was to become the most vehement Confederate in the family, but this spring, in the very week Lincoln went to Washington, she wrote her daughter Mildred:

> I pray that the Almighty may listen to the prayers of the faithful in the land and direct their counsels for good and that the designs of ambitious and selfish politicians who would dismember our glorious country may be frustrated, especially that our own State may act right and obtain the mead promised in the Bible to the peace maker.

Mary Lee had been unable to walk normally for years, but she bore her pain with courage, and she often exhibited a strong will. Mary had loved Robert Lee from childhood, apparently, and had overcome her father's objections to marry him. There was every evidence that they were devoted companions throughout marriage. Lee's letters to her during their young married life had not been passionate, but were filled with expressions of affection, both for Mary and their seven children. He once wrote:

> You do not know how much I have missed you and the children, my dear Mary. . . . I . . . must again urge you to be very prudent and careful of those dear children. If I could only get a squeeze at that little fellow, turning up his sweet mouth to 'keese baba!'

Then there was a hint of the gentle patriarch:

> You must not let him run wild in my absence, and will have to exercise firm authority over all of them. This will not require severity or even strictness, but constant attention and an unwavering course. Mildness and forbearance will strengthen their affection for you, while it will maintain your control over them.

But it was to no avail. The most perceptive of their sons recalled that it was only the father who could command obedience. Yet young Robert never forgot the childhood scenes when Lee tumbled several of his children into bed with him, and made them lie there while he told them stories. He placed his feet in their laps at such times, and literally forced them to tickle his soles as he talked; when they ceased he would nudge them, saying, "No tickling, no story."

Mary had been dowdy and a bit untidy for most of her life, and she was only now beginning to primp and take notice of her appearance. Many years before, writing to prospective guests, Lee had seen fit to warn them that his wife was "somewhat addicted to laziness and forgetfulness" as a housekeeper.[6] Once she had risen from a long illness and, impatient with her snarled hair, had whacked most of it from her head.

But the colonel and "The Mim" were evidently one, and she was soon to organize one of the most faithfully industrious "sewing factories" of the Confederacy in her new home, working for his soldiers at the front.

War closed rapidly upon the Lees of Arlington.

On April twelfth the first shells burst upon Fort Sumter, far away in South Carolina. It was the signal for which the country had waited. The fort surrendered on April fourteenth, and the following day President Lincoln called for 75,000 men to suppress the rebellion which had been thirty years in the brewing. From his Potomac hillside Lee watched. He read *The Alexandria Gazette*, whose longest dispatches were from Richmond, where it was rumored that the convention had closed its doors for secret session. The natural assumption was that secession would follow. Lee learned of the closed meeting on April seventeenth.

On the same day he was called into Washington, by two messages. One was a note from his cousin John Lee, asking him to come tomorrow to meet Francis P. Blair, an old newspaper editor, once chief of *The Congressional Globe,* and a power in the Lincoln administration; Blair was father of the new Postmaster General, Montgomery Blair, who had befriended Lee in St. Louis long before, when he was seeking to tame the flow of the Mississippi.

The other message came from General Scott, a request to report to his office once more.

On the morning of April eighteenth Lee rode down Arlington's hill, across Long Bridge, past squalid cottages on a climbing roadway, along the canal skirting the incomplete monument to Washington, and to the heart of the city. He dismounted at Montgomery Blair's house at 1651 Pennsylvania Avenue, just opposite the War Department, and went in to meet the elder Blair. They talked alone.

Blair did not mince matters. Lee could have command of the enormous Federal army if he wished it. Secretary of War Cameron had ordered this offer of command through Blair, and there was the strong impression that the proposal came from Lincoln himself. Lee dismissed the affair in sparse words:

"After listening to his remarks, I declined to take the offer he made me, to take command of the army that was to be brought into the field, stating, as candidly as I could, that though opposed to secession and deprecating war, I could take no part in an invasion of the Southern states."

Blair did not give up; he pleaded with the colonel for an hour or more. Blair's son, Montgomery, soon had this tale from the old man, and wrote his own version of Lee's words:

"Mr. Blair, I look upon secession as anarchy. If I owned four millions of slaves at the South, I would sacrifice them all to the Union; but how can I draw my sword upon Virginia, my native state?"

Lee also wanted time to talk with his friend General Scott, Blair remembered.

Lee left Blair and went the short distance to Scott's office, and looked for the last time at the familiar face with its eyes embedded in fat. The general lumbered up to meet him, to his height of six feet four and one quarter inches.

Scott was the teacher of Lee's youth, and held his respect. Lee told the general of his refusal of Blair's offer.

"Lee, you have made the greatest mistake of your life," Scott said, "but I feared it would be so."

Scott's aide, E. D. Townsend, whose desk was in the room with the general's round table, wrote:

"I quietly arose, keeping my eye on the general, for it seemed probable he might wish to be alone with Lee. He, however, secretly motioned me to keep my seat."

Townsend recorded the conversation:

"These are times when every officer in the United States should fully determine what course he will pursue and frankly declare it," Scott said. "No one should continue in government employ without being actively employed."

Lee did not respond.

"Some of the Southern officers are resigning," Scott said, "possibly with the intention of taking part with their states. They make a fatal mistake. The contest may be long and severe, but eventually the issue must be in favor of the Union. . . .

"I suppose you will go with the rest. If you purpose to resign, it is proper you should do so at once; your present attitude is an equivocal one."

"The property belonging to my children, all they possess, lies in Virginia," Lee said. "They will be ruined, if they do not go with their state. I cannot raise my hand against my children."

Lee left Scott and visited for a time with his older brother, Sidney Smith Lee, a Navy captain, but neither made an immediate decision about leaving the service or enlisting with Virginia.[7]

As Robert left the capital he saw signs of excitement. The

Washington papers were screaming the news of Virginia's secession, but it was not yet official.

Lee rode into Alexandria the next day. He saw volunteers at drill on vacant lots, and the more polished Mount Vernon Guards, parading under strange new colors. The rooms of the Young Men's Christian Association were filled with women sewing at uniforms.

Lee saw the dread news in print in *The Alexandria Gazette*: Virginia's secession was approved by the convention; it was true. Within a month the people of the state would vote on the act—they were virtually certain to ratify it. He went into a pharmacy shop to pay a household account, and sighed as he stood at the counter:

"I must say that I am one of those dull creatures that cannot see the good of secession."

The merchant was so struck by these words that he scribbled them on his ledger, adding, "Spoken by Colonel R. E. Lee, when he paid this bill, April 19, 1861."[8]

The colonel went home. After supper, while Mary sat in the well-used old family sitting room, he went upstairs to his own room. She listened as he paced the floor above; she waited through long periods of silence.

At last she heard him drop to his knees for prayer. It was after midnight—long after—when he came down with a letter in his hand.

"Well Mary," he said," the question is settled. Here is my resignation and a letter I have written General Scott."[9]

There was a brief note to Secretary of War Cameron, and the longer one to Scott:

Arlington,Va., April 20, 1861

General:

Since my interview with you on the 18th inst. I have felt that I ought no longer to retain my commission in the Army. I therefore tender my resignation, which I request you will recommend for acceptance. I would have presented it at once, but for the struggle it has cost me to separate myself from a service to which I have devoted all the best years of my life and all the ability I possessed.

During the whole of that time—more than a quarter of a century—I have experienced nothing but kindness from my superiors and a most cordial friendship from my comrades. To no one, General, have I been as much indebted as to yourself for uniform kindness and consideration. I shall carry to the grave the most grateful recollections of your kind consideration, and your name and fame will always be dear to me.

Save in defence of my native State, I never desire again to draw my sword.

Be pleased to accept my most earnest wishes for the continuance of your happiness and prosperity, and believe me, most truly yours,

R. E. Lee

Lee next wrote a letter of explanation to his sister Ann—Mrs. William Louis Marshall, whose husband clung to the Union. He enclosed a copy of his resignation to Ann, and wrote in part:

Now we are in a state of war which will yield to nothing. The whole South is in a state of revolution, into which Virginia, after a long struggle, has been drawn; and, though I recognize no necessity for this state of things . . . yet in my own person I had to meet the question whether I should take part against my native State. . . .

I know you will blame me; but you must think as kindly of me as you can, and believe that I have endeavored to do what I thought right. . . .

He also wrote to his brother Smith, explaining that Virginia's secession had forced him to act quickly, and repeating once more the phrase: "Save in defence of my native State, I have no desire ever again to draw my sword."

His sons Rooney and Custis were home now, seeking advice

from their father. Both were solemn, and Custis was actually defiant of the Secessionists; his solution was to fortify Arlington Heights for the Union, and treat the revolutionists as they deserved.

A woman who rode with Rooney on a train that day remembered ". . . the contrast of his deep depression with the prevalent elation and jubilancy. He said the people had lost their senses and had no conception of what a terrible mistake they were making."[10]

A neighbor who talked with one of the Lee daughters described Arlington on this day, April twentieth: "The house was as if there had been a death in it, for the army was to him home and country."

Nearby Alexandria, like most towns of the South, was seized with joyous delirium.

That day, Mary Lee was able to read lavish praise for her husband in the Alexandria paper, whose editor urged Virginia to call Lee to command, if he should leave the Federal army:

> There is no man who could command more of the confidence of the people of Virginia . . . and no one under whom the volunteers and militia would more gladly rally. His reputation, his acknowledged ability, his chivalric character, his probity, honor—and, may we add, to his eternal praise—his Christian life and conduct—make his very name 'a tower of strength.' It is a name surrounded by revolutionary and patriotic associations and reminiscences.

Arlington could not know it, but Virginia had been calling for several days. Two messengers had failed to reach the house. And tonight, Saturday, April twentieth, there was a note from Judge John Robertson, who had come up from Richmond. Lee was asked to meet the Judge in Alexandria the next day. Lee replied that he would meet him after church.

He rode into the town with one of his daughters, and after the service at Christ Church, he was approached by three men. They talked for a long time, first isolated in the crowd of churchgoers, and then alone. No one knew the strange men–Judge Robertson was not among them—but the town assumed they were messengers from Richmond. Lee's daughter waited impatiently in a house across the street.

When Lee left the mysterious men, family and neighbors were still in suspense. This was soon to be ended. That night there was another message from Judge Robertson, saying he had been detained in Washington. He asked Lee to accompany him to Richmond the next day.

Lee accepted without hesitation.

On Monday morning, April twenty-second, hangers-on at the Alexandria station watched the colonel, in a high silk hat, climb aboard to ride to Richmond with Judge Robertson. There was little doubt among the townspeople as to his destination.

The cars jerked him down the line of the Orange and Alexandria Railroad across the landscape so soon to be drenched with blood. At the village of Orange he was recognized, and a crowd clamored for him. He went to the rear of the train and bowed.

At Gordonsville, where he changed to the Virginia Central, he was trapped again, and this time was urged to make a speech. E. P. Alexander, later to become one of his generals, remembered its content:

"He responded briefly, advising his hearers not to lounge about stations, but to be putting their affairs in order for a long and bloody war, which was sure to strain all their resources to support it."

The train shuddered and clanked into motion, and fled southward, trailing a pall of woodsmoke. By late afternoon they were in Richmond, and Colonel Lee was installed in the heart of the city's bustle, at the Spotswood Hotel.

2 SOWING THE WIND

LEE EMERGED from the clatter of the train into a city in the first stages of war madness. Its population of 37,000 was growing so rapidly as to be beyond counting; almost every hour saw new companies of men pour in, by rail and on foot. Men drilled in vacant lots, and there were growing crowds around eating places and hotels.

Virginia did not woo Lee; she simply abducted him. He had no sooner made his toilet after the grimy journey than he was closeted with Honest John Letcher, the loud, earnest, red-faced political lawyer from the Shenandoah Valley who was Governor. Letcher offered command of all Virginia forces, with the rank of major general. Lee accepted.

Letcher quickly wrote a note to the convention, still in session after dark, and Lee's appointment was approved unanimously. Word went to the outposts by telegraph. The most sensitive of these posts was Norfolk, where Virginians had occupied the burned Federal Navy Yard and seized priceless supplies, including about 1,200 big guns. Another was Harpers Ferry, whose terrain Lee had learned in capturing John Brown; there, on the frontier, the Federal arsenal had been seized, with much machinery for making guns.

Before Major General Lee slept that night—if he slept—he might have read *The Richmond Examiner*, which blurted the chilling truth about the state of Virginia's readiness for war: There was a handful of weapons (Lee would find only 60,000 small arms—54,000 of them ancient flintlocks); there were 200 kegs of powder, and 240 more on order.

Yet Governor Letcher estimated that Virginia would be ready for war within four days, and ex-President John Tyler imagined her "clad in steel." Lee must have had the unreal feeling that he had been flung into a swirl of events beyond control of any man.

Unknown to the new general, a veteran of his acquaintance came to town the same day at the head of a corps of cadets from Virginia Military Institute, a soldierly but graceless figure in a Mexican War uniform whose name was soon to spread terror: Thomas J. Jackson. His boy soldiers were already drilling clumsy civilians.

The next morning, April twenty-third, Lee was shown to his office, a single room in the post office building. He went alone to his desk, without staff, aides or secretary, and scratched out his first order, advising the public of his appointment, though his duties were vaguely defined. He was interrupted by four men of the convention who came to lead him into that body's secret session. One of them was Judge John Critcher, from Lee's native county of Westmoreland.

The group entered the Capitol, but was forced to wait in the rotunda for a time. Critcher noted that Lee stared at the marble statue of Washington by Houdon, and he was near enough to hear Lee's grave voice: "I hope we have seen the last of secession."[1] Some of the group were still puzzling over the strange remark when the doors of the hall swung open. They stepped into the chamber, and John Janney, the President, began an obviously prepared speech of soaring rhetoric. Lee saw many friends and acquaintances in the hall; some were strangers, among them the slight Alexander Stephens, Vice President of the Confederacy.

Janney spoke loudly: ". . . in the name of the people of your native state, here represented, I bid you a cordial and heartfelt welcome to this Hall, in which we may almost yet hear the echo of the voices of the statesmen, the soldiers and sages of bygone days, who have borne your name, and whose blood now flows in your veins."

Lee's father had once appeared here in a climactic moment of Virginia history.

Janney began to shout the story of the convention, and said of Virginia: ". . . no spot of her soil shall be polluted by the foot of an invader."

He spoke of Lee's ancestry, and of his career in the Mexican War, and explained that it would be he, not Washington, who would be "first in war, first in peace, first in the hearts of your countrymen."

At the end he cited Washington's admonition that swords should not be drawn from scabbards except in self-defense, and then to Lee said:

"Yesterday, your mother, Virginia, placed her sword in your hand upon the implied condition that we know you will keep to the letter and in spirit, that you will draw it only in her defense, and that you will fall with it in your hand rather than that the object for which it was placed there shall fail."

Lee managed to sound as if embarrassed by the flow of oratory, but he said in slow words:

"Mr. President and gentlemen of the convention, profoundly impressed with the solemnity of the occasion, for which I must say I was not prepared, I accept the position assigned me. . . .

"I would have much preferred had your choice fallen on an abler man. Trusting in Almighty God, an approving conscience, and the aid of my fellow-citizens, I devote myself to the service of my native state, in whose behalf alone will I ever again draw my sword."[2]

The convention left its seats, and men rushed forward to shake Lee's hand. Several men in the chamber, including Stephens, took note of the convincing power and dignity of Lee's words and appearance. But Stephens was one who left the hall in an anxious state of mind. Within a few hours he asked Lee to come to his quarters.

Lee entered the room at the Ballard Hotel and saw the remarkable Georgia orator whose appearance belied his influence and talents. Stephens had lately been sketched by the sharp pen of John Peyton, a North Carolinian:

"A lean, yellow, care-worn man, his back bent forward almost into a hump, his chest bowed inward, one shoulder higher than the other, small arms and wasted legs. . . . His face was . . . withered and twitching, his scanty hair fell on his shoulders in disorder . . . his restless eyes blazed with excitement. His voice . . . was sharp, shrill and squeaky."

The Vice President had a problem. The Confederacy hoped to welcome Virginia into the fold, as soon as its voters could ratify the ordinance of secession. In the meantime, military cooperation between Virginia and the Confederacy was imperative; control in the state must be held by the new government.

But the Confederacy had no higher rank than brigadier general, and Lee, if he sought to exercise his superior rank—well, he could see the point.

Lee saw it instantly, and put the mind of Stephens to rest. Stephens was struck by Lee's sincerity as he said ". . . he did not wish anything connected with himself individually, or his official rank or personal position, to interfere in the slightest."[3]

Stephens was satisfied, and two days later the Virginia convention gave the Confederacy temporary control of Virginia forces, under command of President Jefferson Davis. Lee had been plunged into the nightmare world of government red tape, whose skeins of conflict, confusion and compromise were to entwine the new government until the very end.

As Lee went to work he found a start had been made. Commanders were already at posts on the rivers, most of them Navy officers—his brother Smith among them. Cannon from Norfolk were being hoisted into position, and the store of powder found there was distributed. Small garrisons grew. Lee's old friend Colonel Andrew Talcott, an experienced engineer, was in charge of these defenses; it seemed likely that he might hold the Federal navy to the waters around the still-defiant Fortress Monroe. Lee ordered his commanders on the river fronts to maintain watch, and be ready to defend; they were not to stir the enemy unnecessarily until Virginia was prepared to fight.

Such orders caused dismay among the fire-eating Confederate cadre in Richmond, and the personal emissary of Secretary of War Walker wired to Montgomery dire reports: Lee was quenching the ardor of Virginia; there was a look of treachery here. Lee worked as if unaware of criticism. He had soon moved to rooms atop the Mechanics Institute and began to assemble a staff: Colonel R. S. Garnett, once his West Point adjutant; young Lieutenant Walter Taylor, who would remain to the end; two lieutenant colonels, George Deas and John Washington, the latter an old friend, General Washington's great nephew and last of the Mount Vernon masters of his name. These and a handful of clerks aided Lee to prepare for the inevitable Federal invasion.

As volunteers came, he sent them to outposts, though many carried no guns. Jackson reported and Lee gratefully sent him to the dangerous post at Harpers Ferry. Jackson was to remain there until the Confederacy, without warning, replaced him with Joseph E. Johnston.

Lee was a faithful correspondent to Mary:

I am very anxious about you. You have to move . . . to some point of safety. . . . The Mount Vernon plate and pictures ought to be secured. . . . War is inevitable, and there is no telling when it will burst around you. . . . The war may last ten years. . . .

There is no prospect or intention of the Government to propose a truce. Do not be deceived by it. . . .

You know how pleased I should be to have you and my dear daughters with me. That I fear cannot be.

He acknowledged acceptance of his Army resignation by the United States, sent through Mary, and he sent word to refuse his salary if the government would not agree to date his resignation from April twentieth, when he wrote the letter ending his service.

On May first he had sent out commissions to a set of promising Virginia officers, in addition to Jackson: Joseph Johnston, J. B. Magruder, Dick Ewell, J. C. Pemberton, William Mahone. Not all the helpful veterans were yet generals. One caller was Lieutenant John B. Hood, a tall, thin, shy soldier who had served with Lee in Texas, and was sent to his post at once. Another caller was Lieutenant J. E. B. Stuart, just in from Kansas; this horseman went to Harpers Ferry.

As regiments poured in unexpectedly from the Deep South, Lee began the final mobilization of Virginia, limiting the call to a few counties each day. Somehow, most of them were armed; a few muskets came from North Carolina, and a number of wealthy men raised and armed companies in their counties. Garrisons at the outposts grew, and veteran officers began to supplant the political figures who had first taken command. Jackson reported his strength at Harpers Ferry had grown from 2,000 to 4,500. Everywhere, except in Western Virginia, men flocked to the colors. The outlook in the mountains vaguely troubled Lee, for the western rivers opened the way to Federal invasion of the highlands and the

Shenandoah Valley; as yet, he could not protect that part of the frontier.

On May eighth he wrote Mary that he was grieved she must leave Arlington, adding, "When I reflect upon the calamity impending over the country, my own sorrows sink into insignificance." He urged her to resign herself. He enclosed a check for five hundred dollars, with which she was to pay the children's school expenses. It was the last money he had in the bank, he wrote.

He set up departments on the pattern of the Federal army organization, but they were mere skeletons; Virginia seemed able to arm itself only on the outmoded principle of frontier militia rallying to danger. But order began to emerge before the state took note of it. Batteries were placed on the Potomac, and the York and James were safe against attack by any except great forces. More than 60 big guns were in Norfolk's batteries.

On May fifteenth Lee had begun to concentrate all available men at a railroad junction not far from Alexandria, a village called Manassas. To this place Lee sent the best of the troops emerging half-trained from camps which had sprung up, the largest of them called Camp Lee, on the old Richmond fairgrounds. The commander at Manassas was General P. Saint George Cocke, sent there before Lee had taken command; he was an old West Point man, but lacking in experience. Lee must soon find another commander to meet the expected attack.[4]

Lee still found time to write his family, to inspect the Norfolk defenses, to attend an Episcopal convention. His son Robert, at the University, was spoiling to enter the army, but his father refused. Custis was in Richmond, a captain of engineers; Rooney had the same rank in a cavalry company.

In mid-May came news of two menacing Federal concentrations, one on the Potomac near Washington, another at Fortress Monroe, near Newport News. General Magruder guarded the latter force on the Chesapeake, but Lee saw no easy way to make the

Potomac boundary safe, and as he made the attempt, he had a rude awakening.

Joseph Johnston, already with a Confederate brigadier's rank, was now in Harpers Ferry, having replaced Jackson. Jackson had at first refused to obey the unexpected orders, but soon stepped aside. Now Johnston abruptly informed Lee, for the first time, that President Davis intended to assemble an army at Harpers Ferry, menacing Lee's plan for meeting the enemy at Manassas. Johnston feared Harpers Ferry could not be held, and soon, to the disgust of Jackson and other officers, he abandoned the town and Maryland Heights across the Potomac, saying only, "The want of ammunition has rendered me very timid." The 8,000 troops now under his command moved slightly westward.

Virginia's voters approved secession on May twenty-third. The next day Federals occupied Alexandria. Lee moved three regiments of reinforcements to Manassas. At about this time President Davis and the striking coterie of his leaders came into Richmond— the city chosen as capital over the protest of many strategists, including Davis himself. He was an old friend of Lee, and there were many ties between them from army days when Davis had been Secretary of War.

Davis was a presence not to be forgotten. The English writer Russell had seen him a few days earlier: ". . . a slight, light figure, little exceeding middle height . . . his manner is plain, and rather reserved and drastic; his head is well-formed, with a fine, full forehead, square and high, covered with innumerable fine lines and wrinkles . . . the cheek-bones are too high, and the jaws too hollow to be handsome; the lips are thin, flexible, and curved . . . the eyes deep set, large and full—one seems nearly blind, and is partly covered with a film, owing to excruciating attacks of neuralgia and tic. Wonderful to relate, he does not chew, and is neat and clean-looking, with hair trimmed and boots brushed. The expression of his face is anxious, and he has a very haggard, careworn and pain-drawn look."

The eye was a reminder of the Mexican War; he was also a veteran of the Black Hawk War, a West Pointer long immersed in military affairs. He looked upon himself as an accomplished soldier. He was, many thoughtful men said, the sole cause for the Confederacy, unswervingly devoted to it. He had a well-known gift for controversy, and pride in his own opinion. Though he placed great faith in the talents of Lee, and seldom made decisions without consulting him, there was no predicting whether he would heed his advice.

His cabinet brought color and turmoil to Richmond. There was Judah Benjamin, the attorney general: ". . . most brilliant . . . of the whole of the famous Southern lawyers. A short stout man, with a full face, olive-colored . . . with the brightest large black eyes, one of which is somewhat diverse from the other, and a brisk, lively agreeable manner." He was known as Washington's wealthiest lawyer before the war, but one who lost most of his income at cards.

An observant war office clerk, J. B. Jones, wrote of Benjamin: "Upon his lip there seems to bask an eternal smile; but if it be studied, it is not a smile."

There was Walker, Secretary of War: "Tall, lean, straight-haired, angular, with fiery, impulsive eyes and manner—a ruminator of tobacco and a profuse spitter . . . ardent, devoted to the cause."[5]

There was Stephen R. Mallory of the Navy, a round man with a solid neck, huge head, grizzled hair ". . . his ideas seemed to be confused, and the right word never to be had at the right moment. What he did say was commonplace."

The Secretary of State was R. M. T. Hunter, called for his prewar fanaticism, "Run Mad Tom," who had little to do, and was charged with "dreaming the day away." And finally there was the pale, stout Georgian Robert Toombs, a disheveled man of intellectual powers who fretted at inaction.

The Confederacy came into a huge camp, Richmond grown beyond recognition, with troops from every state of the South thronging through it, committing occasional outrages, forever being sent on to the field where they expected the enemy.

On May twenty-eighth, anxious about the northern border of Virginia, Lee went by train to Manassas, where he had placed South Carolina's General Bonham in command. Lee's judgment that the junction should be strengthened grew; he decided that Bonham should be replaced, as well.

He returned home to the news that a little force in Western Virginia had retreated from Grafton, opening the route to the conquest of that whole area of the state. Lee's adjutant general, Colonel Garnett, was made brigadier general and sent to save the west. Garnett seemed to have no illusions. This officer, ". . . proud, reserved and morose, as cold as an icicle to all but his wife and children," had told friends quietly the night before leaving Richmond: "They have not given me an adequate force. I can do nothing. They have sent me to my death."[6]

Lee was aware that the mountain country was by no means secure, but he had first to deal with the northern border, or all was lost. Davis agreed with him as to the importance of Manassas, and together they chose General P. G. T. Beauregard, hero of Fort Sumter, to head the army there. Beauregard had just arrived in the city, through a continuous ovation; crowds had howled for speeches, women threw flowers, a mob sought to carry him from the Richmond station to the Spotswood, but he escaped it, in a carriage with his staff, still tagged by the crowd and a band.

On June second Beauregard took command of 6,000 men at Manassas; his army would grow rapidly. Almost at once, however, he caused alarm in Richmond. Before headquarters caught its breath he asked for reinforcements of 10,000, and threatened retreat if he did not get them. He talked of selling his life as dearly as possible. He also raised the first public cry over the inefficiency of the commissary general, Colonel L. B. Northrop; Beauregard charged that he could get no food, since Northrop would not allow him to get it in the field, and none was sent from Richmond. Northrop, a West Point mate of President Davis, soon became a favorite butt for Richmond jokes.

By this time Davis had entered the Richmond social whirl; his wife was seen everywhere behind her smart team and the Spotswood suite was thronged with parties night after night. Mrs. James Chesnut, wife of a South Carolina Congressman, wrote fully of the "miniature world" of the Spotswood, with its pushing crowds of contractors, hangers-on, job-seekers, soldiers, planters.

In late June, Mrs. Chesnut came near the throne:

"In Mrs. Davis' drawing room last night, the President took a seat by me. . . . He talked for nearly an hour. He laughed at our faith in our own prowess. We are like the British; we think every Southerner equal to three Yankees at least, but we will have to be equivalent to a dozen now. After his experience of the fighting qualities of Southerners in Mexico, Mr. Davis believes that we will do all that can be done by pluck and muscle, endurance and dogged courage, dash and red-hot patriotism, and yet his tone was not sanguine. There was a sad refrain running through it all.

"For one thing, either way, he thinks it will be a long war. That floored me at once. It has been too long for me already. Then he said that before the end came we would have many bitter experiences. He said that only fools doubted the courage of the Yankees, or their willingness to fight when they saw fit. And now we have stung their pride, we have roused them till they will fight like devils."

Mrs. Chesnut saw Richmond changing as more men hurried to the north: "Noise of drum, tramp of marching regiments all

day long, rattling of artillery wagons. . . . Troops pass every day.
They go by with such a gay step . . . as we lean out of the windows.
Such a shaking of handkerchiefs. We are forever at the windows."

Lee became slightly ill in early July. He wrote Mary: "As
usual, in getting through with a thing, I have broken down a little
and had to take to my bed last evening, but am at my office this
morning." He searched the town for a copy of the popular new
song "Dixie" for her, and said there was none to be found. He
said he was "very anxious to get into the field," but that his movements depended upon President Davis. Lee had turned over his
Virginia troops and organization to the Confederacy. His own position was somewhat vague, but he had raised 40,000 men in about
four weeks, with almost 200 guns. There was a semblance of safety
on all but one border front, the expected Federal offensive had
been delayed; the state was as nearly war-ready as he could make
it. There were glaring weaknesses, but he would seldom render
more effective service as a soldier.

War now loomed—more than one war, in fact. Mrs. Chesnut
one day saw her husband return from Manassas, where he was
aide to Beauregard. Before she had a chance to speak with him
Davis called him into a room, and, with Lee and General Samuel
Cooper, the Adjutant General, they disappeared. All afternoon
the leaders conferred.

Chesnut had brought an absurd plan of battle from Beauregard, who thought the Federals would strike south in two columns.
Johnston should send 20,000 men to Beauregard (Johnston had not
nearly that many men), and the combined force would crush one
enemy column. Then Beauregard would send 10,000 men back to
Johnston, who would wipe out the enemy in his neighborhood of
Winchester. In turn, more troops would be shuttled farther westward, where Garnett could deal with General George McClellan.
That was not all: The two western forces would unite and invade

the north, hitting Washington from the north; Beauregard would come sweeping up from the south, ending the war. The conference could not have dallied long over this plan, but sought to work out a practical defense for Manassas.

Mrs. Chesnut learned little from her husband: "The news does not seem pleasant. At least he is not inclined to tell me any of it. He satisfied himself with telling me how sensible and soldierly this handsome General Lee is. General Lee's military sagacity was his theme."

The council had decided to combine the armies of Beauregard and Johnston when it became feasible; if they were concentrated too soon, Federals at Winchester might invade the Shenandoah Valley. The timing of the move was left to the President.

Lee wrote Mary: "I do not know what my position will be." He would not know for a long time. He made it clear to his wife that a rumor naming him commander-in-chief was false; only Davis bore that title, he wrote in unconscious irony.

Now the drift of affairs made Lee a sort of untitled commander of Eastern Virginia, for on June tenth the first serious brush of the war came near Newport News, at Big Bethel. A force of the Federal General Benjamin F. Butler, seven full regiments, ran into a brash party of 1,400 Confederates under D. H. Hill, and through confusion fired into their own lines, killing many bluecoats. At the end a charge of the Rebels, chiefly North Carolinians, rolled back the enemy. Casualties were almost 100 in the Federal ranks; the Confederates lost eight men. This brought joy in Southern towns as with macabre pride the first Confederate battlefield corpse was mourned—but it opened the eyes of Richmond headquarters to incomplete defenses in the east, and Lee turned to helping Magruder throw up vast lines across the peninsula, concentrating the earthworks at Williamsburg and Yorktown.

Lee was soon improving the Richmond defenses, too, and in these days, more by accident than design, Davis occupied himself by building up the army at Manassas for its approaching crisis, and left Lee to his own work—now that he had chosen the ground for defense and predicted where the major enemy blow would fall.

Almost as if by intuition, Lee telegraphed Garnett to beware of surprise Federal attacks in the mountains. Before his message had reached its man, there was word of disaster from Western Virginia: Garnett was dead after a shrewd flank attack by General McClellan's forces. It was a fulfillment of Lee's fears, and made him anxious to visit the scene himself. That was now impossible, for though the Federals in the west, if they chose, could push into the Shenandoah, the army to the north was the key to survival. Everything depended upon the army at Manassas.

Lee could make only feeble attempts to reinforce the western army. He assigned General W. W. Loring to that command, a West Point veteran who had long directed Federal campaigns against Indians in New Mexico. Before he could leave Richmond, there was electrifying news:

On July seventeenth Beauregard wired that the enemy was advancing. The news found Davis in the midst of one of his painful attacks of neuralgia, but he rallied to order Johnston to leave Winchester and hurry to Manassas for battle.

The reinforcements made a dramatic dash across the Virginia hills, urged by the impatient General Jackson, who himself stood sentry when the troops fell to sleep after a killing march. The men at last reached the railroad, and by noon on Saturday the vanguard poured out on the broiling plain at Manassas.

While these men marched, and Beauregard fenced with the Union pickets, Davis became more and more fretful, and on Sunday morning boarded a train for the scene of action, as if the familiar scent of battle had been too much for him to resist. He ordered Lee to remain in Richmond to direct affairs there.

Sunday was a long day for Richmond. Rumors were terrifying:

The army was routed, Richmond would be invaded at any hour, the generals were dead or captured. It was long after dark when the first official word came to headquarters from Davis:

> We have won a glorious though dear-bought victory. Night closed on the enemy in full flight and closely pursued.[7]

The city became hysterical with the news. It seemed the war was over. Since the middle of the afternoon, after long hours of heavy firing and butchery up and down the shallow Bull Run, the Union army under General McDowell had been checked. The Confederates were on the point of utter defeat, it seemed, when from the railroad came the last of Johnston's reinforcements to turn the tide. The blue waves of infantry had halted and panic followed, with thousands surging to the rear, overrunning the massed carriages of Federal Congressmen and Washington society come to see the end of the rebellion.

The rout of the enemy streamed into Washington itself. Beauregard was a hero become a god; there were others: On a hot hillside South Carolina's General Bee, just before he fell, had rallied his troops, pointing to Jackson: "There stands Jackson like a stone wall!" Troops had rallied and an unforgettable name was created. Richmond celebrated, only slightly subdued by the pleadings of some frantic men who came for stretchers, bandages, medicines and doctors. There was carnage on the field that defied description, but there was victory.

Lee himself telegraphed Beauregard:

> I cannot express the joy I feel at the brilliant victory of the 21st. The skill, courage and endurance displayed by yourself excite my highest admiration. You and your troops have the gratitude of the whole country.

His message to Johnston was even more lyrical:

I almost wept for joy at the glorious victory. . . . The feeling of my heart could hardly be repressed on learning the brilliant share you had in its achievement.

It developed that Beauregard had staged an almost flawlessly dramatic performance: A beautiful young girl had ridden to headquarters, unrolled her long hair, and produced a note from Mrs. Rose Greenhow, the Confederate agent in Washington: the Yankees were coming.

Beauregard had plunged into action, alternately cowed, shouting that he was beaten, and would sell his army dearly in suicidal lunges, and boastful, saying to his staff: "Now, gentlemen, let tomorrow be their Waterloo." He had sent out an indecipherable order of battle. Orders were not delivered, or they were bungled. But in the end, after stout fighting, and with the arrival of reinforcements, Beauregard had triumphed. At the instant of victory Davis had come up through the stragglers of the rear, at first fearful of defeat. For many reasons, or no reason, there was no pursuit of the enemy. Stern officers like Jackson were grumbling in their tents that the war might have been won that night.

Casualties were horrible to a nation unprepared: The Federals had 1,500 dead and wounded, and lost more than 1,400 as prisoners (these were soon herded through Richmond throngs which chanted: "Live Yankees! Live Yankees!"). The Confederates had lost some 2,000, of which 1,500 were wounded. But Beauregard had seized treasures, too: 6,000 small arms, 54 field guns, 500,000 rounds of ammunition, endless stores.

Davis returned to Richmond in the first of the trains that bore the wounded; hospitals overflowed and the suffering men were carried into homes, churches, cellars.

Mrs. Chesnut spoke for thousands of the city's women: "A military funeral passed the hotel. The empty saddle and the led war horse; we saw and heard it all. Now it seems we are never out of the sound of the Dead March in *Saul*. It comes and it comes until I feel inclined to close my ears and scream."

Richmond's joy waned as it cared for wounded and buried the dead.

Mrs. Chesnut heard rumors that Jeff Davis was already feuding with several of his leaders, and there was a universal chorus: Why did not Davis grasp final victory at Manassas? A story crept out that Beauregard had urged pursuit, but that Davis checked it. The President was so disturbed he asked Beauregard to deny the rumor, in writing; the general obliged him. Mrs. Chesnut heard one of the inner circle: "Many here already hate Jeff Davis."

It was about now that Mrs. Chesnut had her first glimpse of Robert Lee: "He sat his horse very gracefully, and he was so distinguished. . . . As he left us I said eagerly, 'Who is he?' 'You did not know? Why, that was Robert E. Lee, the first gentleman of Virginia.'"

Mrs. Chesnut looked after the rider with a cool eye: "All the same, I like Smith Lee better, and I like his looks, too. Besides, I know him well. Can anybody say they know his brother? I doubt it! He looks so cold, quiet and grand."

She also wrote: "Fitzhugh Lee and Rooney are being promoted hand over fist, and Custis Lee is aide de camp to the President, they say because his father wishes it."

There was some basis for the gossip: Custis was in Richmond working for Davis, chiefly with the engineer corps; Rooney was a major of cavalry, now in western Virginia. If Lee was concerned about the appearance of their rise, however, he must have reflected that many lesser men were already installed as general officers, many of them inept political leaders lost in a perplexing new world.

As Mrs. Chesnut gossiped, Lee was preparing for a journey to the west. Davis had consented to allow him to go there in hopes of winning the imperilled mountain counties. He was armed with no impressive authority, and bore no orders for command. The probable result of his modest refusal to advance himself, this ambiguity was to plague him and render him helpless.

Just before he left Richmond Lee wrote Mary:

> That was indeed a glorious victory and has lightened the pressure upon our front amazingly. Do not grieve for the brave dead. Sorrow for those they left behind. . . . I wished to partake in the former struggle, and am mortified at my absence, but the President thought it more important that I should be here.
>
> I could not have done as well as has been done, but I could have helped. . . . So the work is done I care not by whom it is done. . . . My whole time is occupied, and all my thoughts and strength are given to the cause to which my life, be it long or short, will be devoted. . . .

He was hardly out of the city when Beauregard set off a storm. The Creole wrote from Manassas:

> The want of food and transportation has made us lose all the fruits of victory. We ought at this moment to be in or about Washington. . . . Only think of the brilliant results we have lost by the two causes referred to.[8]

A secret session of Congress heard his letter, and a furore resulted. There was a hostile, if short-lived, investigation of the Davis administration. Davis sought to placate Beauregard with: "Enough was done for glory," but the rift was there, and would not heal. Soon both Davis and Beauregard were interviewing witnesses to the July thirteenth conference, when the Creole's fantastic battle plan had been abandoned. Beauregard hotly inquired of a South Carolina colonel, Joe Kershaw, why he sent a copy of his military report to the critical *Charleston Mercury* before it went to headquarters. There was a noisy squabble over the affair.

With this advent of Confederate cannibalism in Richmond, Lee was climbing the Virginia ridges on the western reaches of the Virginia Central Railroad. He led a small and unimpressive party on his foray to save the frontier: . . . Colonel Washington and Walter Taylor, by now a captain, and two slaves—his body servant, Perry, and Meredith, a cook. In the baggage car he had one horse among the party's few mounts, his bay stallion called Richmond, given to him by friends shortly after he arrived in the capital. Lee was not fond of this "troublesome fellow" who disliked to be near strange horses, and when in company would squeal in protest.

Lee had looked forward to seeing Rooney in the hills, and perhaps getting a glimpse of his younger son, Rob, as he passed through Charlottesville. The train paused in the college town briefly, however, and Lee had time to do no more than find out that "he was at the University and I could not stop."

3 *A DISMAL DEBUT*

LEE AND his little escort left the railroad at the foothill village of Staunton, where he saw scattered companies of the western army, most of them unarmed and undisciplined. Lee went on horseback toward Monterey in the mountains.

It began to rain soon after they took the road on July twenty-ninth, but it was not unpleasant and the general admired the scenery. He could not know that he had already met an enemy who was to prove more deadly than Union troops, and that the shower was the beginning of rainfall which would virtually deluge him for three months.

He remembered his last passage of this road, and he preserved the thought for Mary:

> A part of the road, as far as Buffalo Gap, I passed over in the summer of 1840, on my return to St. Louis, after bringing you home. If any one had then told me that the next time I travelled that road would have been on my present errand, I should have supposed him insane.

Lee soon entered the theater of war in Western Virginia, amid scenery of breath-taking beauty, but a land cruel to armies, a jum-

bled terrain of heavily timbered ridges, smothered in laurel and rho-
dodendron. These counties, so vital a stake to the Confederacy,
were almost isolated from the rest of Virginia by the mountain
barrier; there were few good roads, and no railroads. Most of
the people were hostile and suspicious of Confederates. It was a
country of few slaves and small farms.

It was here that the Federals under McClellan had won their
first victory, and here McClellan, now gone triumphantly to eastern
command, had left behind a small bluecoat force to threaten the
state.

At Monterey, Lee had a cheering reception from General Henry Jackson, who seemed capable despite his gentle, bookish ways;
he had been a Yale scholar, a poet, a United States Minister to
Austria. It was Jackson who had first proposed that Lee visit the
west, and for two or three days of this week, as Lee rode endlessly
into the mountains, peering with his field glasses down the long
vistas, Jackson accompanied him.

Lee saw that Jackson's estimate of the terrain was correct: Its
key was Cheat Mountain, whose pass had been taken by the Federals. They waited there now, a bluecoat force of undetermined
size; Lee rode for miles through the wet scrub, wearing the patience
of Taylor and Washington, stirred by a desire to get at the Federals,
and seeking the way.

With Jackson's help he concluded that a road leading through
the village of Huntersville to the rear of Cheat Mountain might
be made a path of victory. If they could turn the mountain, and
oust the Federals, there were bright prospects of clearing Virginia.

It was now fourteen years, almost to the day, since Lee as a
young staff officer had shown Scott's army the path to victory in
Mexico, sending it to the gates of Mexico City; that had been a
campaign begun amid peaks more towering and forbidding than
these, and yet Lee, somehow, had always found a route to the vulnerable flank of the enemy.

He went ahead with Washington and Taylor and the Negro servants into Huntersville, a "wretched and filthy town" filled with the army's sick. Huntersville had a chilly welcome for Lee. General Loring, who was struggling with his command from the village, could not overcome his visible surprise; it had been less than two weeks since Lee had sent him from Richmond to save the frontier, and now here was the staff chief, come to hold his hand. As a veteran with a long and honorable record, made while Lee was enjoying some of the Army's more comfortable posts, Loring was filled with resentment.

Loring had a sensible enough scheme: He would march his 8,000 men to the rear of Cheat Mountain, where two regiments were already in advance, under Colonel William Gilham. When the Cheat Mountain force of the enemy had been overcome, he would march to nearby Beverly, and the region would be made safe.

Loring was not moving, however, and there were dangers. Gilham had already been seen by the Federals, who were now fortifying the neglected road. If the Confederates waited much longer, the attack would not be possible over that route. Loring dallied.

It was an open secret that Loring was throwing away the opportunity by his timidity. Major A. L. Long of Loring's staff wrote that "it was obvious to all those about the general" that there must be a speedy movement: "Yet notwithstanding the great value of time . . . he seemed to regard the formation of a depot of supplies at Huntersville and the organization of a supply-train as a matter of first importance. He appeared to overlook the fact that the line from Huntersville to Beverly, only forty miles long . . . abounded in beef and grain."

Lee quickly discovered the trouble, but could not bring himself to discipline Loring, whose fears of advancing without mountains of supplies were absurd. Lee did not so much as force the issue to candid discussion. He could not even press Loring for details. Major Long wrote:

> After remaining several days at Huntersville without gaining any positive information from Loring in regard to the time of his probable advance, he proceeded to . . . Valley Mountain.

It was an incredible victory for the timorous officer over Lee, an incident that was to assume greater proportions as this war dragged on; in his first brush with a disobedient general officer, Lee found himself too gentle, his modesty too genuine, to grasp the situation with the hand of command. It was Loring who, within a few months, and in these very mountains, would so infuriate the stern Stonewall Jackson that he would attempt to resign from the army when Loring appealed to Richmond from a Jackson order.[1]

Lee wrote to Mary, however, with little more than a hint of his troubles:

> It is so difficult to get our people, unaccustomed to the necessities of war, to comprehend and execute the measures required. . . .

> The measles are prevalent throughout the whole army, and you know that disease leaves unpleasant results, attacks on the lungs, typhoid, etc., especially in camp, where accommodations for the sick are poor.

It was ludicrous, of course, but Lee left Huntersville with his party almost as if he fled from the necessity of dealing with Loring. He went ahead to Valley Mountain. He scouted every road or path outside the Federal lines, and it was not long before he discovered that Loring's delay had made impossible the advance by road against Cheat Mountain. He sought some other means of attack. He once wrote Mary:

> It has rained, I believe, some portion of every day since I left Staunton. Now it is pouring, and the wind, having

veered around to every point of the compass, has settled down to the northeast. . . . Colonel Washington, Captain Taylor, and myself are in one tent.

He told her of finding their son Rooney, now a major of cavalry:

He is very well and very active, and as yet the war has not reduced him much. He dined with me yesterday and preserves his fine appetite. Today he is out reconnoitering and has the full benefit of this rain. I fear he is without his overcoat.

Lee had seen some of Mary's friends, he wrote, and mentioned that a Federal commander nearby was their old friend J. J. Reynolds, the old West Point professor of philosophy who lived in a cottage "with his little, pale-faced wife."

Rooney had discovered Reynolds a day or so earlier when he carried a flag of truce between the lines—so the news was out that Lee opposed the Federals in the hills, and was soon printed in Northern newspapers. Rooney was told by Reynolds that the enemy was quite confident, and had from 12,000 to 30,000 men on and around Cheat Mountain.[2]

He soon afterward wrote his daughters, openly complaining:

It rains here all the time, literally. There has not been sunshine enough since my arrival to dry my clothes. Perry is my washerman, and socks and towels suffer. But the worst of the rain is that the ground has become so saturated with water that the constant travel on the roads has made them almost impassable, so that I cannot get up sufficient supplies for the troops to move. It is raining now. Has been all day, last night, day before, and day before that too, etc., etc. But we must be patient. It is quite cool, too. I have on all my winter clothes and am writing in my overcoat.

His horse, Richmond, he said ". . . has not been accustomed to such fare or treatment," and he "complains some." The horse was not gaining weight, he added. It was not surprising. Lee was riding almost every day. The army marveled at the sight of the stout figures of Lee and Washington, followed by Taylor, as they clambered far up over crags and exposed rocks, poking about for a means of hitting at the enemy.

Rooney and his horsemen aided them in the task of scouting. Lee's huge young second son, who was to rise swiftly in the service, and seldom draw the army's resentment, was described by an officer as: ". . . an immense man, probably six feet three or four inches tall. . . . I wondered how he could find a horse powerful enough to bear him upon a long ride . . . his complexion was florid. His hands and feet were immense, and in company he appeared to be ill at ease. His bearing, however, was excellent, and his voice, manner, and everything about him bespoke the gentleman."[3]

Rooney, unlike his older brother Custis, had shown no interest in West Point, and had been educated at Harvard, where he pulled a stroke oar on the crew. He was a young man of a sober, quiet manner, but apt to roar with laughter at the jokes of others. He was master of the historic White House plantation below Richmond, where George Washington had married Martha Custis. Just now there was enough to occupy father and son in the hostile terrain, which grew more forbidding.

Captain Taylor remembered seeing "double teams of horses struggling with six or eight barrels of flour, and the axle of the wagon scraping and leveling the road-bed." But slowly, day by day, Loring was pushing up his men to Valley Mountain, and soon the little band would be ready to launch Lee's attack.

Daily, too, their numbers became less; measles and typhoid raged. The North Carolina 16th Regiment already had two thirds of its men down with various fevers. Lee tried in vain to improve camp conditions to reduce sickness, and wrote Mary: "They bring it on themselves by not doing what they are told. They are worse than children, for the latter can be forced."

Lee gave the troops a sign that he knew how to handle camp discipline. He was busy scouting near an outpost one day when a squad of his soldiers thronged around, watching him, peering in the direction he turned his glasses, unconscious of their intrusion. Lee asked one of them:

"What regiment do you belong to?"

"First Tennessee, Maury Grays."

"Are you well drilled?"

"Yes, indeed."

"Take the position of a soldier."

The man came to attention.

"Forward march," Lee ordered. "By the right flank, march, Double-quick, march." The soldier paced off toward his camp, and his mates followed him. The general's privacy was invaded no more.[4]

Toward the end of August affairs seemed to improve slightly. The news that Lee's rank as full general had been confirmed seemed to make Loring more docile, and co-operation on preparations for attack improved. The news from Richmond added that four other officers were now full generals: Samuel Cooper, Albert Sidney Johnston, Joseph Johnston and Beauregard. Lee was senior to all except Cooper and Albert Johnston. There was also an understanding letter from Cooper, giving assurance of President Davis' awareness of his difficulties. The President wished him to come to Richmond as soon as possible, but only when he had seen to it that the west was secure.

Lee felt better days coming: "I feel stronger, we are stronger. . . . Now . . . a battle must come off, and I am anxious to begin it. Circumstances beyond human control delay it. . . ."

He had by now discovered a route to the Cheat Mountain road; his path would mean a wild scramble through the underbrush for troops, but they could advance along the ridges of the mountain and be upon the Federals. He had only to find a way to thrust another column against the enemy, and he could order forward the men. The answer came unexpectedly. Loring sent up Colonel Albert Rust of an Arkansas regiment, along with a surveyor who had found a passage to the tallest crest of Cheat Mountain, from which he could look down on the fortifications of the Federals on the center crest. If an army was led to that spot, it could sweep the enemy off the mountain. It was the answer Lee needed.

He questioned Rust with care, and the colonel corroborated the surveyor's story; he had gone up with the man a second time, to see for himself. The enemy's trenches and a blockhouse were in clear sight of the position, which had been reached by climbing up from the Greenbrier River. Lee seemed convinced. If he could coordinate an attack from that sector with one along the route he had found himself, victory was at hand. He seemed then to abandon his caution.

"If we attack from there," Rust said, "I have one favor to ask—I want to lead the column from the height."

Lee agreed, though he did not know Rust. He began to complete plans for his offensive, and gradually, as if gaining confidence, took over the details of command.[5]

On September eighth the army began its bizarre little campaign. With Cheat Mountain as the first objective, and the clearing of the Tygart's River valley as the second, the army would divide:

Rust was to lead 2,000 men to the top of the mountain, and on September twelfth open the action by firing on the enemy, driving them off the road at the crest. That would enable the second division to move.

General Jackson would wait on the turnpike east of the mountain and when the way was clear, he would march up the road to the site of battle.

On the west of the mountain, a force under General S. R.

Anderson would creep along the route Lee had found on the ridges and block escape in that direction.

Farther west, the remainder of the force would sweep down Tygart's River, taking Federal outposts. Cavalry under Rooney Lee would cover this flank.

As officers studied the movement they saw its simplicity; perhaps they did not see that lack of co-ordination would mean certain failure. The army in the sodden camps soon got a curious order from Lee, urging "the troops to keep steadily in view the great principles for which they contend and to manifest to the world their determination to maintain them. The eyes of the country are upon you. The safety of your homes and the lives of all you hold dear depend upon your courage and exertions. . . . The progress of this army must be forward."[6]

It was painfully forward it turned out as the ranks left camp on September ninth—and it was not easy for men in ranks to keep sight of their companions, much less to remain in view of the "eyes of the country." One who marched with them said, "It was no uncommon thing for a mule to slide twenty feet down a slope, and I could see strong men sink exhausted trying to get up the mountain side."

One soldier would never forget it: ". . . I never saw as much mud. It seemed to rain every day and it got to be a saying in our company that you must not halloo loud, for if you should, we would immediately have a hard shower, and when some of the men on their return from picket had to shoot their guns off to get the load out, it brought on a regular flood. Granville Gray always said it rained thirty-*two* days in August. . . . I saw dead mules lying in the road, with nothing but their ears showing above the mud."[7]

Somehow the advance went on, though one force ran into such terrain that the cannon were abandoned. The columns spent the night in the cold mountains, the rain having spoiled the rations carried by the men; the muskets were wet and some powder was ruined. They were forbidden to light fires. One man wrote: "Here we tried to sleep, but the rain poured so, and the torrents ran down the mountain with such a flood of water that we would have been drowned had we lain on the ground."[8]

The next day the separated forces went into position. Fog hung over the hills most of the day, and when it cleared for a time Lee had through his glasses "a tempting sight," a glimpse of the Federals in camp. Morning would bring action.

But the slow hours brought only daylight and silence from the dripping peaks. In both east and west the army was waiting; Anderson had cut the road below the enemy, and two forces had seized Federal pickets without giving a general alarm. Still there was no sound from the crest where Rust lay, and the expected volleys of fire did not come.

As he waited Lee was drawn down to the west, where a few scattered shots were fired. He rode Richmond into the midst of a Federal outpost which had tangled with his own horsemen, but he escaped into the woods. He then tried to salvage the day. If Rust did not come into action, the battle plan was useless; but they might sting the Federals west of the mountain, and take a few of them out of action. He found the officers sullen and defiant: the place was impossible, the rain was too hard, the men were in no condition for attack. Orders were passed in confusion, and within a few hours it was obvious that the army could not move this day, however the commander felt about it.

For a day or two the army lay there. Lee sent scouts to find other means of attack, among them Rooney and Colonel Washington, who were riding with a handful of men when an ambush fell upon them. Washington was killed, and Rooney and his riders barely escaped. The enemy sent forward the colonel's body.

Lee wrote a letter of sympathy to Washington's daughter Louisa, expressing his grief at the loss.

On September seventeenth he wrote to Mary, and the detail

with which he described his plan of attack and its failure made clear his disappointment. He added:

> I can not tell you my regret and mortification at the untoward events that caused the failure of the plan. I had taken every precaution to ensure success and counted on it. But the Ruler of the Universe willed otherwise. . . . We are no worse off now than before.

His dismay was equally plain in a letter to Governor Letcher, in which Lee took pains to point out the trials of the troops in reaching their positions, and his chagrin at failure, saying:

> It is a grievous disappointment to me, I assure you. But for the rain-storm I have no doubt it would have succeeded. This, Governor, is for your own eye. Please do not speak of it; we must try again.

Lee discovered that it was not the storm which had cost him victory, but the strange timidity of Colonel Rust. He had reached his position on schedule, and helped to snatch some of the Federal pickets from their posts and bear them in silence to the rear. But then, when the chattering bluecoats began to tell him tales of Federal strength in the lines before his eyes, Rust quailed. The Federals said that 4,000 to 5,000 men awaited him in the trenches—there were in truth just 300. Rust held his men quietly in the woods, thankful that the word from the enemy had come in time to save him from disaster.

Lee could only march the troops back to their camps. Word of failure got back to Richmond somehow. One newspaper told the capital that his plan of attack had been sent to the War Department, and was a model bit of strategy; another paper lectured Lee that: ". . . in mountain warfare, the learning of books and of the strategists is of little value."[9]

Lee was through on the northern end of the hill defenses. It was too late in the season to mount an offensive, and for the present he could not move the troops to advantage. There were insistent calls for him from the southern end of the mountain line, in the Kanawha Valley, where two bickering generals from the world of politics were staging a comic, but perilous, rivalry. The generals were Henry A. Wise, the former Governor of Virginia, and John B. Floyd, also an ex-Governor, and Secretary of War under Buchanan. These two, operating as independent war lords, had come together in the region opposing the enemy under General Rosecrans.

Their dispatches and complaints had been fluttering to Richmond as they argued and even when the enemy was driving at their heels, they would not co-operate. Still savagely disputing, they had fallen back with their armies to an eminence called Sewell Mountain. Floyd did not like the site, and pulled back to Meadow Bluff, a dozen miles away. His old position was seized by the Federals, and Wise, screaming epithets, was almost isolated with his little force of some 2,000 men.

It was toward this unpromising theater that Lee rode in advance of Loring's men. He arrived at Floyd's camp September twenty-first, with only Captain Taylor, the Negroes and some cavalrymen at his side.

About this time Lee began to grow a beard, and it was probably as he arrived at the new camp, for he had ridden across country and had no baggage wagon when he reached Floyd; his effects did not appear until September twenty-sixth, and by then he may have given up shaving as much for the sake of warmth as for lack of his razor. He wrote Mary:

> It is raining heavily. The men are all exposed on the mountain, with the enemy opposite to us. We are without tents, and for two nights I have lain buttoned up in my overcoat. To-

day my tent came up and I am in it. Yet I fear I shall not sleep for thinking of the poor men.

And a little later he told her that his appearance had undergone a startling change.

I have a beautiful white beard. It is much admired. At least, much remarked upon.[10]

The state of the army he had come to aid was ludicrous, and surpassed even his recent trials. For the commands of Wise and Floyd sat in the mountains, so far apart as to endanger both, and Lee could not make out, in all the squabbling, just where military necessity called for concentration.

The two generals all but drove Lee mad with their tug of war, and their alternate shrill claims that the enemy was advancing and threatened one of the commands. Lee ended it at last by ordering Floyd to march up to the side of Wise—just as there came an order from Benjamin, the new Secretary of War in Richmond, a providential order calling Wise to the capital. For a time it seemed that Wise would defy even that, but Lee advised departure, and the old warrior hurried to the east.

About this time Lee saw the horse of his dreams, when Major Thomas Broun, of the Third Virginia, rode through the camp. One of Lee's soldiers described the mount: "No pedigreed, wide-nostrilled, round-barrelled, healthy, comfortable, gentleman's saddle horse. Gray, with black points, he was sound in eye, wind and limb . . . ready to go . . . without a single fancy trick, or the pretentious bearing of the typical charger."

But Lee saw him with a fonder eye:

Fine proportions, muscular figure, deep chest, short back, strong haunches, flat legs, small head, broad forehead, delicate ears, quick eye, small feet & black mane & tail. Such a picture would inspire a poet. . . .

> But I am no artist . . . & can therefore only say he is a
> Confederate *grey.*

Lee approached Major Broun and asked about the horse,
studying him in admiration. He had been bred by Andrew Johnston
near Blue Sulphur Springs. In both 1859 and 1860 he had won
first premium at the Greenbrier County Fair. He came of the good
stock of Gray Eagle. His name was Jeff Davis.

Broun said more: The horse needed "neither whip nor spur,
and would walk his five or six miles an hour over the rough mountain roads. . . ."

Broun had paid $175 in gold for the horse, which was just a
little over four years old and sixteen hands high. Lee called it "his
colt."

"I'll need him before the war is over," he told Broun. He
looked fondly after the gray as he disappeared. For days afterward,
whenever he saw the colt ridden by Broun's brother, "he had something pleasant to say . . . about 'my colt.'"

This was the mount to be known as "Traveller." But Lee did
not yet own him. He was forced to buy a new horse to fill his needs,
and found the best he could in the area— a lesser mount known as
The Roan. The two horses, Richmond and Roan, now carried
Lee about his rounds.[11]

It looked as if there would be no battle for Lee to ride through.
His army had few supplies to spare, and lived almost hand to
mouth. And Lee knew that attack in these hills, with their killing
slopes and blind flanks, would be perilous indeed.

He spoiled for a fight, however, and once wrote Floyd: "I begin
to fear the enemy will not attack us. We shall therefore have to
attack him."

But there were several signs that Rosecrans was pulling his
forces together for an assault, and Lee waited. In the end he waited
too long.

One morning a young officer, Lieutenant T. C. Morton of the 26th Virginia, came through the strange press of men and wagons, his company lost as it sought the ordnance train to which he had been sent for powder. He asked men along the way: "Where's the ordnance train? Who's the ordnance officer?" No one seemed to know.

Morton caught sight of Lee:

"A martial figure standing in the rain by a log fire before a small tent, with his breeches tucked in his high cavalry boots, his hands behind his back. A high, broad-brimmed black hat, with a gilt cord around it, on his head."

Morton calmly introduced himself and asked, "Where's the ordnance train? I don't know the officer."

Lee turned on the young man with eyes he would not forget.

"I think it very strange, Lieutenant," Lee said, "that an officer of this command, which has been here a week, should come to me, who am just arrived, to ask who his ordnance officer is, and where to find his ammunition.

"This is in keeping with everything else I find here—no order, no organization; nobody knows where anything is; no one understands his duty; officers and men are equally ignorant. This will not do."

But he pointed out the ammunition train and sent the lieutenant away with, "I hope you will not have to come to me again on such an errand."

Morton was soon to see Lee in a different mood, however. A sergeant of his company had word of diphtheria in his family, and he applied for leave; he was afraid to approach Lee himself, and Morton took a letter from him to the General. Morton watched:

"The expression of his face softened like that of a woman. Handing back the letter he said, 'I wish, Lieutenant, I could send your man home to his sick children. But, my dear sir, we all went into this struggle expecting to make sacrifices. . . . Your Sergeant must make his. He cannot go now. Every man is wanted at his post. Tell him that as soon as possible, he shall have his leave."[12]

On that night, October sixth, wheels rumbled on the mountain roads, and Lee's pickets thought the enemy was to attack at last. When daylight came, the frowning hill was empty, and the Federals were gone. Lee sent men after them but the chase was slow, and there were new problems of food, of discipline and of bad roads. There was word of an attack on the northern end of the line, and fears were raised for safety of the vital railroad from Staunton. Nor was that all: Back in Richmond, newspapers, curiously enough, were publishing in detail Lee's plans of campaign.

He wrote Mary on October seventh, the day after his final disappointment:

> . . . There was a drenching rain yesterday, and as I had left my overcoat in camp I was thoroughly wet from head to foot. It has been raining ever since, and is now coming down with a will. But I have my clothes out on the bushes and they will be well washed. . . .
>
> I wish [the enemy] had attacked us, as I believe he would have been repulsed with great loss. . . . When day appeared, the bird had flown, and the misfortune was that the reduced condition of our horses . . . exposure to cold rains in these mountains, and want of provisions . . . prevented the vigorous pursuit. . . .

The campaign was over. Lee stayed on for a few days; the weather was now so bitter that he and Taylor slept together, using the blankets of both piled atop them. On October twentieth, he ordered Floyd to fall back and join General H. R. Jackson to the north, and the officer grumblingly did so. Four days later it became clear to all how miserable had been the Confederate failure: Not only was the country here abandoned to the Federal army, but the people voted overwhelmingly to separate themselves from Virginia and establish the free state of West Virginia, in the Union.

On his way back to Richmond, Lee gave no sign that he was aware the South had lost faith in him and that critics were howling on every side. His loyal nephew, Fitz Lee, heard some of the things men said of the general in these days: "a showy presence," "a historic name," "too tender of blood." There was another name of derision, more memorable: "Granny Lee."

Lee and Taylor and the servants passed through Charlottesville on October thirtieth, and this time he saw young Rob, who seemed stunned at his father's appearance, and at his beard, in particular. Lee entered Richmond the next day. He had been gone three months; it seemed years.

He went first to report to Jefferson Davis, who seemed as friendly as ever. As they talked, Lee rather provokingly refused to say what Davis wished to hear about the campaign in the mountains until the latter gave his word to make the matters confidential. At last Lee spoke freely, giving him details of the nightmare of stubborn officers, bleak terrain and constant blunders. Davis was much impressed by this stand of Lee, and he later said:

> He came back, carrying the heavy weight of defeat, and unappreciated by the people . . . for they could not know . . . that, if his plans and orders had been carried out, the result would have been victory. . . .
>
> I should not have known it had he not breathed it in my ear only at my earnest request, and begging that nothing be said about it.
>
> The clamor which then arose followed him when he went to South Carolina, so that it became necessary on his departure to write a letter to the Governor of that State, telling him what manner of man he was. Yet, through all this . . . he stood in silence, without defending himself . . . for he was unwilling to offend any one who was wearing a sword and striking blows for the Confederacy.[13]

Thus Davis unwittingly placed his finger on the chief weakness of his greatest general, one which he would not overcome even in the darkest days ahead.

Lee tried to get away to visit Mary, who was visiting at Shirley, a river plantation down the James, but when he went to the landing he found that no government boat was making the trip that day—the passenger boats had left in the morning. Lee went to his stable and had a horse saddled, but changed his mind; it was too near night, and the roads were strange to him. He might go later.

Two days afterward he was called to Secretary Benjamin's office for a long talk over the discouraging state of affairs. South Carolina was now the chief concern, for a large Federal fleet had appeared off Charleston. The next day Davis ordered him to South Carolina, where he would be in charge of defenses.

Remembering the western mountains, Lee for the first time spoke boldly to Davis: "Just what will my authority be?"

And Davis, surprised, gave him full assurance; he would be in complete command, and Richmond's authority was at his call. The President had only now begun to muse that Lee did not understand his position in the Confederate scheme.[14]

The Richmond Examiner gave Lee a farewell as he boarded a southbound train on November sixth. The editor expressed the hope that Lee would be more successful with the spade than he had been with the sword.

Charleston was blazing with excitement when Lee, Captain Taylor and the servants came into the railroad station: A Federal invasion was under way. Lee left immediately for the scene, on Port Royal Sound, the state's finest harbor, in which lay large Beaufort Island. At Coosawhatchie, a tiny station, the party dismounted; there was furious firing seaward, but none of the few soldiers about could explain the situation. Lee rode out to see for himself, but it was nightfall before he learned that the enemy fleet had blasted the guns of two tiny forts and was in control of the sound.

Lee ordered the island garrisons pulled back to shore, and went to find quarters at Coosawhatchie.

The house was isolated, small and abandoned, but Lee chose it at once. He settled there with Taylor, Perry and Meredith, and soon added others to his staff, Captains Thornton Washington and R. W. Memminger. Several other officers attached themselves, among them Major Long, who had come down from Western Virginia, and Captains Joseph Manigault and Joseph Ives from the South Carolina department. Lee set the staff to work immediately on the problem of defending the wandering, bay-cut coastline from Charleston to Savannah, which must be held in the face of the enemy's complete control of the sea.

Major Long pictured headquarters: "The table service consisted of a neat set of tin-ware, plates, dishes and cups made to fit into each other for convenience in packing. The bill of fare corresponded in frugality to the plainness of the furniture. The general occupied the head of his table, and always seasoned the meal with his good humor and . . . jests, often at the expense of some member of the staff who seemed to miss the luxuries of the table more than himself."

There was little leisure, however. Lee rode through the sandy low country; he went twice to Savannah in the first weeks, and from reports of his staff and volunteers, built a picture of his problem. He acted swiftly. He ordered stone, rubble and other debris piled into the black rivers near their mouths to prevent Federal boats from approaching the inland railroad bridges; he put men to work on the forts of Charleston and Savannah, increasing their guns until they seemed impregnable. He had just over 12,000 troops, but some 5,000 of them were defending Savannah, and could not be moved. He built a force, with Richmond's permission, by delaying troops passing through these states, and put them on temporary duty. He brought together scattered bands, and camped them on the railroad, where they could meet any Federal threat.

As Lee worked, the enemy seemed disposed to wait; the blue-coat regiments sweltered in their troop ships offshore, the sleek steamers moved up and down on blockade duty, and affairs were quiet.

On November fifteenth Lee wrote to his daughter Mildred, as if he were still in despair:

> Another forlorn hope expedition. Worse than West Virginia. . . . I have much to do in this country.

From Savannah, a week later, to his other daughters, he revealed homesickness:

> I wish I could see you, be with you, and never again part from you. God only can give me that happiness. I pray for it night and day. But my prayers I know are not worthy to be heard. . . .
>
> I am so pressed with business. . . . I have been down the coast to Amelia Island to examine the defenses. They are poor indeed, and I have laid off work enough to employ our people a month. I hope the enemy will be polite enough to wait for us. . . . It is difficult to get our people to realise their position.

About this time the romantic poet of South Carolina, Paul Hamilton Hayne, caught sight of Lee as he inspected Fort Sumter with his officers, and was impressed: "In the midst of the group, topping the tallest by half a head was, perhaps, the most striking figure we had ever encountered, the figure of a man seemingly about 56 or 58 years of age, erect as a poplar, yet lithe and graceful, with broad shoulders well thrown back . . . unconscious dignity, clear, deep, thoughtful eyes, and the quiet, dauntless step of one every inch the gentleman and soldier."

Now Lee met an old friend—the beautiful horse Jeff Davis, transferred to the state with his master from the West Virginia campaign. Lee saw him one day at Pocotaligo, a hamlet on an estuary of Broad River, as he rode the line of defenses. Young Captain Joseph Broun was riding the animal. Lee approached him.

"Ah, my colt," he said, and began to reminisce about the animal.

Broun offered to give him the horse. Lee shook his head. "I can't accept him. But if you will willingly sell him to me, I will gladly use it for a week or so to learn its qualities."

So the big gray was sent to Lee's stables at Coosawhatchie, and went into service. He suited the general perfectly. He put the horse, which he now called Greenbrier, to some stern tests.

On November twenty-fourth, the Federal fleet had struck near Savannah, and put troops ashore on Tybee Island. Lee drove his regiments to harder work with shovels on the sandy parapets. On one day he rode 115 miles, 35 of these on Greenbrier.

In the middle of December, Lee, Taylor, Ives and Long were spending a night in a Charleston hotel, the Mills House, when the great Charleston fire began to sweep the city. The officers heard fire alarms before going to bed, but paid little attention. In the middle of the night they were aroused, and Lee, Long and others climbed to the roof and looked out:

"More than one-third of the city appeared a sea of fire, shooting up columns of flame that seemed to mingle with the stars . . . extending back more than a mile, stores and dwellings, churches and public buildings were enveloped in one common blaze."

Soldiers came to fight the flames, which were now endangering the hotel itself. Lee and his party escaped, aiding women and children down the back stairs through a cellar. Lee took a baby in his arms, and Long seized another, and the group went off in a horse-drawn omnibus in a shower of sparks to spend the night at the large home of Charles Alston on the Battery.[15]

With Christmas approaching, Lee at last returned the fine Greenbrier to Captain Broun with a note: The horse suited him well, but he could no longer keep so valuable an animal in such dangerous times, unless it were his own. Broun wrote to his older brother, ill in Virginia, who replied that the horse was to be given to the General; if he would not accept it, the price would be $175, just what he had cost the Brouns. Lee paid $200, carefully estimating that inflation of currency had added $25 to the value.

Soon the name Greenbrier was abandoned, and "because he was such a good traveller," the horse became known to Lee and others as "Traveller." Not even this seemed to satisfy Lee's love of horseflesh. One hostler at army stables complained that the "durned old fool" was "always a-pokin' round my horses as if he meant to steal one of 'em."

On Christmas Day Lee wrote a long letter to Mary, who was at the White House with Rooney, Annie and Charlotte:

> I cannot let this day of grateful rejoicing pass, dear Mary, without some communication with you. I am thankful for the many among the past that I have passed with you, and the remembrance of them fills me with pleasure.

He advised her to give up thoughts of Arlington, except, "They cannot take away the remembrance of the spot," and said he wished that he might buy Stratford, his birthplace:

> I wish I could purchase Stratford. That is the only other place I could go now. . . . You and the girls could remain there in quiet. It is a poor place, but we could make enough corn bread and bacon for our support, and the girls could weave us clothes. I wonder if it is for sale and at how much. Ask Fitzhugh to try to find out.

He then tried to disillusion Mary in her hopes for war between England and the United States because of the recent Federal seizure of the Confederate ministers to Britain, Mason and Slidell:

> You must not build your hopes on peace on account of the United States going into a war with England. She will be very loath to do that, notwithstanding the bluster of the Northern papers. Her rulers are not entirely mad. . . . We must make up our minds to fight our battles and win our independence alone. No one will help us. . . . But we must be patient.

Shortly after the new year came in Lee inspected defenses of the Florida coast. There, on Cumberland Island, he spent a few moments which must have been some of the most moving of his life. Here was the old house Dungeness, once the home of General Nathanael Greene, with whom Lee's father had fought in the Revolution. And Lighthorse Harry's grave was here in the Greene cemetery.

It was just a few days before Robert's fifty-fifth birthday. He had last seen his famous father in 1813, when he was six years old, and the handsome, mercurial old soldier, beset by debtors, had disappeared from the child's life into the West Indies.

Lee went through the crumbling old Greene mansion with Long at his heels, Long recalled: " . . . a road shaded with live-oak and magnolia . . . grounds dotted with olive, orange and lemon trees . . . a dilapidated wall enclosing a neglected cemetery. The general then, in a voice of emotion, informed me that he was visiting the grave of his father. He went alone to the tomb, and after a few moments of silence plucked a flower and slowly retraced his steps. . . . We returned in silence . . . and no allusion was ever made to this act of filial devotion."

Lee himself wrote Mary:

> The spot is marked by a plain marble slab, with his name, age, and date of his death. Mrs. Greene is also buried there,

and her daughter . . . and her husband. . . . The garden was beautiful, enclosed by the finest hedge I have ever seen. It was of the wild olive.

The work of the fortifications was still so slow as to perplex him, and the enemy was more active, and had now crowded near to Savannah. From other sections of the Confederacy, the news was even worse. Two forts in the west, Henry and Donelson, had fallen, and Tennessee might well be lost. Equally as depressing was word that Roanoke Island, on the ragged North Carolina coast, had been occupied by the Federals, and the railroad south from Richmond was becoming exposed.

Richmond ordered Lee to withdraw all his island forces to the mainland and to surrender most of Florida to the enemy, sending the troops to the west. Lee had scarcely done this when he had a telegram from Davis:

> If circumstances will, in your judgment, warrant your leaving, I wish to see you here with the least delay.

He left behind him fantastically long lines of earthworks in South Carolina and Georgia, and men in such numbers as to defend them with reasonable hope of success, but he did not deceive himself. There was indeed, as he wrote: "More here than I can do, and more, I fear, than I can well accomplish."

On March third he left Savannah by train with his faithful companions, Taylor, Meredith and Perry, with Traveller and Richmond in the baggage car—and three days later was in Richmond.

4 "HIS NAME MIGHT BE AUDACITY!"

LEE HIMSELF had not changed more than the Richmond of early spring, 1862. There was strangeness everywhere, as if he had come to the wrong city. It was grimy, lay under an atmosphere of smoke, and swarmed with strangers—hard, pushing people about some mysterious business. Girls flocked to and from government departments. Many of the buildings rumbled and hummed, and through windows could be seen hundreds of women bending over benches in the cartridge factories; there was a pounding and wheezing of foundries and lathes and wood-working plants.

The shops were there, more of them than ever, and they had an air of plenty. Their windows displayed French perfumes and wines, the finest hams, ducks, partridge, oysters and terrapin. French and English prints were there, reminders that lanes to Europe were open.

Despite the Yankee blockade, one window was crowded with gleaming new pianos. But there were a few signs of distress even here. Dandelion coffee was proclaimed "equal to the best Java," and prices were climbing. Butter was an unheard-of fifty cents a pound.

The ordnance department called on citizens to give up their souvenir pistols and muskets for unarmed soldiers. Lee would discover the reality, and approve a remarkable order sending General Jackson 1,000 pikes, crude spears for an army short of firearms.

The full tide of bickering broke on Lee when he examined the official records. Davis was in a feud with the proud Joseph E. Johnston, now in command at Manassas; the President was assailed by Robert Toombs, who had left the Cabinet for the field, and by Vice President Stephens as well.

"The President," Mrs. Chesnut's diary revealed, "is accused of making a place for his brother-in-law, Dick Taylor. After all, it is only transferring Walker, a Georgian, to a Georgia regiment, and giving Walker's regiment . . . to Dick Taylor. . . . Walker says he has disciplined and trained this regiment, and now Dick Taylor will have all the benefit of his work. Forgetting their country, quarreling for their own glory! For shame!"

President Davis was still pale from a long illness of the winter, and was now completely blind in one eye, which had become a stone-gray orb. He seemed as energetic as ever, though he now said, "Events have cast on our arms and hopes the gloomiest shadows."

The Davis family had moved from the Spotswood to the Brockenbrough mansion, with rooms forty feet square, mantels of Carrara marble adorned with Greek sculpture. A handsome cream rug lay in Mrs. Davis' parlor, which was usually thronged with people. Lee saw the President often in these days and it was not long before he understood the bleakness of the situation.[1]

Not only had the fall of Forts Henry and Donelson cost parts of Kentucky and Tennessee; Fort Columbus, high up the Mississippi, was now gone, and the line of the great river as far south as Memphis was crumbling. Hope of foreign intervention was faint; King Cotton, rather than saving the Confederacy, had fallen. England seemed in no mood to force the blockade to reach the cotton supply, and the useless bales piled up. Cotton was now five cents a pound, and slaves were selling for a trifle.

There was much, Lee learned from Davis, that the public could not be told. The powder supply was so low that no major battle could be fought, and muskets were depleted. The ironclad *Merrimac*, so promising under her new name, *Virginia*, could not lift the blockade; she was a victim of the Federal *Monitor*.

Davis was vexed by the timidity of Joseph Johnston at Manassas, who was constantly threatening to retreat, despite the President's opposition. After weeks of this, that army had fallen back to the line of the Rappahannock River.

Affairs of politics were little better, Davis confided to Lee. Congress had literally chased Benjamin from the war department, and he had substituted George Randolph, who was popular in Richmond. For a time it appeared that Lee might be made Secretary of War, but Davis had greater need of him. After an internal wrangle with Congress, Davis vetoed a bill that would have given Lee full authority in the field. Davis named Lee "commander," to be posted at Richmond, where he would be "under the direction of the President," an assignment vague enough to allow Davis to retain full authority.[2]

Lee wrote Mary, revealing that he was not deceived by Davis' reluctance to share his power:

> I have been placed on duty here to conduct operations under the direction of the President. It will give me great pleasure to do anything I can to relieve him and serve the country, but I do not see either advantage or pleasure in my duties. But I will not complain, but do my best.

Mary was still at the White House below Richmond, and Lee wrote that he would make a place for her in the city if she wished to come, saying, "No one can foresee what may happen. . . . I shall, in all human probability, soon have to take the field."

The general left his duties for a few hours on March fifteenth to help his son Robert, who was on his way to join the Rockbridge Artillery. Robert seemed overjoyed to see his father, whom he found "as sweet and loving . . . as in the old days."

Lee went with Robert to get his clothing and equipment for army service, and "took great pains" to see that each item was suitable. They bought little, but even so, Robert was to find that his father had oversupplied him, and that many things were to be discarded in action.

Lee saw him off to join Stonewall Jackson in the Shenandoah Valley, and wrote to Mary, saying that they must be resigned and adding that he hoped Rob would be a good soldier.

There were now many conferences, and Lee began to learn the labyrinthine ways of Davis in dealing with his political generals and cabinet officers. In his slow, gentle fashion Lee tried to impress sound strategy upon the President. Lee had no command, and was quick to perceive that his hope of aiding the cause lay in planting ideas with Davis and hoping that they would bear fruit before ruin fell upon them.

On March twenty-fourth there was an abrupt end to Lee's delicate fencing with Davis. A score or more of Federal troopships had docked at Fort Monroe, and invasion by a major force was threatened in Tidewater Virginia. Lee began to issue orders, and to guide Davis, with a new confidence of manner; delay might well be fatal. The scattered commands of the Virginia coast were sent reinforcements, and defenses of the rivers were tightened. Lee expected the blow to fall on the peninsula between the York and James, where Magruder commanded, and he sought troops for him.

He proposed the daring transfer of Johnston's army from the north to the peninsula. Johnston resisted, though he had been told to expect an order to move. Lee did not protest, but nibbled away at Johnston's force, taking the small groups the commander was willing to spare. Magruder grew slowly in strength and soon had over 31,000 men.

At last, with news from the west worsening daily (Albert Sidney Johnston was killed in the bloody battle at Shiloh on April sixth; two days later the last fort on the Upper Mississippi had fallen to the Federals), Lee ordered Joseph E. Johnston to move his men to the peninsula, and to report to Davis in Richmond. Behind in the north was left only the little band of General Dick Ewell, who was to aid Stonewall Jackson in the Valley if needed.

Johnston was a rather austere Old Army man who had out-ranked Lee in prewar days, and had been deeply hurt when Davis made him inferior in rank. He had recently been described by a South Carolinian who met him on a hunting trip:

"We all liked him, but as to hunting, there he made a dead failure. He was a capital shot . . . but with Colonel Johnston the bird flew too high or low, the dogs were too far or too near. Things never did suit exactly. He was too fussy, too hard to please, too cautious, too much afraid to miss and risk his fine reputation for a crack shot. . . . Unless his ways are changed, he'll never fight a battle. You'll see. He is as brave as Caesar, an accomplished soldier, but he is too particular."[3]

Joe Johnston was soon to prove the accuracy of this sketch. He conferred briefly with Lee and Davis, and on April thirteenth went east, to his large command of the Virginia front. He lost no time in stirring a tempest.

Johnston took a quick look at the defenses on the lower penin-sula and hurried back to Richmond, where he frightened Davis with his tale: Magruder's men were weak and dispirited and could not fight; if they could, the earthworks would be of little value, because the enemy could force his way up the rivers and cut off the entire command. Davis should at once concentrate every soldier in the Eastern Confederacy, from Georgia northward to Virginia, and this huge force should smash McClellan. Pull back in the east, and surrender Norfolk and the peninsula to the enemy; the army should retire to the Richmond trenches to prepare for decisive battle.

The surprising thing was that Davis sat in a day-long conference over Johnston's plan. He called in Lee early in the morning, and they sat with Johnston, Secretary Randolph, and two generals in from the front, James Longstreet and Gustavus W. Smith. They debated all day, with Lee and Randolph arguing that the plan of Johnston would end the Confederacy. Smith supported Johnston. Longstreet did not advance an opinion. It went on until one A.M. when, at last, Davis overruled Johnston, ordered him to defend the lower peninsula, and ended the singular conference.[4]

Johnston returned to his command once more.

Johnston's coming did not diminish Lee's chores. He had assembled a staff about him, an informal group of young men, most of them from civilian life. Long had come up from South Carolina as his military secretary, and his aides were Walter Taylor and a newcomer, an engineer and the son of an old friend, T. M. R. Talcott. They had been joined by Charles S. Venable and a Baltimore lawyer with a gift for rhetoric, Charles Marshall.

One of the first chores the staff helped Lee to handle was the conscription act, which he had urged on Davis and all who would listen—and which was finally passed in weakened form by Congress. It would take into the army all men between eighteen and thirty-five, and though it was imperfect, should fill the brigades Lee foresaw would be needed for survival.

Military operations put the small staff to a test. In the Shenandoah, General Jackson's little command drew the attention of Lee.

On March twenty-third, Jackson had attacked the Federals at Kernstown and been beaten off, but Lee was aware that Stonewall had checked the enemy and increased their respect for the tiny valley force. Now he suggested reinforcements for Jackson, so that General Banks and his Union force might be kept busy, and other reinforcements prevented from joining the attack on Richmond. Jackson could take Ewell's men. Lee put his proposal in words welcome to Stonewall:

> The blow, wherever struck, must, to be successful, be sudden and heavy.

Jackson was soon off through the hill country, and for long days was out of touch with Richmond.

On Sunday, April twenty-eighth, more bad news came to Richmond. With the tolling of church bells, a report reached the city that New Orleans had fallen to a Federal fleet.

But the next day Lee was writing Jackson another gently urgent dispatch out of which a campaign was to grow. He did not conceal the limits of Confederate manpower, but said:

> A decisive and successful blow at Bank's column would be fraught with the happiest results . . .

On May twenty-third, Jackson fell upon Banks in a surprise attack, mauled his outpost at Front Royal, set his main army to flight, half destroyed his wagon train—and in full-scale battle at Winchester put the Federals into panic. The war had seen nothing like this; Richmond rejoiced, and the tide appeared, at last, to be turning. Jackson's victories, so reports said, had astounding effect in the North. Washington was fearful of attack. The large army of General McDowell, near Fredericksburg, was held for the defense of Washington, instead of joining the push on Richmond.

This thrust improved Lee's frame of mind, of which he had recently written: "We have received some heavy blows lately, from the effects of which, I trust, a merciful God will deliver us." The latest of these blows had come from Johnston, who had never accepted the President's decision that the lower peninsula must be defended. On May first he had notified Davis that he would evacuate Yorktown, center of his line at the water front. Despite Lee's arguments and the prospect of losing Norfolk, Johnston fell back up the peninsula on May fourth, without notifying Richmond. As the army swarmed along the sandy swamp roads, Federal gun-boats cut their way up the rivers, and some were within thirty-seven miles of Richmond.

That was not all, for in the retreat the Federals slashed at Johnston's rear guard at Williamsburg with such fury that thou-sands were drawn into the bloody little battle and casualties were heavy. No one knew what loss had been sustained, since Johnston had been forced back, leaving his wounded to their fate in a rainy night.

Throughout this action Richmond heard only rumors. Even in these two or three anxious days, however, Lee calmly sent rein-forcements to Jackson in the hills.

On May eight, Johnston sent an angry letter to headquarters accusing Lee of interference in his command, blaming others with his defeat: "My authority does not extend beyond the troops im-mediately around me. I request therefore to be relieved of a merely nominal geographical command." Lee replied with a deftly con-ciliatory letter, indicating that he knew well Johnston's quick tem-per, and valued him despite that fault.[5]

The situation continued to darken. Norfolk was lost and John-ston's army was a mere thirty miles from the capital. Lee and Davis hastened to complete batteries of big guns at Drewry's Bluff on the James to hold off enemy boats, and had the river blocked with every available obstruction. The enemy reached the bluff on May fifteenth, but after a noisy battle between an ironclad and the batteries, the Federal craft withdrew.

Johnston now retired to the line of the Chickahominy, and was still difficult in dealings with Richmond. Davis asked him to report for a conference. Johnston did not reply, nor answer even a second request. Davis and Lee rode to investigate and found the army in poor condition. The President pointed out to Johnston that the turnpike into Richmond lay open for the enemy, so far as he could see. Davis was almost right, for on May twenty-fourth the enemy occupied the village of Mechanicsville just five miles from Richmond. The situation was maddening to Davis, and his patience wore so thin that Lee volunteered to make peace. He rode out to Johnston and pulled from him the admission that he planned to attack on May twenty-ninth.

There were long days while Richmond waited, for outposts from the north brought news that McDowell's army had marched from Fredericksburg; it would soon be upon Richmond and fall on Johnston's rear. There were frenzied dispatch riders from Richmond to the front, but there seemed nothing to do in preparation for the crisis. Davis and Lee went out to Johnston's army, and while there got word almost too good to be true: McDowell's army, with the road to Richmond open, had been halted and returned to Fredericksburg. The magic of Jackson's attacks had made the North fearful, and saved the city.

Johnston delayed another day, arguing strategy with his generals. On May thirtieth, Lee could stand inaction no longer. He was spoiling to be at the front. Long carried a note to Johnston from Lee, "to tell him that he would be glad to participate in the battle. He had no desire to interfere with his command, but simply wished to aid him on the field to the best of his ability and in any manner."

This aroused no enthusiasm in Johnston, who replied only that Lee was welcome to come to the field; he also needed reinforcements, he said.

May thirty-first, a Saturday when clouds hung low over Richmond and the country to the east, was to be a strange day in the annals of the Confederacy—and one of the most memorable. In the early morning Lee went out with some of his staff to Johnston's headquarters on Nine Mile Road. The roads were bordered with standing water; it had rained more than three inches late the previous afternoon, and continued all night. The Chickahominy had not been so high in twenty years; it overflowed its banks in front of Johnston's army.

Johnston seemed to have little time to explain to Lee—or to know quite what was happening in the tangles of undergrowth bordering the river. From the coming and going of officers, it was clear that a full-scale army movement was under way.

The troops were hurrying to attack Federals south of the Chickahominy, on the theory that reinforcements from the huge enemy army could not come to their aid across the swollen stream. Johnston had given his generals their assignments: Longstreet, Magruder, Gustavus Smith and D. H. Hill. They were to converge on the enemy flank, which was presumed to be exposed. The plan seemed sound. Its chief objective was the seizure of a lonely village called Seven Pines.

By noon it appeared that something had gone wrong, but Johnston gave no indication of his troubles, and Lee learned nothing of the details.

At three P.M., when firing broke out in the distance, Lee knew that it was musketry, and that large bodies of troops were in the fight. He said as much to Johnston.

"No," Johnston said, as if his plan of battle made that impossible. "It could be nothing but artillery fire."

The difficulties of the day, it developed, were caused by Longstreet, who misunderstood or disobeyed orders, and rather than advancing directly toward the enemy down Nine Mile Road, had cut over to the Williamsburg Road. His passage had blocked other brigades and snarled the plan of battle, with the result that isolated bodies of troops went through the brush to face the enemy alone. The men of D. H. Hill attacked the Federals, but could not budge them; reinforcements went in and were mauled.

Almost at the first sounds of battle Davis rode to Johnston's headquarters. Here Lee and Davis and an assembly of staff officers saw Johnston behave curiously. Young Major E. P. Alexander, an artilleryman, watched.

"General Johnston saw Mr. Davis approaching, and . . . sought to avoid a meeting by mounting quickly and riding rapidly to the extreme front."

The group stared after the field commander as he disappeared. Lee and Davis rode off down an overgrown roadway, and into the thick of firing. Near here, in the morning, General John B. Gordon's troops had charged, swept over and taken some breastworks on the outer ring of McClellan's defenses. Gordon's coat had been ripped by bullets, and most of his staff killed; General Rodes, the brigade commander, was wounded. Gordon passed his brother, lying among the dead, evidently breathing his last. He did not stop. Gordon was seldom to see harder fighting in his long career: "At this time my own horse, the only one left, was killed. . . . McClellan's men were slowly being pressed back into and through the Chickahominy Swamp, which was filled with water; but almost at every step pouring terrific volleys into my lines. My regiment had been in some way separated from the brigade. . . . My field officers and adjutants were all dead. . . . Fully half of my line officers and half my men were wounded or dead. A furious fire still poured from the front, and reinforcements were nowhere in sight. . . . In water from hip- to knee-deep, the men were fighting and falling, while a detail propped up the wounded against stumps or trees to prevent their drowning."[6]

Not far away Wade Hampton, going into battle, had ridden down the front of the 16th North Carolina, shouting, "Do not fire a shot until you can feel the enemy on your bayonets! Forward!"

Isolated brigades pawed at the enemy in the watery groves, and casualties increased though no ground was won. Lee and Davis were helpless to find a key to the situation; Richmond officials, including Congressmen, milled about them. Davis made an attempt to command men into action himself, to drive out the Federal batteries pouring such galling fire into the flank, but he was too late. The army retreated a short distance at dusk. Confused messages came to headquarters, and for a time there was no word from Johnston.

A dispatch rider said General Hampton had been wounded. Another, following him closely, said that General Johnston was seriously wounded.

The field commander had been far in advance of the troops, heedless of danger; he had refused to move to the rear. He got a flesh wound in the shoulder from a musket ball. A moment later a shell fragment struck his chest, knocking him from his horse. He was put in an ambulance, but could not bear the jarring motion over the bad roads, and was then carried out on a litter. The night was pitch black in the swamps, and everywhere was the cry of the wounded.

Lee and the President greeted Johnston as he was moved out in the rear. Still conscious, but weak, the wounded general was taken away.

As Lee and Davis tried to puzzle out the results of the day and make plans for the morrow, General Smith, the ranking officer, reported and described the costly fighting on his wing. Davis pressed him for his plans, since he would logically inherit command. Smith's nervous, hesitant replies made Davis wary. He did not like to hear rambling talk of pulling back even closer to Richmond.

No one was near Lee and Davis as they rode slowly through the swarm of vehicles carrying the wounded into Richmond—not near enough at least to hear Davis' few words, surely brief, quiet ones, which placed Lee in command of the army he would make famous. His most devoted biographer was to render them:

"General Lee, I shall assign you to the command of this army.

Make your preparations as soon as you reach your quarters. I shall send you the order when we get to Richmond."⁷

They reached the city amid a moving spectacle. Hospitals were already crowded, for sick men by the hundred had fallen out of Johnston's army in the rainy season. New regiments from the South were just moving into town, and cheering throngs greeted them. These new soldiers marched toward the battlefield as the tide of wounded began to arrive. Alexander Hunter, a Texas private, saw them:

"Long lines of ambulances coming from the opposite way toiled slowly along . . . the long, torturing way marked by the trail of blood that oozed drop by drop . . . or else might be seen a wagon-load of dead piled one upon another, their stiffened . . . feet exposed to view. . . . The more slightly wounded were made to walk, and long lines of them could be seen hobbling along the street, their wounds bound up in bloody rags. The citizens turned out in full force and did all in their power. . . . Ladies stood in front of their homes with waiters of food and drink, luxuries and wine, which they dealt out unsparingly. . . .

"For days and nights wagons and ambulances never ceased to empty their wretched loads before the doors of . . . hastily improvised hospitals . . . the long procession of wounded, nearly five thousand, young, middle-aged and white-haired . . . hurt in every conceivable manner. . . . In one day Richmond was changed from a mirth-loving, pleasure-seeking city into a city resolute and nerved to make any sacrifice. . . ."

Lee was up most of the night, preparing for the expected battle of the next day; he had his first dispatch from General Smith on the field at five in the morning. It soon became apparent that the Union troops were not coming forward seriously, for the skirmishing was light. And Smith was pacified a bit by Lee's generous dispatch of the morning, which ended: "It will be a glorious thing if you can gain a complete victory. Our success on the whole yesterday was good, but not complete."

The new commander seemed to overstate the case, for long bickering arose among generals as to the responsibility of the fumbling of Seven Pines. That very day, in fact, Longstreet showed his temper in a dispatch:

> Can you re-enforce me? The entire army seems to be opposed to me. We cannot hold out unless we get help. We can fight together, we can finish the work today and Mac's time will be up. If I can't get help, I fear that I must fall back.

The army had gained little from Seven Pines; the loss in officers was appalling. One South Carolina colonel reported: "In my two color companies out of 80 men who entered, 40 were killed or wounded, and out of 11 in the color guards 10 were shot down." Three brigades alone had more than 2,700 casualties, or 44 per cent of their strength. D. H. Hill was to report testily that it took all of the day to pull back together thirteen brigades. At one in the afternoon Lee went out to the field with his staff, his first appearance as commander of the army he that day had styled The Army of Northern Virginia.

In the afternoon Lee sent out an order to the troops, announcing his coming as commander:

> The unfortunate casualty that has deprived the army in front of Richmond of the valuable services of its able general is not more deeply deplored by any member of his command than by its present commander. He hopes his absence will be but temporary, and while he will endeavor to the best of his ability to perform his duties, he feels he will be totally inadequate to the task unless he shall receive the cordial support of every officer and man.
> ... he feels assured that every man has resolved to maintain the ancient fame of the Army of Northern Virginia and the

reputation of its general and to conquer or die in the approaching contest.

This rather heroic address did not seem to stir the troops, and the change of command passed without excitement in Richmond, except for some lavish praise of Johnston in newspapers. *The Richmond Examiner* saluted Lee: "Evacuating Lee, who has never yet risked a single battle with the invader, is commanding general."

Lee turned his attention to the enemy, who lay quietly. Confederate casualties at Seven Pines were greater, but their charges had torn McClellan's ranks and made him cautious. The Rebels had captured ten guns, 500 muskets, 400 prisoners. The flooded country seemed as likely to hold McClellan as a battle; the rains continued.

On June second, Lee wrote Rooney's wife Charlotte, modestly speaking of his new command:

> I wish that mantle had fallen upon an abler man, or that I were able to drive our enemies back to their homes. I have no ambition and no desire but the attainment of this object, and therefore only wish for its accomplishment by him that can do it most speedily and thoroughly.

The next day he issued orders designed to "drive our enemies." He put engineer officers to work on a series of earthworks for the city which would make it secure, with the thought that he must pull the army from its gates if he were to strike. The army was not accustomed to such bold thinking.

Lee's dispatches of the week showed he had not forgotten Jackson in the west, who was now getting into position for even more brilliant attacks; Lee asked Davis to help get larger re-enforcements for Stonewall. He also gave Davis an estimate of his own opponent, George McClellan, and forecast the coming campaign for Richmond:

McClellan will make this a battle of Posts. He will take position from position, under cover of his heavy guns, and we cannot get at him without storming his works, which with our new troops is extremely hazardous. You witnessed the experiment Saturday.[8]

He told Davis that Richmond could be defended under siege by no fewer than 100,000 men, and added in plain language that he was building a line to hold with a small force, so that he could sweep in upon a flank and "bring McClellan out."

The exchanges with Davis show a candor and intimacy of relationship, and Lee's apparent interest in everything connected with his army. He must have known of the experimental Confederate repeating cannon at Seven Pines, and he now told Davis of his scheme to have made a heavy iron "battery on trucks," on which he could mount a heavy railroad gun; he might thus prevent McClellan from bringing up heavy siege guns. He wrote of the miserable roads in the front: "You have seen nothing like the roads on the Chicky bottom. Our people are opposed to work. Our troops, officers, community and press. All ridicule and resist it. It is the very means by which McClellan has and is advancing. Why should we leave to him the whole advantage of labor?"

Now there was further electrifying news from Jackson.

Stonewall had fallen back from Winchester by day and night marches to escape the trap being closed on him by two Federal armies, and in the rugged country just south of the Massanutton Mountains, he had turned. Incredibly, he had whipped first one of the pursuing armies and then the other, putting them to flight, once more clearing that area of the Shenandoah. The twin victories of Cross Keys and Port Republic were the climax of a campaign won against fearful odds by a little army of 17,000. The Confederacy had at last a genuine hero.

Lee had become, in these weeks, "The King of Spades," as he

drove troops to the Richmond defenses, and the hostile *Richmond Examiner* crowed: "General Jackson's two maxims, 'to fight whenever it is possible,' and in fighting, to 'attack at once and furiously,' are worth all the ditches and spades that General Lee can display on this side of the Chickahominy."

But the men continued to work in the sweltering days, and trenches ran in mazes before the city; earthworks rose. Lee wooed his men with better food, more clothing, all the arms he could find for them. Federals reported that Rebels taken prisoner "improved in appearance, cadaverous looks became rare."

Lee was often among the ranks. One of his young gunners recorded his first appearance as commander:

"General Lee first appeared before us in citizen's dress, in white duck with a bob tail coat; jogging along without our suspecting who he was. We thought at first he was a jolly easy going miller or distiller on a visit as a civilian to the front, and perhaps carrying out a canteen of whisky for the boys. He showed himself good-natured . . . stopping once to reprove, though very gently, the drivers for unmercifully beating their horses when they stalled; and walking about and laughing at one of Artemus Ward's stories; and kept in a good humor about it the rest of the day."

Lee lost no time in trying to win his officers. The stolid Longstreet was at first a bit reticent. After all, he complained, though a change would be "a happy relief from the . . . halting policy" of Johnston:

> The assignment of General Lee to command . . . was far from reconciling the troops to the loss of our beloved chief. . . Johnston. . . . All hearts had learned . . . to love him dearly.

More than that, Longstreet grumbled:

> Lee's experience in active field work was limited to his West Virginia campaign . . . which was not successful . . .

officers of the line are not apt to look to the staff in choosing
leaders . . . either in tactics or strategy. There were, therefore,
some misgivings.

These began to disappear almost with Lee's coming to command. He called an extraordinary conference of all his general
officers—about 40 of them. They swarmed to the place of meeting,
a house known as The Chimneys, out the Nine Mile Road. There
was a chattering hubbub, for everyone in the army seemed to be
there, down to the very brigadiers. Longstreet revealed his surprise:

> This novelty was not reassuring, as experience had told
> that secrecy in war was an essential element of success; that
> public discussion and secrecy were incompatible.

But Longstreet watched and listened with care as Lee talked
with his commanders with his subtle charm. "Old Pete" must
have enjoyed a slow inward grin as the conference went on. For
though Lee talked, and presented the problems of the army seriously, as if he sought advice, Longstreet could see that he divulged
nothing. The secrets he imparted were harmless enough for the
ears of the enemy. The lesser officers did not appreciate the skill
of the performance. Longstreet recorded it: "As he disclosed nothing, those of serious thought became hopeful, and followed his wise
example. The brigadiers talked freely, but only of the parts of
the line occupied by their brigades; and the meeting finally took
a playful turn."

For the first time, after these innocent moments with the new
commander, the field officers who were to lead the Army of Northern Virginia felt themselves vital parts of the growing force; they
had the feeling that the commander knew their problems and
valued their opinions. Even Robert Toombs was being won, that
violent man who had for weeks been shouting publicly to his troops

of "West Point men holding the army from battle, digging and throwing up lines of sand."

Lee persisted in his skilled probing of the generals. W. H. C. Whiting, for one, seemed depressed by the casualties his division had suffered among the bogs of Seven Pines; he was a highly intelligent, educated man, but, Longstreet observed, "the dark side of the picture was always more imposing on him." Before Whiting and the rest had left him, Lee knew a great deal about their temperaments and the condition of their troops. He soon broke up Whiting's division, sending part of it to A. P. Hill. The rest, with new troops chosen by Whiting, marched out westward, to reinforce Jackson after the victory at Port Republic. The rumor swept Richmond's streets: The next offensive would be in the Shenandoah.

Lee did not rest, the watchful Longstreet saw: "He ordered his engineers over the line occupied by the army," to reinforce it. And: "Lee was seen almost daily riding over his lines, making suggestions to working parties and encouraging their efforts. . . . Above all, they soon began to look eagerly for his daily rides, his pleasing yet commanding presence, and the energy he displayed in speeding their labors."

The young gunner, E. P. Alexander, was scornful of this digging and impressed by newspaper critics in Richmond, who said that Lee's work was proof enough that he would not be an aggressive fighter. One day Alexander met Colonel Joe Ives, who had served with Lee, and was now on the staff of Davis.

"Ives," Alexander asked: "tell me this. We are here fortifying our lines, but apparently leaving the enemy all the time he needs to accumulate his superior forces, and then to move on us in the way he thinks best. Has General Lee the audacity that is going to be required for our inferior force to meet the enemy . . . to take the aggressive, and to run risks and stand chances?"

"Ives' reply was so impressive," Alexander wrote, "that it has always been remembered. . . . He reined up his horse, stopped in the road, and, turning to me, said: 'Alexander, if there is one man in either army . . . head and shoulders above every other in audacity, it is General Lee! His name might be Audacity. He will take more desperate chances and take them quicker than any other general in this country, North or South; and you will live to see it, too.' "9

Lee was already in the midst of work which would convince Alexander.

First, he had begun with his scouts and cavalrymen to sniff about the fringes of McClellan's vast and formidable position. To the southeast there was no question of attack, for impassable White Oak Swamp shielded his flank. The Chickahominy, however, still split McClellan's army, and if the wing to the north could be pried loose, then the entire Federal force might be hurled back. It could not be attempted until Lee knew the situation.

He called to the task one of his old West Point cadets, the youngster who had aided him in catching old John Brown at Harpers Ferry, almost three years before: James Ewell Brown Stuart. Jeb Stuart was just such a commander as the wild young Virginia horsemen could worship, a general not yet thirty, given to wearing jaunty plumes, flowing scarlet-lined capes, fashionable jack boots, and to leading a gay band of musicians who were forever playing corn-shucking tunes, with bones and banjo. His troopers wailed their infectious hymn: "Jine the Caval-ree!"

Stuart, whose rust beard now covered the weak chin that had won him the nickname "Beauty" at West Point, was already a hero; he had met the enemy hand to hand, and had himself captured almost 50 Yankees at the little battle of Falling Waters the year before. Lee, until now, had not been his kind of a general, but this week he had given him an assignment to his liking.

So Stuart was off, on June twelfth, and his 1,200 riders plunged into the swamps. For more than two full days they were gone, as if they had been swallowed by the dark waters. But when Stuart reappeared, his worn, mud-soaked riders having entered history, he brought the news Lee wanted most to hear. The cavalry had made the entire circle of the Federal army, easily thrusting off the little cavalry opposition they had stirred, and after splashing the bad roads and fording full creeks and rivers, had found McClellan's right, and it was exposed. Beyond the Federal flank was a high, commanding ridge. From this wing, the enemy was pushing his supply wagons through terrible roads from Rooney's old home, White House on the Pamunkey. Lee determined to attack, and turned to prepare the army.

He would need Jackson, and despite Stonewall's reticence to leave the field where he was winning laurels in independent command, and despite the risk of opening that section of the state to Federal attack, Lee finally ordered Jackson to Richmond. Congressman Boteler, probably speaking Stonewall's mind, had protested mildly to Lee, that bringing Jackson to the capital "will be putting all your eggs in one basket."

Lee replied: "I see that you appreciate General Jackson as highly as I myself do, and it is because of my appreciation of him that I wish to have him here."

In the end Jackson, telling not even his chief lieutenants of his move, flung a cavalry screen behind him and moved across Virginia. He had Dick Ewell swearing as the army marched: "Dammit, Jackson is driving us mad. He don't say a word . . . no order, no hint of where we're going."

Jackson had a saying appropriate to the streaming of his army this week: "If my coat knew my plans, as Frederick the Great once said, I would take it off and burn it. And if I can deceive my friends, I can make certain of deceiving my enemies."

Lee's order had said, "Will meet you at some point on your approach to the Chickahominy." And the commander drew his detailed plan. When it was ready he explained it to Davis, who finally approved, despite its boldness: The entire army, except for a fragment to the south under Magruder, would leave its trenches, with

Richmond lightly defended in its rear, and fall on the exposed 25,000 on McClellan's right. The Federals had some 105,000 troops in the front, and Lee could count no more than 85,000 in his ranks.

Davis had protested mildly: If McClellan did not behave like an engineer officer, and hold to his lines, he would strike the south end of Lee's line while the move was under way.

Lee bristled: "If you will hold as long as you can at the entrenchments, and then fall back on the detached works around the city, I will be on the enemy's heels before he gets there."[10]

As Jackson's troops neared, coming across Virginia, Lee went to peer at the point of planned attack. One afternoon he took Long with him north of the Chickahominy, and they rode as near as they dared to the enemy flank. Absently Lee asked, "Now, Colonel Long, how can we get at those people?" He was silently answering his own question.

Longstreet came to the same conclusion at about the same time, he recalled:

"The day after Stuart's return I rode over to General Lee's headquarters and suggested that General Jackson be withdrawn from the Valley to take position on our left . . . and was informed that the order for Jackson was sent when Whiting . . . was sent to join him."

Longstreet seemed overjoyed at the prospect before them, and he was in such an unusually gay humor that he went about merrily quoting Stuart, who said, when congratulated upon his historic ride:

"Well, I left a general behind me."

"Who?"

"General Consternation."[11]

On the afternoon of June twenty-third a bearded horseman with yellow dust thick on his uniform dismounted before Lee's headquarters and, being told that the commander was busy, propped himself against the fence and nodded, an ancient forage cap pulled down over his nose—Jackson.

He was found there by D. H. Hill, his brother-in-law, and the two went in to Lee. Couriers rode for Longstreet and A. P. Hill. Jackson began to relax. He drank a glass of cold milk and leaned forward to hear Lee's brief explanation of the attack: Jackson's troops would move in on the north, to hit the flank while the other units of the army struck below him, nearer the Chickahominy. Down roughly parallel roads the divisions would advance in unison. Lee left them to further discussion, as if he had complete faith that these veteran commanders would agree on details of the attack. Longstreet turned to Jackson:

"You have distance to overcome, and in all probability the enemy will try to halt you. Your move is the key. You set the hour when the troops can join."

"The morning of the twenty-fifth," Jackson said, without pause.

"I don't know," Longstreet said. "The roads are bad. You had best take a little more time. We can adjust our movements to yours."

"All right," Jackson said. "The morning of the twenty-sixth."

Lee soon returned, but did not question his lieutenants. Jackson rode away to put his men in motion.

5 THE SEVEN DAYS

IN THE drizzling rain of June 25, 1862, Federal balloons hanging to the east of Richmond seemed closer yet, and the capital could almost feel the eyes of enemy scouts upon it.

There was an undercurrent of talk. Everyone knew by now that the President had sent his wife and children to Raleigh, in North Carolina, for safety.[1] And the clerks whispered that government files had been packed for removal.

The army seemed confident enough, as its men cooked their three days' rations, knowing that trouble was coming. Most of them seemed hardened to battle. Reverend Joseph Stiles, a Presbyterian minister, rode his sulky to the front lines seeking his son Robert, a major, and held a prayer service in sight of the enemy. A Federal battery dropped a few shells about the group, but the minister would not open his eyes from prayer, nor would his congregation—except for Robert, who saw his companions, still with eyes shut, down on hands and knees scrambling for a protective tree or stump.

Stiles came upon some enemy wounded with ranks of the Louisiana Tigers, who had been recruited from New Orleans prisons. One of the Federals writhed, begging, "Some one put me out of my misery!"

One of the Tigers leapt forward: "Certainly, sir!" and before he could be halted, brained the man with his musket butt and glared about him. "Any other gentlemen like to be accommodated?"[2]

During June twenty-fourth and twenty-fifth Jackson had been moving on the upper edge of the Confederate front, and had camped, late by five or six hours, in the hamlet of Ashland. The men from the Valley had, in fact, the longest approach march to make, through country strange to them, and were dead tired from campaigning and crossing the state. There were no adequate maps. General Richard Taylor complained: "Confederate commanders knew no more about the topography, the whole of it within a day's march of the city of Richmond, than they did about Central Africa."[3]

Jackson, however, seemed to know where he was. Stuart had joined him to cover his flank. Stonewall notified Lee that he would hurry by starting his troops at two thirty A.M. on the twenty-sixth, and he had been snapping at his brigadiers to push them. There was a slight change in Jackson's order, but it would not prevent him from coming in, high to his left, to get behind Beaver Dam Creek, so that there need be no fighting for the heights along the stream; that would also mean bloodless occupation of the village of Mechanicsville, where the enemy had stout lines.

Lee's new chief of staff, Colonel R. H. Chilton, had sent out the order of battle, which seemed clear enough. Running from left to right, the advancing divisions would be commanded by Stuart and Jackson—north of Mechanicsville—D. H. Hill, A. P. Hill and Longstreet. When Jackson's guns opened, the divisions would plunge down their assigned roads, clearing the Chickahominy bridges, and striking an enemy expected to be forced from his lines.

Early in the morning, about eight, most of Lee's troops were in position, and the long wait for Jackson began. Lee watched from heights above Mechanicsville. Nothing happened. By early afternoon Davis had come with a scattering of officers and politicians. In the river bottoms ahead, men lay in line. A little after three P.M. Lee and his staff saw with relief the quick blooming of smoke in the distance, and in their field glasses made out the reassuring sight of blue infantry falling back. Men of A. P. Hill's division were up and across the open toward Mechanicsville. D. H. Hill and Longstreet were pressing behind; snarled columns halted other troops, and time was wasted while a bridge was repaired. The enemy did not flee on schedule.

As men moved into the village, they came under heavy artillery fire. Davis got across the river even before Lee, while some of the troops were still wading. It became obvious to Lee that something had gone wrong. He ordered A. P. Hill to halt. As he went forward men were dropping among the scattered outbuildings, and in the open fields. Lee saw Davis in the midst of it. A Richmond diarist later recorded the scene:

"General Lee was evidently annoyed . . . he turned his back for a moment, until Colonel Chilton had been dispatched at a gallop with the last direction to . . . the attacking brigade; then, facing the cavalcade and looking like the god of war indignant, he exchanged with the President a salute, with the most frigid reserve. . . .

"Looking at the assemblage at large, he asked in a tone of irritation, 'Who are all this army of people, and what are they doing here?'

"No one spoke or moved, but all eyes were upon the President. . . . The President twisted in his saddle, quite taken aback at such a greeting. . . . After a painful pause the President said deprecatingly, 'It is not my army, General.'

" 'It certainly is not my army, Mr. President . . . and this is no place for it.'

" 'Well, General, if I withdraw, perhaps they will follow,' and, raising his hat in another cold salute, he turned his horse's head."[4]

But when Davis was screened from Lee by bushes, he reined his horse and the entire staff remained on the battlefield.

Lee soon found his trouble: Men were being dashed against the strong enemy line on Beaver Dam Creek, which had not been turned. Jackson had not been heard from. Lee got from A. P. Hill the dismaying news that he had attacked without hearing from Jackson, fearing that otherwise the battle plan would fail. Lee contained his wrath, and turned to rescuing exposed segments of his command, already suffering heavy losses. Night fell upon the unexpected battle at Mechanicsville. Almost 1,400 men had fallen with little gained. It was too late to hear from Jackson, and Lee gave orders for attack in the morning, and went to bed in a house near Mechanicsville.

There was some firing in the early morning, but Lee quickly saw that the enemy had abandoned the strong line of Beaver Dam Creek; perhaps they had fallen back upon finding Jackson on the flank. In any event, the army went forward. An artillery duel broke out near Gaines' Mill, and more troops converged on the spot along swampy roads. Progress was slow and underbrush screened Lee's vision. During the morning Stuart's horsemen clashed with large bodies of Federal cavalry armed with lances, and drove them off. Even the massed infantry was attacked by these bold, picturesque horsemen, many of whom were shot down in the random attacks. Not until after noon, when Lee had sent Walter Taylor to find him, did Jackson appear. His gunners had already challenged the enemy near the mill. Lee found him about one P.M. and the generals sat on a stump, near a church east of Beaver Dam Creek.

Lee's staff stared at the unkempt Valley conqueror, and Jackson's worn men eyed the glittering young officers from headquarters. Lee himself looked so much the ordinary soldier that the Reverend Dabney, Jackson's chief of staff, did not recognize him. There was little time for a report in this conference; Lee only later learned of the difficulties of Jackson's march and his mysterious failure to attack the day before. Now there was work to be done, and Lee sent Jackson to direct affairs of his front.

Furious fighting ensued, and the thickets literally shook with the storm of bullets and shells. On A. P. Hill's front the infantry had groped through to the site of Gaines' Mill, and the gray ranks were driven back time after time. Longstreet's men were thrown in, and for hours these troops fought an unequal battle. Jackson had been lost for a time, in a misunderstanding with a local guide; D. H. Hill had been delayed on a road by cannon fire.

At last the army heard from the men of the Valley, a rousing Rebel Yell from the Stonewall Brigade which drove Federals through the swamp. Jackson had been directing affairs, waving one of his usual lemons, and he now threw it away. He at last got all his fourteen brigades into line, and the general advance began.

Lee found him once more in a road.

"Ah, General," Lee said, "I am glad to see you. I had hoped to be with you before now."

Jackson did not make a clear reply; he muttered what might have been an apology for his second tardiness of the day.

"That fire is very heavy," Lee said. "Do you think your men can stand it?"

"They can stand almost anything. They can stand that."[5]

In the final attack of the day, ended by darkness, the Confederates dashed forward and threw the Federal line into panic at some points. It was costly: One Texas regiment lost every field officer; in another, 600 of 800 men had fallen. The army, almost incredibly, had lost 8,000 men, and Jackson's wing alone had 3,700 casualties. The failure to concentrate, even when he could gain victory, was making Lee pay dearly. But the men were jubilant; the great army of the enemy had run, and would soon be trapped.

Lee spent most of the morning of June twenty-eighth puzzling over the intentions of the enemy. Before long great clouds of dust rose over the swamps. The enemy was moving hurriedly, as if Mc-

Clellan feared himself outnumbered. Lee sent Stuart's riders down river to the White House, and ordered Jackson to have Ewell's infantry press down the Chickahominy banks. From every scout reporting Lee had the same news: Federals had burned the bridges, crawled out of last night's lines, and disappeared. They had left vast piles of stores and debris.

During the day Lee encountered his son Robert, whom he had not seen since he sent him off to join Jackson in the west. He sought out the Rockbridge Artillery. Young Robert remembered it:

"Most of the men were lying down. . . . I had crawled under a caisson and was busy making up many lost hours of rest. Suddenly I was rudely awakened by a comrade, prodding me with a sponge-staff . . . and was told to get up and come out, that someone wished to see me.

"Half awake, I staggered out, and found myself face to face with General Lee and his staff. . . . I was completely dazed. It took me a moment or two to realize what it all meant, but when I saw my father's loving eyes and smile it became clear to me that he had ridden by to see if I was safe and to ask how I was getting along.

"I remember well how curiously those with him gazed at me, and I am sure that it must have struck them as very odd that such a dirty, ragged, unkempt youth could have been the son of this grand-looking victorious commander."

On the field they had fought over yesterday, a maze of bogs and thickets, the Texas troops had won the day with a furious charge.

Today Jackson rode this ground, seeing the brush and trees slashed to stumps and ribbons by the fire, still sprinkled with bodies of the Texas dead. "The men who carried this position were soldiers indeed," he said.[6]

Lee allowed most of the men to rest during the day, until further word from the front made the situation clear: McClellan was retreating southward, and had abandoned his base of supplies. The Union army was falling down the Peninsula, or was making for the James River, to change base. In either case, Lee had driven it from its campaign to seize Richmond by the direct route. He put everything into the chase.

Jackson was ordered to cross the Chickahominy at Grapevine Bridge. Near White Oak Swamp he would join with General Magruder's troops, who had remained on the south end of the line. Jackson was to strike at McClellan's rear, while Longstreet and A. P. Hill worked their way southward over the river and along parallel roads to come into the Federal front. The enemy should be caught as he was crossing the swamp.

Sunday was a long day, however. Jackson was again delayed; his men labored all day at the Grapevine Bridge, and it was three A.M. Monday when D. H. Hill's men passed over it. In the late afternoon of Sunday, Magruder had attacked the enemy at Savage's Station, not far from Jackson; but when a messenger asked Jackson for help, he was given the strange reply that Stonewall had "other important duty" to perform—perhaps the repairing of the bridge. Magruder, at any rate, had fought a vastly superior Federal force alone, with little profit, and the army's foremost units had made but five miles for the day. Once more, concentration had been impossible.

Lee wrote Magruder: "I regret very much that you have made so little progress today in the pursuit of the enemy. . . . I must urge you . . . to press on his rear rapidly and steadily. We must lose no more time or he will escape us entirely."

McClellan was already across White Oak Swamp, and the plan of assault was amended.

Lee showed no strain, despite the heavy mental and physical demands upon him. Robert Stiles saw him on the fearfully hot Sunday:

"A magnificent staff approached . . . and riding at its head, superbly mounted, a born king among men. At that time General Lee was one of the handsomest of men, especially on horseback,

and that morning every detail of the dress and equipment . . .
was absolute perfection. When he recognized Jackson he rode
forward with a courier, his staff halting. . . .

"The two generals greeted each other warmly. . . . They stood
facing each other, some thirty feet from where I lay. . . . Jackson began talking in a jerky, impetuous way, meanwhile drawing a dia-
gram on the ground with the toe of his right boot. He traced two
sides of a triangle . . . then starting at the end of the second line
began to draw a third. . . . This third line he traced slowly and
with hesitation . . . looking up at Lee's face and down at his dia-
gram, meanwhile talking earnestly; and when at last the third line
crossed the first . . . he raised his foot and stamped it down with
emphasis, saying, 'We've got him'; then signalled for his horse . . .
vaulted awkwardly into the saddle, and was off. Lee watched him a
moment . . . he mounted, and he and his staff rode away."

Stiles found Jackson: "Worn down to the lowest point of flesh
consistent with effective service. His hair, skin, eyes, and clothes
were all one neutral dust tint."

Jackson went on to the strangest day of his military career. His
task was simple, though it was not easy. He was to press the enemy
rear, crossing White Oak Swamp, and moving south. As he did
so, A. P. Hill and Longstreet would move on perpendicular lines,
pushing eastward.

Lee had once more fashioned a trap. By morning of June
thirtieth he had 44,000 men concentrated below White Oak Swamp,
ready to sweep on McClellan's flank; Jackson had 25,000 with
which to force the swamp against a force thought to be small. There
was a new prospect of victory.

In the early morning Lee and Longstreet and Hill sat their
horses in a broom-sedge field, waiting to hear the guns of Jackson,
who was no more than four miles away. The hours passed. On
Lee's front Federal artillery became active. President Davis appeared, and found Lee in an exposed place.

"Why, General, what are you doing here? You are in too dangerous a position for the commander of the army."

"I am trying to find out something about the movements and plans of those people. But you must excuse me, Mr. President, for asking what you are doing here, and for suggesting that this is no place for the commander in chief of all our armies."

"Oh, I am here on the same mission that you are," Davis said.

They began to talk over the situation. A. P. Hill appeared, outraged at their exposure:

"This is no place for either of you, and as commander of this part of the field, I order you both to the rear."

"We will obey your order," one of them said, and Lee and Davis turned back a few yards. The firing became even hotter, and Hill galloped to them once more, obviously angry.

"Didn't I tell you to go away from here? And didn't you promise to obey my orders? Why, one shell from that battery over yonder may deprive the Confederacy of its President and the army of its commander."

And Hill persuaded the two to fall back out of sight, to a place of greater safety.[7]

To his left, through the open, Lee saw long trains of McClellan's 5,000 wagons crossing a height known as Malvern Hill. It was the site of an estate once owned by his grandfather. Some of the artillerymen of Holmes' command asked permission to blast the wagons, and when Lee gave the order, six of them began firing. They drew down upon that wing of the army a fierce cannonade, some of it fired by gunboats far down beyond the hill in the James River. The six guns were soon wrecked, and troops in the woodland were frightened by the crashing shells, as they toppled limbs and trees upon them. There was a momentary panic, such a confusion of flight that Lee, in alarm, sent six brigades of Magruder's troops to the aid of Holmes—and for a time this force of 18,000, as General Alexander noted, was out of action.

Longstreet took command of the infantry at hand, and Lee urged him forward. There was now only the barest chance of crippling the disappearing enemy. No one knew what had become of Jackson. Only light artillery fire had been heard from over White Oak Swamp. There could be no longer delay.

At last, at five o'clock, with shadows growing long, brigades hurried over the heavily wooded ground of Frayser's Farm, which lay near the tiny settlement of Glendale. The infantry pushed back enemy outposts, but were often separated from commands by isolated fields in the thick woods. One of Longstreet's Virginia brigades, under General Kemper, took heavy punishment when it chased impulsively beyond connecting troops into the open, where it seized most of a Federal battery. But no sooner had the troops taken the big guns than they were swept by fire from three sides. These men and some Alabamians charged into deadly fighting with strong Pennsylvania regiments, and struggled for three hours or more; two brigades had been caught and held by the stubborn Federals, and when they pried free, their casualties were heavy. The affair went like that until after dark, hand-to-hand fighting until the Federals had broken, mistakenly supposing that Confederate reinforcements had come. Lee rode with Longstreet at the end, seeing that the thrust had not seriously damaged McClellan's army.

He heard nothing of Jackson, and he was never to have a satisfactory explanation of the aggressive Valley fighter's failure. The story could be pieced together only in part:

Longstreet had sent a messenger to Jackson, who lay on the edge of White Oak Swamp, but he learned little; Jackson had been delayed by picking up prisoners, and reached the swamp bridge only at noon. There did not seem unusually heavy opposition in the thickets to halt him.

General A. R. Wright was sent by Huger to Jackson, to scout the area, and Wright asked Jackson for orders; Stonewall replied, strangely, that he had no orders. Wright went away and not far from Jackson's position was able to find a route leading through the swamp. Jackson, who was halted at the swamp's edge, made no effort to find alternate roads.

Colonel T. T. Munford of Jackson's cavalry, whom Jackson had sent over the swamp in the morning, crossed without difficulty, but Stonewall had not pushed his infantry in his track, as he ordinarily would have. More curious, when Munford sent word of a path through the bog, Jackson did not reply. He remained seated on a log during a desultory cannonade, sometimes asleep, sometimes awake.

General Wade Hampton had also tried to stir Old Jack. He later recalled that he found a good crossing of the swamp, suitable for men and big guns, and went to Jackson with his story:

"He asked if I could make a bridge across the stream. . . . He directed me to make the bridge . . . a bridge was made in a few minutes. On my return to our side of the swamp, I found General Jackson seated on a fallen pine. . . . I reported the completion of the bridge and the exposed position of the enemy. He drew his cap down over his eyes which were closed, and after listening to me for some minutes, he rose without speaking, and the next morning we found Franklin with the rest of the Federal troops concentrated on Malvern Hill."[8]

There was wonderment in the army. If Jackson had not been physically exhausted, or perhaps touched by fever, maybe it was true what they said, that he did not intend that *his* command should do all the fighting. There was gossip that he had been slow to act on Sunday, when he should have crossed the Chickahominy with dispatch, because he could not fight on the Sabbath—yet he had won victories on Sunday in the Valley.

In his staff relations, and in his reports as well, Lee was to display no vexation over Jackson's failures, or the failures of others this week. Of the day just ended he wrote: "Could the other commands have cooperated in this action, the result would have proved most disastrous to the enemy."

That night he could do no more. Perhaps there would never again be such an opportunity to destroy a Federal army. Tomorrow he must see.

At daylight the advanced infantry could make out the long, ugly hump of Malvern Hill, in their eyes just another of the unlovely landscapes to which the Army of Northern Virginia had become accustomed in this week of endless days. In the first hour of gray light, Jackson crossed the swamp. The other outlying divisions came up, and Lee's forces were belatedly concentrated.

Longstreet and Magruder met Lee at the Long Bridge Road. Longstreet noted that Lee was bitterly disappointed, and could not conceal it, even behind the mask of composure he wore this morning. Old Pete was touched, and remembered that Lee's bearing, and obvious suffering, "drew those who knew his plans and purposes closer to him."

As these officers talked a Federal surgeon approached and asked Lee's help in care of his wounded. The doctor said he had been with General McCall's division of Pennsylvanians. McCall had been captured, and Longstreet joked with the surgeon:

"McCall is safe in Richmond; but if his division had not fought so stubbornly on this road, we would have captured your whole Army. Never mind—we will do it yet."

Lee did not seem amused. He was feeling a bit sick and was so weary that he was not sure whether he could direct the army; he asked Longstreet to ride with him in case he had to transfer command to him. They soon met D. H. Hill, who had a report from a scout that the enemy's position on Malvern Hill was impregnable. "If McClellan is there in strength, we had better let him alone," Hill said.

Longstreet laughed. "Don't get scared, now that we have got him whipped."[9]

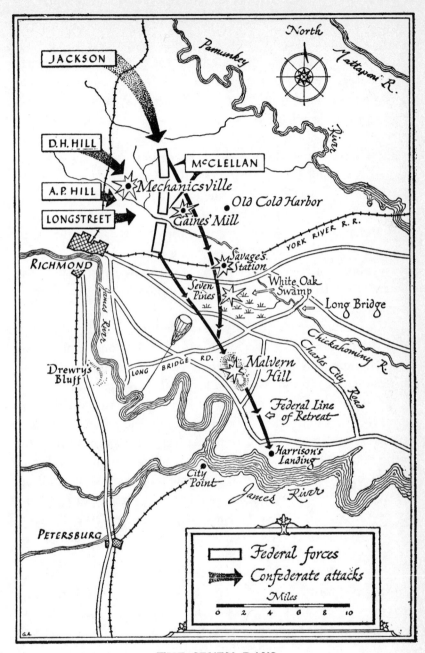

THE SEVEN DAYS

Lee's temper did not improve. While troops were on the road to the base of Malvern Hill, General Jubal Early ran afoul the commander. Early was afraid the enemy would escape, he said.

Lee snapped at him. "Yes, he will get away because I cannot have my orders carried out!"[10]

Inspection of the Federal position did not cheer Lee. Strong infantry—more than three corps, it turned out—protected a mass of artillery along the crest of the hill, some 150 feet above the marshy creek bed where the Confederate front must lie. Confusion had already beset Lee's command, for Magruder was on the wrong road and in the end would spend most of the day in the dense woodlands, finally to receive the wrong order of attack. Lee was casting about for a means of striking when Longstreet proposed an artillery duel from favorable ground he had found. Lee ordered guns into position.

The response was pitifully weak. Both General Pendleton of the artillery corps and Jackson's chief gunner, Colonel Crutchfield, were ill and out of action. The guns had to be brought up slowly, over paths cut through woods. The result was that a mere three guns first opened on the magnificent Federal batteries, which stood wheel to wheel between two farm houses on the hill. The thickets prevented Lee from moving along his front, but he could hear the results as the enemy blasted his guns into silence; some of Jackson's cannon, opening later, suffered the same fate from poor handling. It was an ominous beginning, and Lee had already ordered the troops to charge the exposed slope of the hill, upon hearing a signal —a yell from Armistead's brigade. This was intended only if the artillery fire had been successful.

Lee met Jackson and Ewell in the morning as the guns rolled. A dispatch informed them that guns in nearby woods were being overcome by enemy fire. Jackson impulsively rode off in the direction the rider had come. Lee called after him to leave the task to Crutchfield, not knowing he was ill, but Jackson rode on in the open, where shells burst about him. Lee sent a courier with a peremptory order to return, and Jackson came back to his side. Stonewall soon suggested a flank attack. After some hours of confusion Lee found a likely spot for such an attack on the left, but just as he was ordering it, word came from the far end of the line that General Whiting could see Federals retreating, and that Armistead's men had gone forward. Lee could not see these things, but assumed them to be correct, and ordered an advance.

The army's tragedy of errors was complete when Magruder received belatedly the early order, and pushed his men into the open, just under the mouths of the Federals guns, which dropped hundreds of men in furious target practice. D. H. Hill's regiments now came out in support, and for more than three hours, until dark ended it, there was senseless slaughter of brigades hurled up the 800 yards of open slope, one after another. One command would advance a few yards and lie down, or break for the rear; another would pass to a protective hollow near the top; other men came on behind and order disappeared. When reserves were called, as General Early wrote, they could hardly make their way for men streaming rearward: "A large number of men retreating . . . a very deep ditch filled with skulkers."

Lee could not stop it in time, nor, indeed, could he make out what was happening for most of the waning hours. Men who survived the war would remember the experience of the endless din of Federal guns, from midafternoon until after dark. Hundreds of wounded cried from the slope in the night.

There was an undercurrent of grumbling among Lee's generals, and criticism of the attack which had so cruelly punished the army. There were tales that Magruder had been drinking. Lee must have been near the collapse of his unfailing reserve, for he sought Magruder, as if to lash at him for the day's failure—a course strange for him. Captain John Lamb of Magruder's staff was a witness:

"I wish to say that General Magruder was perfectly sober the whole day. I did not leave his side, except to carry some order; I spread his blankets that night, and, lying near by, heard the whole conversation between him and General Lee in regard to the fight."

Lamb recalled this brief, revealing exchange:

"General Magruder, why did you attack?"

"In obedience to your orders, twice repeated."

Lee said no more; he would soon see Magruder leave the command in an atmosphere of strained relations.[11]

D. H. Hill, who had lost 2,000 of his 6,500 men, wrote of the day: "As each brigade emerged from the woods, from 50 to 100 guns opened upon it, tearing great gaps in its ranks; but the heroes pressed on and were shot down by reserves at the guns. . . . It was not war, it was murder."

Morning brought fog and rain. Ambulances went onto the grisly hill, which, though most of its scattered forms were dead "had a singular crawling effect" from the wounded who struggled there. Jackson seemed more concerned over the bodies than anyone else. The dead of his command lay everywhere, and "owing . . . to the extreme fatigue and excitement Jackson's troops had been through," the corpses lay in bizarre rigid poses, one with its feet in air, another, with eyes wide, holding up a handful of turf. Jackson sent his troups to work for an hour or more to clean the field, piling the dead in rows, and covering them from sight; he watched the work, and would have not a scrap of clothing or other sign of the dead left in the open. He explained to Captain William Blackford of Stuart's cavalry that he would attack on this ground when the fog rose, and it would never do to give his regiments a sight such as this.

But when the fog lifted, Malvern Hill was empty. The Federals were safe under the big guns of the ships at Harrison's Landing on the James. It seemed that the campaign was over.

Jackson went to headquarters and sat for a time, looking out at the sudden rain which swept the woodlands by the river. Lee was dictating to Taylor. Longstreet burst in, and after an exchange Lee asked Old Peter what he thought of the outcome of the battle.

"I think you hurt them about as much as they hurt you."

Lee's face showed no pleasure at this reply. "Then I am glad we punished them, at any rate."

Longstreet left, and almost immediately President Davis entered the room. Lee was surprised.

"President, I am glad to see you."

Davis saw Jackson, whom he had not met since the days after Bull Run, when they discussed the problems of Western Virginia, where Old Jack had since won his laurels. Jackson bore a grudge against the President, thinking he had unjustly backed General Loring when he was guilty of insubordination against Jackson. In that affair Jackson had attempted to resign from the army. Lee could see that the hurt still rankled. Jackson stiffened; he did not speak, or even move. Lee and Davis shook hands, and Lee turned to Jackson.

"Why," he said, in an effort to make peace, "President, don't you know General Jackson? This is our Stonewall Jackson."

There was a curious exchange: Davis bowed; Jackson saluted.

Lee and Davis held a frank talk before the staff officers who had crowded into the room, and there was silence as the young men eavesdropped on the making of strategy. Little was decided, however, for the confusion in Confederate ranks and the continuing downpour of rain seemed to forbid attack. But when Lee asked Jackson for his opinion, Old Jack said stubbornly: "But they have not all got away if we go immediately after them.[12]

It was too late, however. The army did not lurch ahead in the wet roads until the following day, when Lee discovered the huddled hosts of the enemy at the landing, and for a day he drew the army

closer. Called to the scene, on July fourth, he found the army in
battle formation, but though some of the officers wanted to attack
the enemy and seize a low eminence known as Evelington Heights,
Jackson said his men were in no condition to fight.

After a long reconnaissance which showed the enemy in a
powerful position, Lee reluctantly decided to leave McClellan un-
molested. He had, perhaps, lost his chance the day before when
Stuart had fired rockets down among the Federal camps from
the heights—immediately reminding the enemy that it should seize
that ground, and Stuart's small force had been pushed off.

The Seven Days were over.

The chorus of bickering and jealous charges which now arose
was loud and long, and much of it came to public attention. Animos-
ities between generals were spread in the newspapers, and a number
of high-ranking officers were transferred from the Army of Northern Virginia. The critics might have led the country to believe that
the army under Lee had suffered ignominious defeat, rather than
having driven a vastly superior army from Richmond's gates, on
his heels almost every foot of the way, exacting heavy toll. The Confederacy seemed to sense Lee's deep feeling of failure, of what
might have been, if his orders could have been obeyed—on almost
any of those gun-roaring days in the swamps.

Perhaps he had expected more than a new army could provide
in co-ordination, in intricate staff work, in making a way through
strange, virtually unmapped country. He soon wrote Mary:

> I have returned to my old quarters and am filled with
> gratitude to our Heavenly Father for all the mercies He has
> extended to us. Our success has not been so great or complete
> as we could have desired, but God knows what is best for us.
> Our enemy met with heavy loss, from which it must take him
> some time to recover, before he can recommence his operations.

Casualties exceeded anything the Confederacy had dreamed of: 3,200 dead, 16,000 wounded, about 1,000 missing—20,000 in all. The Federal loss was unknown, but thought to be greater. It was in truth 15,700.

Still, the enemy had been driven. Lee had captured priceless fortunes in arms—35,000 muskets and other small weapons, and 52 pieces of artillery. And there was the remaining force of McClellan's great army, safe under the big guns, evidently demoralized—at least with such a harmless look now that Lee pulled away from the scene more and more troops, sending them near Richmond to rest and refit. He had concluded that McClellan would not cross the James and drive toward Richmond from the far side, but for a time he waited to see.

He once more saw young Robert, and wrote:

> Rob came out to see me one afternoon. He had been much worn down by his marching and fighting, and had gone to his mamma to get a little rest. He was thin but well ... he had re-joined his company ... as good as new again, I hope, inasmuch as your mother thought, by means of a bath and a profusion of soap, she had cleansed the outward man considerably, and replenished his lost wardrobe.

Rob was off with thousands of other boys now to the west, with Jackson, where a new invasion menaced Virginia.

Sometime during the week of fighting Lee had found that Roan was going blind, and left the horse with a farmer on the Chickahominy, where he could be cared for. Now, almost exclusively Traveller would carry him to war for a while.

Lee was briefly idolized by the Richmond press which had so recently berated him. There was praise on every hand, none higher than that from Jackson, repeated everywhere: "I would follow him blindfolded."

Still there was remorse for the Confederacy in the restrained language of Lee's report on the running battles: "Under ordinary circumstances the Federal army should have been destroyed."

His son Rob had seen something in his father's face: "His great victory did not elate him, so far as one could see."

6 *TURNING TIDE*

MARY LEE returned to Richmond when it had become one great hospital from the fighting of the Seven Days. There was an endless passage of funeral processions and a new quiet, too, noticeable on Sundays. The church bells were gone, made into cannon at the Tredegar iron works, whose furnaces lighted half the city at night with geysers of flame.

After she had passed through most of Virginia, eluding the Federals, Mrs. Lee had been forced to ask permission to pass their lines, and was obliged by gracious officers. She had gone to the home her father had willed to Rooney, the White House on the Pamunkey, and had hardly left when the enemy arrived. The Federals found her defiant note in the doorway:

> Northern soldiers who profess to reverence Washington, forbear to desecrate the home of his first married life, the property of his wife, now owned by her descendants.
> A granddaughter of Mrs. Washington.

Mary remained in the neighborhood with friends, and a Union search party went through that house soon after she arrived.

Mary had been enraged, and wrote a note to the Federal commander:

> Sir: I have patiently & humbly submitted to the search of my house by men under your command, who are satisfied that there is nothing here which they want; all the plate & other valuables have long since been removed to Richmond & are now beyond the reach of Northern marauders who may wish for their possession.
>
> Wife of Robert E. Lee, General C. S. A.

General Fitz-John Porter replied with an offer of protection. Mary accepted a Federal guard, and within a few days requested permission to enter Richmond. General McClellan himself met her at his headquarters and sent her in a carriage with a Confederate escort to Gooch's Farm, where she found Lee. He was depressed at her appearance, for her arthritis had become much worse since he had seen her in April, and she walked with extreme difficulty. The family was together in Richmond for a time; at least Robert and the girls were there. Lee had but a few days to see them.

For six weeks after the gunfire died away at Malvern Hill, he drove his growing staff to the improvement of the army. There was a scramble for uniforms and shoes for poorly clad troops whose enlistment finery was now in rags; captured stores were distributed. Lee began a major reorganization: D. H. Hill commanded the North Carolina department, from Petersburg; Huger and Magruder went out of the army, leaving controversy behind. In almost every regiment new officers were named to replace the fallen. Most important of all, Lee now began seeking a way to evade the Confederate law which had made his army a clumsy band of independent divisions.

He was beset on every side. His strange, fierce lieutenant,

Stonewall Jackson, plagued him about an invasion of the North: They should take every available man across the Potomac, threaten Washington, drive into the heart of the enemy country. It would pull every Federal soldier out of Virginia; McClellan would be no threat because his army was "whipped." More than once Lee was forced to turn Jackson aside with noncommittal replies. And Jackson, for all his hostility toward Davis, appealed to the President over the head of Lee; it was an act which a stern commander might have regarded as insubordination.

Jackson had protested to his friend and messenger, Congressman Boteler: "We are losing valuable time here . . . allowing the enemy leisure to recover from his defeat. . . . Yes—we are wasting precious time and energies in this malarious region that can be much better employed elsewhere."

Reluctantly, Boteler went to Davis with the Jackson scheme. Davis listened, but he had other plans. A new Federal threat had appeared in the north, and Jackson's dream of invasion must wait.[1]

Stonewall was not wrong about the state of McClellan's mind; the Federal army was far from whipped, but McClellan was convinced of the hopelessness of a move against Richmond from his small post on the James. When the Federal commander-in-chief, General Halleck, urged an offensive, McClellan protested that Lee had 200,000 troops in his front, and that he could not launch an attack without reinforcements. Meanwhile, McClellan's men rested under the protection of gunboats, with a small Confederate force guarding them.

Jackson seemed to take no note of his failures of the Seven Days, and the reports of Lee were to bear on them only slightly. Stonewall left a scanty record in a letter to his wife: "During the past week I have not been well, have suffered from fever and debility. . . ."

But it was Jackson to whom Lee turned as a more menacing phase of the war opened.

Federal forces in the Shenandoah Valley had been consolidated
and reinforcements added. The confident commander of this army
joined his men about July first. He was Major General John Pope,
who seemed to feel the hot breath of destiny upon him. He addressed his troops:

"I have come to you from the West, where we have always
seen the backs of our enemies; from an army whose business it has
been to seek the adversary and to beat him where found; whose
policy has been attack and not defense. I presume I have been
called here to pursue the same system and to lead you against the
enemy. It is my purpose to do so, and that speedily. . . . I hear constantly of 'taking strong positions and holding them,' of 'lines of
retreat . . .' Let us discard such ideas. The strongest position a
soldier should desire to occupy is one from which he can most easily
advance against the enemy."

Pope was entirely right about affairs in the west, where the
Union appeared to be winning the war, but he drew laughter from
the increasingly confident Army of Northern Virginia. Somehow it
got about that Pope had shouted: "My headquarters are in the
saddle!" and Lee's army laughed over Stonewall's purported retort:
"I can whip any man who doesn't know his headquarters from his
hindquarters."

There was soon grimmer news from Pope's command. One
of his officers entered the village of Luray and took hostages, to be
shot if he lost men to guerrillas; another ordered all Southern men
found in his lines treated as spies, if they did not leave. There were
reports of depredations such as Virginia had not heard before.

When, on July twelfth, Pope's advance took the town of Culpeper, Davis and Lee began to plot his immediate downfall. They
were forced to work under menacing circumstances.

McClellan was still dangerous, so near to Richmond, and must
be watched. A large new force of Federal troops had just come up
from Burnside's army, and lay on transports at Fort Monroe, able

to move quickly in any direction. To the north, McDowell commanded a large force at Fredericksburg—and Pope was moving down into Virginia. There was little time to decide what the enemy was likely to do next. Pope must be halted. Jackson was ordered to move by train to Gordonsville, carrying Ewell's troops with his own. Stonewall probably got the orders in person from Lee on Saturday night, July twelfth.

The night before departure, Jackson's staff heard him make his only defense of his inactivity back in White Oak Swamp. The young men were debating what might have happened, if Jackson had sent forward his men that day, and Stonewall, passing through the room, halted and said with a trace of impatience: "If General Lee had wanted me, he could have sent for me."

Jackson's men began the trip on July thirteenth, and before the end of the week were in camp around Gordonsville, not quite thirty miles south of Pope's position at Culpeper.

For a few days it appeared that war against the enemy was less important than bickering among Lee's own command. An affair of honor erupted between Longstreet and A. P. Hill. John Daniel, editor of the *Richmond Examiner,* had been with Hill's troops at the opening of the Seven Days, and published lavish praises of Hill's generalship, crediting him with the victory won. Longstreet replied with a letter bearing the name of a staff officer, Major Moxley Sorrel, pointing out the errors of Daniel. Hill was enraged and asked to be transferred from Longstreet's command. Lee took no action, and the feud continued.

Hill refused to speak with Sorrel, or even to see him on routine army business. Longstreet placed General Hill under arrest, to be confined to his camp. Friends of the generals began to whisper of arrangements for a duel. This brought Lee into action, and through intermediaries he settled the question and brought peace.[2] Hill was removed from arrest, and on July twenty-seventh his 12,000 men began the march to Gordonsville, where they were to reinforce Jackson.

Hill went off in relief to strengthen the army against Pope, and as he moved Lee wrote a strange letter to Jackson:

> A. P. Hill you will, I think, find a good officer with whom you can consult, and by advising with your division command-ers as to their movements much trouble can be saved you in arranging details, as they can act more intelligently. I wish to save you trouble from increasing your command.

This was plain talk to a veteran soldier; Jackson had known A. P. Hill for many years. Lee was taking note of a flood of com-plaints that Jackson's passion for secrecy kept his officers in the dark until the very moment of action, and giving him a gentle les-son in army administration. But Jackson had no warm welcome for Hill, despite this—or perhaps because of it.

Hill was a thorough soldier, a handsome "man's man,'" as one of his officers saw him, a man with a full, dark, curling beard, a high brow, large nose and mouth; a quiet, uncommunicative of-ficer who looked anything but the stubborn fighter he was. He wore rough clothing, and more often than not wore a red woolen shirt beneath a shell jacket—stars on his collar the only sign of rank.

The departure of Hill did not lessen Lee's troubles. He was called upon almost daily to advise Davis on the war in the west, which did not improve for the Confederates, and Lee could do little better than make obvious suggestions about fighting on fields he had never seen.

He was in the midst of final reorganization of his army, too. To supplant the many divisions which had proved so difficult to co-ordinate in the fighting below Richmond, he established what were, in truth, corps, under Jackson and Longstreet; the Confederacy did not recognize such army units, but they now came into being, known only as "commands." The cavalry was formed into a division, collected from its scattered units, with Jeb Stuart, now a major general, in full command. His brigades were led by Wade Hampton, the fearless and able South Carolina horseman, and Fitz Lee, Robert's nephew and son of Smith Lee.

There was, as usual when a Lee stepped upward, a mutter of protest. But Fitz seemed the very prototype of a cavalry leader to the reckless Virginia boys he commanded: Just thirty years old, a full-bearded bull-voiced bachelor who had left his post as West Point's cavalry instructor to join the Confederacy. There was an air of romance about him which attracted women and cavalrymen as well. He was a veteran of plains warfare, and bore the wound from an Indian arrow in his leg. He was short, thickset, inclined to stoutness, with a square head and short neck.

Jackson's troubles soon vexed Lee once more, but he met them patiently. Stonewall was dissatisfied with his cavalry chief, Beverly Robertson, and wished him removed. Lee hesitated; he did not know W. E. Jones, whom Jackson wished to elevate, and the commander wrote Davis:

> . . . Probably Jackson may expect too much, and Robertson may be preparing his men for service, which I have understood they much needed . . . an undisciplined brigade of cavalry is no trifling undertaking and requires time to regulate.

Lee was also mourning his fine horse Richmond, who died after Malvern Hill. He wrote that he had just resigned himself to the loss of his mare, Grace Darling, taken at the White House by Federals, and then had lost Richmond to some strange malady.

Lee's attention was abruptly riveted on the enemy. About August fifth he had the first piece of impressive news about Federal intentions. It came from Captain John S. Mosby, a cavalryman marked for fame, who had been exchanged after some weeks in prison at Fort Monroe. Mosby had shrewdly looked about him, and talked with Federal soldiers. He reported it as a certainty that the big force of Burnside was to move up the Potomac to join Pope. Before Lee could reach a conclusion on this puzzle, McClellan stirred from his camp on the James.

Lee hurried down the river with three divisions of the 56,000 troops left to defend Richmond, and met McClellan on the old ground of the Malvern Hill battle. There was skirmishing, and Lee studied the impregnable hill for hours, but no battle came. The next morning the enemy had gone back into camp. Lee concluded that this had been a ruse to cover movements to the north. He began to prepare Jackson for battle.

Stonewall now had almost 35,000 men, and was on the move.

Dick Ewell was still protesting—that tiny and profane fighter whose clothes were always too big for him. Ewell was an aggressive officer with a high bald dome accentuated by wisps of hair combed straight forward on the temples, and bristling mustaches. The army, however, had come to respect the old plainsman, who now rode about with an Apache boy at his heels, as he swore at all comers in a piping voice. His reputation won in the Valley had not been diminished in the Chickahominy swamps, where he had led or directed fierce attacks. He was still complaining of Jackson:

"I give you my word," he said to a friend, "I do not know whether we march north, south, east or west, or whether we will march at all. General Jackson simply ordered me to have the division ready to move at dawn. . . . That is almost all I ever know of his designs."

On August seventh Stonewall, having learned from scouts that General Banks, his old Valley opponent, had exposed himself with a fragment of the Federal army, moved forward to attack. He gave precise marching orders, with each division assigned to a place; these orders were changed. A. P. Hill was not aware of the change, and allowed his men to rest, thinking that he was awaiting his proper place in the column. Jackson scolded him publicly, and the two generals kept up an angry correspondence most of the day.

On the same day Lee sent a message to Jackson urging a cautious attack:

> I would rather you have easy fighting and heavy victories.
> . . . I must now leave the matter to your reflection and good
> judgment. Make up your mind what is best to be done under
> all circumstances . . . and let me hear the results.

Jackson made an unpromising start.

Stonewall's men dragged on dusty roads northward in a heat wave; eight men dropped dead of sunstroke or heat exhaustion. Jackson was fretful, and more than half blind. The Federal cavalry cut him off on every hand. Robertson seemed helpless, saying to Jackson that he could get no information because his men were straggling. Stonewall met the enemy unexpectedly on August ninth.

Ewell and Jubal Early found Federals near a hill known as Cedar Mountain, and studied the place for a time before Jackson arrived. He glanced about the country, but did not ride in reconnaissance. A few instructions, a short time with a map, and Jackson took a nap. The army was to pay for his neglect of the terrain.

The Confederate position on the flank of Cedar Mountain was forbidding; guns commanded the approach of the Federals from Culpeper. But on the left, where the line of gray disappeared in a woodland, was a weak flank. Jackson was late in discovering it, and it took the death of a brigadier, Charles Winder, and a surge of blue troops through his lines to point out his error. There were three hours of vicious struggle before the enemy fell back. Jackson's courage and his eye for tactical advantage finally won the day, as he pushed up reinforcements to drive off the Federals, but the action had been costly, and was at best a painful victory. More than 1,200 men were lost to his army; the enemy lost 2,400.

Jackson wrote a laudatory report concerning Winder, who was a promising battle leader, but Winder had had a habit of torturing his men to get discipline, hanging them by their thumbs for hours on end, and one private wrote : "His death was not much lamented by the brigade, for it probably saved some of them the trouble of carrying out their threats to kill him."

Reports from Jackson's battle made Lee more anxious to come to strike Pope's main force. On August thirteenth he ordered Longstreet's ten stout brigades to Gordonsville, and on that day, he had a plausible story from a Federal deserter that a division had left McClellan's army for the north; scouts soon found the story to be true.

Lee could not long remain in Richmond now, with the race under way. He wrote Davis from his headquarters on Nine Mile Road, assuring him of the safety of Richmond under its garrison, and said, almost wistfully:

> Unless I hear from you to the contrary I shall leave for G—— at 4 A.M. tomorrow. The troops are accumulating there and I must see that arrangements are made for the field."[3]

He added in this message word that General Joseph Johnston was recovering and "will soon return to Richmond." There seemed no longer a question, however, that the old commander of the Army of Northern Virginia would supplant the man who had, in less than two months, converted it from a fumbling, retreating, unpredictable force, into a fighting machine which could be hurled across Virginia in defiance of a poised army of invasion.

As he boarded the train for the front on August fifteenth, Lee foresaw a race against time, against the Federal regiments now steaming northward to save Pope. Federals had the same uneasy feeling. McClellan telegraphed Washington just after Lee reached Gordonsville: "I do not like Jackson's movements. He will suddenly appear when least expected." The warning went unheeded.

Longstreet and Jackson met Lee at the Gordonsville station. Lee studied the enemy position: Pope had placed his 40,000 men on the north bank of the Rapidan, with the Rappahannock behind him. He thus lay in the triangle between the two rivers, which joined a few miles to the east. If Lee could strike him with force—and swiftness—from the west, he could break the Federal army against the banks of the rivers. It was a rare opportunity. Orders went out to get the army in motion—but they were not to bear fruit.

The cavalry began to move by fording the high, swift Rapidan. Stuart rode out with them, and because orders were not carried out, and Fitz Lee did not appear, Stuart narrowly escaped capture by hard-riding Federals. The swaggering horseman watched from the woods in chagrin as enemy riders carried off his abandoned cloak and huge plumed hat. He was vexed for weeks by cries from troops: "Where's yer hat?"

Worse than Stuart's adventure, a staff officer was captured, and the enemy took from him a complete copy of Lee's orders for attack. Almost immediately Pope reacted by falling back across the Rappahannock.

Lee rode to a mountaintop with Longstreet to stare down through glasses at the Federal army. Longstreet remembered:

"From the summit we had a fair view of many points. . . . Changing our glasses to the right and left and rear, the white tops of army wagons were seen moving. Half an hour's close watch revealed that the move was for the Rappahannock River. . . . Little clouds of dust arose which marked the tramp of soldiers. . . . Watching without comment till the clouds grew thinner and thinner as they approached the river and melted into the bright haze of the afternoon sun, General Lee finally put away his glasses, and with a deeply-drawn breath, said, 'General, we little thought that the enemy would turn his back upon us thus early in the campaign.' "[4]

It was the loss of a great opportunity for the army, but Lee left no other expression of regret. He issued new orders and sent the army forward to push Pope anew.

He wrote home, a letter full of the details of the strategic situation:

> Here I am in a tent instead of my comfortable quarters. . . . The tent, however, is very comfortable, and of that I have nothing to complain. General Pope says he is very strong, and seems to feel so. . . . I hope he will not prove stronger than we are.
>
> I learn since I have left that General McClellan has moved down the James River with his whole army. I suppose he is coming here, too, so we shall have a busy time. Burnside and King from Fredericksburg have joined Pope, which, from their own report, has swelled Pope to 92,000. I do not believe it, though he is very big.[5]

Lee now had to deal with another problem of discipline among general officers, of the sort he would never learn to solve in soldierly fashion.

It seemed that the blame for Stuart's narrow escape from capture, and the taking of the Confederate orders, resulted from failure to guard a certain ford, which the men of General Toombs were to cover. There was confusion; Toombs, who had been absent, returned to order the guard of the ford removed on his own initiative. He was placed under arrest, but stalked about wearing his forbidden sword, making rebellious speeches to his yelling troops. Lee finally ordered him back to Gordonsville behind the lines.

The armies now began a long, clumsy dance along opposite sides of the Rappahannock, moving upstream, each now and then lunging for an advantage. There were minor skirmishes and a few small-scale battles, flaring briefly, but Lee moved the army through them, seeking his means of major attack before more help came to Pope.

Now that Richmond was safe, he called up the last available men. D. H. Hill, Lafayette McLaws and J. G. Walker brought their infantry from Richmond, Hampton's cavalry came, and from Orange Courthouse the division of General R. H. Anderson.

On August twentieth Lee sent Stuart and 1,200 of his young men across Waterloo Bridge, through Warrenton, and to the enemy rear at Catlett's Station. Only a torrential rain prevented their burning bridges and tearing up the railroad, and they brought back 300 prisoners, in addition to valuable booty from Pope's headquarters' tent. The raiders brought to Lee the letter books of Pope, revealing Federal strength, Pope's concern for his army's safety without further reinforcements, and details of his position. Stuart also brought personal souvenirs including Pope's coat, which he gaily showed to officers of the army. He joked about the exchange of the garment for his captured hat, and went so far as to send a message to the enemy general:

> General: You have my hat and plume. I have your blue coat. I have the honor to propose a cartel for a fair exchange of the prisoners.

Lee determined to repeat the thrust against Pope, but in great strength, using swift infantry marches. And, though the enemy was now alert, Lee planned one of the most daring of his strokes. He ordered Jackson to move far upstream, cross the river, and circle through mountain passes to the rear of the Union army. He was to ruin Manassas Junction station, and prepare for a later assault of the army upon Pope. Hard marching and complete surprise were essential; otherwise, disaster might well overtake the divided army.[6]

Men in Jackson's ranks were soon cooking rations, casting off excess baggage, and gathering a beef herd. Thousands left with no supper, and were off on one of the most dramatic of the Foot Cavalry's marches—some 20,000 to 25,000 strong. The route led through fields of green corn, and men raided them in the brief halts Jackson allowed; they kept a killing pace, and the roads soon swarmed with stragglers. The first day's march took the column twenty-five miles, to the village of Salem. Major Robert Dabney, who until lately had been Jackson's chief of staff, described a scene of this evening:

"As the weary column approached the end of the day's march, they found Jackson, who had ridden forward, dismounted, and was standing upon a great stone by the roadside. His sun-burned cap was lifted from his brow, and he was gazing toward the west. . . . His men burst forth into their accustomed cheers, forgetting all their fatigue . . . but . . . he sent an officer to request that there should be no cheering . . . as it might betray their presence to the enemy. They . . . passed the word down the column: 'No cheering, boys.' But as they passed him, their eyes and gestures . . . silently declared what their lips were forbidden to utter. Jackson turned to his staff, his face beaming with delight, and said: 'Who could not conquer with such troops as these?' "[7]

There was still danger ahead. The flanking force must cross the Bull Run Mountains at Thoroughfare Gap, and if the enemy were alert, this position would be heavily defended. The tempo of the march increased. By noon it was clear that the enemy was unaware of their presence—and, best of all, the mountain pass was clear. Jackson was safely in Pope's rear. In two days Stonewall had taken his corps fifty miles, and now Pope lay between Jackson and Lee. The raiders fell upon the station at Manassas. They tore up the rails, reveled in mountains of delicacies—canned lobster, imported wine and brandy, barrels of coffee, boxes of Havana cigars, pickled oysters. In the end, at sight of oncoming enemy lines, Jackson drove his men from the spoils and burned the Federal warehouses. He had caused the Union a minor disaster: 5,000 pounds of bacon, 2,000 barrels of flour, 2,000 barrels of salt pork, 1,000 barrels of corned beef.

Jackson now withdrew to a position near Groveton, not far

from the old Manassas battlefield, drew his lines along a commanding ridge, and waited.

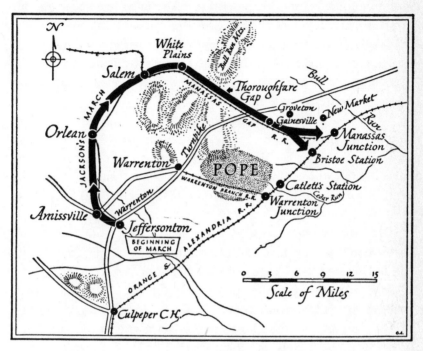

ROUTE OF JACKSON'S SWEEP AROUND POPE—
AUGUST 1862

On the blazing twenty-eighth of August the long blue lines of
Pope advanced on Jackson across a dusty plain. In the rear, Lee and
Longstreet were marching to Stonewall's aid over his own route,
but Lee had now sent all of Stuart's cavalry toward Jackson, and the
main column was blinded. The day before, near Salem, Lee himself had almost been taken by raiding Federal cavalry which swept
down on the army.

Even worse for the Confederates, the enemy was now awake,
and had posted a guard at Thoroughfare Gap. Perhaps Lee's reinforcements would not force their way through in time. A cannonade

announced the attempt to storm the pass in Jackson's rear. The last
Rebel rider to slip through the gap reached Jackson in the late
afternoon, just before the Federal attack struck his men. Stonewall
grinned his relief at news that Lee would have Longstreet's corps
at his side in the morning. He then turned to save himself.

Captain Blackford, of the cavalry, who saw the most of it, said,
"Jackson rode all day in a restless way, mostly alone. When he was
uneasy he was cross as a bear.

"We could almost tell his thoughts by his movements . . . he
would halt, then trot on rapidly, halt again, wheel his horse. . . .
About a quarter of a mile off, troops were now opposite us. All
felt sure Jackson could never resist the temptation, and that the
order to attack would come soon, even if Longstreet was behind the
mountain."

Jackson made Blackford a prophet. "Bring out your men,
gentlemen," he called, and Blackford thought that the troops, rushing out, roared "like cages of wild beasts at the scent of blood."
The brigades went into the open, and in the late sunlight the short,
bloody battle of Groveton opened. The enemy launched the first
charge, and as the blue files stormed over a rise in the ground, a
volley from the Rebels tore them apart. The Federals charged once
more, and fighting swept through an orchard. At the end the lines
were not one hundred yards apart, firing into each other with
terrible accuracy. The Federal Western troops held the famed
Valley veterans at bay, and took a heavy toll.

In the night doctors worked over General Ewell, wounded so
badly that his leg needed amputation. He would be lost to the
service for long months. General Taliaferro was also wounded, two
colonels were dead, and the foremost regiments were mere skeletons; only 69 men of the 21st Georgia regiment were left ready for
duty.

But as night fell, Jackson was at least safe. If Longstreet came,
all would be well. Jackson shifted his men, crowding them along

an old railroad cut on a narrow front. After a quiet morning, the blue lines snaked into position—more than twice his numbers. Jackson sent Stuart to the rear to hurry the reinforcements. Pope's men rushed in.

The enemy poured into a gap in A. P. Hill's line, and in the railroad cut men fought for their lives; wave after wave of Federal infantry charged the spot. General Maxcy Gregg held his men as they wavered, urging them to die there rather than break the line. Ammunition was gone, and men fought with bayonets and even stones. Ham Chamberlayne, in a Virginia regiment, would recall:

"They threw against our corps, all day long, vast masses of troops. . . . We got out of ammunition; we collected more from cartridge boxes of fallen friend and foe; that gave out, and we charged with . . . yell and steel. All day long they threw their masses on us; all day they fell back shattered and shrieking. When the sun went down, their dead were heaped in front of the incomplete railway, and we sighed with relief, for Longstreet could be seen coming into position on our right. The crisis was over . . . but the sun went down so slowly."[8]

It had been a near thing for Jackson, and even in this tense moment, on the field where he had finally concentrated his army, Lee faced a rebellion of sorts from Longstreet.

As the reinforcements came near Jackson's fighting troops Lee urged Longstreet to move into position and charge. Old Pete stubbornly held back; he in fact refused. He later wrote: "I suggested that, the day being far spent, it might be well to advance before night on a forced reconnaissance, get our troops in the most favorable positions, and have all things ready for battle the next morning."

Lee had an amusing encounter with his son Rob on this evening. Rob recalled:

"As we were ordered to cease firing from the last position we took, and the breathless cannoneers were leaning on their guns,

General Lee and staff galloped up, and from this point . . . scanned the movements of the enemy. . . . The General reined in Traveller close by my gun, not fifteen feet from me. I looked at them all some few minutes, and then went up and spoke to Captain Mason of the staff, who had not the slightest idea who I was. When he found me out he was greatly amused. . . . I had been marching night and day for four days, with no opportunity to wash myself . . . my face and hands were blackened with powder-sweat, and the few garments I had on were ragged and stained with the red soil. . . . When the General after a moment or two, dropped his glass to his side, and turned to his staff, Captain Mason said:

" 'General, here is some one who wants to speak to you.'

"The General, seeing a much-begrimed artilleryman, sponge-staff in hand, said:

" 'Well, my man, what can I do for you?' I replied: 'Why, General, don't you know me?' and he, of course, at once recognized me, and was very much amused . . . and most glad to see that I was safe and well."[9]

The guns rolled until after midnight, and on the Confederate lines more troops continued to crowd into position, until some 54,000 were ready.

The mood in Federal headquarters was still optimism. Pope had just wired Washington that he had "intercepted the retreat of the enemy . . . and I see no possibility of his escape."

A staff officer of Pope's, David Strother, had a glimpse of Fitz-John Porter as he carried an order from the commander:

"It was broad daylight when I reached Porter's quarters. . . . I found the handsome general lying on his cot, covered with a blanket of imitation leopard skin. . . . I read the message, then handed it to him. . . . We believed Jackson separated from the main army of Lee . . . and . . . desired to . . . crush him before Lee came up. . . . The General, who was busy writing dispatches on the corner of the. . .

table, looked up and asked, 'How do you spell "chaos"?' I spelled the word letter by letter."[10]

The word was appropriate to the scorching thirtieth of August.

The morning passed with nothing more alarming than an occasional burst from Federal artillery, which fired the browned grass of the open fields and added dancing waves of heat to the smoky scene. Alexander Hunter marched with Hood's men as the order for attack came:

"How the shells rained upon us . . . the living wall kept on . . . until it seemed as if we were walking on torpedoes. . . . Though the shells were tearing through the ranks, the men did not falter. . . . We followed unwaveringly our Colonel . . . straight across the plain toward the battery . . . though the balls were tearing a way through flesh and blood."

Federal ranks, driven back, returned to the charge, and the brigade about Hunter was scattered. Reinforcements came, and then:

"A fusillade of musketry . . . was raining lead all around. Every man with his head bent sideways and down, like people breasting a hailstorm, for soldiers always charge so, and the Gray and Blue met with a mighty shock. A tremendous sheet of flame burst from our line."

This was a small part of the struggle now flaming on the broad landscape. Lee sat Traveller on a knoll, overlooking it. The commander stared after some wagons passing up toward the guns, and said to an officer, "I see that some of those mules are without shoes. I wish you would see to it that all of the animals are shod at once."[11] He turned without a pause to seize the chance for victory he saw on the field before him.

Lee judged that the force of Jackson's infantry charge, aided by the savage fire of Longstreet's massed guns, presented the opportunity to end the fighting.

He ordered Longstreet to attack at once, sent him support from the rear, and the gray mass moved onto the field behind the struggling men of Jackson. The Federals, who had begun to fall away on Jackson's front, were now pressed back by Longstreet's attack, but it was not easy, and for a time Federal guns dropped many from Longstreet's ranks. Old Pete would blame Jackson for that error:

"Jackson failed to pull up even on the left, which gave opportunity for some of the enemy's batteries to turn their fire across the right wing. . . . It was severely threatening upon General Lee . . . who would ride under it, notwithstanding appeals to avoid it."[12]

Longstreet gave the commander a bit of protection by riding through a ravine, from which they emerged to see the weary, thinned ranks boiling about the Chinn House on the old Manassas field, and then, about dark, nearing the old Henry House, scene of such furious fighting in the first big battle of the war.

Private Hunter had a last look at the field: "A vast panorama stretched out on an open plain with patches of wood here and there . . . and with but two or three hills in the whole range of sight. . . . It was unutterably grand. Jackson could be seen swinging his left on his right as a pivot, and Longstreet with his entire corps in the reverse method. The whole Yankee army was in retreat, and certainly nothing but darkness prevented it from becoming *une affaire flambée*."

Longstreet described the final moments:

"Thickening clouds hovering over us, and a gentle fall of rain closely following, the plateau was shut off from view, and its ascent only found by groping through the darkening rainfall. As [the enemy] retired, heavy darkness gave safe conduct to such of his columns as could find their way through the weird mists."

Lee's tent was pitched in the open, and by a leaping fire he wrote to Davis:

This army achieved today on the plains of Manassas a signal victory over combined forces of Generals McClellan and Pope. . . . We mourn the loss of our gallant dead in every conflict, yet our gratitude to Almighty God for his mercies rises higher and higher each day, to Him and to the valour of our troops a nation's gratitude is due.[13]

Lee sent Colonel Long of his staff to inspect the field as best he could, and to make a report. There were ample signs of heavy Federal losses, and the enemy had withdrawn entirely. The field was littered with debris, and among this Confederates found 25,000 small arms and 23 big guns. The Federal loss in men had been about 15,000; the Confederate casualties were about 8,000.

Among the commanders coming to report to Lee was young Hood, who gave an ecstatic description of the enemy retreating over Bull Run, with the army's battle flags in hot pursuit.

"God forbid that I should ever live to see our colors moving in the opposite direction," Lee said.

Morning found the exhausted army all but bogged in the swimming roads; rain streamed upon them, the streams were high, and Bull Run would soon be impassable, since the bridges were out. There seemed little chance to overtake or destroy the Federal army, as Lee had wished for today. He appeared early, bundled in a rubber suit and a rubber cape. Longstreet saw the morning as: ". . . nasty and soggy. . . . General Jackson was called to headquarters early. . . . Upon receiving General Lee's orders to cross Bull Run . . . and march . . . to intercept the enemy's march, he said, 'Good!' and away he went, without another word, or even a smile. . . . I was ordered to look after the dead and . . . wounded, till Jackson could have time to stretch out on his new march, and then to follow him."

During the day the men of D. H. Hill finally approached, coming up from Richmond, and were to be left on the field to aid the wounded. Before they came in Lee had a couple of adventures. He first clashed with a sergeant of a Mississippi regiment who wandered over the wet field. Lee called sharply; "What are you doing here, sir, away from your command?"

"That's none of your business, by God," the ragged soldier said.

"You are a straggler, sir, and deserve the severest punishment."

The sergeant shouted in rage. "It's a damned lie, sir. I only left my regiment a few minutes ago to hunt me a pair of shoes. I went through all the fight yesterday, and that's more than you can say; for where were you yesterday when General Stuart wanted your damned cavalry to charge the Yankees after we put 'em to running? You were lying back in the pine thickets and couldn't be found; but today, when there's no danger, you come out and charge other men with straggling, damn you."

Lee laughed and rode off. Behind him an officer baited the sergeant, who thought he had been talking with "a cowardly Virginia cavalryman."

"No, sir, that was General Lee."

"Ho-o-what? General Lee, did you say?"

"Yes."

"Scissors to grind, I'm a goner!" The sergeant tore out of sight along the muddy road.[14]

On August thirty-first Lee received a painful injury. As he stood by the usually calm Traveller in a woodland, there was a shout that enemy cavalry was upon them. Men ran about, and Traveller shied. Lee, made clumsy by his rubber trousers, lunged forward for the reins and was pulled violently to the gound. Officers brought a surgeon from a nearby Georgia regiment, who found small bones broken in one hand, and the wrist of the other badly strained. Under protest Lee was put into an ambulance, his hands useless in splints.

In this condition he got a report of the battle of Stuart and Jackson with the enemy rearguard at Chantilly, not far ahead. There had been a brief but furious clash in a thunderstorm, with little advantage on either side. The Federal General Phil Kearny had been killed; the next morning his body was sent through the lines by Lee.

Stuart was sent splashing ahead of the army once more, as Lee persisted in his idea of continuing attack, but now the enemy was gone, streaming back toward the earthworks protecting Washington. It became clear that the campaign which had begun so unpromisingly under Richmond's gates had come to an end.

In the west, it might be that the war was being lost, but the Army of Northern Virginia had made a new war for the Confederacy. The state was virtually free of invaders, and Lee's army, tested in the savage fighting of more than half a dozen major battles, began to appear invincible. There was riotous rejoicing in Richmond, and congratulatory telegrams poured upon headquarters.

But Lee, though he began now to lay bold plans for the invasion which Jackson had longed for, realized the true state of his victorious regiments. He confided to Davis:

> The army is not properly equipped for an invasion. . . . It lacks much of the material of war, is feeble in transportation, the animals being much reduced, and the men are poorly provided with clothes and in thousands of instances are destitute of shoes. . . . What concerns me most is the fear of getting out of ammunition.

And yet, though he saw these things, and though the country behind was alive with his stragglers, Lee made ready to strike into the country of the enemy.

7 'THE FAMISHED REBEL HORDE"

No ONE had ever seen such an army.

As Lee gave it a day of rest about Chantilly, it had none of the look of conquerors, even in the eyes of worshipful Virginians on the northern border.

Most of the men were without shoes. The First South Carolina reported 100 of its 300 barefoot; a Charleston newspaper called for 40,000 pairs of shoes for the army.

General Alexander of the artillery found the troops poorly armed: "About one half the small arms were still the old smoothbore muskets of short range, and our rifled cannon ammunition was . . . inferior in quality." He added, "In the matter of shoes, clothing, and food the army was, upon the whole, probably worse off . . . than it had ever been before or ever was again. . . . The lack of shoes was deplorable, and barefooted men with bleeding feet were no uncommon sight. . . . For rations, we were indebted mostly to the fields of roasting ears, and to the apple orchards."

Lee had, in effect, two armies, for the ragged throng was spreading through nearby counties, and 30,000 were stragglers.[1] Jackson had recently had three men shot for leaving his ranks, and had marched his men past the bodies at close range, but the object lesson did nothing to check the wholesale falling away of men. And as news spread that they were to invade Maryland, straggling increased. Especially did the tough mountain troops from North Carolina and southwestern Virginia drop out, for they came from country where Union sentiment had been strong, were opposed to slavery, and fought only to defend their homes, not to invade the North.

Lee wrote Davis in exasperation: "Our great embarrassment is the reduction of our ranks by straggling, which it seems impossible to prevent. . . . Our ranks are very much diminished—I fear from a third to one-half of our original numbers."

Nevertheless, after he had given the men a brief rest, Lee herded them toward Maryland, where he felt that people would rise to aid the Confederacy. There was, in addition, the question of food, for the countryside around Manassas had been picked clean. Invasion would force the Union troops around Washington into a move, for the first time obliged to fight in their own territory. From every standpoint, it seemed wise to cross the Potomac.

September third, 1862, was Lee's day of decision. He probably learned then that George McClellan had succeeded Pope as commander of the Federal forces to confront him. On the same day Lee wrote Davis, saying that he would strike into Maryland unless the President objected. "As long as the army of the enemy are employed on this frontier I have no fears for the safety of Richmond," he added, to allay the President's constant fears for the capital.[2] He hoped to cross Maryland and carry the war into Pennsylvania. On this day it seemed a reasonable goal.

The troops fell into ranks, and the leading files went toward Leesburg, near the Potomac. Jackson led the way. There was already trouble in the ranks, for General Hood was under arrest for his part in an argument over spoils at Second Manassas, and A. P. Hill soon joined him, after a squabble over the slow marching of his men.

Most of the army crossed the Potomac at White's Ford, and for four days the scarecrows splashed through the shallow stream. A few bands enlivened the crossing from each shore, playing "Dixie" and "My Maryland" over and over.

The unkempt troops seemed to some of the officers a magnificent spectacle as the miles of men wound down to the stream and across, going out of sight into Maryland. Heros von Borcke, the Prussian who rode with Stuart, was transported at sight of cavalry crossing:

"A magnificent sight as the long column of many thousand horsemen stretched across this beautiful Potomac. The evening sun . . . burnished them with gold, while the arms of the soldiers glittered and blazed. . . . There were few moments . . . of the war, of excitement more intense . . . than when we ascended the opposite bank to the familiar but now strangely thrilling music of 'Maryland, My Maryland.' "

But the candid eye of a young boy who watched on the Maryland side, saw this army as it was:

"They were the dirtiest men I ever saw, a most ragged, lean and hungry set of wolves. Yet there was a dash about them that the Northern men lacked. They rode like circus riders. Many of them were from the far South and spoke a dialect I could scarcely understand. They were profane beyond belief and talked incessantly."[3]

Lee rode down to the Potomac with A. P. Hill and found hundreds of Hill's troops lying in the roadway. Hill ordered them to get up, but Lee would not permit it. He was only now beginning to ride once more, clumsily, but he reined Traveller out of the road.

"Never mind, General," he said to Hill, "we will ride around them. Lie still men." He splashed into the water, followed by the young men of his staff.

The army settled about the town of Frederick, under Lee's orders forbidding pillage; guards were placed to inspect the passes of troops. Lee's headquarters were under canvas in a pleasant oak

grove just outside the town. Despite a stream of visitors, Lee attempted to remain near his tent, giving his injuries a chance to
heal. Almost as soon as they camped Jackson was also hurt.

Maryland admirers had presented Stonewall with a rangy gray
mare, and when he had mounted her, the animal reared, throwing
Jackson to the ground. The general was briefly unconscious, and for
a time was unable to move. Later in the day he got about painfully,
a semi-invalid. Longstreet was also hobbling, the result of a blis-
tered heel. The three senior commanders were thus indisposed—
but that did not deter visitors to the oak grove.

Incidents of September sixth seemed proof that Maryland
would have a warm welcome for the troops. Two pretty society
girls from Baltimore raided headquarters in an open carriage, and
when they had Stonewall pointed out to them, in the words of the
watching Kyd Douglas: ". . . rushed up to him, one took his
hand, the other threw her arms about him, and talked with the
wildest enthusiasm, both at the same time . . . they were driven
away, happy and delighted; he stood for a moment cap in hand,
bowing, speechless, paralyzed."

The girls went to Lee's tent, where they were received in much
more urbane manner by the commander.

The army was already beginning to feel a new pinch for food
and supplies in Maryland, which was not hostile, but seemed indisposed to feed the hungry invaders. Lee had hopes of winning
the state by a political maneuver, since its people had from the
outset shown Southern sympathies. He thought that Enoch Lowe,
an ex-Governor with a large following in Western Maryland, and a
known Confederate supporter, might come into camp and urge the
people to aid the Army of Northern Virginia. But Lowe did not
come, and Lee concluded that he should make some public statement to Marylanders. He had Charles Marshall, the Baltimore

lawyer on his staff, draw his appeal, a somewhat flowery, though calm and sensible document. It opened with:

"It is right that you should know the purpose that brought the army under my command within the limits of your state. . . . The people of the Confederate States have long watched with the deepest sympathy the wrongs and outrages that have been inflicted upon the citizens of a commonwealth allied to the States of the South by the strongest social, political and commercial ties. They have seen with profound indignation their sister State deprived of every right and reduced to the condition of a conquered province."

He offered to throw off the Northern "yoke," and ended with:

"This, citizens of Maryland, is our mission. . . . No constraint upon your free will is intended; no intimidation will be allowed within the limits of this army, at least. Marylanders shall once more enjoy their ancient freedom of thought and speech. We know no enemies among you, and will protect all, of every opinion. It is for you to decide your destiny freely and without constraint. This army will respect your choice, whatever it may be; and while the Southern people will rejoice to welcome you to your natural position among them, they will only welcome you when you come of your own free will."[4]

While he was in this mood, Lee wrote to the anxious Davis, back in Richmond, proposing that the Confederacy make an offer of peace, based on recognition of Southern independence. He argued that this could not be construed as begging for an armistice, since his army was now in position to "inflict injury upon our adversary." An offer now, he thought, would prove to the world the sincere desire of the Confederacy for any honorable peace, and shift the burden of war guilt to the North. He also looked forward to political developments in the North: "The proposal of peace would enable the people of the United States to determine at their coming elections whether they will support those who favor a prolongation of the war, or those who wish to bring it to a termination."

Lee was given little time to pore over these lost hopes. The Federal garrisons behind him, at Harpers Ferry and Martinsburg, still held firm. He had thought they would be abandoned with his crossing of the river. He had already decided that these outposts must be taken before he could strike farther north, and had, in fact, attempted to persuade Longstreet to attack them before they went to Frederick. In a singular revelation of his stubborn resistance to Lee's will, Longstreet wrote:

"Riding together before we reached Frederick, the sound of artillery fire came from the direction of Point of Rocks and Harpers Ferry, from which General Lee inferred that the enemy was concentrating his forces . . . and proposed to me to organize forces to surround and capture the works and garrison.

"I thought it a venture not worth the game, and suggested, as we were in the enemy's country and presence, that he would be advised of any move we made in a few hours . . . that the Union army, though beaten, was not disorganized."

Longstreet continued to marshal the reasons why the move should not be made: The excellence of Federal officership, the worn condition of the Confederate troops, and so on. In short, Old Pete responded with one of his aggressive dissents which were to play a historic part in the career of the army. It was Longstreet who recorded the final decision to divide the army in the threat of enemy attack, hoping to concentrate once more before McClellan stirred from the Washington trenches:

"As the subject was not continued, I supposed that it was a mere expression of passing thought, until . . . upon going over to headquarters, I found the front of the general's tent closed and tied.

"Upon inquiring of a member of the staff, I was told that he was inside with General Jackson. As I had not been called, I turned to go away, when General Lee, recognizing my voice, called me in.

"The plan had been arranged. Jackson, with his three divisions, was to recross the Potomac by the fords above Harpers Ferry

. . . McLaws' division by Crampton's Gap . . . J. G. Walker's division to recross at Cheek's Ford and occupy Loudon Heights, these heights overlooking the positions of the garrison of Harpers Ferry; D. H. Hill's division to march by the National Road over South Mountain . . . and halt at the western base, to guard trains, intercept fugitives from Harpers Ferry, and support the cavalry, if needed; the cavalry to face the enemy and embarrass his movements. I was to march over the mountain to Hagerstown.

"As their minds were settled firmly upon the enterprise, I offered no opposition further."[5]

These orders went into effect. Lee's plan was to clear the rear lines by this division of force, and when the task was completed, bring the army together near Hagerstown, from which Harrisburg, the Pennsylvania capital, would be within striking distance.

Lee had yet to explain it to the commanders involved, and when he called General Walker to his tent, the latter betrayed his frank astonishment.

Lee smiled. "You doubtless regard it as hazardous to leave McClellan on my line of communication and to march into the heart of the enemy's country?"

Walker nodded.

"Are you acquainted with General McClellan? He is an able general, but a very cautious one. His enemies among his own people think him too much so. His army is in a very demoralized and chaotic condition, and will not be ready for offensive operations— or he will not think it so—for three or four weeks. Before that time I hope to be on the Susquehanna."[6]

The troops began to move. The entire army left Frederick, each division toward its goal.

Longstreet recalled the scene in the town as they wound out to the west: "It was a rollicking march, the Confederates playing and singing, as they marched through the streets of Frederick, 'The Girl I Left Behind Me.' "

On September eleventh Jackson recrossed the Potomac, and found that the enemy had abandoned Martinsburg, its garrison retreating to Harpers Ferry. The other movements went off as scheduled, and there was a slow closing in on Harpers Ferry.

Behind, in Frederick, the army had left one of those trifling castoffs of war on which battles and campaigns may turn. Two forgotten sheets of soiled paper, lying on the odorous Confederate camp ground, were to end Lee's invasion of the north.

The order for dividing the army this week was sent to Lee's generals as Special Order 191; it set forth clearly details of the movements, the objectives, the time and place of reconcentration. In short, it told everything. But there was one bit of confusion.

D. H. Hill had been under Jackson's command until they had crossed the river, and Stonewall was naturally concerned to see that Hill had a copy of the order. Jackson copied it in his own hand, and sent it to Hill's headquarters. Hill, it seemed, already had a copy from Lee, and some staff officer, noting the duplication, wrapped one copy about three cigars, thrust the package into his pocket, and in the hurry of leaving, the cigars and their remarkable wrapping were dropped on the Frederick campsite. (Longstreet had thought the order so vital that, after reading it, he chewed it to bits.)[7]

The Federal army crept into Frederick on September thirteenth, and in the grove where the 27th Indiana happened to camp Private B. W. Mitchell picked up the cigars, made out the confidential nature of the order, and passed it up along the chain of command. It was soon in McClellan's hands, and the importance of the little document was recognized. The Federal army began to move with unaccustomed haste. McClellan advised Washington of his find, and caution was over; the advance of the heavy infantry regiments was flung down the road toward D. H. Hill's vulnerable division at South Mountain to the growing dismay of the confident general of the invaders.

Hill had been told to expect nothing more than a cavalry stab at his position, but he soon looked down from his hills to see something else entirely: "The marching columns extended back as far as eye could see in the distance; but many of the troops had already arrived and were in double lines of battle. . . . It was a grand and glorious spectacle, and it was impossible to look at it without admiration. I had never seen so tremendous an army before."

Lee learned of the massing of Federal infantry below South Mountain in the night of September thirteenth. A report from a scout said that some 90,000 enemy troops were at hand. Longstreet was with the commander:

"General Lee still held to the thought that he had ample time. He sent for me, and I found him over his map. He told of the reports, and asked my views. I thought it too late to march on the fourteenth and properly man the pass . . . and expressed preference for concentrating D. H. Hill's and my own force behind the Antietam at Sharpsburg. . . . He preferred to make the stand at Turner's Pass. . . . The hallucination that McClellan was not capable of serious work seemed to pervade our army, even to this moment of dreadful threatening."

Longstreet left Lee and went to his tent, his mind so disturbed over the position of the army that he could not sleep. "At last I made a light and wrote to tell General Lee of my troubled thoughts, and appealed again for an immediate concentration at Sharpsburg. To this no answer came."

By morning, still anxious over lack of word from Jackson at Harper's Ferry, Lee turned to help D. H. Hill defend the rear at South Mountain. He had ordered Longstreet's men to march back from Hagerstown to Hill's aid, and the veterans, hurrying back over roads "dry and beaten into impalpable powder, that rose in clouds," were just in time. Hill was in trouble under courageous Federal attacks.

General Garland's brigade, fighting under Hill, was driven

back by the enemy, lost its commander, and broke for the rear; reinforcements barely managed to hold the line, with the aid of artillery from the summit of the pass. On every hand the bluecoats came forward, and Hill's men fought until ammunition was out in many regiments, and the commander rode down the lines shouting that the men must use stones to hold the position. Shortly after three P.M., when full Federal reinforcements were at hand, Longstreet's column came to the summit, and Hill was no longer in danger of a rout. Firing went on without pause until long after dark.

Lee watched the last of the fight here. In midafternoon he had sat Traveller at the roadside as his troops went up into the hills, and had an exchange with his Texas brigade. The men yelled to him, "Give us Hood!"

Lee lifted his hat. "Gentlemen, you shall have him," he called.[8]

And a few moments later, when Hood approached, still under arrest from the affair at Second Manassas, Lee urged an apology from his young lieutenant of the old days in Texas:

"General, here I am just upon the eve of entering into battle, and with one of my best officers under arrest. If you will merely say that you regret this occurrence I will release you and restore you to the command of your division."

Hood would not relent, even in the sound of gunfire, and Lee, once more unable to bring himself to administer discipline to rebellious commanders, gave another sign of his chief weakness in the field. He surrendered to Hood.

"Well," he said, "I will suspend your arrest till the impending battle is decided." And Hood rode amid his cheering men to take part in the heavy skirmishing.

When night fell on the mountain, Lee had gained little but protection of his rear; each side had suffered almost 2,000 casualties, and in addition most of one Confederate brigade had been captured. Lee had no way of discovering what had happened to McLaws, but he realized his position would now be dangerous. He sent off a message to that commander whose opening words told the story of Lee's growing concern: "The day has gone against us and this army will go by Sharpsburg and cross the river."

In a council of war his officers agreed with the commander that South Mountain could no longer be held. The army must fall back, and if Jackson and the other separated forces did not return soon, it must indeed retreat into Virginia. Late in the night a dispatch from Jackson announced that Harpers Ferry should fall the next day; if that came to pass, the situation might be improved after all, and Lee could remain north of the river.

This seemed less reassuring as the night wore on; under a bright moon the column marched westward from South Mountain in dust which rolled off in great waves through half-darkness, and lay like the threat of a storm until daylight. At about dawn the leading men crossed Antietam Creek, a slow little stream that crept down out of Pennsylvania, running southwest to empty into the Potomac. Behind it to the west, wrapped about in serpentine turns of the Potomac, was the country village of Sharpsburg. The Antietam was arched by four stone bridges in this region, one of them soon to become famous as a bloody landmark. Four roads fanned out of Sharpsburg, the northernmost leading to Hagerstown, and just west of that road was a small white Dunkard church, with a woodland nearby.

The troops filed over the creek and turned left and right as directed by officers, forming their lines. They saw to the east wide fields of corn, now ripening, and orchards nearing harvest time. There were patches of woodland on the landscape, which along the stream became heavy forests, running down to the borders of the Potomac.

Lee betrayed his anxiety during the morning of September fifteenth by taking personal charge of placing the men coming out of the hot road. One of the veterans remembered his looking at the row of hills between the creek and village, and saying, "We

will make our stand on those hills." It was a skimpy line at best.
The ranks lay along a ridge on which were outcroppings of lime-
stone; their line was drawn with its right a mile southeast of the
village, and the left, three miles away, curved back toward a bend
of the Potomac. In that quarter Lee held his cavalry and its artillery.

There were just 18,000 men in the line, and on the roads to the
east, hurriedly approaching, was the Federal army, estimated at
90,000. In that situation Lee received a dispatch from Jackson—a
stirring message that Harpers Ferry had fallen, and that most of
Jackson's men could march to Lee in the evening; A. P. Hill's
troops would be left to guard the prisoners. Jackson had captured
11,000 men, 13,000 muskets and other small arms, 72 field guns,
and plentiful stores.

Lee looked up from the dispatch. "That is indeed good news.
Let it be announced to the troops."

He was still worried about McLaws, who had been through a
brief fight in his part of the attack on Harpers Ferry, and was now
presumably free to return. Lee now called him with an insistent
message:

> Withdraw immediately from your position on Maryland
> Heights and join us here. If you cannot get off any other way,
> you must cross the mountain. The utmost despatch is re-
> quired.

Lee spent the hour after noon in further inspection of his
line. He saw to the placing of all artillery to be squeezed into position—and those guns left over he sent across the Potomac under
General Pendleton as a reserve.

Heads were constantly turning east, where a new dust cloud
was now unmistakable, and at two P.M. the first of the bluecoats
appeared. Within plain sight the ranks turned to right and left, far
beyond the Antietam, and Federal gun crews unlimbered their
field pieces and sent horses trotting rearward. A slow, almost harm-

less artillery duel opened, rising and falling through the heat of the afternoon.

Most of the day was spent in watching the massing of the enemy who were not yet ready for their assault. Stuart reported to Lee, having ridden across the country in advance of Jackson, and he gave the commander details of the fall of Harpers Ferry.

Just before noon of the next day, while the enemy accommodatingly rested, Lee greeted the advance of Jackson, coming up from its victory. He shook hands with Jackson and General Walker, and congratulated them on the capture of Harpers Ferry. Lee was now completely confident of his ability to meet McClellan, whose troops were still content to rake the Confederate position with sporadic gunfire. Still, the ranks even now held only 25,000 men, so that the odds against Lee were very nearly four to one.

Walker, who certainly remembered the recent scene in the headquarters tent at Frederick when he was informed of the daring army maneuver, was struck by Lee's bearing today:

"If he had had a well-equipped army of 100,000 veterans at his back he could not have appeared more composed and confident."[9]

The commander, however, soon sent riders hurrying across the Potomac to summon A. P. Hill, in a last attempt to reconcentrate the army before the obvious assault fell upon it. Even if he could gather all of the men together here, he would have but 40,000 in line.

Because Lee directed Jackson's veterans toward the left of his line, they must have seemed the most stalwart of troops to him; but a Federal reporter who had seen them the day before thought Jackson himself "seedy, and in general appearance in no respect to be distinguished from the mongrel, barefooted crew who follow his fortunes . . . such a looking crowd! Ireland in her worst straits could present no parallel, and yet they glory in their shame."[10]

Hood's troops had felt the only Federal thrust of the day, a

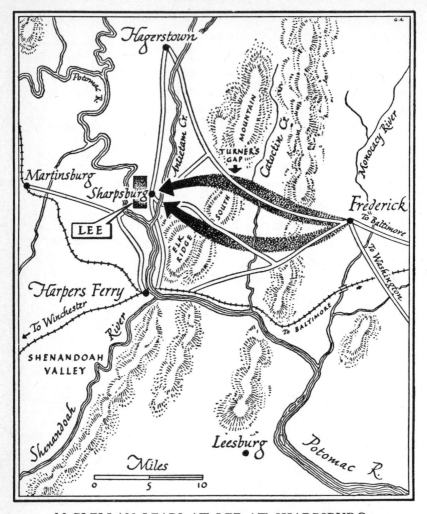

McCLELLAN LEAPS AT LEE AT SHARPSBURG

noisy and brief attack which did not budge the lines of veterans and gave Lee no concern.

A light rain sifted over the armies at dark, and quiet fell with thousands of camp fires sparkling over the hills. Nervous pickets

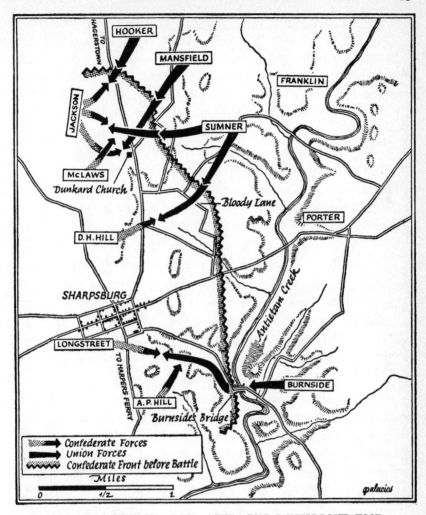

THE BLOODIEST DAY—ATTACKS WITHOUT END

fired a few shots. It was still dark when the thunder of a battle swept on Lee's position.

Lee slept little during the night. By four thirty in the morning of September seventeenth, the fire had become so intense that the opening of a full engagement surely waited only the first light of day; skirmish lines were rattling steadily. Lee ordered Pendleton to send up more of his guns and watch the fords with care, thinking despite his confident mood of the possibility of hurried retreat over the Potomac. He might well have done so. If either of his flanks had been turned, the enemy could cut off his army. If his lines were driven back by frontal assault, as they could be in face of such odds, he would be broken against the river bank.

When it was just daylight, Lee had the good news that McLaws and Anderson, with their divisions, were in the village; now only A. P. Hill was missing. At almost the same time he was told of a disaster on the left. Here was none of the fencing, of charge and counter charge and gallant lines meeting, that the Army of Northern Virginia had been accustomed to in the months just past; those old scenes were bloody enough, but this morning brought something brutal and new.

A corps—it turned out to be Hooker's—lashed out at Jackson's and D. H. Hill's sector of the line, and almost without hesitation overwhelmed this front. Three brigades were torn apart and swept aside. The old Valley division was clawed from its position and the enemy already had stabbed far down the Hagerstown Road and was nearing the Dunkard church. Lee's headquarters were stunned, but the commander went to work in singular calm. Hood's men were already going up from the rear to meet this threat. Lee hardly hesitated; he ordered three brigades pulled from the right of his line, already thinly held, and sent to the aid of Jackson, where the front must be held, or all would be lost. Anderson and McLaws were ordered to hurry from the village. So the first crisis came with Lee crowding more than half of his twenty-four brigades into one mile of the four-and-a-half mile front.

Young James Graham, in the ranks of the 27th North Carolina, recalled starting that day with a canteen of water from a mud puddle in a farmer's barnlot, because the Marylander had broken his pump rather than furnish the Rebels water. During the day even this tasted good to Graham and his companions, for they were pushed into the thick of it when Jackson's front caved in:

"Forming in a corn field we advanced under a heavy fire of grape and canister at a quick step . . . and halted at a rail fence . . . we had suffered heavily . . . the enemy were piled two or three deep in some places. . . .

"Colonel Cooke ordered us to fall back some twenty steps in the corn field and lie down, so as to draw them on. . . . At the first fire . . . nearly every horse and more than half of their men fell . . . numbers of them surrendered to us . . . two or three hundred took shelter behind a lot of haystacks, and fastening white handkerchiefs to their muskets and bayonets, held them out offering to surrender. . . .

"In a short while all our ammunition was exhausted. . . . Four or five times . . . General Longstreet sent couriers telling Colonel Cooke to hold his position at all hazards, that 'it was the key to the whole line.' Colonel Cooke's reply was always, 'Tell General Longstreet to send me some ammuniton. I have not a cartridge in my command, but will hold my position at the point of a bayonet.'

"The regiment entered the battle with 325 officers and men and lost in killed and wounded 203, about 63 per cent. One company went in 30 strong and had but five left at the end of the day."[11]

Longstreet was stirred to admiration by the sight of Cooke's men, and the general went himself to hold the horses of his staff officers while they fired the two remaining guns in Cooke's position. Longstreet recorded it:

"That little battery shot harder and faster . . . we sought to make them believe we had many batteries behind us. . . . General Chilton, General Lee's chief of staff, made his way to me and asked, 'Where are the troops you are holding your line with?' I pointed to my two pieces and to Cooke's regiment, and replied, 'There they are; but that regiment hasn't a cartridge.'

"Chilton's eyes popped as though they would come out of his head; he struck spurs to his horse and away he went to General Lee. . . . In this desperate effort the lines seemed to swing back and forth for many minutes, but at last they settled down to their respective positions, the Confederates holding with a desperation which seemed to say, 'We are here to die.' "

More than one such miracle saved Lee's line, as he pulled troops from quieter sectors and hurried them to threatened points. Jackson fell back around the Dunkard church, and at last was holding his own. This was due more to the incredible slowing of the triumphant Federal attack than to the staying power of the thinning gray lines, for McClellan, or his headquarters staff, seemed determined to make attacks in piecemeal, first at one point and then at another, and this strange pattern of assault enabled Jackson to survive, and Lee to move his few pawns.

Officers on the field aided in the furious improvisation. D. H. Hill's troops were flung back in a frontal attack, and when an open gap invited the pouring Federal troops, Hill himself led a tiny party of 200 to hang onto the line, seeing to the turning of a few guns upon the blue infantry, and to the very placing of individual soldiers. Hill soon fell wounded; on the Federal side both Hooker and General Mansfield, who launched the first attacks, were casualties.

Lee, riding back and forth in his effort to husband his strength and prevent the snapping of his line, was more than once simply carried on the flood of battle, and beyond his resources. When D. H. Hill was fighting for his life, Lee could no longer find reserves to send to his aid; and as the crisis mounted there, a heavy burst of firing to the right became so ominous that he had to ride away to the scene of the new threat.

John B. Gordon, one of Lee's fiercest generals, who was wounded five times that day, watched the troops of the Confederate left regain their ground at last, "enthused by Lee's presence . . . and, with a shout as piercing as the blast of a thousand bugles, they rushed . . . upon the exulting Federals, hurled them back. . . . Again and again, hour after hour, by charges and counter-charges, this portion of the field was lost and recovered, until the green corn that grew upon it looked as if it had been struck by a storm of bloody hail."

Gordon then saw the battle swing upon his own men, in one of the five separate assaults McClellan made, which ran from left to right of the Confederate line. Lee was near Gordon as it began; the division commander recorded:

"Up to this hour not a shot had been fired in my front. There was an ominous lull on the left. From sheer exhaustion, both sides, like battered and bleeding athletes, seemed willing to rest. General Lee took advantage of this respite and rode along his lines on the right and center. . . . With that wonderful power which he possessed of divining the plans and purposes of his antagonist, General Lee had decided that the Union commander's next heavy blow would fall upon our center. . . . We were cautioned to be prepared for a determined assault, and urged to hold . . . at any sacrifice. . . . It was evident . . . that my small force was to receive the first impact. . . .

"To comfort General Lee . . . and especially to make . . . my men still more resolute . . . I called aloud to these officers as they rode away: 'These men are going to stay here, General, till the sun goes down or victory is won.' "

Lee had scarcely left the spot when the new Union attack came, mounted by what Gordon saw as "fresh troops from Washington," neat in white gaiters, with brand-new flags over them, coming out at parade step. Gordon was soon shot in a leg:

"My men were falling under the death-dealing crossfire like trees in a hurricane. The persistent Federals, who had lost so heavily . . . seemed now determined to kill enough Confederates to make the debits and credits of the battle's balance-sheet more even. Both sides stood in the open at short range . . . and the firing was doing a deadly work."

Gordon was hit for the third time, and thought the day would never end: "I looked at the sun. It moved very slowly; in fact, it seemed to stand still."

Gordon was at last borne off on a litter, unconscious, and was not there to see whether his men made good their promise to Lee. At the end, his next in command, attempting to straighten the line to meet the enemy, gave a mistaken order to about face and march to the rear—and the resulting sight led the brigade to a hurried retreat. Miraculously, the Federals did not attack, and the gap was once more closed.

As Lee moved continually toward his right, where massing Federals across the Antietam seemed to promise that the lull would soon end, he had another encounter with Robert, who passed with the survivors of his battered gun crew. The son recalled:

"Our battery had been severely handled, losing many men and horses. Having three guns disabled, we were ordered to withdraw, and while moving back we passed General Lee and several of his staff, grouped on a little knoll near the road."

Captain Poague of Robert's Rockbridge Artillery battery reported to Lee and asked for orders. The commander glanced over the group of weary gunners, "his eyes passing over me without any sign of recognition," Robert recalled. Lee ordered Poague to take the best of the horses and the one gun which was in good order, and go back to the front, sending other guns to the rear.

Robert approached his father: "When he found out who I was, he congratulated me on being well and unhurt."

"General, are you going to send us in again?" Robert asked.

"Yes, my son. You all must do what you can to help drive these people back."

Lee stared after the party as it went up into the firing, the filthy young men tagging after the lone gun; it was a sight he would not forget.

A new storm of firing drew Lee farther to the right, where, in the hollow formed by the creek, the enemy was coming across the stone bridge to be known afterward as Burnside's Bridge, for the Federal commander who lost so many of his men there. Robert Toombs commanded men just above the bridge, and his regiments had driven back half-hearted Federal attempts at crossing in the morning. He could not stem the rush of early afternoon. The Union infantry, already in line, stormed up the slope toward the ridge of the right flank as if nothing could stop them. Every man was now engaged, and in places the line was wavering back toward Sharpsburg itself; some companies were again out of ammunition. And near the climax, Lee learned that the day's victory was gone, when Jackson reported that an effort to turn the Federal right could not be made as ordered, for any attack would be thrown into the mouths of ranked enemy guns. There seemed no hope.

David Thompson, a young New Yorker who came up the slope with Burnside's men, carried the memory of these moments for life:

"... the firing grew more rapid. ... Human nature was on the rack, and there burst forth from it the most vehement, terrible swearing I have ever heard. ... I only remember that as we rose and started all the fire that had been held back so long was loosed. In a second the air was full of the hiss of bullets and the hurtle of grapeshot. The mental strain was so great that I saw ... the whole landscape for an instant turned slightly red.

"... the regiment ... had gone in on the run, what there was left of it, and had disappeared in the cornfield ... there was nothing to do but lie there."[12]

Just then, in the Confederate rear, Lee saw the sight he had waited for during the hours of fury. Incredibly, the men of A. P. Hill were coming, having made the seventeen miles from Harpers Ferry

in about seven hours. Lee made the discovery with the aid of Lieu₄
tenant John Ramsay of the 10th North Carolina, who was coming
up with a battery through Sharpsburg, on his way to the front. Ramsay carried a telescope. Lee halted him. Ramsay remembered how
approaching Federals vexed him:

"General Lee . . . said, 'What troops are those?', pointing. I
drew my telescope from the case and handed it to General Lee.

"He held up his wounded hand (fingers in bandages) and
said, 'Can't use it. What troops are those?' "

Ramsay studied the distant group. "They are flying the United
States flag," he said.

Lee pointed to another line of soldiers, at right angles to the
first body.

"What troops are those?" he asked Ramsay.

"They are flying the Virginia and Confederate flags," Ramsay
said.

Lee replied with such calm that Ramsay noted nothing unusual in his manner: "It is A. P. Hill, from Harpers Ferry. Take
your guns and fire on those people."

"But, General, as soon as we fire we will draw the enemy's fire."

"Never mind me."

Lee sat in this position while Federal shells replied to the battery at his side; two gunners were killed in the first exchange. But
the enemy group was breaking up under Ramsay's firing.

"Well done," Lee said. "Elevate your guns and continue the
fire until these troops come near your line of fire, then change your
position to the ridge on the right, and fire on the troops beyond the
creek."[18]

Lee rode away with his staff. He soon saw A. P. Hill, riding
with his sword in hand, his jacket stripped off, conspicuous in his
red woolen shirt. The new brigades swept through Sharpsburg,
flung off the first lines of the enemy, and stormed along the right
flank, restoring the line and taking the day's last terrible casualties.

Firing rattled on through a red sunset, and there was an occasional volley after dark, but there was a truce for the night, and lights bobbed over the field where the war's bloodiest day had been fought. The Confederate dead and wounded were about 10,000; the Federal, over 12,000. The Federal attacks, though fierce, had been so poorly timed as to give Lee's talent for improvisation on the field full play.

Lee's headquarters tents were pitched between Sharpsburg and the river for the night, and here, as reports came in, he tried to estimate the day's losses and determine what could be done for tomorrow. His generals, as they came, were almost unanimously for an immediate retreat over the Potomac, back into Virginia. Lee gave no sign that he planned to move from the field, and though McClellan had used little more than half his strength, and the Confederate line was pitiably weak, Lee planned to hold his ground.

Despite the loss, fearful in officers, the army's mere survival seemed a miracle. Jackson had said, "God has been very kind to us this day." But three generals were missing that night—dead or dying, Starke, G. B. Anderson and Branch. Still Lee did not seem depressed as he made plans.

He missed Longstreet. Jackson, A. P. Hill, D. H. Hill, Hood, and the others were at hand, but Old Pete had not been seen since sunset, when Major Venable had caught sight of him. The stubborn fighter soon put in an appearance. He wrote:

"I rode for general headquarters to make report, but was delayed somewhat, finding wounded men hidden away under stone walls and in fence corners, not yet looked after, and afterwards in assisting a family whose home had been fired by a shell, so that all the other officers had arrived and made their reports, and were lounging about on the sod, when I rode up.

"General Lee walked up as I dismounted, threw his hands upon my shoulders and hailed me with, 'Here is my old war-horse at last!' "

One witness recollected—his memory perhaps colored with the passage of years—that Lee said something like this to his generals:

"Gentlemen, we will not cross the Potomac tonight. You will go to your respective commands, strengthen your lines . . . collect stragglers and get them up. . . . If McClellan wants to fight in the morning, I will give him battle again. Go!"[14]

No other officers recalled such an uncharacteristic speech by Lee, but there was accuracy in description of the night's work. Lee had stragglers picked up by guards at the fords, set his officers to feeding the men, having cooked rations from the rear carried out to the front lines. He posted artillery in new positions, and with daylight waited for McClellan to move. The Federal army did not stir, and the two forces lay in the heat of the long day, burying dead and caring for wounded. In the late afternoon, when McClellan seemed to be getting reinforcements, Lee determined to retreat into Virginia during the night. He put Stuart across first with the cavalry, and had the horsemen wait on the Virginia shore, ready to protect the rear of the column.

At nine in the evening, Longstreet remembered, the road was clear, and the Army of Northern Virginia began the move back into the Confederacy, its first invasion at an end.

General Walker saw Lee at the crossing, near dawn of September nineteenth:

"I was among the last to cross the Potomac. As I rode into the river I passed General Lee, sitting on his horse in the stream, watching the crossing of the wagons and artillery. . . . He inquired as to what was still behind. There was nothing but the wagons containing my wounded, and a battery of artillery, all of which were near at hand, and I told him so. 'Thank God,' I heard him say as I rode on."

When the Federals discovered the retreat, a small force of cavalry, aided by a few guns, blazed away at the Confederate wagon trains within sight of the river, put many small units to flight, and so disturbed General Pendleton of the artillery that he reported all the reserve guns were captured. A. P. Hill's men were sent in a charge to clear the river bank of a Pennsylvania regiment which had crossed, and a day-long skirmish sputtered across the river, with light casualties. By dark it became clear that the enemy was not going to follow Lee southward.

On September twenty-first Lee wrote to Davis at length, revealing that he was still full of fight despite the bloody end of his scheme of invasion: ". . . it is still my desire to threaten a passage into Maryland, to occupy the enemy on this frontier, and if my purpose cannot be accomplished, to draw them into the Valley where I can attack them to advantage."

He also fixed part of the blame for failure of his campaign:

"A great many men belonging to the army never entered Maryland at all; many returned after getting there, while others who crossed the river kept aloof. The stream has not lessened since crossing the Potomac, . . . some immediate legislation, in my opinion, is required, and the most summary punishment should be authorized.

"To give you an idea of its extent, in some brigades, I will mention that on the morning after the battle of the 17th, General Evans reported to me on the field, where he was holding the front position, that he had but 120 of his brigade present, and that the next brigade to him, that of General Garnett, consisted of but 100 men. . . this is a woeful condition of affairs."

But in an order to his men Lee allowed no such pessimism to creep in:

> Since your great victories around Richmond, you have defeated the enemy at Cedar Mountain, expelled him from the Rappahannock, and, after a conflict of three days, utterly repulsed him on the plains of Manassas. . . . Without halting for repose, you crossed the Potomac, stormed the heights of Harpers Ferry, made prisoners of more than 11,000 men. . . . While one corps of the army was thus engaged, the other insured its

success by arresting . . . the combined armies of the enemy. . . .
On the field of Sharpsburg, with less than one third of his
numbers, you resisted from daylight until dark the whole army
of the enemy and repulsed every attack along his entire front.
. . . The whole of the following day you stood prepared to
resume the conflict on the same ground and retired the next
morning without molestation across the Potomac. . . . History
records few examples of greater fortitude.

8 *LULL AND STORM*

THE ARMY lay for a few days on Opequon Creek near the Potomac, and then, slowly, watching the enemy in its rear, fell back to the area around Winchester. In the last days of September its men were already hopefully building huts for the winter.

Three days after the army had crossed into Virginia, President Lincoln announced his Emancipation Proclamation, but it seemed to stir the Army of Northern Virginia less than it did General McClellan, who put his protest into official dispatches and widened the breach between him and Washington. The enemy also moved slightly, retaking Harpers Ferry and establishing lines along the Potomac.

On October eighth, Richmond was pleased to learn that Lee's force had increased by 20,000 since Sharpsburg, but there was a new concern. Food shortages had become so severe that the War Department notified Lee the ration, already slim, must soon be reduced.

Paper work, which always vexed Lee, was kept from him as long as possible by Colonel Walter Taylor of his staff, but a day of decision came. Taylor recalled:

"On one occasion, when an audience had not been asked of him for several days, it became necessary to have one. The few papers requiring his action were submitted. He was not in a very pleasant humor; something irritated him, and he manifested his ill-humor by a little nervous twist or jerk of the neck and head peculiar to himself, accompanied by some harshness of manner. . . .

"I hastily concluded that my efforts to save him annoyance were not appreciated. In disposing of some cases of a vexatious character matters reached a climax; he became really worried, and, forgetting what was due to my superior, I petulantly threw the paper down at my side and gave evident signs of anger.

"Then, in a perfectly calm and measured tone of voice, he said, 'Colonel Taylor, when I lose my temper, don't you let it make you angry.' "

The commander had an uncanny nose for difficult men who approached him, and, Taylor reported, when he spied some officer or civilian moving toward his tent with the look of trouble about him, Lee would pop into his tent, closing the flap, and calling after him, "Assuage him, Colonel. 'Suage him, and send him away."

Lee was uncertain as to the moves of the enemy. McClellan was lying still, so far as he knew, but there was the possibility that he would move by the water route against Richmond once more, despite Lee's presence so far north. In an effort to solve the puzzle he sent Stuart on one of his favorite diversions, a swift raid into Pennsylvania.

Stuart and 1,800 troopers dashed into Federal territory, moving far ahead of pursuit, to Chambersburg, Pennsylvania, where they sought in vain to destroy an iron railroad bridge the loss of which would have ruptured vital Union movements. They swept back home, the intuitive Stuart studying the country as thoroughly as pursuit would allow. He took Lee information which seemed to rule out a Federal move to the east; Richmond, the conclusion was, could be considered safe. Stuart also brought in 1,200 horses, without which the wagons and guns could hardly have moved during the fall. In addition, he bore some 30 officials from towns along his route, whom he held as hostages.

Lee's headquarters at this time were in a stone-littered field near Winchester. Colonel Long of his staff found a farmhouse, but Lee refused to move out the family, or to impose upon it by taking a few of its rooms. Instead, he moved outside the yard of this place into the field. He seldom greeted visitors without making a joke at the expense of Long, whom he accused of "having set him down there among the rocks in revenge for his refusing to occupy the yard."

Headquarters life was informal, the army noted with pleasure, and only Colonel Chilton of the staff was a West Pointer. Though Lee did not use alcohol, an occasional jar or jug was found at headquarters. Long recalled an instance of Jeb Stuart's visiting Lee with his banjo-picker, Sweeny, shortly after someone had left a large demijohn of liquor outside headquarters. Stuart gave his customary serenade of corn-shucking music, and Lee emerged grinning: "Gentlemen, am I to thank General Stuart or the jug for this fine music?" The company roared at Stuart, himself a teetotaller.

Long noted that Lee was becoming an object of genuine affection for the troops, who usually called him "The Old Man," but to his face, when he appeared in camp, cheered him as "Marse Robert." (In private his staff called him "The Great Tycoon.")

The camp soon had distinguished guests, among them Colonel Garnet Wolseley who left a record of the scene:

"Lee's headquarters consisted of about seven or eight pole tents, pitched, with their backs to a stake fence, upon a piece of ground so rocky that it was unpleasant to ride over it, its only recommendation being a little stream of water which flowed close by the general's tent.

"In front of the tents were some three or four army wagons, drawn up without any regularity, and a number of horses turned loose about the field. The servants—who were, of course, slaves—and the mounted soldiers called couriers ... were unprovided with tents, and slept in or under the wagons. Wagons, tents and some of the horses were marked, 'U.S.' ... No guard or sentries were to be seen ... no crowd of aides-de-camp loitered about. ...

"Lee's staff are crowded together, two or three in a tent; none are allowed to carry more baggage than a small box each, and his own kit is but very little larger. Everyone who approaches him does so with marked respect, although there is none of that bowing and flourishing of forage caps which occurs in the presence of European generals."[1]

Lee was only now recovering from his injury, and he wrote Mary:

> My hands are improving slowly, and, with my left hand, I am able to dress and undress myself, which is a great comfort. My right is becoming of some assistance, too, though it is still swollen and sometimes painful. The bandages have been removed. I am now able to sign my name. ... I have at last discarded the sling.

In less than a week Taylor saw Lee in deep sorrow. His daughter Annie, a great favorite with him, had gone with her mother to Warren Sulphur Springs in North Carolina, and had died there of some fever. Soon after her death on October twentieth, Lee was notified. Taylor was in the tent with him, and saw that Lee read the notice of Annie's death with the same calm with which he glanced over routine correspondence. But a few minutes later, when Taylor came back to the tent, he found Lee sobbing.[2]

It was almost a week before Lee wrote Mary:

> ... I cannot express the anguish I feel at the death of our sweet Annie. To know that I shall never see her again on earth, that her place in our circle, which I always hoped one day to enjoy, is forever vacant, is agonizing in the extreme. But God in this, as in all things, has mingled mercy with the blow in

selecting that one best prepared to leave us. May you be able to join me in saying, 'His will be done.'

He wrote to his brother Charles on the same day, but found himself able to speak of the army's situation:

> I am glad you derive satisfaction from the operations of the army. . . . Nothing can surpass the valor and endurance of our troops, yet while so much remains to be done, I feel as if nothing had been accomplished. But we must endure to the end, and if our people are true to themselves and our soldiers continue to discard all thoughts of self . . . I have no fear of the result. We may be annihilated, but we cannot be conquered. No sooner is one army scattered than another rises up. This snatches from us the fruits of victory and covers the battle-fields with our dead. Yet what have we to live for if not victorious?

On the day these letters were written, McClellan ended Lee's suspense by crossing the Potomac. Lee had already taken tentative steps to receive him, by throwing a long thin line down the ninety-five mile front from Fredericksburg to Martinsburg. He now sent Longstreet forward to Culpeper.

Two days after this move, on November fifth, the Federal command was abruptly changed; McClellan was out and Ambrose Burnside was in. "I hate to part with McClellan," Lee said, "for we always understood each other so well. I fear they may continue to make these changes until they find some one I don't understand."[3]

By November tenth Lee had 70,000 in his ranks. Army morale was good. Revivals swept the camps, inflaming thousands of men with a fervor in which religion was mingled with Confederate patriotism. Lee's generals allowed men to escape daily drills to attend services.

He took note of vice in camp in a formal order.:

> The commanding general is pained to learn that the vice of gambling exists, and is becoming common in this army.

There were also important changes of command. The army was at last, and legally, divided into corps under Jackson and Longstreet, who were promoted to Lieutenant General. The cavalry was divided into four brigades; one of the new brigadiers was Rooney Lee, and Robert left the artillery to become a lieutenant on his staff. Lee gave his youngest son a horse and a sword as he went off on a new series of army adventures. The horse on which Rob rode to Fredericksburg was Traveller, to be left for the commander in that town. Robert found that the famous mount was not quite what he seemed in his majestic appearances with his father:

"Traveller would not walk a step. He took a short, high, trot . . . and kept it up to Fredericksburg, some thirty miles. Though young, strong and tough, I was glad when the journey ended."

There were some signs of enemy movement and the army prepared for action once more. Longstreet's men marched off toward Fredericksburg on November fifteenth, about 3,500 of them still without shoes.

Lee had watched the opening Federal moves from Culpeper, after making a brief trip to Richmond the first week in November to consult with President Davis on possible reinforcements for his army. From the railroad town in the foothills Lee puzzled over the intentions of Burnside for more than a week. First signs were withdrawal of enemy flanking troops in the hills to the west, and the appearance of patrols near Fredericksburg. These signs had grown unmistakable, and Lee was already moving when he learned that Sumner's corps of the Federal army was marching on Fredericksburg itself.

Lee rode toward the town on the south bank of the river and arrived there on November twentieth, finding the familiar streets teeming with refugees going downriver. He had a Mississippi regiment in the town, and there was danger of its bombardment by Federals from heights over the river. He waited for the next move of Burnside from the steep hills back of the town, where Longstreet's corps was in camp, busy with fortifications.

On November twenty-ninth, Jackson appeared at Lee's tent in the Wilderness, having brought in his corps from the Shenandoah Valley. He was sent to the rear with his men, for Lee had serious doubts that Burnside would give battle on the forbidding terrain by the river.

Jackson's troops, many still poorly clothed, went into camp near Guiney's Station on December first. The next day Lee wrote Mary:

> I tremble for my country when I hear of confidence expressed in me. I know too well my weakness, and that our only hope is in God.

He was still brooding over the loss of Annie, and a bit earlier had written his daughter Mary:

> In the quiet hours of the night, when there is nothing to lighten the full weight of my grief, I feel as if I should be overwhelmed. I have always counted, if God should spare me a few days of peace, after this cruel war was ended, that I should have her with me, but year after year my hopes go out, and I must be resigned.
>
> General Burnside's whole army is apparently opposite Fredericksburg, and stretches from the Rappahannock to the Potomac. What his intentions are he has not yet disclosed. . . . He threatens to bombard Fredericksburg, and the noble spirit displayed by its citizens, particularly the women and children, has elicited my highest admiration. They have been abandoning their homes night and day during all this inclement weather . . . with only such assistance as our wagons and ambulances could afford—women, girls, children, trudging through the mud and bivouacking in the open fields.

In a state of uncertainty Lee made the army as nearly ready as possible, and down the lines heavy works grew, chiefly of earth, but dotted by bulwarks of logs and timber. His spies were at work on both enemy flanks, and in the hazy night of December tenth, in the bitter cold, the voice of a woman called across the river that the Yankees were cooking rations, preparing to march. Just before five A.M. the night was disturbed by the signal guns, two rolling cannon shots: the enemy had been seen, beginning an effort to cross the Rappahannock and approach the frowning hills of the Confederate line.

Lee was aroused soon after, and found the news from water-front commanders. Mississippians in the town heard the enemy at work on bridges in the fog, and the voices of command. Lee was soon satisfied that Burnside was moving to the south of the river, but he was yet positive that he would not attack the literally unas-sailable Confederate position.

The morning wore on with a sputtering of fire rolling up from the river, echoing in the fog. The Federals were putting three bridges over the Rappahannock, and two of them were being challenged by infantrymen in Fredericksburg's streets. Lee sent word to Jackson's corps to join the line on the hilltops, but there was little else to be done. Lee waited on a high knoll; his glasses were of no use in the mists. At least one of the bridges was nearing the southern shore, and there seemed no way to halt the enemy advance. In the middle of the morning, when the fog thinned, enemy guns roared across the river on Stafford Heights. Shells fell thickly on the Confederate lines, and scores of the big guns were turned upon Fredericksburg. Lee, though his outposts were using the town to fire upon the enemy, blazed in wrath:

"Those people delight to destroy the weak and those who can make no defense; it just suits them!"[4]

General Alexander looked down upon the valley:

"The city, except its steeples, was still veiled in the mists. . . . Above it and in it incessantly showed the round white clouds of bursting shells, and out of its midst there soon rose three or four columns of black smoke from houses set on fire. . . . The atmosphere was so perfectly calm and still that the smoke rose vertically in great pillars for several hundred feet. . . . The opposite bank of the river, for two miles to the right and left, was crowned . . . with blazing batteries, canopied in clouds of white smoke.

"Beyond these, the dark blue masses of over 100,000 infantry in compact columns, and numberless parks of white-topped wagons and ambulances massed in orderly ranks, all awaited the completion of the bridges. The earth shook with the thunder of the guns, and, high above all, a thousand feet in the air, hung two immense balloons. The scene gave impressive ideas of the disciplined power of a great army, and of the vast resources of the nation which had sent it forth."

There was still no indication that this vast army was to be flung in a suicidal lunge against Lee's hills, but before dark the Federals had finally crossed, using boats to put small parties ashore. A growing number of the blue regiments huddled out of sight in the cold evening, sheltered from the hillside by groves of trees.

Shortly after noon, while Lee and Jackson were staring down on the enemy preparations, Heros von Borcke came with a message from the flank, in obvious excitement. The cavalryman offered to lead them to a post from which they could see. The two generals, accompanied only by von Borcke, came at last to an isolated barn, where they saw the enemy a few hundred yards below: Men poured over a pontoon bridge, and wagons, artillery, horses swarmed among them. There were batteries of guns already on the south shore, and infantrymen were digging long pits for defense.

Lee seemed more than half convinced, now, that Burnside would attack. He seemed pleased at the prospect. "I shall try to do them all the damage in our power when they move forward," he said.

Jackson's men came in during the day, and were placed on the rugged sloped of the right, in a position so strong that many men and guns had to be held in reserve to the rear; there was one strip

of unprotected woodland on the front of A. P. Hill, which was assumed to be impassable. The army waited through a bitterly cold
night; fires were not permitted in the darkness.

When Lee went to bed every available man was in place along
the ridge—an army 78,000 strong. Below them in the dark river
bottom were 100,000 Federals, with 25,000 more just over the Rappahannock.

Morning brought the inevitable fog; the front had literally
disappeared as Lee rode among the camp fires. He soon met with
his lieutenants. Jackson was astonishingly dressed in finery, new
uniform, new hat, saber and spurs—even riding a new, bigger, more
handsome horse. The troops had not seen him in a new uniform
since the war opened. There was much raillery at Jackson's expense
among the general officers. Stonewall seemed embarrassed: "It's
some of the doing of my friend Stuart, I believe," he said.

Lee asked for opinions on the day's tactics. Jackson spoke immediately for attack. The enemy could be flung into the river, he
said, and a Confederate advance would be screened by the trees of
the riverside. Lee shook his head; he preferred to meet attack in
his lines. As the commander left them, Longstreet was baiting Jackson:

"Ain't you frightened, General?" Old Pete asked.

"Perhaps I'll frighten them after a while," Jackson said.

"Jackson, what are you going to do with all those people over
there?"

"Sir, we will give them the bayonet."[5]

The commanders separated and went to their fronts. At about
ten o'clock the fog lifted and the forming Federal assault columns
were revealed beyond the range of Lee's guns. They moved closer
on the plain below, and at ten thirty Longstreet got an order to
test the ranges of his best field pieces along their carefully laid zones
of fire. The guns blazed away, and the enemy lines plunged forward.
They came in earnest, at first on Jackson's front, against the lines

of A. P. Hill; Stonewall's estimate was that they were 55,000 strong in that sector. But they soon came to a halt. Two tiny guns of Stuart's horse artillery, commanded by young John Pelham, the handsome favorite of the army, raced into the open in front of the lines and, moving about, halted the entire Federal attack. For long moments Pelham's guns challenged the heavier enemy, until sixteen guns were turned against him. Despite insistent orders from Stuart, Pelham remained in the open. Lee, watching, murmured in admiration: "It is glorious to see such courage in one so young." Pelham finally fell back, and the enemy advanced.

The lines came nearer the wooded front. They were within less then eight hundred yards when the artillery flared up and down the lines, knocking great gaps in the blue ranks; the enemy fell back.

Now it was the turn of Longstreet's men on the left with the center of the assault against forbidding Marye's Heights, which loomed above open country. It was made more terrible by a sunken road beneath it, with a stone wall alongside the road; Confederate infantry waited at the fence, and guns supported them from every eminence above.

As Longstreet saw it: "The troops that had been lying concealed in the streets of the city came flying out by both roads in swarms at double time and rushed toward us. Every gun that we had in range opened . . . and ploughed their ranks by a fire that would test the nerves of the bravest soldiers. . . . Frequently commands were broken up by this fire and that of other long-range guns, and sought shelter, as they thought, in the railroad cut, but that point was well marked, and the shots were dropped in . . . with precision, often making wide gaps in their ranks.

"One shell buried itself close under the parapet at General Lee's side, as he sat among the officers of his staff, but it failed to explode."

That was not to be Lee's only narrow escape on the day of slaughter.

In early afternoon the Federals returned to the attack on Jackson, this time refusing to be halted by artillery, though they left hundreds of blue bodies in the open. Lee's glasses were turned on the narrow piece of swampy woodland left unguarded by Hill's men, for here the Federals disappeared under the trees; it seemed that the line had been pierced. Lee saw some of his men trailing out as prisoners. Reports from the line told Lee almost nothing. Fighting raged in the woods, hand to hand, but no one could make out how things were going—until, abruptly, in the faint sound of the Rebel Yell, the Federal tide poured back from the cover, and joined an ebb of retreat.

Almost at the same instant, the greatest of attacks against Marye's Heights was at its peak. Lee stared down at the new column of advancing men, and then turned back to see the fleeing Federals in Jackson's front. He said to officers nearby:

"It is well that war is so terrible—we should grow too fond of it."[6]

Now, just below him, three brigades in the sunken road and behind the stone wall took the shock of the Federal onslaught. William Owen, with a New Orleans artillery battery, saw things from the wall:

"Looking over the stone wall we saw our skirmishers falling back, firing as they came. . . . They came on at the double quick, with loud cries of 'Hi! Hi!' . . . they crossed the canal . . . and were almost concealed from sight. . . . The enemy, having deployed, now showed himself above the crest of the ridge . . . and at once our guns began. . . . How beautifully they came on! . . . We could see our shells bursting in their ranks . . . but on they came, as though they would go straight through and over us. Now we gave them canister, and that staggered them. A few more paces and the Georgians in the road below us rose up . . . let loose a storm of lead into the faces of the advance brigade. This was too much; the column hesitated, and then, turning, took refuge behind the bank.

"But another line appeared from behind the crest and advanced gallantly, and again we opened our guns upon them. . . . But this advance, like the preceding one . . . doing and daring all that brave men could do, fell back in great confusion."

The attacks went on for an hour or more, one after another, in futile waste of brave troops against impossible odds. The field was all but covered with Federal bodies, and yet none had reached the stone wall at the foot of Marye's Heights. The tide had come so near the wall, however, that Lee seemed concerned.

He turned to Longstreet: "General, they are massing very heavily and will break your line, I'm afraid."

"General," Longstreet said, "if you put every man now on the other side of the Potomac in that field to approach me over the same line, and give me plenty of ammunition, I will kill them all before they reach my line. Look to your right; you are in some danger there, but not on my line."

General Alexander, Old Pete's chief gunner, was no less confident: "We cover that ground now so well that we will comb it as with a fine-toothed comb. A chicken could not live on that field when we open on it."

Lee narrowly missed death again in the afternoon when one of the giant Parrott guns exploded, some fifty feet from him. General Pendleton, who was standing an arm's length from the faulty gun, was merely stunned, but flying fragments threatened the lives of men beyond.

Pendleton described the incident: "General Lee was standing perhaps fifty feet in the rear, and a large piece of the cannon, weighing, we estimated, about a third of a ton, fell just beyond him. . . . Like himself, however, he only looked upon the mass calmly for a moment, and then, without a syllable expressive of surprise or concern, continued the business occupying him at the time."

Still the Federals were not through, and at a little before four in the afternoon, encouraged by the sight of a gun moving to the rear near Marye's Heights, thinking the Rebels retreating, one of the torn blue lines leapt forward. The sunken road and stone wall were as impregnable as ever, and the only result of Burnside's wasteful attacks was to pile the bodies higher on the slopes. Lee pushed fresh brigades to the roadway, and they had furious work until after dark had fallen, and like those who had gone before, simply knelt and fired and reloaded and fired, tearing apart the long blue lines of targets, until they were worn.

A Cincinnati newspaper correspondent with the Federals wrote:

"No troops in the world would have won a victory if placed in the position ours were. . . . It was with a deep sense of relief that I saw the sun go down. . . . But for a time the fury of the fire on both sides was redoubled as the discovery was made by the combatants that their day's work was about done. For half an hour the din was awful, and the smoke drifted through the streets, as sometimes in a city, when there is a high wind and a great dust. There was severe fighting even after dark. . . . Then the big Rebel rifled cannon ceased to mark time, the sputter and crackle of small arms ceased on the center . . . and all was still. . . . The city of Fredericksburg was a trap, and we had plunged into it. . . . The blunder stood revealed."

After nightfall, Longstreet recorded, Lee had a captured Federal message indicating that Burnside would attack Marye's Heights again with daylight. He was convinced a major blow was yet to fall and preparations were made for that emergency.

Below the army was a chorus of howls and moans in the cold night, where Federal wounded were suffering. Joshua Chamberlain, a Union colonel who wandered there, trying to help, heard the sound of them all as "flowing together into a key-note weird, unearthly, terrible to hear and bear, yet startling with its nearness . . .

broken by cries for help . . . begging for a drop of water . . . calling
on God for pity . . . on friendly hands to finish what the enemy had
so horribly begun."

In the early darkness, the garish colors of the Aurora Borealis
burned in the sky over the resting armies and the fields of fallen
between them.

Lee kept his staff at work through the night. He sent a firm
order to Jackson, reminding him to bring up more ammunition,
and rejoiced over the day's fighting—which had cost the Federals
some 12,600 casualties, as against 5,000 for the Army of Northern
Virginia. His order to Jackson read:

> I need not remind you to have the ammunition of your
> men and batteries replenished tonight, everything ready for
> daylight tomorrow. I am truly grateful to the Giver of all
> victory for having blessed us thus far in our terrible struggle.
> I pray He may continue it.

General Maxcy Gregg, wounded in the neglected opening on
Jackson's front, was visited on his death bed by Stonewall during
the night, and the generals, who had long quarreled, made their
peace.

Lee got full reports from his line, no more than two thirds of
which had been engaged; regiments everywhere were in good condition, save on the flanks between Generals Lane and Archer, of
Hill's command, where the Federals had stabbed through, and
where almost all the day's casualties were suffered. By morning
the line had been filled in.

Lee was out riding in the half-light of dawn. He inspected the
pits dug by work parties overnight, and seemed surprised. He said
that the army was as much strengthened as if 20,000 new troops had
come in.

Jackson soon joined the commander, and since the day was
clearer than others of the week, they had no trouble in making out

the sights below. The Federals were still there, but their advanced lines lay flat on the earth, not a man stirring; there were no signs of preparation for attack around the town. In fact, the roads leading into Fredericksburg were barred, as for defense.

General Hood went down the lines with the two commanders, and exchanged guesses with Stonewall as to the number of Federal troops lying exposed below them in lines of more than a mile. About 50,000 were there, the council agreed.

An uneventful night had passed, and there had been no change in Federal lines; Lee seemed unable to leave the front, where he studied the Federal lines in disbelief. He had said to Longstreet: "General, I am losing faith in your friend Burnside."

He was joined on a hill by Jackson and D. H. Hill, and the latter had a report that the enemy had gone.

"Who says they're gone?" Jackson asked.

"Colonel Grimes."

Stonewall turned to Bryan Grimes, who was with Hill. "How do you know?"

"I have been down as far as their picket line of yesterday, and can see nothing of them."

Jackson ordered him to push his picket line as far as possible, and Grimes left, noting disappointment in the faces of the commanders.[7] It was not long before the report was confirmed: Burnside had pulled across the Rappahannock under cover of rain and darkness. Both Lee and Jackson expressed regret. Stonewall said, "I did not think a little red earth would have frightened them. I am sorry I fortified."

Lee wrote to Mary in the night, complaining of the lost chance to give the enemy a decisive defeat:

> I had supposed they were just preparing for battle, and was saving our men for the conflict. Their hosts crown the hill and plain beyond the river, and their numbers to me are unknown. Still, I felt a confidence we could stand the shock, and

was anxious for the blow that is to fall on some point, and was prepared to meet it here. . . .

This morning they were all safe on the north side of the Rappahannock. They went as they came—in the night. They suffered heavily as far as the battle went, but it did not go far enough to satisfy me. . . . The contest will now have to be renewed, but on what field I cannot say.

He then wrote of the freeing of the slaves as provided by the will of old Mr. Custis:

As regards the liberation of the people, I wish to progress in it as far as I can. Those hired in Richmond can still find employment there if they choose. Those in the country can do the same or remain on the farms. I hope they will all do well and behave themselves. I should like if I could to attend to their wants and see them placed to the best advantage, but that is impossible.

Lee soon left his restless patrolling of the riverside front, and went to his winter quarters at Hamilton's Crossing. On December sixteenth he sent Stuart and Jackson down the river to check a possible attempt at a crossing by Burnside, but the report which prompted the maneuver proved to be false. The army could only wait for the move Lee was certain must come soon.

Headquarters was not an impressive sight. Colonel Long wrote:

"It consisted of four or five wall tents and three or four common tents . . . on the edge of an old pine field . . . the branches of the old field pine served to fortify the tents against the cold of winter and to make shelter for the horses."

Even in the snowy weather, Lee managed an air of cheerfulness. One day officers saw a demijohn carried into his tent, and the thirsty among them wondered what unexpected treasure the commander had stocked for them. Lee smilingly called them in, and sent his mess steward, Bryan, for the jug.

"Perhaps you gentlemen would like a glass of something," Lee said.

The officers seemed eager to join, but could not hide long faces when Bryan poured buttermilk for them. No one enjoyed the joke more than Bryan, the general's devoted steward, an Irishman, a foraging genius whose given name was Bernard Lynch.

In these weeks, with famine threatening, Lee acquired a trusted friend. Someone brought him the princely gift of a flock of chickens, and the staff enjoyed many meals from it. One of the flock, Bryan noticed, deserved a better fate than the pot.

Every day a lone hen laid an egg, and would choose no other spot than the general's tent, beneath his cot. Long remarked on it: "Every day she would walk to and fro in front of his tent, and when all was quiet walk in, find a place under his bed, and deposit her egg; then walk out with a gratified cackle."

Lee always left open the tent flap for the hen, to which he became attached. For many weeks she roosted in a baggage wagon, and in the spring, when the army broke camp, she rode with the army's wagons to battle. She was to serve through several campaigns, and though the noise of battle would disturb her laying habits, she remained faithful.[8]

On Christmas Day Lee wrote Mary:

> I will commence this holy day by writing to you. My heart is filled with gratitude to Almighty God. . . . What should have become of us without his crowning help and protection? Oh, if only our people would recognize it and cease from vain self-boasting and adulation, how strong would be my belief in final happiness and success to our country!
>
> But what a cruel thing is war. . . . I pray that on this day, when only peace and goodwill are preached to mankind, better thoughts may fill the hearts of our enemies and turn them to peace. Our army was never in such good health and condition since I have been attached to it. I believe they share with me

my disappointment that the enemy did not renew the combat on the 13th. I was holding back all that day and husbanding our strength and ammunition for the great struggle for which I thought I was preparing. Had I divined what was to have been his only effort he would have had more of it. My heart bleeds at the death of every one of our gallant men.

He also wrote his daughter Mildred, in a North Carolina school:

> I cannot tell you how I long to see you when a little quiet occurs . . . my heart aches for our reunion. Your brothers I see occasionally. This morning Fitzhugh [Rooney] rode by with his young aide-de-camp [Rob] at the head of his brigade, on his way up the Rappahannock. You must study hard, gain knowledge, and learn your duty to God and your neighbor; that is the great object of life. I have no news, confined constantly to camp and my thoughts occupied with its necessities and duties. I am, however, happy in the knowledge that General Burnside and his army will not eat their promised Xmas dinner in Richmond today.

Lee took part in a strangely elegant Christmas at the headquarters of Jackson, in Moss Neck, the home of a planter, Richard Corbin, near the banks of the Rappahannock. Lee joined Jackson, Stuart, Pendleton, von Borcke and young Pelham and others of Stuart's coterie, and took along two of his aides as well, Colonels Venable and Marshall.

Jackson astounded them with the feast: turkeys, pails of oysters, ham, cake, wines, butter, biscuit, pickles. The officers ate in a room decorated with Christmas greens, and after Pendleton had asked grace, fell to laughing and joking, with Lee joining the baiting of Jackson, chuckling over the sight of white-aproned Negro waiters.

"You people are only playing soldier," he told Stonewall. "You must come to my quarters and see how soldiers ought to live."[9]

He continued to write Mary of his simple life:

> We had quite a snow day before yesterday, and last night was very cold. It is thawing a little this morning, though the water was freezing as I washed. I fear it will bring much discomfort to those of our men who are barefooted and poorly clad. I can take but little pleasure in my comforts for thinking of them. A kind lady—Mrs. Sallie Braxton Slaughter—of Fredericksburg, sent me a mattress, some catsup and preserves during the snowstorm. You must thank Miss Norvell for her nice cake, which I enjoyed very much. I had it set out under the pines the day after its arrival, and assembled all the young gentlemen around it; and though I told them it was a present from a beautiful young lady, they did not leave a crumb.

He complained to her that he needed a good servant, since Perry, who had come from Arlington with him, was

> ... very slow and inefficient, and moves very like his father Lawrence. He is also very fond of his blankets in the morning, the very time I most require him.

Lee was soon to be disturbed from such peaceful scenes, and he hinted at times to come, in drafting praises for the army in the battle of Fredericksburg:

> The war is not yet ended. The enemy is still numerous and strong, and the country demands of the army a renewal of its heroic efforts in her behalf. . . . The signal manifestations of Divine mercy that have distinguished the eventful and glorious campaign of the year just closing give assurance of hope that, under the guidance of the same Almighty hand, the coming year will be no less fruitful . . . and add new lustre to the already imperishable name of the Army of Northern Virginia.[10]

9 *CHANCELLORSVILLE*

MORE THAN one Confederate in the wretched camps along the Rappahannock thought of Valley Forge when snows drifted against the mud-wattled huts, and the only signs of life were wisps of smoke torn from chimneys, or an occasional stumbling figure, wrapped in rags.

There was, somehow, a high state of morale. There were frequent snowball battles, some of them involving whole divisions, with the fighting becoming as intense as if the enemy had come. In the worst of the winter a fresh wave of revival preaching swept the camps, and preachers came from many parts of the South to labor for the souls of the soldiers. Once, both Lee and Jackson sat on a log to hear a sermon by The Reverend B. T. Lacy, chief of Stonewall's chaplains, and Captain James Smith watched the commanders weep at Lacy's description of the peaceful homes the soldiers had left behind.[1]

The gulf between the Confederacy-at-home and the men of the army became plain to Lee when, on January fourteenth, he was called to Richmond with D. H. Hill, to confer with President Davis. The city had changed enormously. Prices were soaring and the Confederate currency was rapidly deteriorating. Apples were $2 a dozen, soap $1.25 per cake, oysters $5 a gallon, coal $14 per cartload, wood $18 a cord. Yet seats at the leading theatre were in demand at $5, and good hotel meals were $25. A Congressman's pay was $2,700 a year; a free Negro bootblack earned $10 a day.

President Davis, however, was full of optimism: "We are strong and growing stronger," he had said. He had convinced himself through arithmetic. The South had thus far spent $170,000,000 on the war, against the North's $500,000,000. Gold was selling at 200 in New York. Rumors from the North had so excited the city that peace seemed near. Confederate bonds were bringing prices equal to those of United States bonds in New York exchanges. Riots had broken out in New York, as if in protest against the bloody repulse at Fredericksburg. There were thought to be new signs that England would recognize the Confederacy, and that officials would soon meet to plan peace. A glimpse of Lee in Richmond streets was enough to set the city buzzing anew over that rumor.[2]

Lee returned to camp in mid-January to find Burnside stirring despite the fearful weather, and he set things in motion to receive him. He had found Jackson and Longstreet locked in an argument; Stonewall thought the Federals would lunge downstream, and clung to his opinion despite Longstreet's feeling that no army could pass the many full tributaries in that marshy area. Lee quickly ended the quarrel, and sent a couple of brigades to strengthen pickets at Banks Ford and United States Ford. Burnside attempted his move on January twentieth.

Confederate pickets heard the enemy, and called over the river in derision, "We'll come help you move, if you'll promise to come on across here!" It was an echo of Jackson's grim remark: "My trust is in God. I wish they would come!"

A Federal officer described the move:

"Herculean efforts were made to bring pontoons . . . into position to build a bridge or two. . . . Double and triple teams of mules were harnessed to each boat, but it was in vain. Long stout ropes were then attached to the teams, and a hundred and fifty men put to the task on each. . . . Floundering through the mire for a few feet, the gang of Lilliputians, with their huge ribbed Gulliver, were forced to give over. . . .

"Morning dawned upon another day of rain and storm. . . . An indescribable chaos of pontoons, vehicles, and artillery encumbered all the roads—supply wagons upset by the roadside, guns stalled in the mud, ammunition trains mired . . . and hundreds of horses and mules buried in the liquid muck. . . . It was no longer a question of how to go forward—it was a question of how to get back . . . the army floundered and staggered back to the old camps."[3]

Lee strengthened his earthworks along the Rappahannock. The works rose and fell with the terrain, a sprawling, turning, bristling chain of tiny forts set in ribbons of trenches. It could be lightly held in the weather of this winter.

There were troubles for the commander: Jackson and General E. F. Paxton argued over whether deserters must be shot; General W. R. Jones was charged with cowardice in action, and Stonewall stood firmly for his trial; Jones otherwise squabbled with officers; General Ike Trimble raised controversy.

Trimble, who felt that he had been unfairly passed over for promotion, especially when Arnold Elzey became a major general, wrote to Richmond, complaining of Elzey's addiction to liquor. He raged at Jackson, who did not speak up for his immediate promotion, saying that Stonewall knew nothing of any troops, except the old Stonewall Brigade.

There were further squabbles, in which Stuart figured largely, as generals sought to claim credit for exploits in the recently ended campaign. Lee appeared to maintain his calm, and even to work a sounder organization from each small crisis of command.

Burnside was removed as Federal commander on the Rappahannock on January twenty-fifth, and Joseph Hooker replaced him

—a corps commander of tough fighting qualities who now began to issue grand orders and threats of annihilation for Lee's army.

On February sixth Lee gave his daughter Agnes an insight into his camp life:

> My movements are so uncertain. . . . The only place I am to be found is in camp, and I am so cross now that I am not worth seeing anywhere. Here you will have to take me with the three stools—the snow, the rain, and the mud . . . we are now in a floating condition. . . . Our horses and mules suffer the most. They have to bear the cold and rain, tug through the mud, and suffer all the time with hunger. . . . I have no news.
>
> General Hooker is obliged to do something; I do not know what it will be. He is playing the Chinese game, trying what frightening will do. He runs out his guns, starts his wagons and troops up and down the river, and creates an excitement generally. Our men look on in wonder, give a cheer, and all again subsides. . . .
>
> I wish you were here with me today. You would have to sit by this little stove, look out at the rain, and keep yourself dry. But here come, in all their wet, the adjutants-general with the papers. I must stop and go to work. See how kind God is: we have plenty to do in good weather and bad.

One man in the ranks wrote home about this time: "You need have no apprehension that this army will ever meet with defeat while commanded by General Lee. General Jackson is a strict Presbyterian, but he is rather too much of a Napoleon Bonaparte in my estimation. Lee is the man, I assure you."[4]

Lee was forced to reduce his army in mid-February. He sent Fitz Lee with cavalry to strengthen the little army in the Shenandoah, opposing the Federal General Milroy, and moved Pickett with his division below Richmond, to help protect the coast, about which President Davis was now concerned. A few days later, Hood's division followed Pickett's; and then Longstreet was sent along to assume the new coastal command. This left Lee with no more than

58,ooo men on the river; if scouts and spies were to be trusted, Hooker had more than 130,000 men on the opposite bank.

Lee wrote Mary of continued bad weather, on February twenty-third:

> The weather now is very hard upon our poor bushmen. This morning the whole country is covered with a mantle of snow fully a foot deep. It was nearly up to my knees when I stepped out this morning, and our poor horses were enveloped. We have dug them out. . . . I fear our short rations for man and horse will have to be curtailed. Our enemies have their troubles too. They are very strong immediately in front, but have withdrawn their troops above and below us. . . . I owe Mr. F. J. Hooker no thanks for keeping me here. He ought to have made up his mind long ago what to do.

It was not only the enemy he blamed for the discomforts and shortages of the army. In a letter to Custis he blazed forth with unaccustomed anger:

> What has our Congress done to meet the exigency, I may say extremity, in which we are placed? As far as I know, concocted bills to excuse a certain class of men from service, and to transfer another class in service, out of active service, where they hope never to do service.

By March twenty-seventh, when signs of spring were about, Lee's mood was again that of dignified acceptance of the army's fate, but he did not attempt to hide his displeasure at the new reduced ration in a report to Richmond:

> The men are cheerful, and I receive but few complaints, still I do not consider it enough to maintain them in health and vigor, and I fear they will be unable to endure the hardships of the approaching campaign. Symptoms of scurvy are appearing among them, and, to supply the place of vegetables,

each regiment is directed to send a daily detail to gather sassafras buds, wild onions, garlic, lamb's quarter, and poke sprouts; but for so large an army the supply obtained is very small.[5]

At the end of March, Lee became ill, and had such pains of the chest, back and arms that Dr. Lafayette Guild, his medical director, ordered him taken to a house near Guiney's Station, the home of the Yerby family. Here Lee was forced to lie for several days, complaining that doctors were "tapping me all over like an old steam boiler before condemning it."

He had not recovered when the stirring of the enemy on the Rappahannock forced his return to duty.

Confederate pickets could follow every move of Hooker's big army, for they were in daily touch with the enemy, and on friendly terms. The Rappahannock was dotted with tiny sailing vessels on any clear day, miniature schooners made in huts during the winter. They carried tobacco, Richmond newspapers and other treasures to Yankees on the north bank, and were sent back with loads of coffee, sugar and other foods.

Almost as soon as Federal orders for cooking eight days' rations were passed, Lee knew of them, and pickets shouted across to the Yankees, deriding them. Lee warned the Secretary of War that his men were not fully prepared—even those left to him, now that Longstreet's two big divisions were too far away to greet the enemy: "I am painfully anxious lest the spirit and efficiency of the men should become impaired," he wrote, "and they be rendered unable to sustain their former reputation, or perform the service necessary for our safety."

Despite that, Lee added, he thought that Hooker would "find it very difficult to reach his destination."

He had given up his room at the Yerby house after his illness, in favor of Mrs. Jackson, who had come up to visit Stonewall. She was a short, plump, rather pretty North Carolina girl, carrying a baby daughter in her arms. Lee met her at church, and paid a visit in the farmhouse later. Mrs. Jackson was impressed by Lee:

"I remember how reverent and impressive was General Lee's bearing, and how handsome he looked, with his splendid figure and faultless military attire."

On Wednesday, April twenty-ninth, Jackson and his wife were aroused by a banging on their door not long after dawn. A courier from General Early asked Jackson to come with him. Stonewall told his wife that this probably meant Hooker was crossing the river, and he left her wih a brief kiss. The house was soon under cannon fire, and Mrs. Jackson and her baby were taken away.

Lee was asleep in his tent when the news came, brought by Captain James Smith of Jackson's staff. Smith remembered the scene:

"I entered his tent and awoke the general. Turning his feet out of his cot, he sat upon its side as I gave him the tidings from the front. Expressing no surprise he playfully said, 'Well, I thought I heard firing, and was beginning to think it was time some of you young fellows were coming to tell me what it was all about. Tell your good general that I am sure he knows what to do. I will meet him at the front very soon.'"[6]

Jackson had found Sedgwick's men coming to the south of the river below Fredericksburg, where they dug in, using almost the same position as in the battle of December. Lee and Jackson studied the Federals from the heights, uncertain of the enemy's plan. In the afternoon, however, Lee had word from Stuart: A large Federal infantry column had crossed high up the Rappahannock, and had turned back southeastwardly, toward fords of the Rapidan. Stuart had taken prisoners from three corps. There was no longer much doubt that Hooker planned a huge flank attack; already there was danger that Stuart's force might be cut off from the main army. Lee moved to prevent it by turning Dick Anderson's division, which was on the riverside above Fredericksburg, in the path of the enemy column approaching from the west. Within three hours, near mid-

night of April twenty-ninth, Anderson's first companies were taking
shelter from a rainstorm in a clearing in the scrubby area known as
the Wilderness, in the vicinity of a house and some outbuildings
called Chancellorsville.

Though he felt a minor return of his illness during the morning, Lee went out with Jackson to take another look at the enemy
near Fredericksburg. The two disagreed as they had in December:
Stonewall urged attack, but Lee could not bring himself to risk
throwing his men down from the protective slopes to the flats by the
river. Jackson was given time to study the landscape, however, to
see if an attack was feasible. Lee left him and began hurrying aid
to Anderson, in the tangled country to the left. He had seen to the
digging of earthworks near Chancellorsville when Jackson reported
that he had finally been convinced; Stonewall agreed that it would
be unwise to attack at Fredericksburg; that position would now become the rear, as Lee swung his main force to meet Hooker in the
forbidding woodland.

Jackson was ordered to support Anderson, and at eight A.M. of
May first, he was on the skirmish line. The screen of woods ahead
concealed Federals in some numbers. General McLaws had also
come up with a division in the early morning. Jackson quickly ordered an end to the digging of trenches, and pushed the lines forward. Thus the main forces of the two armies moved together over
a terrain blinding to both. Colonel Taylor described the situation
of the enemy, now that Hooker had successfully forced Lee from his
strong position:

"...a position of great natural strength, surrounded on all sides
by a dense forest filled with tangled undergrowth, in the midst of
which breastworks of logs had been constructed with trees felled
in front so as to form an almost impenetrable abatis. His artillery
swept the few narrow roads by which his position could be approached from the front, and commanded the adjacent works."

Jackson soon satisfied himself that the left flank of the enemy would not permit attack. At a little after eleven A.M. the first big gun fired from the Federal position. McLaws and Anderson soon became engaged. Jackson was puzzling over a means of getting at the enemy when he had a message from Stuart:

General: I am on a road running from Spotsylvania c.h. to Silvers, which is on Plank Road three miles below Chancellorsville. . . . I will close in on the flank and help all I can when the ball opens. . . . May God grant us victory.

Jackson replied:

I trust that God will grant us a great victory. Keep closed on Chancellorsville.

Lee soon rode up. He had left General Early on the river to hold the rear at Fredericksburg, strengthening him with one extra brigade and reserve artillery. He asked for a report on the Wilderness front. Jackson described the puzzle: The enemy was in strength, but now seemed timid, after the advance in huge numbers. His left flank could not be attacked; perhaps there was room for maneuver on the right.

Lee and Jackson rode for a short distance together, and then Stonewall left the commander. Troops cheered Lee:

"There was a sudden outburst . . . of tumultuous shoutings . . . and very soon General Lee, with a full staff, galloped to the front. . . the General seemed to be unusually impressed . . . he lifted his hat . . . above his majestic head as far as we could see him . . . the men greeted him, shouting, 'What a head, what a head! See that glorious head. God bless it, God bless it!' "[7]

Lee left this emotional scene to scout the enemy lines, and while he was hidden in the thickets, Jackson was given full view of the Federal lines by a South Carolina captain, Alex Haskell, who called him to another hill: "Ride up here, General, and you will see it all."

A. P. Hill joined Jackson, and with their staffs they stared over the scrub thickets to the lines of Federals beyond Chancellorsville, thick columns of bluecoats, digging away at their earthworks, as if to make a stand. It was clear that the mere 50,000 Lee had brought out to meet the enemy could not storm this position. Jackson peered for a long time, as if he could not be satisfied, and at last ordered Captain Haskell to hold the position until night. He sought Lee.

The commanders tried to make one more inspection of enemy lines before darkness fell, but a concealed sharpshooter continually cut twigs about them, and they escaped the humming bullets in a pine grove. Lee took a seat on a log and asked Jackson to sit beside him. They talked of the Federal actions of the day, and Jackson described the advance of Stuart on the enemy right, which had halted with exchanges of artillery fire. Then, despite what he had seen of enemy breastworks in the front, Jackson said that Hooker was feinting, or making some sort of deceptive maneuver. "None of them will be on this side of the river tomorrow," he said.

"I hope you may be right," Lee said, "but I believe he will deliver his main attack here. He would not have gone to such lengths and then give up without effort."

A fire was lighted in the grove, and Lee and Jackson continued a long conversation, which sometimes seemed wandering as they canvassed the means of attack. Lee left nothing to chance, and when it was suggested that a frontal assault might be feasible, after all, he sent out two capable engineers, Colonel T. M. R. Talcott from his own staff, and Captain J. K. Boswell, from Jackson's. These two crept through the underbrush in full moonlight for their inspection. The conference continued in their absence.

Stuart arrived with news: Fitz Lee had found the Federal flank in the air in the woodland near Wilderness Church. The cavalryman was not certain whether good roads led to the position, and Lee sent him off into the night to investigate.

Lee bent over his map by lantern light.

"Jackson," he said, "how can we get at those people?"

"You know best," Stonewall said. "Show me what to do, and we will try to do it."

Lee paused and with his finger indicated a route sweeping around the enemy right. The gesture cut across country on the map, where roads were unmarked. Lee explained what he wanted, and ended, "General Stuart will cover your movement with his cavalry."

Jackson smiled a little, rose and touched his cap. "My troops will move at four o'clock," he said.[8]

Talcott and Boswell had already reported the hopelessness of an attack in front, where earthworks, combined with cover of heavy trees which would make artillery ineffective, would doom any attacking regiments.

Lee and Jackson separated and lay on the ground. Lee was soon disturbed. Stuart had sent Chaplain Lacy of Jackson's corps to him, to report on his intimate knowledge of roads in the area. Lee was soon convinced that Jackson would find a way to the Federal flank in the morning, and he dismissed Lacy. He fell asleep under his cloak at the foot of a tree. He was found there by Captain Smith, whom he had sent for some information from A. P. Hill. Lee sat up.

"Ah, Captain, you have returned, have you? Come here and tell me what you have learned on the right." He pulled Smith to his side, heard his report on minor details, and thanked him.

"I'm sorry you young men about General Jackson didn't save me annoyance by finding that enemy battery that held us up. The young men now are not what they were when I was a boy."

Smith remembered: "Seeing immediately that he was jesting and disposed to rally me, as he often did young officers, I broke away from the hold on me which he tried to retain, and, as he laughed heartily through the stillness of the night, I went off to make a bed of my saddle blanket."

The night had become colder, and Jackson soon woke up sneezing. He had refused the offer of a cape from a staff officer, but found it about him when he sat up; Jackson wrapped the coat around young Sandie Pendleton, who slept against a tree, and went to a fireside, sitting on a cracker box with his hands held over the flames.

Chaplain Lacy came to him, and on the box the friends discussed the roads of the woodland beyond. Jackson asked for a route of attack.

Lacy told Jackson that one of the sons of Charles Wellford, who lived nearby, should be able to guide him into the proper path. Jackson had his map-maker, Jed Hotchkiss, shaken awake, and sent him off with Lacy to find a suitable passage for men and guns.

When Lacy and Hotchkiss returned, excited, Lee had joined Jackson. Wellford had shown Hotchkiss a covered route.

Hotchkiss pulled up another cracker box and unfolded a map, on which he had drawn the turning of a trail through the woods. It ran southwest from the Catherine Furnace, joined Brock Road to the west, and cut across to a point not far from Wilderness Corner.

Lee did not look long at the map, but turned to Jackson. "General Jackson, what do you propose to do?"

"Go around here." Jackson's finger traced the trail drawn by Hotchkiss.

"And what do you propose to make this movement with?"

"With my whole corps."

Lee looked back to the map. "And what will you leave me?"

"The divisions of Anderson and McLaws."

If there was a trace of surprise on Lee's face at the proposal that he fling most of his men through the forest on a flank attack of undetermined length, while holding off the whole army of Hooker with a few more than 14,000 men, no bystanders could detect it. Lee's voice was calm. "Well, go on."

Jackson left him to get his troops under way.

It was late, after five o'clock, when the head of his column moved out on the roadway, the regiments followed by guns and heavy wagons. Near seven o'clock, Lee rode over to talk with Jackson. They were not near enough to their staffs for the young men to overhear their words. Jackson pointed down the road ahead, and Lee nodded toward the forest. Jackson went out of sight. It was their last meeting.

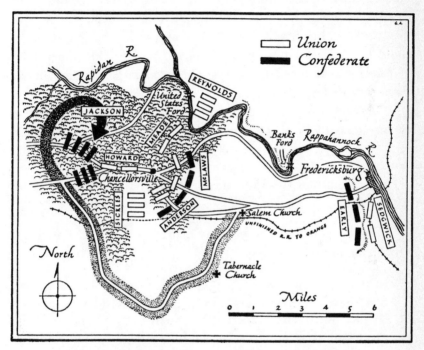

CHANCELLORSVILLE–JACKSON'S ATTACK

Lee had already begun to thin his line to cover Jackson's deserted front; the men were in some places six feet apart with no one behind them.

The orders of the day were simple, despite the army's dangerous position. Early, in the rear at Fredericksburg, was ordered to hold his lines, unless he saw enemy troops being moved from his front toward Chancellorsville; in that event, Early was to pull one brigade from his line and send it to the aid of Lee. If the enemy disappeared entirely at Fredericksburg, Early was to come to Lee's side with his entire force. Colonel Chilton was sent rearward to pass the order to Early.

In effect, Lee waited in the forest with one long skirmish line, on the chance that Hooker's force of more than 50,000 around Chancellorsville would not stir. He knew little of Federal dispositions this morning, but it was clear the enemy was in great strength; he could not know that, as Jackson moved on his wide sweep with 28,000 men, another fresh corps, almost as large, was moving to Hooker from Fredericksburg.

Lee wrote to Davis, explaining the moves which had led to Chancellorsville the day before, and reporting on the move of Jackson:

> I am now swinging around to my left to come up in his rear.

He revealed some uncertainty of the success of the attack at this hour, adding:

> It is plain that if the enemy is too strong for me here, I shall have to fall back, and Fredericksburg must be abandoned. If successful here, Fredericksburg will be saved and our communications retained. I may be forced back . . . but in either case I will be in position to contest the enemy's advance upon Richmond. I have no expectations that any re-enforcements from Longstreet or North Carolina will join me in time to aid in the contest at this point. . . . If I had with me all my command I should feel easy, but, as far as I can judge, the advantage of numbers and position is greatly in favor of the enemy.[9]

There was little idle waiting. The Federals suspected that something was awry on their flank. Their artillery began a broken chorus before ten o'clock, and did not cease entirely; within an hour there was heavy skirmishing. This became more intense, and by noon men around Lee heard the sounds of a pitched infantry fight. Lee sent his left wing brigade to help beat off the attack, which had been against Stonewall's wagon train as it passed an exposed spot. The line under Lee was now stretched even more.

In the Federal lines, men were almost immediately aware of Jackson's move, and at first accurately gauged the peril of Hooker's army. At eight o'clock an officer in front of General Sickles' corps reported a long column of men and wagons passing. A battery went up, and after some delay fired a few rounds on the Confederates. An hour and a half after this first report Hooker's headquarters advised General Howard, commanding on the far right: "We have good reason to suppose the enemy is moving to our right."

Just before eleven o'clock General Howard replied that he had strengthened his position, and that he, too, saw a Rebel flanking movement under way. He saw so many wagons in Jackson's column, however, that he changed his mind. The enemy must be retreating, not attacking.

Men at Hooker's headquarters saw him as he got the first puzzling reports. Hooker spread a map on his cot. "It can't be retreat," he said. "That is not Lee, retreat without a fight. If not retreat, what is it? Lee is trying to flank me."

This conviction was short-lived even at Federal headquarters, and despite the insistence of front-line officers, who beseiged Hooker with warnings all afternoon, the official Federal opinion was firm—Lee had been maneuvered out of position and was pulling back.

Jackson's column spent most of the day in a quiet, hot march. The route was about twelve miles in its rough curve around to the Federal flank, and though only a short part of it led out of the well-used roads, wagons and big guns held back the column. There was almost no sign of Yankees; a cavalry screen was doing its work well.

Jackson had chosen men to prod stragglers with bayonets; even this did not save a few losses, for a Georgia colonel wrote: "Many fell . . . exhausted, some fainting and having spasms; only a few had eaten anything since the day before."

But Stonewall did not relent. His physician, Dr. Hunter McGuire, saw him that day: "Never can I forget the eagerness and intensity of Jackson on that march. . . . His face was pale, his eyes flashing. Out from his thin lips came the terse command: 'Press forward. Press forward!' . . . He leaned over on the neck of his horse, as if in that way the march might be hurried. . . . 'Press on, press on,' was repeated again and again."[10]

Jackson's advance reached the plank road west of Chancellorsville in the early afternoon, and near here Fitz Lee had glimpsed the unsuspecting enemy. He led Jackson to a knoll near a farmhouse, Fitz recalled:

"The soldiers were in groups, laughing, chatting, smoking . . . feeling safe and comfortable. In the rear of them were other parties driving up and slaughtering beeves. . . . I watched him [Jackson] closely. His eyes burned with a brilliant glow, lighting up a sad face; his expression was one of intense interest . . . and radiant at the success of his flank movement.

"To my remarks he did not once reply during the five minutes he was on the hill; and yet his lips were moving."[11]

Jackson almost immediately wrote a dispatch to Lee.

The commander, waiting, had just heard with relief the dwindling fire in the lines nearby, when he got Jackson's message:

> Near 3 P.M.
> May 2d, 1863
>
> General,
>   The enemy has made a stand at Chancellors which is about 2 miles from Chancellorsville. I hope as soon as practicable to attack.

I trust that an ever kind Providence will bless us with great success.

Respectfully,

T. J. Jackson,
Lt. Genl.

Genl. R. E. Lee
The leadg division is up & the next two appear to be well closed.

T. J. J.

Lee studied the lengthening shadows with concern; a bit more, and it would be too late for Jackson's attack, and to delay until to-morrow would mean certain discovery of the new position, and more dangerous hours for the army. There was not a sound from the march of Stonewall across the forest.

Colonel Chilton reappeared, riding in from Fredericksburg with word of a catastrophe. He explained that he had given the message to Early, and Early was retreating, having abandoned the heights over the river, and was coming in, followed by the Federals. Lee wasted no time in probing the misunderstanding of verbal orders. He called up General McLaws, and sat by the road with him as he explained that his command must be withdrawn to meet the new flank threat from General Sedgwick's corps. McLaws must hurry, or disaster would strike the army, whether or not Jackson now attacked.

Lee also passed word for an immediate charge of his files through the thickets, to divert the attention of the enemy at hand. Major Robert Stiles caught sight of him in this moment of danger, and recorded Lee's calmness of manner:

"I was standing in the shade of a tree near our guns . . . when my attention was called to a horseman coming at full speed . . . and as he drew near I saw it was Brother William . . . the consecrated, courageous chaplain of the Seventeenth Mississippi. . . . He did not have a saddle . . . his horse was reeking with sweat and panting. . . .

When his eye fell upon General Lee he made directly for him, and I followed as fast as I could. He dashed to the very feet of the commanding general, and . . . began to tell of dire disaster at Fredericksburg—Sedgwick had smashed Early and was rapidly coming on in our rear.

"I have never seen anything more majestically calm than General Lee was. . . . Something very like a grave, sweet smile began to express itself on the General's face, but he checked it, and raising his left hand gently . . . he interrupted the excited speaker:

"I thank you very much, but both you and your horse are fatigued and overheated. Take him to that shady tree yonder and you and he blow and rest a little. I'm talking to General McLaws just now. I'll call you as soon as we're through.' "

Brother William then assailed Stiles with his story of Fredericksburg, until:

"Marse Robert now called for Brother William, and as he approached greeted him with a smile, saying:

" 'Now what were you telling us about Major Sedgwick?'

"Brother William again told his tale of woe—this time with somewhat diminished intensity and less lurid coloring. When he had finished the General thanked him, saying again:

" 'I am very much obliged to you; the Major is a nice gentleman; I don't think he would hurt us very badly, but we are going to see about him at once. I have just sent General McLaws to make a special call upon him.' "

Lee turned back to his own front, confident that he could predict the rapidity and strength of the advance of Sedgwick, whom he had known so well in the old army. The steady firing of men in the thickets, and a chorus of yells, told him that the skirmishers of Hooker were being held at bay.

Then there was an arresting sound from far across the woodlands, growing into a roar. Jackson had attacked.

Lee gave orders to press the attack in his front—if possible, all the way to the breastworks of Hooker's main line. It was already becoming dark, but the fury of sound coming to him at headquarters made it clear that Jackson was wrecking the union flank.

Among the thousands of brave Federal troops, now fleeing as they were assailed in the exposed flank, were dozens of diarists who described the panic of these last hours of daylight. One was Colonel Charles Morse, of a Massachusetts regiment:

"What was our surprise when we found that instead of a fight, it was a complete Bull Run rout. Men, horses, mules, rebel prisoners, wagons, guns . . . were coming down the road in terrible confusion, behind them an unceasing roar of musketry. We rode until we got into a mighty hot fire, and found that no one was attempting to make a stand, but every one running for his life. . . . I found General Hooker sitting alone on his horse in front of the Chancellor House . . . he merely said, 'Very good, sir.' I rode back and found the Eleventh Corps still surging up the road and still this terrible roar behind them. Up to this time, the rebels had received no check."

Another who recorded was Captain Hartwell Osborn, a Federal cavalryman:

"Along our front deer and wild game came scurrying . . . firing increased and soon came nearer. The right was steadily falling back . . . the whole clearing became one mass of panic-stricken soldiers flying at the top of their speed. . . . The 11th Corps had been routed. . . . Aghast and terror-stricken, heads bare and panting for breath, they pleaded like infants at the mother's breast that we should let them pass to the rear unhindered."

General Alfred Pleasanton, the Federal cavalry commander, gathered a few guns, loaded them with grape, and, with a handful of men halted in their flight, turned to wait for Jackson's charge:

"I suspected deception and was ready for it. They called out not to shoot, they were friends; at the same time they gave us a volley from at least five thousand muskets. As soon as I saw the flash I gave the command to fire, and the whole line of artillery was discharged at once. It fairly swept them from the earth."[12]

It was probably this stand, almost a trifling incident in the blazing forest, which saved the entire Federal army from flight from Jackson, and brought the forces to a standstill as night came down.

On the far side of the Federal lines, near Lee's headquarters, a few Virginia troops had pushed their feint so boldly as to leap the enemy breastworks, and though they had quickly retreated, had deceived the anxious Hooker. As long as Jackson's guns rolled, in the hour after dark, Lee was busy pulling his separated regiments back into line—including the men of McLaws, now back from Fredericksburg road with the rear safe at last. Early's retreat had been ended, and he again shielded the army near Fredericksburg.

There was a glow over the woodland, where thickets were burning, and hundreds of wounded of both armies were whimpering as flames overtook them. But when the guns died down, night noises could be heard around Lee's headquarters, where there was only waiting for tomorrow. There was moonlight, and in the far woods mockingbirds sang; beyond were whippoorwills and owls.

Lee had gone to sleep in a pine grove, under his customary blanket and oilcloth cover. He had slept less than two hours, when just before two thirty A.M., Colonel Taylor's voice brought him to a sitting position.

"Who's there?"

"It's Captain Wilbourn," Taylor said.

Lee asked Jackson's aide to sit beside him. "Tell me about the fight last night," he said.

Wilbourn described the attack, telling how the line of Jackson had swept upon the unsuspecting Federal troops as they were cooking supper, driving everything before them.

But during the night, Wilbourn told Lee, as Jackson rode into his own lines from scouting the enemy, a volley from Confederate troops had wounded Stonewall. Flesh wounds, as far as could be told, in the arms. Surgeons had placed him in an ambulance, and he was now in the rear, under their care.

Lee shook his head, groaning a little. "Ah, Captain," he said, "any victory is dearly bought that takes General Jackson from us, even for a short time."

Wilbourn told him of Jackson's suffering as he moved rearward. Lee rose abruptly.

"Ah, don't talk about it; thank God it is no worse."

The commander said no more, and Wilbourn, thinking he had been dismissed, moved away. Lee halted him. "I want to talk more with you."

He began to question the signal officer of the Second Corps. He learned that General Stuart was now in command of the far flank, since A. P. Hill had also been wounded, though slightly, and General Rodes, who had led Jackson's men into the fight, had bowed to Stuart's seniority.

"Rodes is a gallant, courageous and energetic officer," Lee said. "I will write General Jackson and General Stuart. Where are they now?"

Wilbourn gave the best directions he could, and added, "I think General Jackson planned to take the United States Ford road, and cut them off from the river."

"We must press those people today," Lee said. He was sending out orders even as he pulled on his boots. He gave Wilbourn some breakfast from a basket someone had sent to his headquarters, and soon was writing Stuart:

> It is necessary that the glorious victory thus far achieved be prosecuted with the utmost vigor, and the enemy given no time to rally. As soon, therefore, as it is possible, they must be pressed, so that we may unite the two wings of the army.
>
> Endeavor, therefore, to dispossess them of Chancellorsville, which will permit the union of the whole army.

I shall myself proceed to join you as soon as I can make arrangements on this side, but let nothing delay the completion of the plan of driving the enemy from his rear and from his positions.

I shall give orders that every effort be made on this side at daybreak to aid in the junction.

Before daylight another messenger came to Lee from Jackson's side—Jed Hotchkiss. The young officer told him more of the position of the Second Corps in the tangled woodland, but when he spoke of Jackson's wounds, Lee indicated that he would like to close his mind to all thoughts of the loss of Jackson.

"I know all about it, and do not wish to hear any more—it is too painful a subject."

Hotchkiss left headquarters, carrying a new order for Stuart, a repeated admonition to push the army forward for a junction. Lee also sent his other commanders their orders, and he rode out in the earliest light to see to the attack.[13]

Where Stuart commanded on Jackson's front, a segment some five or six miles from Lee's broken lines, Heros von Borcke witnessed the movement as the cavalry chief, unaccustomed to infantry command, urged the lines forward. They pushed through the debris of the enemy, against the bent line of Hooker:

"The enemy, fully three times our number, occupied a piece of wood extending about two miles from our immediate front towards the plateau and open fields round Chancellorsville. . . . The Federals had thrown up in the wood during the night three successive lines of breastworks, constructed of strong timber . . . mounted by their numerous artillery, forty pieces of which were playing on the narrow plank road. . . .

"All our divisions now moving forward, the battle soon became general . . . the forest seemed alive with shot, shell and bullets, and the plank road . . . was soon enveloped in a cloud of smoke. . . . This road . . . crowded with ambulances, ammunition trains and artillery, the loss of life soon became fearful, and dead and dying men and animals were strewing every part of it. How General Stuart . . . escaped unhurt seems to me miraculous. . . . The shower of missiles that hissed through the air passed round him unheeded; and in the midst of the hottest fire I heard him, to an old melody, hum the words, 'Old Joe Hooker, get out of the Wilderness.' "

A Prussian military observer at Lee's headquarters, Captain Justus Scheibert, was astonished to hear Lee speaking calmly of the future education of the young men in the ranks, after the war should end. The battle roared all about them.

Until the enemy held the Confederate tide for a few moments, at midmorning, von Borcke was riding everywhere in the confusion:

"The woods had caught fire in several places from the explosion of shells . . . the conflagration progressed with the rapidity of a prairie fire, and a large number of Confederate and Federal wounded . . . too badly hurt to crawl out of the way, met a terrible death. The heartrending cries of the poor victims seem still in my ears. . . .

"The enemy had in the meanwhile been strongly reinforced, and now poured forth from their third line . . . a fire so terrible . . . that the first two divisions staggered . . . and in vain even was it that Stuart, snatching the battle flag from the hands of the color bearer and waving it over his head, called on to them as he rode forward to follow him. Nothing could induce them again to face that tempest of bullets, and that devastating hurricane of grape and canister. . . . At this critical moment, we suddenly heard the yell of Rodes' division behind us, and saw these gallant troops, led by their heroic general, charge over the front lines, and fall upon the enemy with such impetus that in a few minutes their works were taken, and they were driven in rapid flight from the woods."

At ten thirty Stuart had a message from Lee: The wings were

linked at last. Stuart sent von Borcke to the commander for final instructions:

"I found him with our twenty-gun battery," the German remembered, "looking as calm and dignified as ever, and perfectly regardless of the shells bursting round him, and the solid shot ploughing up the ground in all directions.

"General Lee expressed himself much satisfied with our operations, and entrusted me with orders for Stuart, directing a general attack with his whole force, which was to be supported by a charge of Anderson's division."

This combined attack finally drove the enemy from his major position, and the climax was almost too much for von Borcke:

"A more magnificent spectacle can hardly be imagined than that which greeted me when I reached the crest of the plateau ... the long lines of our swiftly advancing troops stretching as far as the eye could reach, their red flags fluttering in the breeze, and their arms glittering in the morning sun; and farther on, dense and huddled masses of the Federals flying in utter rout towards the United States Ford, whilst high over our heads flew the shells which our artillery were dropping amidst the crowd of the retreating foe. The Chancellorsville House had caught fire, and was now enveloped in flames."

Lee ordered the army to halt for a rest.

This was victory indeed, and Lee rode into the scene on Traveller as if aware that this was to be for him the supreme moment of the war. Colonel Marshall was there to record the reaction of the troops when they caught sight of Lee, with the symbol of triumph, the burning Chancellor house, between him and the streaming blue lines of retreat:

"The fierce soldiers, with their faces blackened with the smoke of battle, the wounded, crawling with feeble limbs from the fury of the ... flames, all seemed possessed with a common impulse. One long, unbroken cheer, in which the feeble cry of those who lay helpless on the earth blended with the strong voices of those who still fought, rose high above the roar of battle and hailed the victorious chief.

"He sat in the full realization of all that soldiers dream of—triumph; and as I looked on him in the complete fruition which his genius, courage and confidence in his army had won, I thought that it must have been from some such scene that men in ancient days ascended to the dignity of gods."

Lee was watching the flames consume the Chancellor House when a rider approached him, and passed to him a message from Jackson. Lee could not open it with his gloved hands, and passed it to Marshall, who broke the seal and read it.

The wounded Stonewall offered congratulations on the victory; he had already lost an arm by amputation.

Marshall turned to see Lee's face:

"I shall never forget the look of pain and anguish that passed over his face as he listened. With a voice broken with emotion he bade me say to General Jackson that the victory was his, and that the congratulations were due to him.

Marshall dismounted and wrote the dispatch:

> General:—I have just received your note, informing me that you were wounded. I cannot express my regret at the occurrence. Could I have directed events, I would have chosen for the good of the country to be disabled in your stead.
>
> I congratulate you upon the victory, which is due to your skill and energy.[14]

Lee also had Marshall write a message announcing victory to send to President Davis, and had scarcely seen it finished when he had news of final disaster from Fredericksburg, where the earlier error in orders had been rectified by hurrying Early's troops back to their position on the hills above the river. Now they were turned out, by a Federal flank attack, and Lee's army was between Hooker and Sedgwick.

The ever-present von Borcke was at headquarters when this word came:

"This startling intelligence, rendering our position now a very precarious one, was received by our commander . . . with a quietude and an absence of all emotion which I could not but intensely admire. . . . He quietly made his dispositions, ordering McLaws' division to march to the support of Early, who had been retreating to Salem Church—a place about five miles from Fredericksburg."

Lee and Stuart were soon seated by a fire near the Chancellor House, in early darkness. Lee was disturbed frequently during the night by dispatch riders from every direction. Von Borcke had found, among other loot of the day, a box of good candles, which now lay just outside the Confederate picket lines, somewhere near the positions of the enemy. He went after them: ". . . crawling cautiously through the bushes, and, favored by the darkness, succeeded in finding the box . . . without attracting the attention of the enemy's videttes. On reaching the temporary headquarters, and presenting my prize to General Lee, he eyed me with his calm penetrating glance, and said, 'Major, I am much obliged to you; but I know where you got these candles, and you acted wrongly in exposing your life for a simple act of courtesy."

Headquarters had little rest this night. Once a shell burst in a cherry tree nearby, showering branches and pieces of wood for many yards around. Not far away was a barn full of Federal wounded, who moaned and cried most of the night. It was perhaps the plight of these men which decided Lee to insist upon the removal of his own wounded lieutenant, Jackson.

Stonewall had resisted being moved, saying that the Federals, if they captured him, would give him kind treatment, but Lee sent a second order to have him carried out of danger, to Guiney's Station, and Jackson rolled off in an ambulance on a long, slow day's ride. He went to the Chandler farm, where doctors placed him in an outbuilding, made him comfortable, and settled down to wait for his recovery. Mrs. Jackson was summoned from Richmond.

The fighting changed for Lee on May fourth. The enemy was yet to be whipped, and since Hooker was showing no disposition to attack, Lee moved Anderson's division to reinforce Early and Mc-Laws, who were holding on not far from Fredericksburg, along Hazel Run. The march of Anderson was slow, and the morning hours dragged by, testing Lee's temper. Without Jackson, the army seemed unable to carry out his orders for swift movements, and perhaps even yet the fruits of victory, which had seemed so near, would be denied the army.

In the end it was six o'clock before Lee could mount an attack against Sedgwick; it did not drive the enemy as he had hoped, and darkness fell on an inconclusive action. He put the artillerymen to shelling Banks Ford, in the rear of the enemy, but both this day and the next seemed, from Lee's headquarters, to be filled with slow marches and wasted opportunity. He was ready for an attack all along his line in the first hours of May sixth—but his skirmishers found empty woods in front. The enemy had gone.

It was General Dorsey Pender who caught the force of Lee's anger, when he reported Sedgwick had escaped over the river:

"Why, General Pender! That is the way you young men always do. You allow those people to get away. I tell you what to do, but you don't do it!"

And then, though he realized it was too late, he urged Pender forward in a scolding voice: "Go after them, and damage them all you can!"[15]

But it was all over, and after his men had spent several hours scurrying through thickets after the wounded, and burying the dead, Lee pulled his pickets back from the river banks and put the army on the march back to the position at Fredericksburg; the men marched in a driving rain.

On May seventh Lee telegraphed Davis a brief final report of the end of the battle, with restraint concealing his chagrin:

> After driving General Sedgwick across the Rappahannock on the night of the fourth instant I returned on the fifth to Chancellorsville with the divisions of Generals McLaws and Anderson. Their march was delayed by a storm which continued all night and the following day. In placing the troops in position on the morning of the sixth to attack General Hooker it was ascertained he had abandoned his fortified position. The line of skirmishers was pressed forward until they came within range of the enemy's batteries planted north of the Rappahannock which . . . completely commanded this side. His army therefore escaped with the loss of a few additional prisoners.

He also wrote Davis that he was in desperate need of an enlarged cavalry command, and asked for large reinforcements of his infantry, with an eye still on invading the North. His modesty came to the fore in a way that must have been startling to Davis, when he spoke of bringing up Beauregard's troops from the south:

> But it will be better to order General Beauregard in with all the forces which can be spared, and to put him in command here, than to keep them there inactive and this army inefficient from paucity of numbers.[16]

If something near despair was in these words, it may well have sprung from the news of Jackson, who was now in serious condition. Chaplain Lacy saw Lee early on the seventh, as he came in search of another doctor to assist those working with Stonewall. He quietly told Lee that Dr. McGuire, called about daybreak to give Jackson relief from pain in his side, had discovered pneumonia. It appeared that the army might lose the Valley conqueror and the hero of Chancellorsville. Lee sent Lacy away:

"Give Jackson my affectionate regards, and tell him to make

haste and get well, and come back to me as soon as he can. He has lost his left arm, but I have lost my right."

Mrs. Jackson had arrived at Guiney's Station, and was shocked at sight of her husband. He was already talking of death, reading the seriousness of his condition in the number of doctors at hand. He had requested those about him to sing hymns, and protested that he was ready to die. For a day he had rallied, and then declined once more.

On Sunday, not long after Stonewall had said weakly, "It's all right; I always wanted to die on Sunday," Lee's great commander had gone. His last words were: "Let us cross over the river, and rest in the shade of the trees."

Lee went to church, to hear a sermon by Chaplain Lacy, and had sought the preacher before he returned to Guiney's Station: "When you return I trust you will find him better. When a suitable occasion offers, give him my love, and tell him that I wrestled in prayer for him last night, as I never prayed, I believe, for myself."[17]

Lee felt that he could not leave Fredericksburg, with the enemy still just across the river, able to strike in any of several directions—and with Longstreet's corps well on the road from Tidewater Virginia to join him.

In midafternoon he had the news he had dreaded for several days: Jackson was dead.

The next day, on May eleventh, Lee wrote Mary:

> In addition to the deaths of officers and friends consequent upon the late battles, you will see that we have to mourn the loss of the great and good Jackson. Any victory would be dear at such a price. His remains go to Richmond today. I know not how to replace him. God's will be done! I trust He will raise up some one in his place.

Kyd Douglas of Jackson's staff came to headquarters, asking Lee to allow the Stonewall Brigade or a part of it to march in Jackson's funeral procession in the capital. Lee refused him gently. Douglas recalled his words:

"I cannot even leave my headquarters long enough to ride to the depot and pay my dear friend the poor honor of seeing his body placed upon the cars. . . . Those people over the river are showing signs of movement."

On the same day Lee wrote a general order to the troops:

> With deep grief the commanding general announces to the army the death of Lieutenant General T. J. Jackson . . . The daring, skill and energy, of this great and good soldier are now, by the decree of an all-wise Providence, lost to us.
>
> But while we mourn his death we feel that his spirit still lives, and will inspire the whole army with his indomitable courage and unshaken confidence in God as our hope and strength. Let his name be a watchword to his corps, who have followed him to victory on so many fields. Let his officers and soldiers emulate his invincible determination to do everything in the defense of our beloved country.

Lee could not pause: Dick Ewell became chief of Jackson's old Second Corps, and a third corps was organized, under A. P. Hill. These two, with Longstreet, were responsible to Lee for the new army organization. Lee had in mind for it, as it reached a strength of 65,000 men, his old, daring plan of invasion, just such a plan as Jackson would have urged.

Now he had a letter from Rooney, evidently concerned lest his father share Jackson's fate:

> I hear from every one of your exposing yourself. You must recollect, if anything should happen to you the cause would be very much jeopardized. I want very much to see you. May God preserve you.

Lately, almost as if in answer, Lee had said to a warning of caution, "I wish some one would tell me my proper place in battle. I am always told I should not be where I am."

10 *GETTYSBURG*

In the last days of May Lee revealed a mood of vague unrest which sometimes seemed a premonition that things were not right with the army, though it was reaching a peak of strength, in numbers, morale and equipment. It was as if the commander could not put the loss of Jackson from his mind.

One glimpse of him in his tent on the Fredericksburg heights was preserved by a distant cousin, young Randolph McKim, an army chaplain:

"As I talked with him after dinner, he cast his eyes across the Rappahannock to the camps of General Hooker's army and said to me, 'I wish I could get at those people over there.' "[1]

He had, in fact, already begun the moves which would draw the Federal army north of the Potomac at full speed. He had sent Stuart and most of the cavalry westward to Culpeper. He seemed determined to make no more futile stands in the bleak country south of the Rappahannock, where the terrain was likely to rob him of victory—where even a defeated enemy could recoup losses by crossing the Rappahannock once more.

He thought the army ready, but was troubled about it. He had lately written General Hood:

I agree with you . . . that our army would be invincible
if it could be properly organized and officered. There never
were such men in an army before. They will go anywhere and
do anything if properly led. But there is the difficulty—proper
commanders—where can they be obtained? They are improving—constantly improving. Rome was not built in a day, nor
can we expect miracles in our favor.

He had in mind regimental and brigade officers, probably, but
in these days he was given many opportunities to detect in Longstreet a state of mind which might menace the future of the army.
Lee did not record any such impression, but Old Pete's inclination
to challenge the judgment of Lee was now unmistakable.

Longstreet muttered to himself about the elevation of Ewell
and A. P. Hill to his own level: ". . . the fact that both the new lieutenant generals were Virginians made the trouble more grievous.
. . . General D. H. Hill's . . . record was as good as that of Stonewall Jackson, but, not being a Virginian, he was not so well adver-
tised."

Longstreet, of course, did not face Lee with direct criticisms of
this sort, but when he rejoined the army, Old Pete found many flaws
in the victory of Chancellorsville and of Lee he wrote: "In defensive
warfare he was perfect. When the hunt was up, his combativeness
was overruling."

Longstreet, in passing through Richmond from his post in
Eastern Virginia, had swollen his self-importance by an interview
with Secretary of War Seddon, whom he had urged to change the
strategy of the entire conflict: since Vicksburg on the Mississippi
was in dire straits, Joseph Johnston's army and that of Longstreet
should be sent to reinforce Bragg in Tennessee. This large combined force would sweep Tennessee, and go in triumph to the Ohio
River, thereby saving Vicksburg. He came into camp and urged
this view upon Lee, who did not respond as Longstreet would have
liked:

". . . he [Lee] was averse to having a part of his army so far beyond his reach. He reflected over the matter one or two days, and then fell upon the plan of invading Northern soil. . . . His plan or wishes announced, it became useless and improper to offer suggestions leading to a different course."

Longstreet, however, was not one to cease resistance to a plan he did not favor. "All that I could ask was that the policy of the campaign should be one of defensive tactics; that we should work so as to force the enemy to attack us." In short, a campaign of bold aggressiveness, tempered with the utmost caution. Longstreet dedicated himself to imposing that strategy upon Lee.

The commander was called to Richmond, and spent three days after May fourteenth there, conferring with President Davis and his cabinet; Lee gave his advice on the plight of Vicksburg, which was to urge Johnston to attack Grant. While he was there the cabinet gave its blessing to another invasion of the North.

Ewell reported to camp on May twentieth, minus his leg, but with a pretty bride. Veterans looked him over and decided that he had lost some of the fight he had shown before being wounded at Second Manassas; there were men in the ranks who did not approve of his marital status.

On June second, informed that Federal forces were being evacuated from below Richmond, Lee determined that his opportunity for invasion had come—the capital seemed safe enough. He called a council of war for that day. Ewell was ordered to take his corps over the mountains to the vicinity of Winchester, where a small Federal army lay; there might then be a way to turn northward. Longstreet renewed his objections:

"I . . . remarked that if we were ever going to make an offensive battle it should be done south of the Potomac—adding that we might have an opportunity to cross the Rappahannock near Culpeper Court House and make a battle there."

Lee had no intention of fighting south of the border river, however. For three days he pulled segments of the army from the Fredericksburg positions and moved them toward Culpeper, after Ewell had gone ahead. By June sixth, with only A. P. Hill's corps left in the line, Lee broke camp. His wagons lurched in the roads after the army, from one of them his faithful hen peering out at the disappearing and familiar landscape of the winter and spring.

Lee joined the men of Longstreet and Ewell at Culpeper the next day. He had no fear that Hooker, left behind him, would prove troublesome. Just before taking the road he wrote Mary:

> General Hooker has been very daring the past week, and quite active. He has not said what he intends to do, but is giving out by his movements that he designs crossing the Rappahannock. I hope we may be able to frustrate his plans in part if not in whole. . . . I pray that our merciful Father in Heaven may protect and direct us! In that case I fear no odds and no numbers.

The village of Culpeper became for a brief time a recruiting center, and hundreds of men came in daily, especially to the cavalry, bringing fresh horses. Stuart's headquarters were in a grove of hickory and poplar trees, amid rolling clover fields, with a bright mountain stream nearby; many soldiers turned to fishing. Stuart seized the opportunity to stage a spectacle, and on June eighth Lee rode out with him, in company with Hood's Texas brigade, to see the cavalry in review—two lines of them sitting horses under a hot sun in a huge green field. Heros von Borcke described the morning scene:

"As our approach was heralded by the flourish of trumpets, many of the ladies of the village came forth to greet us . . . and showered down flowers upon our path. . . . Not less grateful to our soldiers' hearts were the cheers of more than 12,000 horsemen, which rose in the air as we came upon the open plain near Brandy Station, where the whole cavalry corps awaited us, drawn out in a line . . . at the extreme right of which twenty-four guns of our horse artillery thundered forth a salute."

Lee and Stuart galloped the long lines in the sun, and then the cavalry squadrons moved, and passed in review:

". . . first by squadrons, and at a walk, and the magnificent spectacle . . . impressed one with the conviction that nothing could resist the attack of such a body of troops. The review ended with a sham charge of the whole corps by regiments, the artillery advancing at the same time at a gallop, and opening a rapid fire upon an imaginary enemy."

Lee was not carried away as was Stuart's Prussian aide. He made a note of the poor fit of the saddles made in Richmond, and of the inferior carbines carried by the riders. He joked with Stuart, who had come out with a wreath of flowers around the neck of his horse, placed there by admiring Culpeper women: "Take care, General Stuart," he said. "That is the way General Pope's horse was adorned when he went to the battle of Manassas."[2]

The gay von Borcke noted the day's climax:

"The day wound up with a ball; but as the night was fine we danced in the open air on a piece of turf near headquarters, and by the light of enormous wood fires, the ruddy glare of which . . . gave to the whole scene a wild and romantic effect."

The next morning brought a startling end to celebrations. Thousands of enemy cavalrymen poured over the Rappahannock fords on a huge raid, and though Stuart had rushed men to meet them, one of his brigades had been overwhelmed. Cannon fire drove back this enemy charge, sprinkling the broad field with bluecoat bodies—but this was only the beginning.

The cavalry clash became the greatest of the war, and raged most of the day on the river banks, in charge after gallant charge, often with Stuart's full strength engaged. Lee called up an infantry brigade to help Stuart, and went toward the scene of action. He had a shock: Rooney was being borne to the rear with a serious leg wound. His son assured him that he would soon be back in action, and was carried away. The fight was over in the last hours of daylight, and though casualties were light and the Federals had retreated, there were ominous signs at Brandy Station, for the strong, well-mounted and daring enemy cavalry brigades were now a match for Stuart's men, and were evidently spoiling for fight; in this arm, Lee no longer had superiority.

He wrote to Mary:

> My supplications continue to ascend for you, my children, and my country. When I last wrote I did not suppose that Fitzhugh [Rooney] would so soon be sent to the rear disabled, and I hope it will be but for a short time. I saw him on the night after the battle—indeed, met him on the field as they were bringing him from the front. He is young and healthy, and I trust will soon be up again. He seemed to be more concerned about his brave men and officers who had fallen in the battle than himself.

Rooney was sent to the home of a friend not far from Richmond, accompanied by Rob.

Lee also wrote to Rooney's wife, Charlotte, expressing regret that he sent her a wounded husband, but added:

> As some good is always mixed with the evil in this world, you will now have him with you for a time, and I shall look to you to cure him soon and send him back to me.

He then turned to his bold scheme of invasion. He sent Ewell's corps over the Shenandoah near Front Royal, where it was to advance on Winchester, and, if feasible, drive north into Pennsylvania. Ewell marched on June eleventh. The rest of the army would await developments. If all went well, A. P. Hill would come up from Fredericksburg, northward through the Valley, with Longstreet's corps turning in the same direction, but marching east of the Blue

The Custis mansion, Arlington, and its devoted owners, Robert E. and Mary Ann Randolph Custis Lee. The house is shown in 1864, under Federal guard. Lee's portrait is by Matthew Brady, made in 1850, when he was 43; Mrs. Lee's was probably taken soon after the close of the war, when arthritis had taken its toll.

ANTIETAM: THE DUNKARD CHURCH

The photograph of Antietam casualties was made by a Brady assistant, James Gardner, September 18, 1862. Center, the cooking utensils, mess kit and chest in daily use at Lee's frugal mess. Of the articles pictured below, Lee used only the boots, pistol and uniform; others are typical Confederate equipment.

LEE'S CAMP CHEST

BATTLE TRAPPINGS

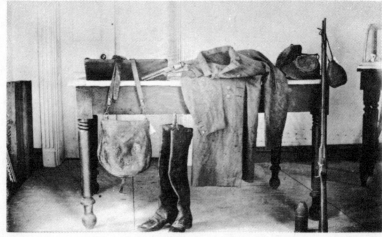

SIX WHO RODE TO FAME WITH LEE

Cook Collection, Valentine Museum

JAMES LONGSTREET

Cook Collection, Valentine Museum

JUBAL EARLY

Meserve Collection

JAMES E. B. STUART

Valentine Museum

RICHARD S. EWELL

Confederate Museum

DANIEL H. HILL

Valentine Museum

A. P. HILL

Courtesy of the New York Historical Society, New York City

A GREAT VICTORY AND A TRAGIC LOSS: THE DEBRIS OF CHANCELLORSVILLE

The Stone Wall and Sunken Road at Fredericksburg [left], which formed Lee's distant rear during Chancellorsville. Early's men, driven from here, left these casualties May 3, 1863. Before this position in the previous December, Ambrose Burnside wasted 5,000 Federal lives in vain attacks.

The men above, shot at about the time Jackson was wounded in his hour of greatest triumph, were part of the ruinous price the Confederacy paid in 1863. The photograph of Jackson, was taken just two weeks before his death. Lee was at his best as a military diplomatist in dealing with the strong characters of Jackson and Jefferson Davis.

Bettmann Archive

STONEWALL JACKSON

Cook Collection, Valentine Museum

JEFFERSON DAVIS

Culver

LEE IN THE FIELD, 1862

This famous photograph, believed to be "the only one" taken in
the field, is now credited to Minnis and Cowell of Richmond.
The enterprising researcher, Roy Meredith, assigns it to the
Virginians rather than others once thought to have made it. This
was probably made in the winter of 1862.

Above, a camera of July 3, 1863, reveals in stark eloquence a part of Lee's cost at Gettysburg, before it became apparent that this was the point from which Southern hopes receded. Below, the McLean house at Appomattox, from a photograph of April, 1865. Lee and Grant met in the first-floor room to the left; porch and yard were crowded by officers.

Matthew Brady besieged Lee in his temporary Richmond home about April 15, 1865. Lee at first declined: "How can I sit for a photograph with the eyes of the world upon me as they are today?" But Mrs. Lee and others prevailed upon him. At right, one of the rare profile views; below, with his son Custis (at his right) and the assistant adjutant general, Colonel Walter H. Taylor. In his new uniform worn at Appomattox, Lee somehow managed mingled expressions of dignity and defiance.

Ridge. Stuart's cavalry would screen the advance along the line of protecting hills.

Lee gave another sign that he was aware of the growing forces against them, and the darkening of the Confederacy's future. He wrote President Davis, urging him to try to use Northern sentiment for peace to reach some kind of an agreement. He revealed no lack of faith in Southern armies, but was candid enough to admit a sense of approaching disaster:

> We should not . . . conceal from ourselves that our re-
> sources in men are constantly diminishing, and the dispro-
> portion in this respect between us and our enemies . . . is
> steadily augmenting.

In short, Lee warned Davis, if the war stretched out much longer, the Confederacy was doomed. In this letter he did not blink at giving up Southern "independence" in exchange for peace:

> Nor, do I think we should . . . make nice distinctions be-
> tween those who declare for peace unconditionally and those
> who advocate it as a means of restoring the Union, however
> much we may prefer the former.[3]

He told Davis that he believed the Southern people would give support to a peace movement, despite their evident ardor for the war.

With this cool statement of conviction that the war was prob-ably lost—though without a hint of despair in his words—Lee was off on the most fateful thrust of his career. He sent Longstreet's corps northward to a point near Manassas Gap, with orders for A. P. Hill to pass westward behind it, heading for the Valley. On June sixteenth, he had good news from Ewell: The enemy had been driven from Winchester.

The army streamed northward in its three separate corps, with

the cavalry swarming about the Blue Ridge. For a time the intentions of the enemy were unknown—and Hooker seemed puzzled
over Lee's complex movements. It was now that Stuart, improving
on the boldness of Lee's plan, suggested that he take most of his
cavalry to Hooker's rear, and peck away at the enemy until that
army followed Lee to the north. The commander agreed to this,
but urged Stuart to come to him quickly in the event Hooker did
cross the Potomac.

Hooker's confusion over Confederate tactics was humorously
pointed out by President Lincoln this week, in an exchange of telegrams:

"Where is the Rebel army?"

"The advance is at the fords of the Potomac and the rear at
Culpeper Court House."

"If the head of the animal is at the fords of the Potomac and
the tail at Culpeper Court House, it must be very thin somewhere.
Why don't you strike it?"[4]

Hooker tried, as Lee neared the Potomac, and the presence of
Federal infantry gave cause for alarm, but still the Confederates
poured over the river.

Lee worried a bit over Stuart and his plan, and wrote him in
detail on June twenty-second, advising him that the first concern
must be to keep the cavalry force near the invading army. He
warned him not to allow Hooker to cross the Potomac ahead of him,
and place his army between Stuart and Lee:

> Do you know where he is and what he is doing? I fear he
> will steal a march on us, and get across the Potomac before we
> are aware. If you find that he is moving northward, and that
> two brigades can guard the Blue Ridge and take care of your
> rear, you can move with the other three into Maryland, and
> take position on General Ewell's right, place yourself in com-
> munication with him, and guard his flank.

Two days later, though an aide protested that Stuart surely understood the urgency of screening the main army, Lee reiterated his fears in a dispatch to the cavalry chief, over and over insisting upon the move that would mean safety for the army. His concern was clear in several phrases:

> I think you had better withdraw this side of the mountains tomorrow night, cross at Shepherdstown next day, and move over to Frederickstown. . . .
> In either case, after crossing the river, you must move on and feel the right of Ewell's troops. . . .
> I think the sooner you cross into Maryland, after tomorrow, the better. . . .
> Be watchful and circumspect in all your movements.[5]

Lee crossed the Potomac without illusions. He warned Davis once more:

> I have not sufficient troops to maintain my communications, and, therefore, have to abandon them. . . .
> I think I can throw General Hooker's army across the Potomac. . . if I can do nothing more and have to return.

And, clearest of all, he wrote:

> It is plain that if all the Federal Army is concentrated upon this, it will result in our accomplishing nothing and being compelled to return to Virginia.[6]

Lee had adventures along the route. One or two women, friendly to the Southern cause, shouted greetings to him, and brought flowers for Traveller's neck, which the General accepted only for a courier to carry. In the Maryland village of Elizabethtown, Lee met Leighton Parks, a boy who had seen him on the previous invasion of the state. Parks had a vivid memory of the day:

"They were different from the corps we had seen the year before. These men were well clad and shod . . . with flags flying, and bands playing 'Dixie,' 'Dixie,' all day long. . . . They had the air of men who were used to conquer. . . .

"It was on the Williamsport pike . . . that we met General Lee . . . His staff was brilliant in gold lace, but he was very simply dressed. No one could have seen that man without being greatly impressed with the dignity of his bearing and the beauty of his face.

"His hair . . . was almost entirely white, and . . . he had aged greatly in the short space of time . . . since the battle of Antietam. I could not help thinking of Washington as I looked at that calm, sad face."

Lee declined the request of some Hagerstown women for a lock of his hair, pleading that his was thinning, and suggesting that they take some of the plentiful yellow curls of General Pickett.

He reached Chambersburg, Pennsylvania, before there was reaction from the enemy. One soldier-diarist recalled that "ladies frequently came out of their houses to show their feeling of hostility." As the army moved on a Pennsylvania road a pretty girl ran down the steps of a large house. The diarist pictured her:

"Standing on the terrace in front, she waved a miniature flag in the faces of our troops. Behind her, applauding her act, was grouped a party of ladies, all richly and fashionably attired. . . . The troops passed by quietly, offering no insult to the flushed beauty as she flaunted her flag in their faces.

"At that moment General Lee rode up. His noble face and quiet, reproving look met her eye, and the waving flag was lowered. For a moment she looked at him, and then, throwing down the miniature banner, exclaimed audibly, as she clasped her white hands together,

"Oh, I wish he was ours!'"[7]

Lee had issued strict orders against plundering, though one reason for invasion was to feed the army from the enemy country; foraging was to be done under direction of officers. Colonel A. J. L. Fremantle, the British observer, was of two minds about the behavior of Lee's troops this week, for he wrote once:

"So completely was the country through which the Confederate army passed robbed and plundered, that all the cattle and farm horses having been seized by General Ewell, farm labor had come to a complete standstill."

But again he noted:

"I saw no straggling into the houses, nor were any of the inhabitants disturbed or annoyed by the soldiers. . . . I witnessed the singular good behavior of the troops."

But Lee saw enough of looting to prompt him to issue another order on June twenty-seventh, generally congratulatory to the troops, but once reminding them:

> There have, however, been instances of forgetfulness on the part of some that they have in keeping the yet unsullied reputation of this army, and that the duties exacted of us by civilization and Christianity are not less obligatory in the country of our enemy than in our own.

Even the most watchful of enemy civilians, including Jacob Hoke of Chambersburg, a storekeeper, could cite but few instances of outrage. One man had been killed by stragglers, after other deserters had robbed him of his money.

As Lee entered Chambersburg, Hoke reported the disappearance of the town's remaining store of goods. Confederate soldiers thronged stores, buying with their scrip every item in sight, especially soap and wool scraps for their cartridge packing. They were gay, Hoke noted, always chattering: "We'll be buying this stuff in Philadelphia, next week," and, "I reckon they'll have this stock in Harrisburg."

Early one morning A. P. Hill appeared on the street, and went into a store, where a photographer asked when Lee would appear. Hill said he was expected at any moment, and the photographer made ready, opening his studio window and thrusting out a camera, just as Lee trotted into the street. The picture was not to be, however. Soldiers lining the street stood, shouting, "See, we're going to have our pictures taken," and the photographer could not see Lee.

From Friday, June twenty-fifth, until the following Wednesday, June thirtieth, Lee and his staff camped in tents in a grove on the pike leading toward the village of Gettysburg.[8]

General Hood joined him there, and reported:

"I found him in the same buoyant spirits which pervaded his magnificent army."

Lee was supremely confident, speaking with Hood:

"Ah, General, the enemy is a long time finding us; if he does not succeed soon, we must go in search of him."

These were words Hood liked to hear: 'I assured him I was never so well prepared or more willing.'"[9]

While Lee was in this camp his men depleted the town's supplies, taking the entire stock of dry goods and grocery stores, and breaking into the cellars of homes. Hoke recorded the looting of his family cellar, and the loss of canned fruit and kegs of molasses. The army made a find of 2,000 hats here, as well.

Lee soon learned of the molasses. He was "delighted" to have the thick syrup with his hot corn bread, but when a staff officer told him that there was but a small supply, which would not last the army a week, Lee's reaction was quick.

"Then I direct, Colonel," he said, "that you immediately return every drop you have, and send an order that no molasses shall be issued to officers or men, except the sick in hospital."

Lee was visited in the grove by a Chambersburg woman, Mrs. Ellen McLellan, who went to ask Lee for flour. She was at first afraid to pass the Rebel troops alone, but at last, with her young daughter, went through to Lee's tent, finding everything in "perfect order":

"Even the horses were picketed so as to do no damage to trees. . . . I found the general seated with his officers at the table. . . . I told him starvation would soon be at hand upon many families unless he gave us aid. He seemed startled by this announcement, and said that such destitution seemed impossible in such a rich and beautiful grain-growing country."

Mrs. McLellan explained that growing grain did not help many who were in need.

"He then assured me that he had turned over the supplies of food that he had found to his men, to keep them from ravaging our homes. He said, 'God help you if I permitted them to enter your houses. Your supplies depend upon the amount that is sent in to my men.' "

As she left, the woman asked for his autograph.

"Do you want the autograph of a rebel?"

"General Lee, I am a true Union woman, and yet I ask for bread and your autograph."

"It is to your interest to be for the Union, and I hope you may be as firm in your principles as I am in mine," Lee told her.

He jokingly told her that his autograph would be a dangerous possession for her, but he finally gave her one, and, changing the subject, began to speak of peace:

"He assured me that war was a cruel thing, and that he only desired that they would let him go home and eat his bread there in peace. All this time I was impressed with the strength and sadness of his face."

One onlooker who came to stare curiously whispered of Lee, "What a large neck he has!"

A loyal soldier replied, "Yes. It takes a damn big neck to hold his head."

Lee was becoming anxious to hear from Stuart. In conversation one day this week, General Ike Trimble found the commander vaguely troubled.

"Our army is in good spirits," Lee said, "Not overfatigued, and can be concentrated on any one point in twenty-four hours or less. I have not yet heard that the enemy have crossed the Potomac, and am waiting to hear from General Stuart. When they hear where we are, they will make forced marches to interpose their forces between us and Baltimore and Philadelphia. They will come up . . . broken down with hunger and hard marching, strung out on a long line and much demoralized, when they come into Pennsylvania. I shall throw an overwhelming force on their advance, crush it, follow up the success, drive one corps back on another . . ."

Lee showed Trimble his battle map; his thick finger stabbed at the little town of Gettysburg. "Hereabout," Lee said, "we shall probably meet the enemy and fight a great battle, and if God gives us the victory, the war will be over and we shall achieve recognition of our independence."

If he could hear from Stuart. . . .

When news came on the night of June twenty-eighth, it was not from Stuart—and it could not have been worse. Colonel Moxley Sorrel of Longstreet's staff told the story:

"I was aroused by the provost guard bringing up a suspicious prisoner. It was Harrison, the scout, filthy and ragged, showing some rough work and exposure. . . . He . . . described how the enemy were even then marching in great numbers in the direction of Gettysburg. . . . Harrison's report was so exceedingly important that I woke General Longstreet, who immediately sent the scout to Lee. The general heard him with great composure and minuteness. It was on this, the report of a single scout, in the absence of cavalry, that the army moved."

This was the first intimation Lee had that the enemy were north of the Potomac, and now they were almost upon him. The infantry was well concentrated, though Ewell's advance was well along toward Harrisburg. But the cavalry, without which his intelligence would be slow and unreliable, was gone. Stuart had not reported since leaving the army, and Lee could not yet know that the horseman had crossed the Potomac on the east flank of the Federal army, even nearer to Washington, and had passed through the suburb of Rockville, skirmishing and seizing prisoners.

Lee wasted no time. He ordered Ewell, who was nearing Carlisle, to turn back, coming by Gettysburg or Cashtown. A. P. Hill and Longstreet were to move to the village of Cashtown from Chambersburg, and reinforcements were called up from Virginia. There were virtually no cavalrymen with the army, and officers were forced to mount men on artillery and wagon horses to do the day's foraging from nearby farms. Still Lee seemed in a confident mood; he was concentrating on Cashtown, a village west of Gettysburg.

One of his veterans recalled Lee's announcement of the changed plan, as he walked with officers before his tent: "Tomorrow, gentlemen," Lee said, "we will not move to Harrisburg as we expected, but will go over to Gettysburg and see what General Meade is after."[10]

The army had only recently learned that Hooker had been deposed, and George Meade, a corps commander at Chancellorsville, had assumed Federal command. Lee saw little benefit to him in the change. He told his staff: "General Meade will commit no blunder in my front, and if I make one he will make haste to take advantage of it."

On June thirtieth Lee rode with Longstreet's corps on the road east toward Cashtown, and spent the night there, at the site of an abandoned sawmill. He was there when he got ominous news: A. P. Hill reported that one of his brigades, North Carolinians under Pettigrew, had moved from Cashtown to Gettysburg during the day, looking for shoes. They had brushed with Federal cavalry—and beyond the town, they said, had plainly heard the drums of enemy infantry. Lee was incredulous that the enemy had moved so fast, but did not seem alarmed.

July first was clear and cool. Lee was up early, and Longstreet found him:

"He was in his usual cheerful spirits . . . and called me to ride with him. My column was not well stretched on the road before it encountered the division of Edward Johnson (Second Corps) cutting in on our front, with all of Ewell's reserve and supply trains."

Lee ordered Longstreet's corps to halt and allow Johnson to pass. Longstreet dismounted to wait with his men.

"After a little time General Lee proposed that we should ride on, and soon we heard reports of cannon . . . as it increased he left me and rode faster for the front."

It was two in the afternoon before Lee saw his troops firing on the enemy. From a hill he looked down on the terrain about Gettysburg, a broad landscape of open fields, marked by stands of woodland, with the village lying in a shallow valley between two prominent ridges. He was three miles west of the town, and his troops were not far beyond him. It was evident that they were not finding the enemy easy to handle. Cannon fire was slowing; Confederates were filing into lines for an attack, and the Federal skirmishers were far away over the fields. Lee was soon advised of the situation.

General Heth of A. P. Hill's corps had pushed two brigades almost into Gettysburg in the morning, but after hard fighting had fallen back. Casualties were fairly heavy; General Archer had been taken by the enemy. More Federal troops were coming up, and already outflanked the Confederates. Lee studied the scene with glasses. It did not seem promising, and his eye found no prospect of victory. An accident of battle snatched the decision from him.

North of Gettysburg, with a yelling chorus, a long line of Confederates fell on the Federal flank; the enemy line turned to meet this new threat. Lee could soon see that it was General Rodes' division, coming in at the moment of crisis as part of Ewell's march down from Carlisle. But soon, with troops scattering and the attack lacking co-ordination, the advance of Rodes' men slowed.

General Heth went to the rear and found Lee.

"Rodes is heavily engaged," he said. "Had I better not attack?"

"No," Lee said. "I am not prepared to bring on a general engagement today. Longstreet is not up."

Heth had scarcely returned to his troops before a new turn of the accidental battle changed the situation—still another gray attack broke against the Federals. Lee learned that Early's division had also arrived, and had been flung against the enemy on the left of Rodes. Ready or not, the fight was becoming a general engagement. Lee sent Heth's troops forward, and put General Pender's division on their right flank. The whole line went toward Gettysburg in a new fury of firing. Things gave the promise of victory, but at close range, the troops found that the Army of Northern Virginia had seldom seen such a day as this.

Heth said: "The fight was without order or system . . . we . . . stumbled into this fight. . . . I found in my front a heavy skirmish line and two lines of battle. My division swept over these without halting. My loss was severe. In twenty-five minutes I lost 2,700 men. . . . The last I saw or remember of this day's fight was seeing the enemy in my front . . . routed, and my division in hot pursuit. I was then shot and rendered insensible for some hours."[11]

The scene was equally fierce from the Federal view, and was recorded by a young gunner in blue, Augustus Buell:

"All our infantry began to fall back. The enemy . . . at last made his appearance in grand shape. . . . First we could see the tips of their colorstaffs coming up over the little ridge, then the points of their bayonets and then the Johnnies themselves, coming on with a steady tramp, tramp, and with loud yells. . . . 'Load . . . Canister . . . Double! . . . Ready! . . . By piece! . . . At will! . . . Fire!'

"Directly in our front the Rebel infantry had been forced to halt and lie down, by the tornado of canister that we had given them. But the regiments to their right kept on, as if to cut us off. . . .

"Then ensued probably the most desperate fight ever waged between artillery and infantry at close range without a particle of cover on either side.

"Our burly corporal, bareheaded, his hair matted with blood from a scalp wound, wiping the crimson fluid out of his eyes to sight the gun . . . the steady orderly sergeant . . . profanely exhorting us to 'feed it to 'em, God damn 'em! Feed it to 'em!'

"Men were reeling and falling; splinters flying from wheels and axles where bullets hit; in rear, horses tearing and plunging, drivers yelling, shells bursting, shot shrieking overhead . . . bullets hissing, humming and whistling everywhere; cannon roaring—all crash on crash and peal on peal, smoke, dust, splinters, blood, wreck and carnage indescribable. But not a man or boy flinched or faltered.

"For a few moments the whole Rebel line seemed to waver . . . but their line came steadily on. Orders were given to limber to the rear. . . . We got off by the skin of our teeth and before sundown were in position on the north brow of Cemetery Hill."

Lee watched the last stages of the Federal flight from the ridge just east of Gettysburg, and as thousands of Yank prisoners streamed past him to the rear, he ordered guns turned on the enemy position, which lay along forbidding slopes to the south of the town. The hills were the key to the terrain, he saw, and Lee made an effort to push the weary enemy from them. He asked for A. P. Hill, but got the message that he had been sick during the afternoon. Hill's men were worn and scattered by the fighting, and in no condition to send against two Federal corps.

Lee ordered Ewell to undertake the final task of the day. He called Colonel Walter Taylor to him. Taylor recalled:

"He then directed me to go to General Ewell and say to him that, from the position which he occupied, he could see the enemy retreating over those hills, without organization and in great confusion; that it was only necessary to press 'those people' in order to secure possession of the heights, and that, if possible, he wished to do this. . . .

"I proceeded immediately to General Ewell and delivered the order of General Lee . . . and returned . . . and reported that his order had been delivered. General Ewell did not express any objection . . . but left the impression upon my mind that it would be executed."

But Ewell, exercising his discretion, ordered his troops to halt, and the hills were not stormed. An aggressive field officer, General John B. Gordon, fumed:

"I was ordered to halt. The whole of that portion of the Union army in my front was in inextricable confusion and in flight . . . my troops were upon the flank and sweeping down the lines. The firing upon my men had almost ceased. Large bodies of the Union troops were throwing down their arms and surrendering. . . . In less than half an hour my troops would have swept up and over those hills. . . . It is not surprising that . . . I should have refused at first to obey the order."

Gordon finally ended his advance, after receiving Ewell's fourth order to halt.

Men in the army were already saying in this moment, "If Jackson had been here!" But Gordon and Ewell, despite their disagreement, were not in bad humor. They rode together in Gettysburg, in the last hour of fighting. Gordon recalled:

"I heard the ominous thud of a Minié ball as it struck General Ewell at my side. I quickly asked: 'Are you hurt, sir?' 'No, no,' he replied. 'I'm not hurt. But suppose that ball had struck you; we would have had the trouble of carrying you off the field, sir. You see how much better fixed I am than you are. It don't hurt a bit to be shot in a wooden leg.' "

As the battle died away, at about five o'clock, Longstreet rode to Seminary Ridge in search of Lee. The commander was busy at the moment, and Longstreet turned to study the Federal position with his glasses. He saw what the gunner, E. P. Alexander, described well:

"The enemy's line . . . upon the natural ridges overlooking the open country . . . resembled a fishhook, with its convexity toward us, forcing upon our line a similar shape with the concavity toward them. Their lines were interior and shorter, being scarcely three miles in length . . . our exterior lines were about five miles. . . . Their left which was the top of the fishhook shank, rested on Big and Little Round Top mountains, and their right, which was the 'point' of the 'fishhook' was on Culp's Hill over Rock Creek. Both flanks presented precipitous and rocky fronts, screened from artillery fire by forest growth . . . the two flanks approached and each was able to reenforce the other."

Having studied this line, Longstreet turned to Lee with a singular proposal.

"We could not call the enemy to a position better suited to our plans. All that we have to do is to file around his left and secure good ground between him and Washington. We can get in strong position and wait, and if they fail to attack us we shall have everything in condition to move back tomorrow night in the direction of Washington, selecting beforehand a good position."

Lee's face must have revealed his astonishment at this plan to make a dangerous flank march by the enemy position, in the face of reinforcements of unknown size approaching from the east.

He gestured, striking with his fist in the air. "No," he said. "If he is there tomorrow I will attack him."

Longstreet was persistent. "If he is there tomorrow, it will be because he wants you to attack. If that height has become the objective, why not take it at once?"

"No," Lee said, "They are there in position, and I am going to whip them or they are going to whip me."

Longstreet, who carried wounded feelings from Gettysburg, re-called: "I saw he was in no frame of mind to listen to further argu-ment at that time, so I did not push the matter, but determined to renew the subject the next morning."[12]

Colonel Long of Lee's staff returned to headquarters with re-port of a reconnaissance of the Federal line; he confirmed the im-pression that it was extremely strong. This seemed to decide the is-sue for Lee. He turned to Longstreet, and to A. P. Hill, who had come up at last:

"Gentlemen," he said, "we will attack the enemy in the morn-ing as early as practicable."

Stonewall Jackson's old aide, Captain James Power Smith, came from Ewell with word that Cemetery Hill might be taken from the Federals, if Lee could take the higher ridge in front. Lee gazed at the terrain. "I suppose this is the higher ground to which these gentlemen refer," he said. "You will find that some of those people are there now."

He sent Smith off with a shake of his head. "Our people are not yet up, and I have no troops with which to occupy this higher ground."

Longstreet's troops were not up, though they had been in bet-ter position to arrive than most of the others of the army, and Lee now asked Old Pete how far away his brigades were. Longstreet said only that General McLaws with his division was some six miles out of town. Lee asked him to hurry his movement, but did not press him, and gave no sign that his lieutenant's behavior seemed strange or distasteful to him. Longstreet left headquarters.

Lee went to Gettysburg in the evening, and under an arbor behind a small house on the Carlisle Road, he talked with Ewell, Early and Rodes. Despite his victory, Ewell seemed strangely sub-dued. He seldom spoke, as Lee asked the officers of their losses, posi-tions and opinions, and remained quiet as Early spoke with fiery conviction—as if he, and not Ewell, were the corps commander.

Lee saw signs of the afternoon's troubles, when Ewell's timidity had enraged many officers, including Gordon and irascible old Ike Trimble, who was reported to have flung down his sword and threatened never to fight under Ewell again. If Lee ever questioned Ewell's ability to handle a corps, or to carry out discretionary orders with sound judgment, he must have done so that night. He at last came to the point.

"Can't you, with your corps, attack on this flank at daylight tomorrow?"

Ewell did not reply. Instead, Early began to outline their difficulties of strength and terrain. Lee's only sign of chagrin was a deepening of his reserve; he bowed his head and spoke without looking into the faces of his officers. He proposed the withdrawal of the end of Ewell's line, which circled the edge of Culp's Hill, but Early, declaring that his men did not relish retreat, asked to be allowed to remain there.

Lee came slowly to his conclusion: if this wing could not attack, and A. P. Hill's men were worn and out of position, there was one recourse. He spoke deliberately:

"Well, if I attack from my right, Longstreet will have to make the attack." He paused. "Longstreet is a very good fighter when he gets in position and gets everything ready, but he is so *slow*."[13]

Early noted the emphasis of Lee's remark, and thought the commander in "pain" as he spoke. It was Lee's only recorded criticism of the increasingly stubborn Old Pete in these days.

For the rest of the evening Lee worked over the plan of battle. Almost all of his infantry would be in line before noon the next day. Pickett's division, still at Chambersburg awaiting Imboden's cavalry, was the far outpost. Stuart at last reported; he was in Carlisle, and though ordered to Gettysburg, could not arrive in time for action tomorrow. Lee discussed affairs fully with Longstreet and A. P. Hill, and was talking with them when a message from Ewell arrived: Culp's Hill had been found unoccupied by scouts, and could be seized in the morning. Lee replied with an order approving the seizure. There was no recorded discussion of the possibility of taking the knoll in darkness.

Lee slept in a house near an orchard on the Chambersburg road. He was with Colonel Long just before falling asleep.

"Colonel Long," he asked, "do you think we had better attack without the cavalry? If we do so, we will not, if successful, be able to reap the fruits of victory."

"It would be best not to wait for Stuart," Long said. "It is uncertain ... when he will arrive.... The cavalry had better be left to take care of itself."

Lee breakfasted in the pre-dawn darkness. In the first moments of daylight he anxiously studied the line of Cemetery Ridge, and satisfied himself that the enemy had not been reinforced; in some sectors there were no Federals. There was yet time to sweep the line of hills. Ewell was presumably ready on the left, and A. P. Hill's men, now stronger, lay along Seminary Ridge facing the enemy center, ready for an emergency. Lee could see no movement to the right, where Longstreet's corps should be moving.

He sent to Ewell, asking if he could shift his troops to the right, where he might attack in Longstreet's place. The message had hardly left headquarters when word came that Longstreet was moving up. Then Old Pete himself arrived and immediately reopened the argument of the day before.

Lee gave him a polite hearing, but at sight of more bluecoats swarming onto the ridge opposite the town, his impatience drove him to leave Longstreet. He walked down among the grove of trees nearby. General Hood had a close look at him in these moments:

"General Lee, with coat buttoned to the throat, sabre belt buckled round the waist, and field glasses pending at his side, walked up and down in the shade of the large trees near us, halting now and then to observe the enemy. He seemed full of hope, yet, at times, buried in deep thought.

"Colonel Fremantle, of England, was ensconced in the forks of a tree not far off, with glass in constant use, examining the lofty position of the Federal army. General Lee was, seemingly, anxious that [Longstreet] should attack that morning. He remarked to me:

"'The enemy is here, and if we do not whip him, he will whip us.'"

A few minutes later Hood spoke with Longstreet, at a short distance from Lee.

"The general is a little nervous this morning," Longstreet said. "He wishes me to attack. I do not wish to do so without Pickett. I never like to go into battle with one boot off."

Longstreet soon dared open insubordination. Lee had been waiting for the divisions of Hood and McLaws of Longstreet's corps to reach their positions, with increasing alarm, since many of the posts he had chosen for them were filling with Federals. McLaws finally arrived and Lee gave him quick orders:

"General, I wish you to place your division across this road." He showed McLaws the spot on his map. "And I want you to get there if possible without being seen by the enemy. Can you do it?"

McLaws said he would try. Lee said he was sending an engineer officer to find a concealed path, and McLaws said, "I will go with him."

Longstreet interrupted the conversation, speaking sharply to McLaws: "No, sir. I do not wish you to leave your division." Old Pete stabbed at the map himself. "I wish your division placed so."

Lee's soft reply betrayed no wrath. "No, General," he said "I wish it placed just opposite."

Still Longstreet was not through. McLaws asked once more for permission to go with Lee's engineer, as he had proposed. "No," Longstreet said, shortly. Lee did not speak up this time, and the confused McLaws left, to hold his division nearby. Lee passed off this defiance so calmly that officers at hand took no note of it.

Lee now rode off to Ewell's flank, but could not find his corps commander, and went with General Trimble to climb the high tower of the Gettysburg almshouse and spy upon the enemy line. He had a wistful sound as he spoke to Trimble of what might have been.

"The enemy have the advantage of us in a short and inside line," he said, "and we are too much extended. We did not—or could not—pursue our advantage of yesterday and now the enemy are in a good position."

He soon found Ewell, and repeated his orders to him; everything depended upon Longstreet. Though he waited almost half an hour on this flank, there was no word from Longstreet, and not a sound indicating that the First Corps had begun its movements. He left, riding back to his headquarters site on Seminary Ridge. A gunner he met on the route was impressed by Lee's anxiety:

"Do you know where General Longstreet is?" Lee asked.

The colonel rode off at his side, in an effort to locate Old Pete for him, and recalled of this ride:

"General Lee manifested more impatience than I ever saw him exhibit upon any other occasion; seemed very much disappointed and worried that the attack had not opened earlier, and very anxious for Longstreet to attack at the very earliest possible moment. He even, for a little while, placed himself at the head of one of the brigades to hurry the column forward."

Colonel Long now saw Lee's vexation grow.

"What *can* detain Longstreet?" Lee asked. "He ought to be in position now."[14]

A little after ten, when he had word that Longstreet's corps was coming forward, Lee appeared to relax somewhat. He rode to a point which Longstreet must pass, but saw nothing to encourage him. In his front he noticed that a peach orchard he had marked

for Longstreet's position was now filled with Federals, and that the
enemy strength continued to grow. He rode to the rear, and at about
eleven o'clock found Longstreet—who had done almost nothing to
push forward his men.

Most of Longstreet's corps had been up since shortly after daylight, within sight of the enemy, and had not been moved. Lee left
Old Pete at about two o'clock, for the last time entrusting the attack
to him. It was almost an hour before the troops of Hood and Mc-
Laws moved to attack on the right—the long line of the Confederates now faced the full strength of the Union army, all but one
corps of which was waiting in formidable position.

McLaws' division was in early trouble, the result of losing its
way under Lee's engineer, but Longstreet seemed determined not
to correct the error, since Lee had given the orders, and must bear
the responsibility. It was long before the column was in place to
help carry out the planned flank attack up the road from Emmitts-
burg, which Lee hoped would turn the enemy from the rocky towers
of Round Top.

Hood's men soon ran into deadly firing from above, since the
enemy line from Round Top along the ridge could fire into their
ranks. Hood sent a message to the rear, asking Longstreet's permission to march around the flank, rather than carry out the letter
of orders. But Old Pete's stubborn mood had hardened. His reply
to Hood was: "General Lee's orders are to attack up the Emmitsburg Road."

Hood sent back another officer to renew his request. He got the
same reply, and at last went forward with his men, under protest.
Longstreet made no effort to communicate with Lee, who was within reach. Instead, he rode up to Hood, and in a brief conversation,
as Hood expressed regret at the attack he must make, Longstreet
said, "We must obey the orders of General Lee."

Hood's men stormed out into the peach orchard, their ranks
riddled by the enemy, and Hood was shot down and carried off the

field. It was the opening of a furious three hours. Longstreet's men clawed through fierce opposition to the jumbled boulders of Devil's Den, a craggy outpost near the Round Tops, and almost surrounded the two small peaks themselves. At last, after paying dearly for their unplanned advance, they fanned out across the Emmitsburg Road, and on that flank seemed on the point of driving the enemy; there was stout assistance from a Mississippi brigade in the Peach Orchard. Far down the line, five miles to the left, Ewell's guns were beginning—and Lee, watching the battle unfold, at last, when it was near six o'clock, sent forward Hill's troops in the center of the line. One brigade had fought all the way through the little valley and up the hill held by the Federals, to hold for a time among the enemy guns, but they had to fall back for lack of support. On this rolling farmland the war had reached a new crescendo in the late afternoon. Watching from the Federal lines on the hill, one of Meade's young men, Lieutenant Frank Haskell, watched the fate of General Dan Sickles' exposed corps in the peach orchard:

"We saw the long gray lines come sweeping down upon Sickles' front and mix with the battle smoke. . . . Oh, the din and the roar, and these Rebel wolf cries! What a hell was there down in that valley! . . . The 3rd Corps was being overpowered. Here and there its lines started to break. The men began to pour back to the rear in confusion. The enemy were close upon them and among them. . . . The 3rd Corps, after a heroic but unfortunate fight, was being literally swept from the field. . . .

"The time was at hand when we must be actors in this drama. . . . Now we were in for it. . . . All along the crest everything was ready. Gun after gun, along the batteries, in rapid succession leaped where it stood and bellowed its canister upon the enemy. They still advanced. The infantry opened fire, and soon the whole crest, infantry and artillery, was one continuous sheet of fire. . . .

"All senses for the time were dead but the one of sight. . . . Men were dropping, dead or wounded, on all sides, by scores and by hundreds. Poor mutilated creatures, some with an arm dangling, some with a leg broken by a bullet, were limping and crawling to the rear. They made no sound of pain but were as silent as if dumb and mute. A sublime heroism seemed to pervade all, and the intuition that to lose that crest was to lose everything.

"Such fighting as this could not last long. It was now near sundown. . . . The Rebel cry had ceased, and the men of the Union began to shout, and their lines to advance. The wave had rolled upon the rock, and the rock had smashed it.

"Back down the slope, over the valley, across the Emmitsburg Road, shattered . . . in utter confusion the men in gray poured into the woods."

The Confederate attack, delivered in piecemeal, had failed on the right, and only lightly pressed in the center and on the left. Except for Hood's position, strong around the Round Tops and the Peach Orchard, Lee's army had not improved its line. There were stories of lack of co-ordination and belated attack from all parts of the line. But Lee could not forget the sight of the lone brigade breaking into the Federal center.

After dark Lee gave little time to pondering. If he could throw the combined attacks of all three corps upon the enemy tomorrow, he had no doubt of victory. Stuart was now up with his men, and though weary, was ready to carry out his orders. Since Longstreet had been reinforced by the arrival of Pickett's division, the risks of the coming day seemed rather less.

Lee sent out his orders, verbally: Longstreet to attack on the right, Ewell on the left, at the same time, this to be as early in the morning as was possible. Neither Longstreet nor Ewell reported to headquarters in person. The artillerymen got orders to soften the enemy with a long cannonade.

As the commander went to bed, unknown to him, Longstreet's scouts were feeling through the darkness to the right, where the contentious officer planned to move in the morning, still in defiance of

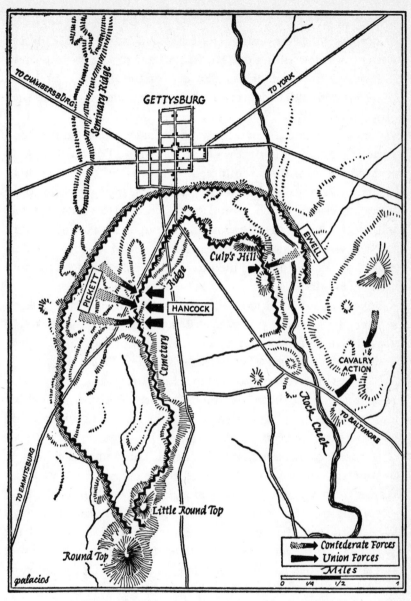

Confederate Forces
Union Forces

GETTYSBURG: BEGINNING OF THE END

Lee's orders; Old Pete clung to his scheme of bypassing Meade and moving toward Washington. He wrote later of Lee in bitterness: ". . . he was excited and off his balance . . . on the afternoon of the 1st, and he labored under that impression until enough blood was shed to appease him."[15]

Daylight brought more delay and defiance. Almost at first light a furious fire broke out on Ewell's sector, where Edward Johnson's advanced division, now reinforced, engaged the enemy without waiting for Longstreet. Lee went to his right, trying in vain to see Pickett's division, which should be in position by now. He met Longstreet, who began once again to insist upon his plan of strategy.

"I have been examining the ground over to the right," Longstreet said. "I am much inclined to think the best thing is to move to the Federal left."

"No," Lee said. "I am going to take them where they are on Cemetery Hill. I want you to take Pickett's division and make the attack. I will reinforce you by two divisions of the Third Corps. [Heth's under Pettigrew and Pender's under Trimble.]"

"That will give me 15,000 men," Longstreet said. "I have been a soldier all my life, in pretty much all kinds of skirmishes. I think I can safely say there never was a body of 15,000 men who could make that attack successfully."

He was not through his argument. He could not attack with so few, and still could not bring the rest of his corps to support them, because the moving of Hood or McLaws would weaken the flank. In short, Longstreet balked at attack. Lee said he would shift enough troops to the aid of Pickett to make the attack as strong as if the whole First Corps were storming the heights. Orders went to Ewell to delay until ten o'clock, when the movements should be completed. Though Longstreet was still grumbling and discontent, Lee went ahead with his plans.

He ordered the men kept behind the ridge, where they could not see the open ground over which they were to charge the Union center; the men in ranks were not deceived, for as they lay in the growing heat, the rumor of the coming assault spread among them; they waited calmly.

Lee rode out in the front with Longstreet to make certain that officers understood the objective, a small grove of chestnut oaks surrounded by low stone walls, on Cemetery Ridge. The attack would be made by 47 regiments, the bulk of them from Virginia and North Carolina. They were to move out when word came from the artillery that the enemy guns were silenced, or nearly so. The signal for the opening of the guns would be two cannon shots. The final consultation was held on a log, where Lee sat with A. P. Hill and Longstreet.

Old Pete had nothing more to say; Hill made a plea that his entire corps be used to support the attacking column, but Lee shook his head.

"What remains of your corps," he said, "will be my only reserve, and it will be needed if General Longstreet's attack should fail."

The three parted with the understanding that when things were ready Longstreet would order the attack, the signal guns would roll.

There was a long wait under the hot sun, the silence broken only by an outburst of firing in the front, when A. P. Hill's men brushed with the enemy over a barn between the lines. This attracted artillery fire, but since ammunition was low, General Alexander soon ordered his guns to cease; Lee was not advised of the shortage of powder and shell.

Noon passed. Things were so quiet that the occasional laughter of men lying behind Seminary Ridge could be heard in the front. When everything was in readiness Longstreet found himself unable to give the order, and sought for a final means to avoid the attack. He tried to pass the responsibility to Alexander, who was to have vivid memories of the day:

"Some half hour or more before the cannonade began, I was startled by the receipt of a note from Longstreet:

> Colonel: If the artillery fire does not have the effect to drive off the enemy or greatly demoralize him, so as to make our effort pretty certain, I would prefer that you should not advise Pickett to make the charge. I shall rely a great deal upon your judgment to determine the matter and shall expect you to let Gen. Pickett know when the moment offers.

" . . . here was a proposition that *I* should decide the question. Overwhelming reasons against the assault at once seemed to stare me in the face."

General Wright, whose brigade had mounted Cemetery Ridge yesterday, was with Alexander, and after conferring with him, Alexander replied to Longstreet:

> General: I will only be able to judge of the effect of our fire on the enemy by his return fire. . . . If, as I infer from your note, there is any alternative to this attack, it should be carefully considered before opening our fire, for it will take all the artillery ammunition we have left to test this one, and if result is unfavorable we will have none left for another effort.

The ever-present British observer, Colonel Fremantle, was near Longstreet when this dispatch was delivered, and he reported Old Pete had gone to sleep in the woods, and was shaken awake to read the message. Longstreet replied with another curious note in this exchange, while the armies waited:

> Colonel: The intention is to advance the infantry if the artillery has the desired effect of driving the enemy's off, or having other effect such as to warrant us in making the attack.

When that moment arrives advise Gen. Pickett and of course advance such artillery as you can use in aiding the attack.

Alexander read this and turned to General Wright: "What do you think of it? Is it as hard to get there as it looks?"

"The trouble is not in going there. . . . There is a place where you can get breath and reform. The trouble is to stay there after you get there, for the whole Yankee army is there in a bunch."

Alexander was still perplexed; he asked officers for all information he could get on the charge, and assumed it was to be supported by the entire army. He looked for Pickett, and found him "both cheerful and sanguine," and, thus reassured, wrote to Longstreet once more:

General: When our fire is at its best, I will advise Gen. Pickett to advance.

Two guns roared in the stillness: the signal for bombardment, and then attack. Alexander looked at his watch. It was one o'clock. The gunnery chief looked up and down the valley, beginning to fill with gunsmoke as the batteries raked the enemy lines; the reply of the Federal guns was ominously strong. Alexander thought of his low supplies: "I dared not presume on using more ammunition than one hour's firing would consume. . . . So I determined to send Pickett the order at the very first favorable sign and not later than after 30 minutes' firing."

He also began to have serious doubts as to the soundness of Lee's plan:

"The Federal line . . . its whole length, about two miles, was blazing like a volcano. It seemed madness to order a column in the middle of a hot July day to undertake an advance of three-fourths of a mile over open ground against the center of that line.

"But something had to be done. I wrote . . . to Pickett at 1:25:

General: if you are to advance at all, you must come at once or we will not be able to support you as we ought. But the enemy's fire has not slackened materially and there are still 18 guns firing from the cemetery.

"I had hardly sent this note when there was a decided falling off in the enemy's fire."

Alexander saw, in great excitement, that the Federal gunners were hitching horses and pulling off their big guns. He wrote Pickett once more at one forty:

For God's sake come quick. The 18 guns have gone. Come quick or my ammunition will not let me support you properly.

Pickett was with Longstreet when he got from Alexander the note urging him to advance, though the 18 enemy guns still fired. Pickett held the note to Old Pete.

"General," Pickett said, "shall I advance?"

Longstreet could say nothing. He looked away. Pickett saluted.

"I am going to move forward, sir," Pickett said. He galloped off.

A sharp-eyed young officer, John Wise, had sketched Pickett:

"A tawny man, of medium height and stout build; his long yellow hair was thick, hanging about his ears and shoulders, suggestive of a lion's mane. He was blue-eyed, with white eyelashes, florid complexion and reddish mustache . . . a gentleman by birth . . . a high and free liver."

Pickett passed Fitz Lee sitting among his cavalrymen and shouted, "Come on, Fitz, and go with us; we shall have lots of fun there presently."[16]

Longstreet rode to the front where Alexander was directing the guns. He heard, once more, that ammunition was running low—and this time the report seemed to strike home.

"Go stop Pickett right where he is," Longstreet ordered, "and replenish your ammunition."

"We can't do that, sir. The train has only a little. It would take an hour to distribute it, and meanwhile the enemy would improve the time."

Alexander was the only recording witness of Longstreet's last struggle:

"Longstreet seemed to stand irresolute (we were both dismounted) and then spoke slowly and with great emotion: 'I do not want to make this charge. I do not see how it can succeed. I would not make it now but that General Lee had ordered it and is expecting it.' "

It was too late now, for as the generals stood there, talking, the first wave of infantry, of Garnett's brigade, passed through the gunners and into the front. Alexander's crews began to hitch their guns for the dash forward. He exchanged a salute with Garnett, a companion of army days on the frontier; Garnett could not walk, just up from a sick bed, but he clung to the saddle to be with the column. He was dressed in an old blue coat buttoned to his chin. A long line began to form along the slope.

Pickett was completing a letter to his fiancée just behind the lines:

. . . I rode with them [Lee and Longstreet] along our line of prostrate infantry. The men had been forbidden to cheer, but they arose and lifted . . . their caps to our beloved commander. Oh, the responsibility for the lives of such men as these! Well, my darling, their fate and that of our beloved Southland will be settled ere your glorious brown eyes rest on these scraps of penciled paper. . . .

The men are lying in the rear, and the hot July sun pours its scorching rays almost vertically down on them. The suffering is almost unbearable.

I have never seen Old Peter [Longstreet] so grave and troubled. For several minutes after I had saluted him he looked at me without speaking. Then in an agonized voice, the reserve all gone, he said, 'Pickett, I am being crucified. I have instructed Alexander to give you your orders, for I can't.'

... I shall never forget the look in his face nor the clasp of his hand, and I saw tears glistening on his cheeks and beard. The stern old war horse, God bless him, was weeping for his men, and, I know, praying too that this cup might pass from them. It is almost three o'clock.

Your soldier.[17]

The men in the long ranks on the hillside managed to look as if they were off on a commonplace errand, standing in the drifting smoke of guns, with their regimental flags lazily stirring. But there had been a certain bravado. Pickett could not restrain himself, and shouted: "Up, men, and to your posts! Don't forget today that you are from Old Virginia!"

In the North Carolina front General Pettigrew, "his face lit up with the bright look" it always had in battle, passed the order: "Now, Colonel, for the honor of the good Old North State, forward!"

The regimental commanders chanted the words all down the line as the first wave stepped out into the valley in the searing sunshine.

There was only an occasional cannon shot, at first, whistling overhead in reassurance; the enemy held his fire. Longstreet watched from a perch on a rail fence, his face inscrutable. For about 200 yards the lines went on without meeting Federal fire. The watchers behind and beyond squinted at the 15,000 through dancing heat waves, some of them knee-deep in ripe grain. Two Richmond newspaper reporters saw it:

"On press Pickett's brave Virginians . . . and now the enemy opens upon them in terrible fire. Yet on, on they move in unbroken line, delivering a deadly fire as they advance. Now they have reached the Emmitsburg Road, and here they meet a severe fire from the enemy's infantry, posted behind a stone fence, while their artillery turn their whole fire upon this devoted band. . . . That flag goes down. See how quickly it again mounts upward. . . .

"The line moves onward, straight onward—cannon roaring, grape and canister plunging and plowing through the ranks—bullets whizzing thick as hailstones in winter, and men falling as leaves fall when shaken by the blasts of autumn. In a double-quick, and with a shout which rises above the roar of battle, they charge. Now they pour in volleys of musketry—they reach the works—the contest rages with intense fury—men fight almost hand to hand. . . . The Yankees flee. . . . Pickett's men deliver their fire at the gunners and drive them from their pieces. I see them plant their banner in the enemy's works. I hear their glad shout of victory!"[18]

But this is only a moment. The advance lashes onto the crest, but cannot remain, and the smoky valley is scattered with the dead and writhing with wounded in the track of the charge. There were some moments of terror on the Federal ridge before it was over. Lieutenant Haskell gave witness: ". . . an ocean of armed men sweeping upon us! . . . More than half a mile their front extends; more than a thousand yards the dull gray masses deploy, man touching man . . . the arms . . . barrel and bayonet, gleam in the sun, a sloping forest of flashing steel. Right on they move . . . in perfect order . . . through orchard and meadow, and cornfield, magnificent, grim, irresistible. . . .

"General Gibbon rode down the lines, cool and calm. . . . 'Do not hurry, men, and fire too fast, let them come close up before you fire, and then aim low and steadily.' . . . Then the thunders of our guns . . . as the range grows shorter and shorter . . . without wavering or halt, and hardy lines of the enemy continue to move on. The Rebel guns make no reply to ours, and no charging shout rings out today . . . but the courage of these silent men amid our shots seems not to need the stimulus of other noise.

"All along each hostile front, a thousand yards, with the narrowest space between, the volleys blaze and roll; as thick the sound as when a summer hail storm pelts the city roofs. . . . The larger part of Webb's brigade—my God, it was true—there by the group of trees and the angles of the wall, was breaking from the cover of their works, and, without orders or reason, with no hand lifted to check them, was falling back, a fear-stricken flock of confusion! The fate of Gettysburg hung upon a spider's single thread. . . .

"As I met the tide of these rabbits (with my sword), the damned red flags of the rebellion began to flaunt and thicken along the wall they had just deserted. . . . The men that had fallen back, facing the enemy, soon regained confidence in themselves. . . .

"The jostling, swaying lines on either side boil, and roar. . . . The frequent dead and wounded lie where they stagger and fall. . . . The men do not cheer or shout; they growl. . . . The line springs— the crest of the solid ground with a great roar, heaves forward its maddened load, men, arms, smoke, fire, a fighting mass. It rolls to the wall—flash meets flash, the wall is crossed—a moment ensues of thrusts, yells, blows, shots . . . followed by a shout universal . . . and the last and bloodiest fight of the great battle of Gettysburg is ended and won."

The broken ranks fell back, dogged and sullen at first, and then faster.

Lee had come, during the last moments of the fight, to Alexander's position—just as the brigade of Wilcox was being sent in, twenty minutes late, to cover the flank and rear of the attack.

The survivors came past him there, or many thousands did— the walking wounded among the first, and many cheered the sight of him on Traveller, even then. Alexander was struck by his mood:

"He . . . spoke to nearly every man who passed, using expressions such as: 'Don't be discouraged.' 'It was my fault this time.' 'Form your ranks again when you get under cover.' 'All good men must hold together now.'"

Lee turned to one of Alexander's staff, Lt. F. M. Colston, when a burst of cheering rang along the front, asking him to investigate. As Colston started forward, his horse reared and balked. Colston began beating the horse with a stick. Lee's reaction was immediate.

"Oh, don't do that. I once had a foolish horse and I found gentle measures so much the best."

General Kemper passed on a litter. Lee rode to him. "General, I hope you are not badly hurt."

"Yes, General," Kemper said, "I'm afraid they have got me this time."

Lee squeezed Kemper's hand. "I trust not," he said, "I trust not." Kemper went off to the rear, seriously wounded.

Colonel Fremantle, who had been out of sight during the charge, came to the center of the line and glimpsed Longstreet seated on his fence. The Britisher thought he was just in time to witness the attack.

"I wouldn't have missed this for anything," he said.

"The devil you wouldn't!" Longstreet replied. "I would like to have missed it very much." He told Fremantle of the brief grasp upon a point of the Federal line and retirement after twenty minutes. Fremantle was struck by Longstreet's calm acceptance of the failure.

Fremantle now moved to the commander:

"If Longstreet's conduct was admirable, that of General Lee was perfectly sublime. . . . He was addressing to every soldier he met a few words of encouragement, such as, 'All this will come right in the end. We'll talk it over afterward, but in the meantime all good men must rally.' The slightly wounded he exhorted to 'bind up their hurts and take up muskets.' "

Lee turned to Fremantle: "This has been a sad day for us, Colonel—a sad day. But we can't expect always to gain victories."

General Wilcox came up, "almost crying," Fremantle saw. Lee shook hands with his officer. "Never mind, General, all this has been *my* fault. It is *I* who have lost this fight, and you must help me out of it in the best way you can."

Fremantle looked in wonder at Lee: "It was impossible to look at him or to listen to him without feeling the strongest admiration."[19]

On the ground near Lee was a wounded Federal prisoner who, recognizing the Rebel commander, stirred and shouted, "Hurrah for the Union!" He seemed frightened when Lee turned toward him, dismounting—and later confessed that he thought Lee meant to kill him.

Instead, Lee shook his hand, "My son, I hope you will soon be well."

The awed Federal could remember only "the sad expression" and Lee's kindness; he sobbed on the bloody ground until he fell asleep, he said.

Pickett passed near them, and Lee went to him, pointing, "General Pickett, place your division in rear of this hill, and be ready to repel the advance of the enemy should they follow up."

"General Lee, I have no division now, Armistead is down, Garnett is down, and Kemper is mortally wounded."

"Come, General Pickett, this has been my fight and the blame rests on my shoulders. The men and officers of your command have written the name of Virginia as high today as it has ever been written before."

There had been scattered fighting down the rest of the line, and during the day Stuart's troopers had met the enemy at a distance, but when the last of the men of Pickett, Pettigrew and Trimble came back into the ranks, it was all over; Lee behaved as if he did not care to hide their failure. He remained on the field only long enough to see Alexander covering the few advanced Federal guns, until they had retired.

He placed the blame on no one but himself, though when Colonel Venable of the staff said bitterly that he had overheard the order directing Longstreet to send the divisions of McLaws and Hood in support, Lee said in anguish, "I know! I know!"

Longstreet had been drinking late this afternoon, and though there was no hint that he was drunk, an officer recalled that Old Pete could not remember whether he had sent an order to McLaws.

Lee ordered the army to prepare for retreat. Soon after dark he rode to find A. P. Hill. While the two talked General Imboden, the cavalryman, came in response to a call:

". . . a single flickering candle, visible . . . through the open front of a common wall tent, exposed to view Generals Lee and Hill seated on camp stools with a map spread upon their knees."

Lee asked Imboden to go to headquarters and wait for him.

It was one o'clock before Lee appeared, riding Traveller alone, at a slow walk, his head forward, musing in the bright moonlight. The horse was obviously worn as he halted before Lee's tent.

Lee tried to dismount, and the effort was so great, Imboden saw, that the cavalryman leaned forward to assist him. But before he could be reached Lee had reached the ground, and for a long moment leaned there, bearing heavily against Traveller, as if to gather breath and strength. Imboden was moved:

"The moon shone full upon his massive features and revealed an expression of sadness that I had never before seen upon his face."

It was a moment before Imboden broke the silence: "General, this has been a hard day on you."

"Yes, it has been a sad, sad day to us." Lee dropped his head, then straightened with a sudden animation:

"I never saw troops behave more magnificently than Pickett's Virginians did today in that grand charge. . . . And if they had been supported as they were to have been . . . the day would have been ours."

There was another silence, and then Lee spoke, more loudly, "Too bad! Too bad! Oh, too bad!"

They went into Lee's tent, where Imboden got orders to cover

the retreat with his horsemen, over the mountain by the Chambersburg road, then down to Williamsport. The train of retreat would
be about seventeen miles long, slow with the wagons of stores and
wounded, and would require all of Imboden's men, with all the
guns Lee could spare.

As Imboden took the night's last look at the commander, he
was given a secret duty—he must carry to President Davis a message of such importance that it could not wait, and must be destroyed if he were captured. It was after two o'clock when Lee went
to his bed.

11 A NEW ADVERSARY COMES

THE WEAK SUN of Independence Day shone on the thousands of bodies strewn between the waiting armies.

Men crawled out to search for food. Young Napier Bartlett, with the Washington Artillery of New Orleans, recalled that: "During the whole of this memorable day, and part of the preceding, the men had nothing to eat, and were very often without water. . . . The last bread we tasted was obtained from the dead Federal infantry, whose haversacks were furnished with three days' rations."

The Confederate survivors watched the enemy from Seminary Ridge, with the right curled down to a small stream, Willoughby Run. Hours passed in quiet.

Major Robert Stiles left a vivid complaint: ". . . the dead bodies of men and horses had lain there . . . under the summer sun for three days . . . corpses swollen to twice their original size, some of them actually burst asunder . . . the shocking protrusion of the eyeballs of dead men and dead horses. Several human . . . corpses sat upright against a fence, with arms extended in the air and faces hideous with something very like a fixed leer. . . . The odors were nauseating, and so deadly that in a short time we all sickened and were ly-

249

ing with our mouths close to the ground, most of us vomiting profusely . . . for the rest of that day and late into the night the fearful
odors I had inhaled remained with me and made me loathe myself."

Lee was busy through the morning, writing orders for the plan
of retreat: Hill, then Longstreet, then Ewell; the wagons of
wounded would follow a different route. There were stragglers by
the thousand, and more than 4,000 Federal prisoners, which Lee
tried to have exchanged during the day; Meade did not agree to relieve him of this burden.

Alexander reported that there was but "one day's fighting" left
in the artillery caissons, and Lee thought of nothing but retreat. As
the hours passed it became clear that the Federals were not to molest
him. At one o'clock in the afternoon a rainstorm broke upon the
field. Imboden, struggling to organize his train of ambulances,
fought against the rain:

"The rain fell in blinding sheets, the meadows were soon overflowed, and fences gave way before the raging streams. During the
storm, wagons, ambulances, and artillery carriages by the hundreds
—nay, by the thousands—were assembling in the fields along the
road from Gettysburg to Cashtown in one confused and apparently
inextricable mass. As the afternoon wore on, there was no abate-
ment of the storm. Canvas was no protection against its fury, and
the wounded men, lying upon the naked boards of the wagon bodies
were drenched, horses and mules were blinded and maddened by
the wind and water, and became almost unmanageable."

Colonel Fremantle saw Lee during the pelting storm, sitting
Traveller for a moment or two atop the ridge, looking calmly across
the valley of defeat. In the evening, when he spoke for a few minutes with Longstreet at his roadside camp, he found Old Pete in a
conciliatory mood. Lee repeated his brief sorrowing refrain:

"It's all my fault. I thought my men were invincible."[1]

Fremantle noted that Longstreet did not take up again his

scheme of moving on Washington, but said that the attack had failed only because it was not made in sufficient strength.

The wagon train began moving back toward Virginia at four in the afternoon. When it was well under way in the rain-swept darkness Imboden pushed along the road toward the head, his orders to keep the wagons moving at all costs. The sights along his way were unforgettable:

"From almost every wagon issued heart-rending wails of agony. For four hours I hurried forward on my way to the front, and in all that time I was never out of hearing of the groans and cries of the wounded and dying. Scarcely one in a hundred had received adequate surgical aid. . . . Many of the wounded in the wagons had been without food for 36 hours. Their torn and bloody clothing, matted and hardened, was rasping the tender inflamed . . . wounds. Very few of the wagons had even a layer of straw in them . . . the jolting was enough to have killed strong men long exposed to it.

"From nearly every wagon as the teams trotted on, urged by whip and shout, came . . . cries and shrieks:

" 'Oh, God! Why can't I die?'

" 'My God! Will no one have mercy and kill me!'

" 'Stop . . . just for one minute! Take me out and leave me to die!'

" 'I am dying! My poor wife, my dear children!'

". . . We must move on. The storm continued, and the darkness was appalling. There was no time even to fill a canteen with water for a dying man; for except for the drivers and the guards, all were wounded and utterly helpless in that vast procession of misery. During this one night I realized more of the horrors of war than I had in all the two preceding years."

With the wounded off, and the infantry march under way, Lee broke camp. When the wagons were loaded and all made ready, there was a frenzied search.

"Where is the hen?" someone yelled.

Officers and servants groped about, searching for her, and even Lee joined them. She was found at last, perched in her usual place in a wagon, ready for the journey.[2]

In two days, by July sixth, both the wounded and the leading infantry had neared the Potomac at Williamsport and Hagerstown. Imboden and his teamsters, lashing their horses, had passed through Greencastle, Pennsylvania where the people of the town, perhaps fifty of them, rushed from the houses after the cavalry vanguard had passed and axed the wheels of the wagons carrying wounded, collapsing them in the road. Imboden brought back horsemen in a fury, arrested all the guilty civilians he could find, to be held as prisoners of war; some wagons had to be abandoned.

All this day and the next Union cavalrymen pecked away at the column. There was constant skirmishing between the cavalry escort and the enemy, and often guns were unlimbered to drive off the tormentors. As the caravan rolled across Maryland, approaching Williamsport, there was word that the enemy held the town, but Imboden pushed on and found the rumor false. He took over Williamsport, and put many of his wounded into homes. He commandeered the kitchens, as well, ordering every home to cook for the wounded, or suffer their houses to be seized.

But the Potomac was at flood stage, more than ten feet over fording level. Imboden knew that he must remain on the north bank for several days before getting all of his train over; he had some 10,000 animals with him, virtually all of Lee's wagons, and the thousands of wounded.

A small vanguard of the enemy appeared behind him on July sixth, but Imboden held it at bay with his cooks, teamsters and walking wounded, until Stuart's cavalry came in at nightfall and drove the Federals away.

Ferry boats gathered from up and down the river carried across the wounded, but it was agonizingly slow work, and only a few passed over each day. Engineers built crude scows to help the passage. Lee arrived, and from the north bank urged haste, for though the Army of Northern Virginia was now near Williamsport, the main Federal army would soon be upon it. By July ninth things were better; the 4,000 Federal prisoners were ferried to the south bank that day. Lee sent Imboden to guard them on the way to Richmond.

Imboden left Lee after a conference at Williamsport headquarters. The commander was in a testy humor, ordering the engineers to give up their work on scows and barges, and turn it over to Old John Harmon, who had been Stonewall's remarkable handyman in the field. As Imboden and Lee talked, Longstreet entered the tent, muddy and wet. Lee greeted Old Pete more cordially than usual, the difficulties of Gettysburg evidently forgotten: "Well, my old war horse, what news do you bring us?"

Imboden was so struck by the cordiality of Lee's manner that he heard nothing of Longstreet's report. This scene seemed proof enough that army gossip about ill feeling between the commanders was false.[3]

There were some anxious days before the river could be crossed by the entire army, but Lee showed his concern only in letters. He wrote to Davis:

> I hope Your Excellency will understand that I am not in the least discouraged, or that my faith in the protection of an all-wise Providence, or in the fortitude of this army, is at all shaken. But, though conscious that the enemy has been much shattered in the recent battle, I am aware that he can be easily reinforced, while no addition can be made to our numbers.[4]

He was more candid in writing to Mary:

> You will . . . learn before this reaches you that our success at Gettysburg was not so great as reported—in fact, that we failed to drive the enemy from his position, and that our army withdrew to the Potomac.

Had not the river risen unexpectedly, all would have been well with us; but God . . . willed otherwise, and our communications have been interrupted and almost cut off. . . . I trust that a merciful God, our only hope and refuge, will not desert us in this hour of need.

It appeared that the army's losses at Gettysburg would exceed 20,000, and that the enemy, though he had lost 23,000 or more, was in much better state. It was a miracle that Meade had not followed closely and fallen upon them. On July ninth, in fact, there was word that the main Federal army was coming up. Enemy parties appeared in strength on the roads from Sharpsburg and Boonsboro. Lee put Longstreet's corps into a defensive line, and there was skirmishing in the rear of the bridgehead which was held for the crossing.

More men were ferried over the river each day and at last, on July thirteenth, Major Harmon completed his rickety bridge, a wandering line of planks laid atop scows and barges. The wagons crept across it at a place called Falling Waters; most of the infantry struggled through a deep ford at Williamsport.

There were some moments of peril on this night of July thirteenth. Lee remained on the north bank.

General Alexander said he had never seen Lee "more visibly anxious" than when he was placing Longstreet's men for defense of the crossing two days earlier, but tonight the commander seemed near the breaking point. He had suffered with rheumatism during the Gettysburg campaign, and the rains increased his pain. He sent Longstreet to the south bank to supervise the crossing there, and Old Pete noted that Lee was "worn by the strain of the past two weeks."

A fresh rainstorm broke on the troops just at dusk. There was no moon, and showers poured on the crossing through the black night. The way to the bridge at Falling Waters was new, cut a day or so earlier, and paved with green logs. Men and wagons crept along it. Alexander's artillery made only three miles between darkness and daylight. Longstreet described part of it:

"The rain fell in showers, sometimes in blinding sheets, during the entire night; the wagons cut deep in the mud . . . and began to stall going down hill. . . . We could keep only three or four torches alight, and those were dimmed at times when heavy rains came. Then, to crown our troubles, a load of the wounded came down, missed the end of the bridge, and plunged the wagon into the raging torrent."

Strangely enough, there rang above the roaring of the Potomac and the rain the cheers and laughter of troops.

Lee was in no such mood, and when Colonel Venable of his staff was so indiscreet as to report in a loud voice, within earshot of troops, that things were going badly, Lee gave him a tongue-lashing. Venable went off to his tent to nurse wounded feelings.

Lee, remorseful, sent for Venable to have a glass of buttermilk with him at headquarters, but though the colonel came, he remained in a bad mood.

A few hours later when Lee found Venable lying asleep in the rain near the thronging ford, he threw his poncho over him. Venable was astonished to find the covering when he woke.[5]

At the last moment there was firing from the rear in the darkness, but the men moved ahead and the rearguard held off the pressing enemy. Lee was obviously relieved, and when Stuart brought him some coffee he gulped it down, saying that he had never been so refreshed by anything.

When the army had reached the southern bank of the river he took time to write Mary once more, upon getting news that Rooney, while recuperating from his wound, had been captured by the enemy. He expressed "great grief," but added:

We must bear this additional affliction with fortitude and resignation, and not repine at the will of God. . . . We must bear our labors and hardships manfully. Our noble men are cheerful and confident. I constantly remember you in my thoughts and prayers.

To Rooney's wife, Charlotte, he wrote that he sympathized with her in her distress "and in the lone hours of the night I groan in sorrow and separation from you," but he assured her that Rooney, in the hands of old army officers and surgeons, would be well cared for.

Lee wrote these cheering letters under difficult circumstances. He had lost General Pettigrew in the final moments of the crossing, when the tiny rearguard mistook a Federal party for one of Confederates, and the enemy came near enough to cause brief havoc. At Winchester, where many of the wounded were taken, General Dorsey Pender died of his wounds. The army was depressed, too, by word of disaster in the west, where the fall of Vicksburg gave the enemy absolute control of the Mississippi.

The army rested about Bunker Hill for a few days, and after the Shenandoah receded crossed into Loudoun County and camped around Culpeper. Lee wrote Mary:

> The army has returned to Virginia. Its return is rather sooner than I had originally contemplated, but, having accomplished much . . . relieving the Valley of the presence of the enemy, and drawing his army north of the Potomac—I determined to recross the latter river. . . . It has been raining a great deal since we first crossed the Potomac, making the roads horrid and embarrassing our operations. . . . We are all well. I hope we will yet be able to damage our adversaries when they meet us, and that all will go right with us.

A few days later he wrote Mary that the army had "labored hard, endured much, and behaved nobly. It has accomplished all that could be reasonably expected." It should not have been expected to do the impossible, he added—as if Gettysburg was much on his mind.

No one was disposed to allow the army to forget that climactic battle. General Pickett, bristling at memory of his defeat, sent in a report charging lack of support in the charge of the third day at Gettysburg, but Lee diplomatically returned it to Pickett: "You and your men have covered yourself with glory, but we have the enemy to fight, and must carefully, at this critical moment, guard against dissensions which the reflections in your report would create."[6] He suggested that Pickett destroy all copies of the report, and this was evidently done. But men were already beginning to say that Pickett was becoming a lesser man than he had seemed in his moment of glory at Gettysburg.

Lee was not unaware of growing criticism of the Gettysburg campaign. He wrote Davis in mid-July that he thought the campaign a "general success," though the army did not win a victory. He added: ". . . with the knowledge I then had, and in the circumstances I was then placed, I do not know what better course I could have pursued."

But by August eighth, in camp at Orange, he had come to the conclusion that he should offer to step aside, and in one of the most remarkable letters of his career wrote Davis:

> The general remedy for the want of success in a military commander is his removal. This is natural, and, in many instances, proper. . . .
>
> I have been prompted by these reflections more than once since my return from Pennsylvania to propose to Your Excellency the propriety of selecting another commander for this army. I have seen and heard of expression of discontent in the public journals at the result of the expedition. I do not know how far this feeling extends in the army. My brother officers have been too kind to report it, and so far the troops have been too generous to exhibit it. It is fair, however, to suppose that it does exist, and success is so necessary to us that nothing

should be risked to secure it. I therefore, in all sincerity, request Your Excellency to take measures to supply my place.
I do this with the more earnestness because no one is more
aware than myself of my inability for the duties of my position.
I cannot even accomplish what I myself desire. How can I ful-
fill the expectations of others? In addition I sensibly feel the
growing failure of my bodily strength. I have not yet recovered
from the attack I experienced the past spring. I am becoming
more and more incapable of exertion, and am thus prevented
from making the personal examinations and giving the personal supervision to the operations in the field which I feel to
be necessary. I am so dull in making use of the eyes of others
I am frequently misled. Everything, therefore, points to the advantages to be derived from a new commander, and I the more
anxiously urge the matter upon Your Excellency from my belief that a younger and abler man than myself can readily be
obtained.

There was a good deal more about the bravery of the army and
the able help he had from others, including praises for Davis and
his co-operation, and ending:

I pray that your efforts may at length be crowned with
success, and that you may live to enjoy the thanks of a grateful people.

Almost immediately he had a reply from Davis, enough to reas-
sure him and push him onward. Davis wrote of the voices of the
critics, and said:

Where am I to find that new commander who is to possess
the greater ability which you believe to be required? I do not
doubt the readiness with which you would give way to one
who could accomplish all that you have wished, and you will
do me the justice to believe that if Providence should kindly
offer such a person for our use, I would not hesitate to avail
of his services. . . .

Our country could not bear to lose you. To ask me to sub-
stitute you by some one in my judgment more fit to command, or who would possess more of the confidence of the
army or of the reflecting men of the country, is to demand an
impossibility.[7]

In short, Davis believed that the hopes of the Confederacy were
bound up in Lee, Gettysburg or no. It would be long, and in darker
days, before he could bring himself to relinquish to Lee powers making him commander indeed, but by now Davis was seeing afresh
the realities of his war. He was no such starry-eyed war-maker as he
had been in the spring of '61, when Beauregard had seemed to him
the reincarnation of Napoleon and the savior of the South. He had
found his field general.

Lee attended to the usual accumulation of detested correspondence. He called for more troops to fill the ranks, and for food
and clothing for men at hand. As always, he advised Davis on the
unpromising operations in the west. For the latter purpose, he
agreed to detach some of Longstreet's troops, and sent Old Pete
with them.

One September day Longstreet left Lee's tent, on his way to reinforce General Bragg in Tennessee. Lee followed him to his horse.

"Now, General," Lee said, "you must beat those people out in
the west."

"If I live," Longstreet said, "but I would not give a single man
of my command for a fruitless victory."

Lee promised him support, and reinforcements to follow up
any victory.

By now General Meade had crossed the Potomac and lay in a
strong position north of Culpeper. Lee's skirmishers had brushed
with Federals occasionally, but he had not given up hope of dealing
Meade a major blow.

From his camp near Orange he wrote Mary:

My camp is near Mr. Erasmus Taylor's house, who has been very kind in contributing to our comfort. His wife sends us every day buttermilk, loaf bread, ice, and such vegetables as she has. I can not get her to desist, though I have made two special visits to that effect.

And again, he wrote of Meade, whose presence in Virginia he seemed to find depressing:

I was out looking at him yesterday from Clark's Mountain. He has spread himself over a large surface, and looks immense, but I hope will not prove as formidable as he looks.

The enemy had given Lee time for refitting, but the ranks, now depleted by the departure of Longstreet, could count no more than 44,000. A direct attack on the big Federal army was out of the question, and Lee planned a march by the flank, to move through Culpeper. Before leaving he held a review of his army. Young Robert left a glimpse of it:

"The General was mounted on Traveller, looking very proud of his master, who had on a sash and sword, which he very rarely wore, a pair of new cavalry gauntlets, and, I think, a new hat. . . . The infantry was drawn up in column by divisions . . . their bands playing, awaiting the inspection. . . . General Hill and staff rode up to General Lee, and the two generals, with their respective staffs, galloped around front and rear of each of the three divisions. . . . Traveller started with a long lope, and never changed his stride. His rider sat erect and calm, not noticing anything but the gray lines of men he knew so well. The pace was very fast, as there were nine good miles to go. . . . When the General drew up . . . flushed with exercise . . . he raised his hat and saluted. Then arose a shout of applause and admiration from the entire assemblage. . . . The corps was then passed in review at a quick-step."

After this review Lee rode among the carriages of spectators, and in one found Robert sitting with some pretty girls. The commander shook hands with the onlookers, and soon went to his tent. It was one of his last rides for many days.

He was so plagued with rheumatism that he could scarcely take part in the unfolding movement of the army, which was the flanking march he had ordered—a wide sweep of about forty-one miles to Culpeper. He could not ride, and was forced to follow the regiments in a wagon.

There was a final tragedy before headquarters left Orange. The faithful egg-a-day hen was killed. One day when the general had an important dinner guest the mess steward, Bryan, "very inhumanly" butchered the hen. It was only a day or so after the delicious meal that Lee and the staff discovered Bryan's crime. Headquarters mess was now without its customary morning egg for the commander.

Though Lee rode after the army in a rear wagon, it was soon clear to him that the march against the enemy was futile. Federal cavalry was everywhere, so that the commander knew he was expected. It seemed that Richmond newspapers had warned the Federals by publishing camp gossip of the bold thrust by the small, worn army against the large, amply reinforced invading force.

By the time Lee reached Culpeper, General Meade, seeing the potential danger of the Confederate move, had pulled back from the town, recrossed the Rappahannock, and was in strong position once more.

Lee had a brief skirmish with a town gossip as his wagon jolted into Culpeper.

People flocked about him, especially ladies of the village. Among them was one who chattered in outrage about the friendly relations between pretty girls of the town and the Yankees, who had just decamped. In particular, the woman told Lee grimly, two pretty girls who stood blushing before him had been in the habit of visiting General Sedgwick's headquarters. What did the commander think of that?

Lee's face was solemn enough to frighten the girls, but he said, "I know General Sedgwick very well. It is just like him to be so kind and considerate, and to have his band there to entertain them. So, young ladies, if the music is good, go and hear it as often as you can, and enjoy yourselves. You will find that General Sedgwick will have none but agreeable gentlemen about him."

The army got little rest in Culpeper, for Lee's eye detected yet another flaw in Meade's position, and he sent the infantry off again. His bold plans for turning the Federal army out of position seemed interminable. This time, the army was to sweep by fast marches to the neighborhood of Warrenton and take commanding ground. There was constant cavalry action as the move went forward.

Stuart got into a second fight at Brandy Station and gave a good account of himself, but in the confusing marching of the big Federal corps on the roads all about him, he found himself in a trap, caught with most of his troopers between two moving wings of the Federal army, which were going northeast from Warrenton toward Bristoe Station.

To the camp near Warrenton, where Lee remained awake, anxious for Stuart, came one Goode, a scout, who explained the predicament of the cavalry: Stuart was now hidden from the enemy, but could escape only if Lee turned artillery fire on the Federal column near the village of Auburn, creating a diversion. Lee listened to Goode's story and went into his tent. Within a few moments he overheard the scout outside, discussing with one of his aides the situation of Stuart, and telling of the point where cannon fire must be placed to save the cavalry.

Lee instantly reappeared, and shouted in anger, "I will not have scouts talking in my camp, sir!" He disappeared.

Major Venable saw Goode's dismay at the scolding for violating the army rule that such reports must be made only to the commanding general, and went in to Lee, explaining that the man was simply trying to give an accurate point for the artillery fire, in hopes of aiding Stuart. Lee was at once repentant. He popped out of the tent, apologized to Goode and ordered supper for the scout. He placed Goode in his own chair at the mess table, and stood nearby talking with him as he ate.[8]

During the night he sent Ewell's infantrymen out to help Stuart, who in the morning escaped to Warrenton. The pursuit of Meade continued but it ended badly. A. P. Hill was in the lead when the men reached Bristoe Station; he placed two brigades in line to cross a tiny stream, Broad Run, along the Orange and Alexandria Railroad. The enemy appeared to be retreating, and the men were ordered forward. They had arrived in a mood of anticipation. A captain of the 27th North Carolina recalled:

"It was almost like boys chasing a hare. Though the march was very rapid not a straggler left the ranks . . . every man seeming in earnest and confident in the belief that we would soon overtake and capture a portion of the Federal army before us with their wagon train."

These men, looking for loot, were instead torn to pieces by fire from a heavy force of Federals on their flank, and no support was sent to aid them. General Cooke, advancing with his handful under orders, protested mildly: "Well, I will advance, and if they flank me, I will face my men about and cut my way out."[9]

In a brief, painful fight of less than an hour, with the attack exposed to crossfire, the army lost almost 1,400 men. Lee was late in reaching the scene, and when Hill pointed out the scene of the fight and reasons for failure and sought to explain, Lee said only, "Well, well, General, bury these poor men and let us say no more about it."

The campaign had evidently come to an end, with the final fillip given by Stuart and Fitz Lee, who chased back Federal cavalry on a network of roads near Warrenton in a running skirmish known as the Buckland Races; this brought in 250 prisoners, but little else, and the army returned south of the Rappahannock. Lee and the army suffered alike.

In a letter to Mary he said that he had been forced to give up the chase of Meade out of pity for the men:

> It would have only served to fatigue our troops by advancing farther . . . thousands were barefooted, thousands with fragments of shoes, and all without overcoats, blankets or warm clothing. I could not bear to expose them to certain suffering on an uncertain issue.

His rheumatism became worse, but he at first told his wife nothing of it:

> I moved yesterday into a nice pine thicket, and Perry is today engaged in constructing a chimney in front of my tent which will make it warm and comfortable. . . . I am glad you have some socks for the army . . . I wish they could make some shoes, too. We have thousands of barefooted men. There is no news. General Meade, I believe, is repairing the railroad, and I presume will come on again. If I could only get some shoes and clothes for the men I would save him the trouble.

He was well enough on November fifth to review his cavalry for Stuart, and on that day wrote Mary that "I think my rheumatism is better." He had wanted to review the cavalry for some time, but had named this day "with fear and trembling," because for five days he had been so tormented with pain that he could not ride. To his surprise, he got along well at the review—which was also attended by Governor John Letcher, who brought news of Mary.

Two days later Lee went to the Rappahannock, where Federals had crossed at Kellys Ford. Though they faced an entrenched line, where General Rodes' division was on duty, they posed a threat, and Lee remained close at hand to direct affairs. He spent many hours at Rappahannock Bridge nearby, where he had a couple of brigades holding a small area north of the river, with more trenches and field works. As the enemy moved against these, he put over more men, until he had seven brigades in the bridgehead. They seemed safe enough, but on November seventh, just after dark, when Lee had concluded the day's fighting was over, a mass attack captured all but a few of these men; more, Federals in growing strength had crossed near Kellys Ford on quickly built pontoon bridges. For the third time Meade had bested him. He pulled the army out of its comfortable huts and marched it back south of the Rapidan to safety and the long weeks of work were for naught.

Colonel Walter Taylor of the headquarters staff made no effort to conceal his disgust at the failures against Meade, probably typical views of the army:

"Our people were not put into battle correctly . . . by unpardonable mismanagement the enemy was allowed to capture five pieces of our artillery. There was no earthly excuse for it . . . "

The capture of 1,200 men at Rappahannock Bridge, he said, was "the saddest chapter in the history of this army."

A day or so after the army dug in on the Rapidan, and the men began to build new huts for the winter, Lee replied to the President of Richmond's City Council, who had offered him a house for the use of his family:

> I assure you, sir, that no want of appreciation of the honor . . . or insensibility of the kind feeling that prompted it, induces me to ask . . . that no further proceedings be taken with reference to the subject. The house is not necessary for the use of my family, and my own duties will prevent my residence in Richmond. I shall therefore be compelled to decline the generous offer, and that (it) . . . may be devoted to the relief of the families of our soldiers in the field who are now in need . . . and more deserving of it than myself.[10]

Lee was unable to leave the army, with Meade so near, and when called to Richmond to confer with Davis, he asked the President to come to camp instead. They were together for three days, talking over the military situation here and in the west, where things had been growing worse since the surprising victory of Chickamauga shortly after Longstreet's arrival on that front. Lee wanted to give Davis a review of the army, but bad weather prevented it. The troops were still shabby, in any event, and more hungry by the day.

Lee was keenly aware of the failing strength of the men, and most of his concern, in the talks with Davis, was for improving the supplies of food and clothing; he passed clear warnings that the fate of the capital and the entire Confederacy hung upon this. Lee's frugal headquarters mess was in keeping with the suffering of the men.

Meat was served only twice a week in Lee's tent; the commander refused to allow it more often because of the impoverished condition of the army and country. His usual dinner in this camp was a head of cabbage boiled in salt water, with a piece of cornbread.

One day, however, he was expecting distinguished guests, and in "a fit of extravagance," Lee ordered cabbage served with slabs of "middling meat." When the guests had been seated, Bryan brought a platter of cabbage, in a great steaming pile. Atop this rested a bit of the tough red pork, about four inches long and two inches wide. The polite guests, in turn, took cabbage and declined the delicacy of meat, and Lee himself left it untouched.

The next day, remembering the middling, he asked a servant to bring it, and drew the reply, "The fact is, Master Robert, that there was borried middlin'. We didn't have a speck, and I done paid it back to the man where I got it from."[11]

Lee also gave an indication, during these days, that he had by no means forgotten the army's tragedy at Gettysburg. He talked of this to General Henry Heth one day:

"After it is all over, as stupid a fellow as I am can see the mistakes that were made," Lee said. "I notice, however, my mistakes are never told me until it is too late, and you, and all my officers, know that I am always ready and anxious to have their suggestions."[12]

Heth said that Lee thought the Army of Northern Virginia capable of anything at this time, and that he was confident of the future despite the dark outlook.

The commander was, in fact, smarting under the inability of the army to punish Meade since Gettysburg, and more than once he rode down the Rapidan, peering across at the enemy, pondering some means of striking him. One day he went out with Ewell and Early and General John Pegram, followed by a party of staff officers. The group trotted down the line of riverside hills, discussing artillery positions there. Lee halted on a hill from which he had an unusual view of the camps of the enemy across the stream. He swept a hand at the scene, still thinking, perhaps, of the painful loss of men at the Rappahannock Bridge:

"What is there to prevent our cutting off and destroying the people in these nearer camps on this side of that hill, before those back yonder could get to them to help them?"

Early answered him. "This infernal river. How are you going to cross that without giving warning?"

"Ford it, sir. Ford it!"

"What are you going to do with your pneumonia patients?" Early asked.

Ewell and Pegram joined Early, and there was a brief discussion of the possibility of crossing to hit the Federals. Onlookers, including Major Robert Stiles, thought that Lee had not seriously considered the crossing, but was nettled by the recent stabs of the enemy, and looking for the least opportunity of reprisal.

On the cold, foggy night of November twenty-fourth Lee had a report that Federal troops were cooking rations for eight days— a sure sign of coming movement. He made ready for what he had

assumed Meade must do—cross at Germanna Ford and strike
through the Wilderness at the vital Richmond and Fredericksburg
Railroad. That seemed almost the only logical move, for it would
be foolhardy on this terrain to launch an attack on the Army of
Northern Virginia, which could dig in and minimize the Federal
advantage of numbers. Colonel Taylor wrote on November twenty-
fifth:

"We are just on the eve of another move. This morning and
afternoon . . . the enemy is moving down the river, and we have
been busy preparing for a counter-move in the same direction. Matters seem to be drifting toward our old and renowned battlefields,
Chancellorsville and Fredericksburg. . . . There will be a clash somewhere. . . . We have all our arrangements made to move before
dawn in the morning."

Once more the men left their new huts, and were in haste
pushed downriver. Lee, amid the grumbling of his staff, was up at
three A.M. and riding in weather so cold that ice formed in the
beards of the officers. Lee found no enemy at the village of Verdiersville, where he expected him, but he roused Stuart and had him
cover the roads nearby with the cavalry, groping toward Chancellorsville and Spotsylvania Courthouse. In the day's fumbling movements, there were a series of skirmishing actions along the bank of
the Rapidan, and it was some time before Lee could fathom
Meade's intentions. He was becoming convinced, though slowly,
that the big Federal army would not strike for the railroad, after all,
but would come to grips with the Army of Northern Virginia.

Taylor described Lee's Sunday ride along the lines, when he
had finally pulled the army to the west side of Mine Run, and was
waiting for the enemy to come up the Rapidan against it:

"On Sunday, as we were riding down the lines, attended by
General Hill with his staff and others, we came upon a collection of
men engaged in divine worship. We had been riding at a pretty fair
gait, but the general at once halted, and listened to the singing of

the men. He heard the entire hymn, and as the benediction was pronounced, reverently raised his hat from his head, received the blessings, and then continued his ride along the fortifications.

"It was a striking scene. . . . The parapet was crowded with men; here and there at proper intervals waved the battle-flags; and from many dozen embrasures frowned the now silent artillery . . . it was a cheering thing to see that, while ready for action, our men did not forget that, to secure victory, divine help should be implored."[13]

Still the enemy's behavior was puzzling, and the armies now faced each other, furiously digging trenches and throwing up banks of earth. In the bitter night of December first, when the very canteens of the troops had frozen, Lee detached two divisions for use in a flank assault, and put the men in the trenches on the alert for the next day's action.

Daylight brought astonishing news: The enemy had gone. Lee seemed to feel that this was the climax of a wasted fall and winter, and could not conceal his chagrin.

"I am too old to command this army," he said angrily. "We should never have permitted those people to get away."[14]

Colonel Venable, who was at his elbow, thought Lee was feeling something he could not say aloud. "In his heart he was sighing for that 'right arm' which he threw around Hooker at Chancellorsville"—Jackson.

Lee ordered a pursuit in the cold morning, but by the time skirmishers reached the Rapidan, Meade had his columns safely across, and the strange little campaign was at an end. Lee had almost nothing to show for the last maneuver about Mine Run, for all his watchfulness: Some 700 prisoners, 400 horses and mules, about 150 wagons. The enemy's casualties reached about 1,000. Both armies went back to life in the huts and tents.

Lee wrote Mary, explaining in detail the moves of Meade, ending:

I am greatly disappointed at his getting off with so little damage, but we do not know what is best for us. I believe a kind God has ordered all things for our own good.

He was then deep in a serious correspondence with Davis, who was appalled at the collapse of the Confederate effort in Tennessee, where the Union army under Grant seemed to threaten ruin. Lee had given his advice, and suggested a first-rate commander for the western army; Davis countered by proposing that Lee go there. Davis called Lee to Richmond on December ninth—Lee fearful that he was being removed from his army. He gave a hint of this in a message to Stuart as he left: "My heart and thoughts will always be with this army."

He found Mary and their daughter Agnes in cramped quarters, pinched by shortages of food; and Mary was suffering terribly with her arthritis. Lee was himself in pain, but his presence evidently inspired the people of the city, as he appeared on the streets and at church, and on occasion at evening gatherings. The diarist Mrs. Chesnut recorded:

"General Lee told us what a good son Custis was. Last night the house was so crowded Custis gave up his own bed to General Lee and slept on the floor. Otherwise General Lee would have had to sleep in Mrs. Lee's room. She is a martyr to rheumatism, and rides about in a chair. She can't walk.

"Constance Cary says: 'If it pleased God to take poor Cousin Mary Lee—she suffers so—wouldn't these Richmond women campaign for Cousin Robert?'

"In the meantime Cousin Robert holds all admiring females at arm's length."

Mrs. Chesnut did once report, however, that she observed Lee holding hands with the charming Constance.

On December fifteenth Lee inspected Richmond's defenses with Davis, who had by now agreed to place Joseph E. Johnston in command in the west. Lee was free to rejoin his army. He returned to the huts along the Rapidan to share the Christmas holidays with his men. He had hardly arrived when he had news of the death of Rooney's wife, Charlotte, and her two children. He wrote Mary:

> It has pleased God to take from us one exceedingly dear to us, and we must be resigned to his holy will. . . . Thus is link by link of the strong chain broken that binds us to earth, and smooths our passage to another world. Oh, that we may be at last united in that haven of rest, where trouble and sorrow never enter. . . . I grieve for our lost darling as a father only can grieve for a daughter, and my sorrow is heightened by the thought of the anguish her death will cause our dear son, and the poignancy it will give to the bars of his prison.

As the weeks dragged on, the army's suffering increased. In late January, Lee wrote that he had been forced to disperse the cavalry so that forage could be had for the horses: the country was picked clean for many miles. He added:

> Provisions for the men, too, are very scarce, and with very light diet and light clothing I fear they suffer; but still they are cheerful and uncomplaining. I received a report from one division the other day in which it was stated that over four hundred men were barefooted and over a thousand without blankets.

He got occasional gifts from Richmond, chiefly food and clothing. Once, when he got a bag of gloves and socks and a box of coffee from Mary, he returned the coffee, saying that since a friend had given it to her, it was not intended for him. He explained a bit of the lore of army substitutions:

> It is so long since we have had the foreign bean that we no longer desire it. We have a domestic article, which we procure by the bushel, that answers very well. You must keep the good things for yourself.

The army ration of meat was cut in half, and on many days there was none.

Once or twice more during the winter, Lee appeared in Richmond to confer with Davis, and the contrast between camp life and that of the city, which thought itself in dire straits, was striking. Mrs. Chesnut's diary recorded several revealing moments:

"January 21 . . . to the President's reception, and from there to a ball at the McFarlands'. Breckinridge alone of the generals was with us. . . . I had a long talk with Mr. Ould, Mr. Benjamin and Mr. Hunter. These men speak out their thoughts plainly enough: What they said means: 'We are rattling down hill, and nobody to put on the brakes.'

"January 31: Mrs. Davis gave her 'Luncheon to Ladies' on Saturday . . . we had gumbo, ducks and olives, supreme de volaille, chickens in jelly, oysters, lettuce salad, chocolate cream, jelly cake, claret cup, champagne."

On February twenty-third Mrs. Chesnut again saw Lee:

"At the President's. General Lee breakfasted there. A man named Phelan told him all he ought to do, planned a campaign for him. General Lee smiled blandly all the while, though he did permit himself a mild sneer at the wise civilians in Congress who refrained from trying the battlefield in person, but from afar detailed the movements of armies."

In early March Mrs. Chestnut wrote: "Somebody counted fourteen generals in church, and suggested that less piety and more drilling of commands would suit the times better. There were Lee, Longstreet, Morgan, Hoke, Clingman, Whiting, Pegram, Elzey, Gordon, Bragg, and I forget the others."[15]

It was about this time that Meade sought to hoodwink Lee— and did so, briefly, in order to launch a cavalry raid against Richmond. While the Federal army threatened attack on the left flank, and Confederates hurried to meet the threat, some 4,000 bluecoat riders under young General Judson Kilpatrick slipped over the

Rapidan at Ely's Ford, on February twenty-eighth, and dashed through the country toward the capital. It was not easy going for the marauders.

The long column went through Spotsylvania Court House and the Wilderness, with the rain freezing on trees and animals and men suffering—by this time their ranks reduced by 500, because Ulric Dahlgren, the youngest Federal colonel, a charming boy of twenty-one with a wooden leg, took a party off to stab into Richmond and create havoc.

Kilpatrick took the horsemen down to Beaver Dam Station, where an unpleasant night was passed in hanging over fires in an effort to stay alive. The next day, with a few guns, the invaders banged away at the Richmond defenses in front, opposed by gunfire from what they supposed were only government clerks—but they were driven off. By afternoon, when Kilpatrick tried it again he had a nasty surprise: his charge was met by the hard-fighting veterans of Wade Hampton, brought down to meet them. Kilpatrick turned back, wondering what had come of young Dahlgren.

The youthful colonel's column had come to grief after a swift march of burning houses and mills down to the James, where Dahlgren had permitted himself the pleasure of chatting and drinking wine with the wife of Secretary of War Seddon in her plantation house. A young Negro, picked up as a guide, had been hanged by Dahlgren when they came to an impossible river crossing and the riders were forced to turn back, running for life. In the end, with the column split up, Dahlgren had been shot down by the closing Rebels, a finger cut off to steal a ring, his wooden leg taken as a souvenir—and in his pocket were found orders which became a raging sensation in Richmond: the raiders were to burn and sack the city, kill Davis and his Cabinet.

Lee wrote to Meade, asking if this were a genuine document; Meade denied that war had been planned on civilians. There was little further excitement for the winter.

Lee passed his time in the endless paper work of the army, for he had now only Colonels Chilton, Venable, Marshall and Taylor, and five headquarters clerks. They were kept busy with promotions of officers, reorganizing of army units, pleas for more food and clothing and ammunition. They led the same simple life Lee preferred, within sight of the suffering troops.

He went often to the height of Clark Mountain, to stare down at the far tents of the enemy, whose peaceful smoke floated off in strong, crisp winds, promising inactivity until the return of warm weather.

His wife once urged him to add Robert to his staff, and drew this reply:

> In reference to Rob, his company would be a great pleasure and comfort to me, and he would be extremely useful in various ways, but I am opposed to officers surrounding themselves with their sons and relatives. It is wrong in principle. . . . I should prefer Rob's being in the line in an independent position, where he could rise by his own merit and not through the recommendation of relatives.
>
> I expect him here soon, when I can better see what he himself thinks. The young men have no fondness for the society of the old general. He is too heavy and sombre for them.

He soon wrote to Rob, after his nephew, Fitz, had taken his cavalry off on a hard ride—but had hurried back to Charlottesville to attend a ball:

> Tell Fitz I grieve over the hardships and sufferings of his men. . . . I am afraid he was anxious to get back to the ball. This is a bad time for such things. We have too grave subjects on hand to engage in such trivial amusements. I would rather his officers should entertain themselves in fattening their horses, healing their men, and recruiting their regiments. There are too many Lees on the committee. I like them all to be present at battles, but can excuse them at balls.

Mrs. Lee and Mildred, forever sending him socks, gloves and other clothing for the army, always drew his appreciation, but he once or twice complained. He returned to the army from a Richmond visit carrying 67 pairs of socks. He wrote Mary:

> One dozen of the Stuart socks had double heels. Can you not teach Mildred that stitch?

Again he wrote:

> Your note with the socks arrived last evening. I have sent them to the Stonewall Brigade; the number all right—thirty pairs. . . . I have sent to that brigade two hundred and sixty-three pairs. Still, there are about one hundred and forty whose homes are within the enemy's lines and who are without socks. I shall continue to furnish them till all are supplied. Tell the young women to work hard for the Stonewallers.

Growing troubles in Richmond drew his attention now, for the President kept him close to the situation in the south and west, which was still grim and unpromising.

Mrs. Chesnut caught a hint of despair in high places:

"Everybody is in trouble. Mrs. Davis says paper money has depreciated so in value they cannot live within their income, so they are going to give up their carriage and horses."

She also recorded a bit of army gossip she heard from her friend with the imperious manner, General Wade Hampton of the cavalry:

"When I got home, General Hampton came with his troubles. Stuart had taken one of Hampton's brigades and given it to Fitzhugh Lee. General Hampton complained of this to General Lee, who told him curtly: 'I would not care if you went back to South Carolina with your whole division.' Wade said his manner made this speech immensely mortifying.

"While General Hampton was talking to me, the President

sent for him. It seems General Lee has no patience with any personal complaints or grievances. He is all for the cause, and cannot bear officers to come to him with any such matters as Wade Hampton had come to him about."[16]

The sharp-eyed South Carolina woman also found Mrs. Davis "utterly depressed" within a few days, and predicting the fall of Richmond. And the whole town was soon disturbed by the movement of Secretary Memminger's female Treasury Department clerks to Columbia, South Carolina. Mrs. Chesnut said, "that looks squally!"

Near the coming of spring, Longstreet came back to the army, but he lacked the glamor he had when he had gone west, even though he had carried the Gettysburg defeat with him. Affairs had gone from bad to worse in the west, and Longstreet became so involved in bickering between generals that he came back to Virginia with three of his commanders under arrest.

In March came compelling news from the enemy camps: Meade was replaced. The new commander, this one to direct all the Federal armies, was U. S. Grant, the conqueror from the west. The Army of Northern Virginia knew nothing about him, but stories were soon passed among the ragged privates, who could sniff action ahead.

They said that Grant had come down to his new army and had caught sight of Meade's splendid Solferino flag, emblazoned with a golden eagle and a silver wreath, and the grizzled little man, unkempt in a private's blouse and with only the plain stars on his shoulders, had exclaimed to his staff, "What's this: Is Imperial Caesar anywhere about?"

Lee seemed to realize what the coming of Grant meant for the army. He wrote Davis:

Indications that operations in Virginia will be vigorously prosecuted by the enemy are stronger than they were. General

Grant has returned from the army in the West. He is, at present, with the Army of the Potomac, which is being reorganized and recruited. From the reports of our scouts the impression prevails in that army that he will operate it in the coming campaign. Every train brings it recruits, and . . . every available regiment at the North is added to it. . . . everything shows secrecy and preparation. . . . I think we can assume that if General Grant is to direct operations on this frontier he will concentrate a large force. . . . The time is also near at hand when I shall require all the troops belonging to this army.[17]

On April thirtieth he again wrote the President:

Everything indicates a concerted attack on this front which renders me the more anxious to get back the troops belonging to this army.

The extra baggage wagons were sent to the rear, ammunition was passed out, and the army was as nearly ready as Lee could make it. One night, just before the opening of the new campaign, a four-horse wagon drew up at his tent, with the 26th North Carolina's band playing in it. Lee invited the regiment's colonel inside, and candidly talked over the situation.

"We will not be idle many days," Lee said. "Grant is making preparations to cross . . . if I could only strike him with my center, I could make him recross in a way not so pleasant to him. . . . I could reinforce from each wing."

And at last, absently, hearing the loyal band outside, blaring away, he said to the colonel, "I don't believe we can have an army without music."[18]

12 *THROUGH THE WILDERNESS*

THE ARMY had changed almost beyond recognition, as if it had grown old. Lee welcomed back Longstreet's men on April twenty-ninth in a review near Gordonsville, and here men could see a difference in the army. There was none of the old spirit of boyishness; instead, there was a demonstration of affection between Lee and the men which was almost maudlin. Years later General Alexander recalled the moment:

"Lee . . . bares his good gray head and looks at us and we give the 'rebel yell' and shout and cry and wave our flags and look at him once more."

But after that, there was no loud calling during the review. The silence seemed to Alexander "a wave of sentiment . . . the effect was as of a military sacrament."

The young artillery general overheard a South Carolina chaplain, the Rev. Boggs, in conversation with Colonel Charles Venable of Lee's staff, as they watched the men pass before their commander.

"Doesn't it make the General proud to see how these men love him?" Boggs asked.

"Not proud," Venable said. "It awes him."

And a South Carolina private pictured the Old Man overcome by his emotions:

"The men hung around him and seemed satisfied to lay their hands on his gray horse or to touch the bridle, or the stirrup, or the old general's leg—anything that Lee had was sacred to us fellows who had just come back. And the General—he could not help from breaking down . . . tears traced down his cheeks, and he felt that we were again to do his bidding."[1]

Only the day before, Lee had revealed in a letter to his favorite young cousin, Margaret Stuart, that he could glimpse fighting ahead:

> . . . you must sometimes cast your thoughts on the Army of Northern Virginia, and never forget it in your prayers. It is preparing for a great struggle, but I pray and trust that the great God, mighty to deliver, will spread over it His almighty arms, and drive its enemies before it.

It was perhaps the same day that Lee went to the signal station atop Clark's Mountain, where he had gone so often in the winter to look down upon the distant enemy camps. This time he had President Davis with him, on a visit of inspection to the army. They rode to the signal tower with staff officers. Lee pointed out the Federal camp and its recent changes to Davis.

"I think those people over there are going to make a move soon," he said.

He turned to the soldier on duty, Sergeant B. L. Wynn of Mississippi.

"Sergeant, do you keep a guard on watch at night?"

"No, sir."

"Well, you must put one on."

It was not long before the sergeant understood the wisdom of the order.

A day or so later, on May second, Lee returned to the mountaintop, and this time brought all the corps and division commanders. He sat with them as they studied the enemy camps with their glasses, hearing their opinions as to the probable direction of the coming attack by the enemy, which all expected. Despite signs of Federal activity upstream, Lee's hand pointed in the opposite direction, and he told his officers that he expected Grant to move against their right, by way of Ely's and Germanna Fords.

Sergeant Wynn was almost the first man to detect the movement of General Grant, in the last hours of May third:

"About midnight . . . the guard called me to the glass.

"Occasionally I could catch glimpses of troops as they passed between me and their campfires, but could not make out in which direction they were moving."

Wynn's signal lights began to blink in the darkness: "I signaled to General Lee at once what I saw."

There were answering flickers from the grove near Orange Court House where Lee made headquarters, far below Wynn's post:

"He asked me if I could make out whether they were coming toward Germanna Ford or Liberty Mills. I replied that I could not. His next message was that I make a report to him as early in the morning as possible."

At about two A.M. another message blinked from Lee's headquarters to the mountaintop, to be relayed on beyond:

General Ewell, have your command ready to move by daylight.

With the coming of daybreak, May fourth, Wynn and his sleepy assistant were still busy:

"I signaled General Lee that the enemy was moving down the river. Clouds of dust were rising from all the roads leading southeast and toward Fredericksburg, and that Germanna Ford seemed to be their objective point."[2]

With Grant looking over his shoulder as commander-in-chief, Meade had pushed the Federal army forward, across the Rapidan, down the old path of last year's butchery, just where Lee had expected attack to come.

The oncoming Federal army was 102,000 strong, soon to be raised to 116,000. There were 4,000 wagons and 50,000 horses, and all of it, infantry, cavalry and wagon train, passed the Rapidan on May fourth and made twelve miles into the forbidding Wilderness, virtually undisturbed. While Lee was hurrying his columns into position at the end of the day, Grant was announcing his pleasure and surprise to his staff.

About 64,000 Confederates were in the Army of Northern Virginia. Lee had faced such odds before, and now seemed even anxious to meet his new foe in the blind thickets of the Wilderness. His men already sensed that this meeting with the enemy was to be different, however; there was gossip in the ranks that Grant had left all his sutlers behind, with their wagons of luxuries, so that there would be none of that glorious looting. Equally ominous, there would be no further exchange of prisoners. Grant sounded like grim fight, as if the old war had not been to his taste.

Lee rode with Hill's men down the old Plank Road, so familiar to the survivors of Chancellorsville. Near him, on the parallel Turnpike, was Ewell. Altogether, on these roads and nearby, Lee had no more than 30,000 men, including cavalry. Even if the enemy came up unexpectedly, he could muster no more strength until Longstreet came in from Gordonsville.

Lee camped at the village of Verdiersville where he was awake much of the night, reading dispatches. There was a long one, full of unconcealed fears, from President Davis: The enemy had landed a big force below Richmond on the James, at Bermuda Hundred; there was a move by the Federal General Sigel up the Shenandoah, evidently aimed at Lee's western flank. There were other signs of Federal attack in co-ordination. But Lee's attention remained focused on the approaching peril in the Wilderness, which he saw as the true threat to Richmond.

There was a message from Longstreet early in the evening: Old Pete was on the North Anna in camp, and could be with Lee early the next afternoon. That was what Lee wanted to hear—and he immediately sent orders to Ewell: Attack. When Colonel Taylor took the order to Ewell he added verbally, "The General's desire is to bring him to battle as soon now as possible."[3]

There were bleached skulls and skeletons in the greening brush when men made their fires in the undergrowth, and the cries of whippoorwills reminded veterans of the battle of last May in this place, when the army had lost Jackson.

Lee was moving before daylight on May fifth. Prospects seemed to cheer the Old Man, Colonel Venable noted at breakfast:

"General Lee, though generally reticent at table on military affairs, spoke very cheerfully of the situation. . . . He expressed his pleasure that the Federal general had not profited by General Hooker's Wilderness experiences, and that he seemed inclined to throw away . . . the immense advantage which his great superiority in numbers . . . gave him."

Stuart and some of his horsemen led the way down the Plank Road, with A. P. Hill's corps close behind; Lee rode with the vanguard of this infantry. Ewell's corps was on the parallel route of the Turnpike. In the first hours there were no signs of the enemy.

Men of the two armies would not forget this terrain.

A young Confederate who saw it wrote:

"It is in places level and marshy . . . but for the most part rugged or rolling, with very few fields of thin soil, easily washing into gullies, and still fewer houses scattered here and there . . . in some places . . . pine with low spreading branches, through which a horseman cannot force his way without much turning and twisting, but generally the oak predominates. In many places the large trees had been cut down in years past and a jungle of switch had sprung up ten or twenty feet high, more impenetrable, if possible, than the pine. . . . There is no range for artillery."

About noon Lee got first real news of the enemy. Stuart met Federal troopers ahead, and there was firing. An infantry brigade under North Carolina's General Kirkland pushed back the blue horsemen.

A few minutes later Ewell reported that he could see infantry columns from the Turnpike, moving southeast toward the Plank Road.

Lee could not know that Grant, having seen and interpreted his signals, had moved directly upon the Confederate army, seeking battle. Just at noon the prelude came, in heavy firing near Parker's Store. Hill's advance was in furious action. Lee rode up with Hill and Stuart to a knoll to study the situation. The corps of Ewell and Hill were now separated, since their roads had turned apart, and from the gusts of firing in the thickets, no one could make out what was going on. It was clear that the enemy was pouring more and more men into the action, and that battles raged along both the Plank Road and the Turnpike.

General Gordon recorded his remarkable work of this day, May fifth, after he had charged up from the rear, meeting Ewell's men being driven back:

"These retreating divisions, like broken and receding waves, rolled back against the head of my column while we were still rapidly advancing along the narrow road. . . . At this moment of dire extremity I saw General Ewell . . . riding in furious gallop. . . .

" 'General Gordon, the fate of the day depends on you, sir,' he said.

" 'These men will save it, sir,' I replied. . . . Swiftly riding to the center of my line, I gave in person the order: 'Forward!'

"With a deafening yell which must have been heard miles away, that glorious brigade rushed upon the . . . enemy, and by the

shock of their furious onset shattered into fragments all that portion of the compact Union line which confronted my troops."

But this Federal army was somehow different today—Hooker's
men, or Pope's or McClellan's once driven back in one sector,
might have broken down the entire line. Grant's lines did not budge
on either side of Gordon, to his consternation:

"At that moment was presented one of the strangest conditions
ever witnessed upon a battlefield. . . . My command had cut its way
through the Union center, and at that moment it was in the . . .
strange position of being on identically the same general line with
the enemy, the Confederates facing in one direction, the Federals
in the other."

Gordon was perplexed. He could neither advance nor retreat,
and devised a solution to prevent disaster: ". . . before the Union
veterans could recover from the shock, my regiments were moving
. . . right and left, thus placing them in two parallel lines, back to
back. . . .

"This done, the wings were ordered forward, and, with another
piercing yell, they rushed in . . . upon the right and left flanks of the
astounded Federals, shattering them . . . capturing large numbers,
and checking any further effort by General Grant on that portion
of the field."

In other quarters fighting was equally furious. Private Warren
Goss of the Federal army saw much of it:

"No one could see the fight fifty feet from him. The roll and
crackle of musketry was something terrible. . . . The lines were very
near each other, and from the dense underbrush and the tops of the
trees came puffs of smoke, the 'ping' of the bullets and the yell of
the enemy. It was a blind and bloody hunt to the death, in bewilder-
ing thickets, rather than a battle. . . .

"It was next to impossible to preserve a distinct line, and we
were constantly broken into small groups. The underbrush and
briars scratched our faces, tore our clothing, and tripped our

feet. . . . Two, three and four times we rushed upon the enemy, but were met by a murderous fire and with heavy loss from concealed enemies. As often as we rushed forward we were compelled to get back. . . . The uproar of battle continued through the twilight hours. It was eight o'clock before the deadly crackle of musketry died gradually away. . . . The groans and cries for water or for help from the wounded gave place to the sounds of the conflict. . . . Our lines now faced westward."

The brush caught fire in the night, and the wounded who were able limped and crawled away from the flames.

By nightfall Lee was aware of his danger. The wings of Hill and Ewell were now well apart, lying across each of their roads, with a yawning gap between. Longstreet, behind schedule and at some distance from the field, could not come through the rough country in time to plug the hole before dawn brought fresh attacks from the enemy.

All reports were of lines pushed to the utmost, and now lying in such irregular form as to make it impossible to straighten them before morning. A. P. Hill's estimate was that his corps, of less than 15,000, had faced some 40,000 Federal troops.

Lee's tent was placed just off the Plank Road, near the Widow Tapp's house. Hill's men were all about him, and to the northwest was the line of Ewell. The marshy and broken ravine country of Wilderness Run split the line.

Lee did not seem concerned as he received reports. When Generals Heth and Wilcox asked for orders, Lee told them calmly to remain where they were. The first of Longstreet's corps, the division of General Field, was on the move, and would be ready to take its place in line about midnight.

But it was soon apparent that Longstreet was suffering another attack of what the army called "the slows," for which he was becoming famous. His troops had gone into camp about six miles from Hill's flank, and when Lee sent Major H. C. McClellan to hasten General Field's march, Field had stubbornly refused to move. General Longstreet, he said, had told him to wait until one A.M., giving the men a rest before going into the line for action.

Longstreet had not been fully advised of the urgency of the situation, but Lee, who saw that the coming of dawn might bring disaster to the army, was in no mood to reflect upon the causes of delay. Yet, when Major McClellan volunteered to ride to Field once more with written orders, Lee revealed no concern:

"No, Major, it is now past 10 o'clock, and by the time you could return to General Field and he could put his division in motion, it would be 1 o'clock; and at that hour he will move."[4]

The army could only wait and trust that the enemy would not overpower the fragments before Longstreet arrived. Just as the sun rose on May sixth, the storm of a Federal attack broke near Lee's headquarters. Warren Goss described it from the lines of Grant:

"The enemy were at once attacked . . . and driven confusedly through the woods. Their dead and wounded lay thick in the jungle of scrub-oaks, pines, and underbrush, through which we rushed upon them. . . . By six o'clock the rebel lines had been driven a mile and a half and were broken and disordered. The advance of our corps through swamps and tangled thickets, in this hot encounter, had broken our own lines. . . . A halt was ordered."

Messages came to Lee asking help, but for the moment there was no help; he sent back orders to hold as long as possible, with the prospect that Longstreet would soon be at hand. It seemed that his daring in attacking an army of 100,000 with 30,000 might bring ruin. For an hour the wing of A. P. Hill clung to its position, but at last, streaming past Lee, the men of Wilcox went back in hurried retreat. General Alexander was nearby to describe the scene:

"With both flanks broken . . . the men . . . fell back from both flanks into the Plank Road, and came pouring down the road past the open field near the Tapp House, where Lee stood among the

small and scattered pines. Seeing [General] McGowan pass, Lee
rode up and said:

" 'My God! General McGowan, is this splendid brigade of
yours running like a flock of geese?'

" 'General, the men are not whipped. They only want a place
to form, and they will fight as well as ever they did.' "

Lee turned to Colonel Taylor and sent him to Parker's Store,
some two miles to the rear, to prepare the wagon train for flight.
He also sent General Wilcox to urge Longstreet forward, calling
after him, "Longstreet must be here. Go bring him up!"

There was now nothing to hold back the Federals but a little
battery of the Rockbridge Artillery, which tore the thickets with
grapeshot and forced the bluecoats to hesitate.

Then a torrent of ragged men surged around Lee, coming from
the rear, and not far behind them was Longstreet. The leading
brigade cheered as it passed Lee, going to the front through Hill's
retreating men. The commander yelped when he saw they were
from the Texas brigade. He turned Traveller about, waving his
hat like a schoolboy, his reserve gone.

"Hurrah for Texas!" he yelled. "Hurrah for Texas!"

One of the Texans trotted near the commander, and was impressed by the scene:

"The cannon thundered, musketry rolled, stragglers were fleeing, couriers riding here and there . . . minnies began to sing, the
dying and wounded were jolted by the flying ambulances. . . .

"General Gregg and General Humphrey were ordered to form
their brigades in line of battle . . . and we found ourselves near
the brow of the hill. . . . 'General Gregg, prepare to move,' was the
order from General Lee.

"About this time, General Lee, with his staff, rode up to General Gregg—'General, what brigade is this?' Lee said.

" 'The Texas Brigade,' was General Gregg's reply.

" 'I am glad to see it,' said Lee. 'When you go in there, I wish you to give those men the cold steel—they will stand and fire all day, and never move unless you charge them.'

" 'That is my experience,' replied the brave Gregg."

The Texans now got the order to move forward, and the young soldier heard Gregg shout; "Attention, Texas Brigade! The eyes of General Lee are upon you. Forward, march!"

The commander then urged his horse impulsively toward the Texas soldiers, and the watchful young diarist recorded:

"General Lee, in front of the whole command, raised himself in his stirrups, uncovered his grey hairs, and with an earnest, yet anxious voice, uncovered above the din and confusion of the hour:

" 'Texans always move them.'

"Never before in my lifetime . . . did I ever witness such a scene as was enacted when Lee pronounced these words. . . . A yell rent the air that must have been heard for miles around. . . . Leonard Gee, a courier to General Gregg, and riding by my side, with tears coursing down his cheeks . . . exclaimed,

" 'I would charge hell itself for that old man!' . . .

"We saw that General Lee was following us into battle . . . refusing to come back at the request and advice of his staff. . . . The brigade halted when they discovered General Lee's intention. . . . Five and six of his staff would gather around him, seize him, his arms, his horse's reins, but he shook them off and moved forward."[5]

Colonel Venable of Lee's staff was moved by the sight, too, and recorded shouts of the Texas boys: "Go back, General Lee! Go Back!"

Still Lee rode on with them.

"We won't go on unless you go back!"

Venable wrote:

"A sergeant seized his bridle rein. The gallant General Gregg, turning his horse towards General Lee, remonstrated with him. Just then I called his attention to General Longstreet, who sat his horse on a knoll to the right of the Texans. . . . He yielded with evident reluctance to the entreaties of his men and rode up to Longstreet's position."

Venable told Longstreet of Lee's brush with the Texans, and Old Pete added his persuasion, asking Lee to move farther to the rear. The Texans disappeared into the brush, driving back the enemy in an attack which was to claim more than 450 of the 673 attackers.

Fire grew heavier, and a major battle was soon roaring. Both Hill and Longstreet were pushing forward, but with increasing stubbornness the Federal lines slowed the attacks. The lines became more static, and it was evident that the enemy, though strongly reinforced, had been checked. Lee now turned to a bold plan he had conceived in the early morning, even while his troops were in danger of annihilation.

He had sent the new chief engineer, General M. L. Smith, to find some means of turning the Federal left, and at about ten o'clock Smith, the accomplished West Pointer who had won fame by building the Vicksburg defenses, came back with good news: There was an unfinished railroad cut by which troops could be led to the enemy flank. Lee sent Smith to Longstreet, who promptly approved, and sent four brigades under Colonel Moxley Sorrel to the flank. The rest of Old Pete's troops would be ready to give support when firing began.

Lee had by now recovered his customary calm, and when a young courier came to him on a panting horse he scolded the rider for hurrying at the expense of his animal. Lee then reached into a saddlebag and fished out a buttered biscuit, which he fed to the dispatch-rider's horse.

Within an hour, at about eleven, Lee heard with relief the roll of an attack on the enemy's left. There was no need of the messengers; from the progress of firing it was clear that the Federals were being pushed back on their flank. In fact, a panic now swept the enemy, and could not be halted by General Hancock; it had swept so far that it now crossed the Plank Road, and at the moment Grant's army seemed at Lee's mercy. Longstreet prepared to throw the weight of his corps into the assault. It promised to be a repetition of the hour, almost a year ago in these very thickets, when Jackson had struck so fiercely at the enemy flank.

More troops were flung toward the front. As they went up, Colonel William Oates of Alabama had a glimpse of Lee:

"He sat his fine gray horse 'Traveller'. . . his face flushed and full of animation. . . . His eyes were on the fight then going on south of the Plank Road. . . .

"A group of General Lee's staff were on their horses just in rear of him. He turned in his saddle and called to his chief of staff in a most vigorous tone, while pointing with his finger across the road, and said: 'Send an active young officer down there.'

"I thought him at that moment the grandest specimen of manhood I ever beheld. He looked as though he ought to have been and was the monarch of the world.

"He glanced his eye down on the 'ragged rebels' as they filed around him in quick time to their place in line, and inquired, 'What troops are these?' And was answered by some private in the Fifteenth, 'Law's Alabama Brigade.' He exclaimed in a strong voice, 'God bless the Alabamians!' The men cheered and went into line with a whoop. The advance began."[6]

Lee remained in the rear, leaving the entire flank attack to Longstreet. Old Pete rode with a large party of officers, well in advance, with only a Virginia regiment between him and the enemy; the confusing forest closed about them. The general's party was strikingly gay.

Micah Jenkins, the commander of a crack South Carolina regiment, had just spoken to Longstreet with congratulations for the success of the first crushing attack.

"I am happy," Jenkins said. "I have felt despair of the cause for some months, but am relieved, and feel assured that we will put the enemy back across the Rapidan before night."

Jenkins turned to Colonel Moxley Sorrel of Longstreet's staff, throwing his arm about him.

"Sorrel, it was splendid," Jenkins said. "We shall smash them now."

From the roadside tangle there was a blast of fire; the Virginians had opened on Longstreet's party, thinking them Federals. Old Pete swayed in the saddle. Jenkins fell.

Sorrel was at Longstreet's side:

". . . he was actually lifted straight up and came down hard. Then the lead-torn coat . . . close to the right shoulder pointed to the passage of the heavy bullet. His staff immediately dismounted him, at the foot of a branching tree, bleeding profusely."

The bullet had entered Longstreet's throat, and he was almost choked with blood. He managed to blow the crimson froth from his lips with a last message: "Tell General Field to take command, and move forward with the whole force and gain the Brock Road."

Surgeons came. General Field was soon at his side, asking about his chief's condition.

"I will be looked after," Longstreet said. "You take command of the corps and push ahead."

Field went off to untangle his men, who lay in crossed lines, barring the progress of all; the attack slowed as men tended Longstreet. Sorrel was sent to advise Lee.

Old Pete went toward the rear. He would not forget the experience:

"As my litter was borne to the rear my hat was placed over my face, and soldiers by the roadside said, 'He is dead, and they are telling us he is only wounded.' Hearing this repeated from time to time, I raised my hat with my left hand, when the burst of voices and the flying of hats in the air eased my pains somewhat."

The veteran Robert Stiles came upon Old Pete, after he was placed in an ambulance:

"They had taken off Longstreet's hat and coat and boots. The blood had paled out of his face and its somewhat gross aspect was gone. I noticed how white and dome-like his great forehead looked, and . . . how spotless white his socks and his fine gauze undervest, save where the red black gore from his breast and shoulder had stained it . . . he very quietly moved his unwounded arm and, with his thumb and two fingers, carefully lifted the saturated undershirt from his chest, holding it up a moment, and heaved a deep sigh. 'He is not dead,' I said to myself."[7]

But Longstreet was no longer leading the attack, which seemed to slow instantly, and the enemy dug a new line of defense. By the time Lee could herd the army into position for a new assault it was after four P.M., and the waves of gray troops flung forward were broken. Lee then pressed for an attack by Ewell's corps, which might have driven the enemy. General Gordon reported:

"Both General Early and I were at Ewell's headquarters when, at about 5:30 in the afternoon, General Lee rode up and asked:

" 'Cannot something be done on this flank to relieve the pressure upon our right?' "

Gordon listened to the resulting conference until he could contain himself no longer, and then told Lee of the day-long controversy among generals on that flank:

Early in the morning Gordon, led by scouts, had found and carefully inspected an unguarded flank of the enemy where: "There was no line guarding this flank. As far as my eye could reach, the Union soldiers were seated on the margin of the rifle-pits, taking their breakfast. Small fires were burning over which they were boiling their coffee."

But Gordon's call for a flank attack had been refused by General Early, and that officer now explained to Lee that he thought big Federal regiments were in support of the flank, and that to

attack would have invited disaster. Gordon described Lee's reaction
to the squabble:

"The details of the whole plan were laid before him. There
was no doubt with him as to its feasibility. His words were few,
but his silence and grim looks while the reasons for that long delay
were being given, and his prompt order to me to move at once
to the attack, revealed his thoughts almost as plainly as words could
have done."

But it was too late, and though a final Confederate sally put a
Federal corps to flight, the main lines scarcely moved before darkness closed in. The night was again dreadful in many quarters, for
leaves had caught fire, and brush fires swept through the Wilderness, once more claiming the dead and wounded, and filling the
night with currents of bitter smoke.

Lee went to his tent near the Tapp House in an eerie yellow
glow, cast by the fires which swept the forest thickets. Before going
to bed he had serious decisions to make. Casualties had been fairly
heavy; about 7,500, it developed. And though the enemy had suffered much more (over 17,500 in the two days in the Wilderness),
Grant's force was by no means crippled. Lee sent orders to have
the men dig in; the night was spent in entrenching on most of the
front.

Somehow, the enemy had not found the large gap between
the army's wings. Colonel Venable, riding across it with a message
for Ewell, had discovered that only two Federal stragglers occupied
the woodland.

There was little news from Longstreet; the First Corps commander's wounds were serious, but should not be fatal. In any event,
someone else must handle his troops, perhaps for many months to
come. Lee went to sleep with the problem.

Sunrise of May seventh brought a strange calm to the blackened brush. There was a scattering of picket fire, but no attack in
force; it was almost as if the enemy had gone. Lee put his scouts

to work, and gave careful attention to reports from every segment of the front.

Colonel Sorrel was called in the early morning. Lee stood with him under a tree near headquarters.

"I must speak to you, Colonel," he said, "about the command of the First Corps."

He passed over two recent Major Generals, and Sorrel noted how Lee passed over Pickett without a thought of promoting him. Lee mentioned three names as possibilities: Jubal Early, Edward Johnson, Richard Anderson.

"You have been with the corps since it started as a brigade," Lee said to Sorrel, "and should be able to help me."

"Early would be the ablest, but would also be the most unpopular in the corps," Sorrel said. He recalled incidents growing from Early's fits of temper. Lee turned to another.

"And now, Colonel, for my friend Ed Johnson. He is a splendid fellow."

"All say so, General . . . but I think that some one personally known to the corps would be preferred."

Of Anderson, Sorrel said, "We *know* him and shall be satisfied with him."

"Thank you, Colonel," Lee said. "I have been interested, but Early would make a fine corps commander."

Sorrel left with the impression that Early would take over the men of Longstreet, and later in the day was surprised at the order placing Dick Anderson in command.[8]

During the morning Lee had word from Early that aroused his suspicions: The Union troops on the far left had fallen back. This was proof to Lee that Grant was moving—but not retreating. The enemy had cut loose from rear communications at Germanna Ford, and was going somewhere, leaving the reassuring line of the Rappahannock over which Hooker had retreated a year ago. Lee turned to a study of the familiar terrain between him and Richmond in an effort to divine Grant's intentions.

There were two routes for Grant: He might reach downriver to Fredericksburg, clinging to his line of supply with a new, safer base; or he might strike directly for Richmond, passing through a crossroads known as Spotsylvania Court House, which had the advantage of a railroad junction.

The ease with which Lee predicted Grant's goal was marked by Gordon, who was invited to ride out with the commander in the early daylight of May seventh.

Lee fell to talking of Grant. Gordon later declined to quote him exactly, but wrote: "His comments . . . were full and free. He discussed the dominant characteristics of his great antagonist: his indomitable will and untiring persistency; his direct method of waging war by delivering constant and heavy blows. . . . General Lee also said that General Grant held so completely and firmly the confidence of the Government that he could command to any extent its limitless resources in men and materials, while the Confederacy was already practically exhausted in both."

Lee told Gordon that he hoped to be able to check Grant, keeping the Army of Northern Virginia between him and Richmond. A few months of such maneuver, he thought, might bring victory, or peace of some sort. Surely the North would not long bear such casualties as Grant had sustained in the past two days. Gordon thought Lee was not only hopeful, but extremely confident.

Gordon asked what the next move of the enemy would be.

"I am moving the army at once to Spotsylvania," Lee said.

Gordon told him of reports that Grant was retreating, pulling men away from the long front in the Wilderness.

"I have heard so," Lee said, "but they did not impress me much, even coming from my own scouts. The only basis for the rumors is that Grant has pulled back his wagons and ambulances."

Gordon was now listening carefully.

"General Grant is not going to retreat," Lee said. "He will move his army to Spotsylvania."

"Is there any information on that?" Gordon asked.

"Not at all," Lee said. "But that is the next point at which the armies will meet. Spotsylvania is now General Grant's best strategic point. I am so sure of his next move that I have already made arrangements to march by the shortest practicable route, that we may meet him there."[9]

Almost at the moment Lee and Gordon discussed Grant's plans in the forest, the order for a general movement on Spotsylvania had been issued from Federal headquarters.

The prelude of the Wilderness was over, and though its two fierce days had brought the Federal army what would have been stunning defeat a year ago, the enemy was not behaving as of old. Instead of a retreating and confused adversary, the Confederates faced Grant's army as it marched in rapid order, somewhere on the narrow roads out of sight, sliding still down the long road to Richmond by its left.

Lee had begun by having crews of artillerymen cut a road through the brush, giving his army the interior route to Spotsylvania. He did not yet move the entire force, however.

All day, as the commander moved along his line, he got reports of Union withdrawal. Lee was visiting at the headquarters of A. P. Hill when he got a final bit of information: Big guns which had protected Grant's headquarters had just been moved off toward the south. Lee gave orders for Anderson to pull the First Corps out of line at dark and hurry it along the newly cut road through the forest, into the well-used highway to Spotsylvania. The army would follow, with Ewell's corps bringing up the rear. In the first hours of darkness, when the false rumor spread that the enemy had retreated, the army marched amid long cheers. A North Carolina officer recalled the hour of eight P.M., May seventh:

"The rebel yell was raised at some point on the right of the line; at first, heard like the rumbling of a distant railroad train, it came rushing down the lines . . . and passing, it would be heard dying away on the left in the distance. It was renewed three times. . . . It was a yell like the defiant tones of a thunder storm, echoing and re-echoing. It caused such dismay among the Federals that it is said their pickets fired and ran in."[10]

The First Corps marched through the night along a route parallel to that of the enemy, and by eight A.M., May eighth, the first of General Anderson's troops reached Spotsylvania. The enemy was almost immediately in sight; firing broke out; and the two armies began to entrench.

Lee was far behind, in the Wilderness. At daylight he saw that the Federal army was gone beyond a doubt; not even skirmishers remained.

A. P. Hill, whose health had been poor, was unable to take command today, and in his illness rode in the rear. Lee ordered Early to command his corps, and placed John B. Gordon over Early's division. The last of the army marched.

Lee passed by Shady Grove Church on his way to the new fighting, where he had a word of the clash between Anderson and a Federal corps under General Warren. He pressed forward in more haste, and arrived in Spotsylvania at two thirty. He talked with officers during an afternoon lull, and saw to the placing of more men as they arrived at the court house. Opposite them, swarming bluecoats indicated a coming attack. General Sedgwick's corps had, in fact, been brought up to help drive Lee's advance from Spotsylvania. Private Theodore Gerrish described things from the Federal ranks:

"At six o'clock in the evening we were again pushed up to the front, to assault the enemy's position. The troops were in three lines, our regiment being in the third. It was the design of our commander to make the assault under cover of darkness, but unbe-

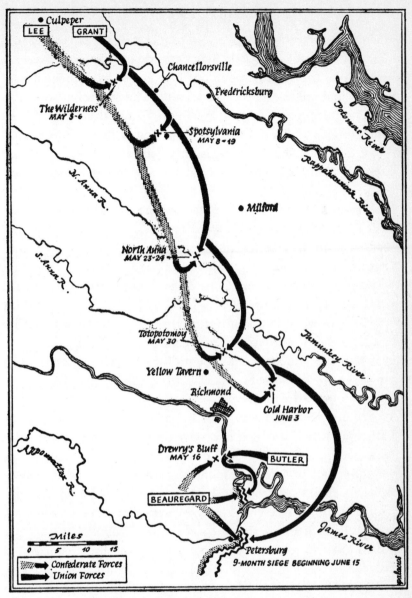

DANCE OF DEATH: GRANT SIDLES DOWN TO
RICHMOND

known to us, the Rebels were also preparing to make an assault.

"Just at dark there was a heavy crash of musketry and a wild, savage yell as they rushed upon our first line of battle, which soon gave way and fell back upon the second. The confusion was indescribable: it was only with the greatest difficulty that we could tell friend from foe. . . . The Rebels came on with terrible energy. We were alone. The other regiments had fallen back. Our men were in just the right mood to fight—weary, hungry, discouraged, mad. . . .

"It was a hand-to-hand conflict, resembling a mob in its character . . . for that hour they were brutes, wild with passion and blood. . . . The air was filled with oaths, the sharp reports of rifles, thuds of clubbed muskets, the swish of swords and sabers, groans and prayers. . . . Federal and Confederate would roll on the ground in a death struggle. Our officers fought like demons. . . . Many of those who were wounded refused to go to the rear but, with blood pouring from their wounds, continued to fight.

"And thus Blue and Gray fought for victory. . . . The lumberman of the North crossed bayonets with the Southern planter, and both lay down to die together."

When night fell the mingled brigades lay over the face of the small ridge which shielded Spotsylvania Court House. Until this moment, at least, Lee had blocked the way of Grant. It had been a near thing, but tonight Richmond seemed safe. Lee went to sleep with the men of Anderson and Ewell in position before the enemy. Even here, he had reserve strength, with Gordon's division not yet in line. A little to the north, camping around Shady Grove Church, was still the Third Corps, ready for use tomorrow, if needed.

But May ninth brought only sharp, brief little stabs at Lee's lines, as the Federal strength grew.

Lee wrote to Davis, commenting on the ominous news that General Benjamin Butler had landed a big Federal force below

Richmond on the James, which he told Davis had "occasioned me great uneasiness." General Beauregard had been called up from South Carolina with reinforcements to check the move. Lee advised Davis on how to meet that threat to the east, and then turned to the Army of the Potomac which he faced, thinking of it always as the major enemy:

> We have succeeded so far in keeping on the front flank of that army, and impeding its progress, without a general engagement, which I will not bring on unless a favorable opportunity offers, or as a last resort. Every attack made upon us has been repelled and considerable damage done to the enemy.
>
> With the blessing of God, I trust we shall be able to prevent Gen. Grant from reaching Richmond, and I think this army could render no more effectual service.[11]

Lee spent May ninth in strengthening his lines along a ridge between the steep-banked streams, the Ny and Po Rivers; men dug and felled trees along this arc, giving the lines a formidable look, with one exception.

Anderson's flank on the left, under command of General Field, had curled back to the north bank of the Po River. The enemy moved against this weak spot on May tenth, but Lee sent reinforcements there, and after a brief clash the Federals withdrew. Lee agreed with Ewell that the line should be improved on this front, and made the only change which seemed logical: A long shift northward, to include higher ground. The move put a bulge in the line, which from its shape the men called the "Mule Shoe." This salient, where General Johnson was in command, was about half a mile wide and more than a mile deep, with irregular sides.

The front of the "Mule Shoe" looked inviting to the enemy, and in the late afternoon of May tenth, after a number of punishing attacks, the bluecoats came over the open with great courage, in the face of heavy musketry and cannon fire, and some of them climbed over the piled bodies of the dead, into the trenches themselves. They paid a fearful price, but they tore a hole in Lee's line, held it a few moments, and fell back stubbornly, taking a number of Rebels as prisoners. Only Lee's wisdom in banking artillery on the flank had broken up a supporting attack and saved the "Mule Shoe" from being torn apart and the army cut in two.

Robert Stiles, the tireless Confederate diarist, was in the thick of it:

"I cannot pretend to identify the separate attacks or to distinguish between them, but should think there must have been at least a dozen of them. . . . While fresh troops poured to almost every charge, the same muskets in the hands of the same men met the first attack in the morning and the last at night; the men. . . were so weary and worn and heavy at night that they could scarcely be roused to meeting the charging enemy. . . .

"Toward the close of the day everything seemed to have quieted down. . . . Someone rose up . . . cried out: 'Hello! What's this? Why, here come our men on a run from—no, by Heavens! It's the Yankees!' and before anyone could . . . start toward the stacked muskets, the Federal column broke over our little work. . . . Quicker almost than I can tell it, our infantry supports . . . fairly tore the head of the Federal column to pieces . . . those who were able to do so turned to fly and our infantry were following them over the intrenchments."

Many men lay exhausted in the lines, double lines where the dangerous exposure of the "Mule Shoe" had drawn Lee's attention.

There was bad news in the evening: A big Federal cavalry raid had swept off to the southeast, apparently heading for Richmond, under a new commander, General Phil Sheridan. Stuart had gathered his troopers, and was somewhere far off to the right of the army in a desperate effort to get between the raiders and the capital.

The raid had already caused serious damage, for at the crossing of the Virginia Central Railroad, the enemy had destroyed more than a million rations, the reserve supply of the army's bread and meat.

At Spotsylvania, however, there was nothing but digging in and waiting.

Lee's first concern was for the "Mule Shoe," and when he went to the tip of the salient after a three A.M. breakfast, he found General Johnson busy. Lee heard Johnson's report that he had scouted the front in person, and found no sign of the enemy, but was not convinced; he expected attack. He had placed artillery thickly on this part of the line.

Dawn of May eleventh seemed slow in coming. The morning was thick with fog, and visibility was poor. But in the afternoon, despite a steady rain, movements of the enemy could be heard.

Near nightfall, at his headquarters just back of the line, Lee had disturbing news which forced a change of plan. Rooney Lee, with his cavalry in the rear of the enemy left, had found that Federal wagon trains were carrying wounded to Belle Plain, above Fredericksburg on the Potomac. That probably meant that Grant was ready to move once more. It could mean retreat to Fredericksburg, which Lee thought unlikely; it might mean another slide past Lee's right, which seemed probable. In any event Lee, though he could not yet afford to leave his line, must be ready for another race. He sent orders to pull out the artillery, particularly the most advanced pieces, which could not be moved in haste. Caution was urged, but as Confederate gunners began to steal backwards with cannon from the tip of the "Mule Shoe," they were observed by a Rebel preparing to desert with darkness, and carry this interesting word to the enemy.[12]

As the hours wore on and men in front heard more sounds of enemy movement, General Johnson became alarmed. For one thing, Yankee bands blared away most of the night. Men were moving into new positions out there in the wet darkness, great bodies of men. Johnson told Ewell of his fears, and asked that guns be replaced on his front.

There was some confusion at headquarters in the night, and officers would not later recall whether Lee ever learned of Johnson's pleas. At any rate, the commander was uncertain whether he faced the greater danger on his front, or on the flank where Grant might slip away. He wanted the cannon replaced in the "Mule Shoe" at daylight.

That order had not been carried out when the night erupted with a general engagement. Lee went to the front almost as soon as musketry broke out. He was stunned to find himself surrounded by Confederates running to the rear. Lee shouted to the men to halt, telling them to form a new line.

Robert Stiles caught sight of him in the dawn:

"We passed General Lee on horseback. . . . His face was more serious than I had ever seen it, but showed no trace of excitement or alarm. Numbers of demoralized men were streaming past him, and his voice was deep as the growl of a tempest as he said:

" 'Shame on you, men; shame on you! Go back to your regiments; go back to your regiments!' "

As he tried in vain to stop the flight Lee was beset by an excited young rider from General Johnson's staff, Major Robert Hunter, who said that the enemy had broken the line at the "Mule Shoe" and were pouring through. Masses of Federals had gathered just outside the lines in the night, and had abruptly stormed the works. Lee sought Gordon, whom he had already given orders to attack in case of such an emergency.

Lee and Gordon soon came under fire, but the Old Man headed Traveller toward the front, before the forming lines.

Gordon saw that Lee meant to lead the charge:

"As he rode majestically in front of my line of battle, with uncovered head . . . Lee looked a very god of war . . . evidently resolved to lead in person the desperate charge and drive Hancock back or perish in the effort....

"Instantly I spurred my horse across Old Traveller's front, and grasping his bridle in my hand, I checked him. Then, in a voice which I hoped might reach the ears of my men, I called out,

" 'General Lee, you shall not lead my men in a charge. No man can do that, sir. Another is here for that purpose. These men behind you are Georgians, Virginians, and Carolinians. They have never failed you on any field. They will not fail you here. Will you, boys?'

"The response came like a mighty anthem . . . 'No, no, no; we'll not fail him. . . .'

"I shouted to General Lee, 'You must go to the rear!'

"The echo, 'General Lee to the rear, General Lee to the rear!' rolled back . . . from the throats of my men; and they gathered around him, turned his horse in the opposite direction, some clutching his bridle, some his stirrups, while others pressed close to Old Traveller's hips, ready to shove him by main force to the rear."

Another of Lee's officers at hand was Colonel J. Catlett Gibson, who called to the men, "Three cheers for General Lee and Old Virginia!" While the men were yelling Gordon dropped Lee's bridle. Nearby troops thought Lee was once more going toward the enemy, and some of them snatched Traveller's reins.

Gibson wrote: ". . . and amid redoubled shouts of 'Lee, Lee, Lee to the rear! Lee to the rear!' the soldiers led him . . . and they passed through in single file, and the field of coming carnage resounded with wild shouts of 'Lee, Lee, Lee!' "

Gordon's attack, with the aid of support thrown in by Lee on each flank, at last restored the center of the line. Lee was soon under fire again, and his men shouted:

"Go back, General Lee! Go back."

"If you will promise to drive those people from our works, I will go back," he shouted.[13]

As the troops trotted ahead, he retired to a nearby battery of guns, where Colonel Venable saw him busy writing and dictating dispatches, in the heaviest of the fire.

The army had never been in such fighting before, and the day's storm in the "Mule Shoe," henceforth to be known as "Bloody Angle," was said by witnesses to be the most severe firing ever known. Throughout the day, with both Lee and Grant feeding in more troops at the "Bloody Angle," and elsewhere, casualties mounted at a sickening rate.

Colonel Taylor wrote:

"Then occurred the most remarkable musketry-fire of the war: from the sides of the salient, in possession of the Federals, and the new line . . . occupied by the Confederates, poured forth hissing fire, an incessant, terrific hail. No living man nor thing could stand in the doomed space . . . even large trees were felled—their trunks cut in twain by the bullets of small arms."

Major Stiles watched Lee during this struggle:

"We passed again within a few feet of General Lee, seated upon his horse on the crest of the hill, this time entirely alone, not even a courier with him. I was much impressed with the calmness and perfect poise of his bearing, though his center had just been pierced by forty thousand men and the fate of his army trembled in the balance. He was completely exposed to the Federal fire, which was very heavy . . . he ordered all his couriers to protect themselves behind an old brick kiln, some one hundred and fifty yards to the left, until their services were required, but refused to go there himself."

The day's fighting restored much of Lee's line at the end, though he had lost General Johnson and most of his men, now captives of the Yankees. Several big guns were lost.

By nightfall, Lee had seen to the completion of a new line of logs and felled trees some 800 yards to the rear of the old parapets. This was the last hope, for though the Federals had been driven out, they clung to the outside of the works by the thousand, stabbing and firing at the Confederates huddled just inside, and the struggle went on as the bodies piled higher, and men fought on the piled corpses. This torture continued, with losses heavy, until late in the night, when the last of the front-line units had abandoned the front of "Bloody Angle" to fall back to Lee's new works.

Lee sent a report to Davis of the gloomy day's work. Besides General Johnson, General George Steuart was also a Federal prisoner. General Junius Daniel was dead, and General Abner Perrin had a death wound. Four other general officers were wounded. Total casualties could not even be estimated, but at least 2,000 men had been captured in the first pre-dawn attack.

There was sad news from the rear. In the midst of a rainstorm Lee was informed that Stuart had been wounded, shot down while warding off General Sheridan's raid, near Yellow Tavern. He was thought to be mortally wounded, and had been taken to Richmond.

Lee read the dispatch, and, folding it, turned slowly to the young officers about him.

"General Stuart has been mortally wounded," he said. "A most valuable officer." He paused, and then said in a trembling voice, "He never brought me a piece of false information."[14]

There was a later message that Stuart was dead, passing with a smile as he lay in the home of a relative in Richmond, saying "God's will be done," and weakly joining in the singing of "Rock of Ages." Stuart, greatest of Lee's horsemen, was gone at thirty-one. The commander turned from a young cavalry officer who came to tell him of Stuart's end. He covered his face with a hand. "I can scarcely think of him without weeping," he said.

It was a glorious new legend for the army, that of Stuart's 4,000 checking the thrust of Sheridan's 12,000, but with Stuart gone, it seemed only disaster. The reckless horseman had declined even brandy at the end, despite his pain, keeping a pledge of boyhood days. And the next day Richmond mourned him, as he lay in a casket under a sword fashioned of lilies, with a crown of bay.

More news came to Lee at Spotsylvania. The Federal cavalry had severed the lines with Richmond, cutting the last railroad left intact. The army must live on the meager rations in its wagon train.

There was one blessing: The roaring, drowning rain, which fell steadily through May thirteenth, and lasted almost without ceasing for four days. The army rested.

Lee was almost as busy as if the army had been in action. He scoured the countryside for supplies, and when three farmers offered 2,000 bushels of corn, he detached a North Carolina regiment to march after it.[15] He was obliged to direct the army almost alone, with Hill still sick, Ewell in dangerous physical condition, Stuart dead, and Longstreet away. Lee delayed naming a successor to Stuart, and in the meantime had all of the cavalry division leaders reporting to him in person.

On May sixteenth, after a long lapse, he wrote Mary:

As I write I am expecting the sound of the guns every moment. I grieve the loss of our gallant officers and men, and miss their aid and sympathy. A more zealous, ardent, brave and devoted soldier than Stuart the Confederacy can not have. Praise be to God for having sustained us so far. I have thought of you very often in these eventful days.

He soon wrote an order to the army on the death of Stuart:

Among the gallant soldiers who have fallen in this war, General Stuart was second to none in valor, in zeal, and in unflinching devotion to his country. His achievements form a conspicuous part of the history of this army, with which his name and services will be forever associated. To military capacity of a high order and to the nobler virtues of the soldier he added the brighter graces of a pure life, guided and sustained by the Christian's faith and hope. . . . To his comrades in arms he has left the proud recollections of his deeds and the inspiring influence of his example.[16]

On May sixteenth, there was a flurry of good news. The upper Shenandoah Valley was free of the enemy, for General Breckinridge, reinforced by the child soldiers of the cadet corps of Virginia Military Institute, had met the Federal Sigel at New Market, driving his troops back in confusion. On the next day General Beauregard had lashed out at the invaders under General Butler, below Richmond, and driven them within a loop of the River James, bottling them in Bermuda Neck where they were no longer a threat.

The Spotsylvania front then erupted once more, though briefly. On the morning of May eighteenth, stepping over the bodies of the fallen of May twelfth, Union regiments charged "Bloody Angle," hoping to take the new entrenchments of the Confederates behind it. But this time the big guns were in place, and the Rebs were alert. The artillery tore the blue ranks apart as they emerged from the woods, and after the place had been strewn with casualties once more, the Federal commander called it off, and quiet returned.

Lee sent Davis a long dispatch on that day, saying that Grant's position was "strongly entrenched, and we cannot attack it with any prospect of success without great loss of men which I wish to avoid if possible."

He added:

My object has been to engage him when in motion and under circumstances that will not cause us to suffer from this disadvantage. I think by this means he has suffered considerably in the several past combats, and that his progress has thus far been arrested. I shall continue to strike him whenever opportunity presents itself.

Lee sent several telegrams to Davis during the day, stressing the coming of reinforcements to Grant, his own lack of strength, and the need to fall back to cover Richmond. He had called to him the only available spare forces in the Eastern Confederacy, the little army of Breckinridge, which had only 2,400 infantry.

In the night of May nineteenth, the enemy began to retire once more, and the next day, after he had ordered Ewell to be ready for attack on Grant's rear, Lee moved the vanguard. He found Grant moving to the southeast, on the north bank of the Mattapony River, passing the villages of Bowling Green and Milford. And Lee, forced to meet him at the nearest possible site of battle, put the whole army in motion. On the evening of May twenty-first he saw the last of them off from Spotsylvania, and leaving the Wilderness behind, rode off toward Hanover Junction. The army was hurrying to reach the line of the little North Anna River before the enemy could cross. The stream was just twenty-three miles from Richmond.

13 *AT BAY*

THE ARMY came to the south across the little river Po, by Mud Tavern, Dickinson's Mill and Pole Cat Creek. It was a strange time for men in the ranks, whose ears still rang with the almost endless roar of firing in the Wilderness. They now had the first quiet in two weeks, and for the first time were out of sight of the enemy.

Looking back, the struggle was beyond belief. On May fifth, the armies had clashed three times; on May sixth, four times; on May eighth, twice; on May tenth, five times; on May twelfth, assaults beyond counting for twenty hours on "Bloody Angle" and two fights on the rest of the line; on May eighteenth and May nineteenth one clash each day. And when Grant's army left the Wilderness, Lee's salvage crews gathered 120,000 pounds of lead, to be recast into bullets and fired at the enemy once more.

The Federals had left hundreds of their dead unburied. They sent about 7,000 Rebels to the North as prisoners, but their own losses were fearful. Grant had suffered over 33,000 casualties in the long battle. Lee had lost a little over 20,000. In Grant's army, brigades which had gone into the Wilderness had emerged the size of regiments, and two divisions had simply disappeared. A historian of the Army of the Potomac would one day work out the grisly arithmetic: Grant had lost 2,000 men every twenty-four hours since he had crossed the Rappahannock to meet Lee.[1]

At Dickinson's Mill, some six miles above the line of the North Anna, Lee rode through his weary men, encouraging them to move ahead to avoid capture by the enemy. He was at this place when he got the welcome news that many of his Wilderness losses had been replaced. The fine brigade of General Hoke would soon be sent by President Davis, and in addition the division of Pickett, which had long been detached for duty in Eastern Virginia. Lee knew that these were the last reinforcements, but he still seemed to be spoiling for a decisive fight with Grant. He wrote Davis at five A.M. of May twenty-second from Dickinson's Mill, explaining his movement:

> The enemy night before last commenced to withdraw from his position. . . . The movement was not discovered until after daylight, and in a wooded country like that in which we have been operating, where nothing is known beyond what can be ascertained by feeling, a day's march can always be gained.

He then gave his reasons for moving toward Hanover Junction, in the vicinity where the North and South Anna Rivers formed the Pamunkey:

> I thought it safest to move to the Annas to intercept his march, and to be within easy reach of Richmond. . . . The Third Corps is moving on my right and I hope by noon to have the whole army behind the Annas. I should have preferred contesting the enemy's approach inch by inch; but my solicitude for Richmond caused me to abandon that plan.

Lee crossed the North Anna early that day, seeing with relief that he had once more outraced Grant to a natural obstacle. He left orders for the army to cross on the two remaining bridges and

fall into line near the south bank of the stream. He made his headquarters at Hanover Junction, about three miles below the river,
and was there for the next day, as the troops filed past, going into
line. It was noon of May twenty-third before the enemy appeared
on the north bank.

Before he caught sight of the first blue infantry he had written
Davis:

> General Grant will have time to recruit and reorganize
> his army, which as far as I am able to judge, has been very
> much shaken. . . . Whatever route he pursues I am in a position
> to move against him, and shall endeavor to engage him while
> in motion.

He then turned to a new and larger field of strategy, whose
possibilities he pointed out to the President. The Federal army
east of Richmond, under Benjamin Butler, seemed to Lee only to
brighten prospects of combining the two Confederate armies, which
were now drawing close together:

> General Grant's army will be in the field, strengthened
> by all available troops from the north, and it seems to me
> our best policy to unite upon it and endeavor to crush it. I
> should be very glad to have the aid of General Beauregard
> in such a blow, and if it is possible to combine, I think it
> will succeed.
> The courage of this army was never better, and I fear no
> injury to it from any retrograde movement that may be dic-
> tated by sound military policy. I do not think it would be well
> to permit the enemy to approach the Chickahominy . . . and do
> not see why we could not combine against him after he has
> crossed the Pamunkey. . . . His difficulties will be increased as
> he advances, and ours diminished.

Then, having pointed out the means of saving the capital and
the hope of defeating Grant, he turned to the task at hand on the

banks of the North Anna. The first blow of the enemy was a barrage against the little force holding the bridges north of the river, an affair which Lee watched with such calm that he astonished onlookers by slowly finishing a glass of milk on the porch of a hospitable house, even after a Federal cannonball had buried itself in the wood just behind him. He went on a brief reconnaissance, but since he had a touch of illness, rode in a carriage. The enemy poured across the river in the afternoon, fording the stream at the site of a mill on A. P. Hill's front—a whole corps. There was an inconclusive fight through heavy woodlands and after dark Grant's infantry surprised the bridgehead forces with an attack in a rainstorm, capturing many of them and forcing the others to flee.

Lee concluded that the enemy might once more be poised to race across the country toward Richmond, and so he turned to the familiar process of preparing the army to fight on its ground, or be ready for the chase, following the lead of the enemy. But in the night he gave Grant one more sample of his talent for choice of terrain:

His lines were open to attack along the river at every point except a ridge near a place called Ox Ford, where the guns commanded the enemy position. Lee shifted his troops, making the strong Ox Ford position the northern apex of an irregular V, with the western leg resting on Little River, and the eastern curling around the railroads at Hanover Junction. With this simple movement he invited attack where the enemy must split his force to assail the whole line, while Lee dealt with him across conveniently short lines of communication.[2]

Lee revealed his feeling about Grant's army in a letter of May twenty-third to Mary: "I begrudge every step he takes toward Richmond."

His illness was becoming acute by now, however, some sort of painful intestinal ailment. He made a last effort to continue direction of the army on May twenty-fourth, riding along the lines where men were digging in, just as the enemy was doing opposite them. He saw that Grant had done as he had hoped, splitting his army and facing the line of the Confederate V down its length. If Lee could mount an attack from either side, the Federals could not reinforce their besieged wing without a double crossing of the river. The opportunity began to fade, however, as the enemy entrenched and Lee's illness grew worse.

He gave a sign of short temper as he inspected the line. When he saw A. P. Hill he scolded him for the failure of the previous afternoon, when Hill had launched piecemeal attacks on the lone enemy corps, and lost several hundred men to no purpose. Lee's voice was sharper than usual:

"Why did you not do as Jackson would have done—thrown your whole force upon these people and driven them back?"[3]

This was the commander's last sally before surrendering to his illness. He spent May twenty-fifth in bed. The lines lay under occasional bursts of skirmishing fire, but at headquarters, many officers suffered from Lee's worsening temper. He would not relinquish command, and could not be afield to direct affairs himself; he saw opportunity slipping away.

He complained to a doctor that he could whip Grant, if given one more chance. His temper flared and he had a spat with Colonel Venable, who was overheard as he emerged from Lee's tent:

"I have just told the old man that he is not fit to command this army, and that he had better send for Beauregard!"

But everyone knew the source of Lee's irritation, and Colonel Venable sketched it clearly:

"As he lay prostrated by his sickness, he would often repeat: 'We must strike them a blow—we must never let them pass us again—we must strike them a blow.' "[4]

For two days Lee was reduced to passing orders from his bed, but there was no improvement in the checkmate he had given Grant. There was no longer a question of attacking the divided

Federal army, for on May twenty-seventh the situation changed completely.

After a movement along the bank of the stream, when Lee thought Grant was perhaps on the direct march to Richmond, the enemy slid away once more. The big Federal columns pulled out of position on the south bank of the North Anna, went over to the north side, and marched once more to the southeast. They were soon reported crossing the Pamunkey River at Hanovertown. Lee once more moved the army in chase. He probably went in a carriage himself, but in the vanguard, with Ewell's Second Corps. Ewell was suffering with somewhat the same ailment, and late on May twenty-seventh was forced to retire to bed himself, with Early in command of his troops.

The army was now moving into familiar territory, just above Richmond, on the flank of the old line from which McClellan had been pried, early in the summer of 1862. The troops came down the south side of the Pamunkey, across narrow Totopotomoy Creek, near the Chickahominy. When the leading columns were just nine miles from the capital, Lee halted them, placing the lines with care on the high ground near Beaver Dam Creek which had once before been so vital, on the day of the bloody storming of Mechanicsville. He waited there until he discovered which route Grant would take toward the city, shrewdly shifting his strength to cover the most likely approaches.

Lee's health was no better, and on May twenty-eighth he took shelter indoors for the first time during the campaign, making headquarters in the home of the Clarke family at a station known as Atlee's, on the Central Railroad north of the Chickahominy. He remained here during most of the next anxious days as he watched Grant's moves. There were serious clashes with enemy cavalry, which now carried the deadly repeating Spencer carbines; but the enemy did not press Lee. There was more trouble from the perplexed Beauregard who, now that Lee was along the Chickahominy, and in the area where Beauregard had agreed to combine the armies, had again become frightened.

Beauregard feared that General Butler, still cooped in an arm of the James at Bermuda Hundred, was preparing to escape, and that the result would be disaster. He declined to send Lee reinforcements, and took refuge in army red tape, so that for several days, at the cost of speed and secrecy, he transmitted all messages to Lee through General Bragg and the War Department in Richmond. This exchange was an example:

> War Department must determine when and what troops to order from here. I send to General Bragg all information I obtain relative to movement of enemy's troops in front.
> —Beauregard.

Lee replied, May thirtieth:

> If you cannot determine what troops you can spare, the Department cannot. The result of your delay will be disaster. Butler's troops will be with Grant tomorrow.

And at the same time he advised Davis:

> General Beauregard says the Department must determine what troops to send from him. He gives it all necessary information. The result of this delay will be disaster. . . . Hoke's division at least should be with me by light tomorrow.[5]

This at last brought action, and the reinforcement of Hoke's men was put on the way from Beauregard to Lee, but this had been accomplished only after Lee's grim insistence, and a conference at Atlee's between Lee, Davis and Beauregard, when the mercurial Creole had displayed grave fears for his own command, and none for that of the main army. He resisted to the last the taking of any of his troops.

As May came to an end it became apparent that Grant was not to hit the lines the army was digging along the Totopotomoy. Lee cast about for means of attacking. He was now at a greater disadvantage, perhaps, than ever. Grant had 112,000 men for the looming battle. And even with the coming of Hoke's 7,000, Lee had no more than 45,000.[6] The Federals had new advantages, for they were by now perfecting their field-telegraph system, and had vastly improved communications. Lee must still depend upon racing mounted couriers under fire. In the days of increasing heat the armies groped southward toward the swampy fields of the Chickahominy. General Alexander saw Lee, not yet recovered from illness, still spoiling for the chance to attack:

"On May 30 . . . a half-mile in front of our line we could see Bethesda Church, an important junction point, well within the enemy's territory. . . . Down a long, straight road, we had seen their cavalry all the morning, and, about noon, a brigade of infantry appeared. Immediately, Lee ordered Early to send a brigade to attack it. Early selected Pegram's brigade, commanded by General Edward Willis, a brilliant young officer. . . . I saw his brigade start on its errand with apprehension of disaster, for it was evident that a hornet's nest would be stirred up. The Federal brigade was quickly routed and pursued, but the pursuers soon encountered a division with its artillery and were repulsed with severe loss. It had 'made a resolute attack' . . . and lost Willis and two of his colonels, killed."

Alexander observed that, though Lee's position would have seemed to be defensive, "never in the war was he so ready to attack upon the slightest opportunity."

It was as if the feel of Richmond at his back made him uneasy, after the succession of failures during the past weeks of blood, when the sliding tactics of Grant and the refusal of Beauregard to help had brought the Army of Northern Virginia to this pass.

Late on May thirty-first Fitz Lee reported the enemy in

strength at Cold Harbor. Lee moved to attack once more with his old audacity; he still rode in a carriage, but seemed no less aggressive. He ordered most of Hoke's men to strike the enemy at Cold Harbor, as early as possible on June first, with the aim of rolling up Grant's flank before it became strong.

This attack, which might have brushed away a cavalry screen and put a strung-out Federal corps at the mercy of Lee's infantry, was a failure. One of the commanders was Colonel Lawrence Keitt of South Carolina, who was seeing his first action at the head of green troops. Keitt rode boldly in the front, and in the open, and was soon killed. His command broke in panic.

Robert Stiles wrote of them: "I have never seen any body of troops in such a condition of utter demoralization; they actually groveled upon the ground and attempted to burrow under each other. . . . We actually spurred our horses upon them, and seemed to hear their very bones crack, but it did no good; if compelled to wriggle out of one hole they wriggled into another."

The Confederate line in this sector was drawn along this road, guarded chiefly by guns brought in by General Alexander. Nearby was a gap between the commands of Kershaw and Hoke, a marshy ravine through which ran a sluggish stream; behind it, along a slope, was a peach orchard. At the end of June first, when the Confederates had concluded the day's fighting was over, the Federals came through the gap and took a number of prisoners before help came from other parts of the line. Darkness fell with the Confederate front intact, except at the marshy gap.

Lee was busy all night, strengthening his line until it was formidable indeed. Near the ruptured gap the gray infantry lay atop a commanding ridge with a swamp bordering it along the front. Alexander directed whispering gunners near the gap in front of the lines, while they put a big gun into ambush, where it was shotted with canister to await the enemy.

June second brought skirmishing but no major action. Lee

put the last of his reinforcements into line, the troops of General Breckinridge who had come down from the Valley. Many men from Richmond were in the rear of the army, the anxious, curious and desperate, come to witness what might be the last stand.

There was hardly a segment of the long, irregular line which Lee had not seen himself; he had selected most of the positions. The men waited in the mud until four thirty A.M., June third, when Grant flung his men into the Army of Northern Virginia in a frontal assault. The slaughter of Cold Harbor had begun.

Horace Porter of Grant's staff wrote:

"I noticed that many of the soldiers had taken off their coats and seemed to be engaged in sewing up rents in them . . . the men were calmly writing their names and home addresses on slips of paper and pinning them on the backs of their coats, so that their dead bodies might be recognized. . . .

"At 4:30 A.M., three columns . . . moved forward to the attack."

Robert Stiles watched from the Confederate lines, as more than 7,000 Federals fell in the first hour:

"For my own part, I could scarcely say whether it lasted eight or sixty minutes, or eight or sixty hours, all my powers being concentrated on keeping the guns supplied with ammunition. . . .

"Here, then, is the secret of the otherwise inexplicable and incredible butchery. A little after daylight . . . infantry discharged their bullets and artillery fired cast-shot and double-shotted canister, at very short range, into a mass of men twenty-eight feet deep, who could neither advance nor retreat, and the most of whom could not even discharge their muskets at us."

Stiles found the musket fire so heavy that "bronze guns looked as if they had had the smallpox, from the striking and splaying of leaden balls against them. . . . One of the guns . . . was actually cut down by musket fire, every spoke of both wheels being cut."

Colonel William Oates would not forget the morning on his part of Lee's line:

"I called out: 'Sergeant, give them double charges of canister; fire, men, fire!'. . . the enemy were within thirty steps. They halted and began to dodge, lie down, and recoil. The fire was terrific. . . . They endured it but for one or two minutes, when they retreated, leaving the ground covered with their dead and dying. There were three men in my regiment killed, five wounded. . . .

"After the lapse of about forty minutes another charge was made. . . . I could see the dust fog out of a man's clothing in two or three places at once where as many balls would strike him at the same moment. In two minutes not a man of them was standing. All who were not shot down had lain down for protection. . . .

"The stench from the dead between our lines and theirs was sickening . . . but we had the advantage, as the wind carried it away from us to them. The dead covered more than five acres of ground about as thickly as they could be laid."

The Federal historian William Swinton wrote of the moments when the worst of it was over, and orders were passed to attack again:

"General Meade sent instructions to each corps commander to renew the attack. . . . The order was issued through these officers to their subordinate commanders, and from them descended through the wonted channels; but no man stirred, and the immobile lines produced a verdict, silent, yet emphatic, against further slaughter. The loss on the Union side . . . was over 13,000, while on the part of the Confederates, it is doubtful whether it reached that many hundreds."

There were attacks without number but none broke the gray line, and the most successful of them only lodged leading regiments where Confederate fire in the flanks could cut men down, and they were forced to fall back, carrying their few prisoners with them.

Porter described Grant:

"At eleven o'clock General Grant rode out along the lines. Hancock reported that the position in his front could not be taken.

Wright stated that a lodgement might be made in his front, but that nothing would be gained by it unless Hancock and Smith were to advance at the same time. . . .

"The general in chief at half past twelve wrote the following order to General Meade: 'You may direct a suspension of farther advance for the present.'

"That evening the general said, 'I regret this assault more than any one I have ever ordered. I regarded it as a stern necessity; but, as it has proved, no advantages have been gained sufficient to justify the heavy losses suffered.' Subsequently the matter was seldom referred to in conversation."

The morning's fury found Lee, in the rear of the lines, in a calm mood which must have astonished his civilian visitors, Postmaster General J. H. Reagan and two of his influential friends. Reagan wrote of finding Lee alone, in heavy fire, and asked him if the artillery fire was not remarkably heavy.

"Yes," Lee said. "More than usual on both sides. That does not do much harm here." He waved his hand toward the front, where Reagan heard musketry sounding "like the tearing of a sheet." Lee added: "It is that that kills men. Grant is hurling columns six to ten men deep against our lines at three places in order to break them."

"General," Reagan said, "if he breaks your line, what reserve have you?"

"Not a regiment," Lee said. "And, that has been my condition ever since the fighting began on the Rappahannock. If I shorten my lines to provide a reserve he will turn me; if I weaken my lines to provide a reserve, he will break me."

Lee told Reagan that he had lost more men to exhaustion and lack of proper food than to enemy bullets. He said he had advised them to eat buds of sassafras and grapevines, but that they were poor substitutes. "Some of the men now have the scurvy," Lee added. He urged Reagan to tell the commissary general to send potatoes and onions to the army as soon as he reached Richmond.

Reagan asked Lee if he could not send his orders to the front as well under cover of timber as in his exposed place.

"It is best for me to be as well to the front as I can," Lee said. "I have as good generals as any commander ever had, and I know it, but still it is well for me to know the position of our lines." He cited the instance of a complexity in lines in front of them. His guests appeared to be impressed.[7]

Lee turned from his well-fed visitors (a Richmond critic of the times had observed that Reagan, in a time of famine when flour brought $500 a bushel, was "as fat as a bear") to plead for reinforcements for the army. He found from prisoners that a corps from General Butler's army was on his front today, and he sent Davis a dispatch, giving him a picture of the lines and a brief, modest review of the repulse of Grant's attacks. He wrote at one P.M., June third, when the tempo of fighting had slowed somewhat:

> So far every attack of the enemy has been repulsed. His assaults began early this morning, and continued until about 9 o'clock. . . .
> General Hoke reports that the troops in his front are said to belong to Butler's forces. . . . I hope that General Beauregard will be able to find out the strength of the enemy in his front, and that he can spare additional reinforcements for this army at once. No time should be lost if reinforcements can be had.

Lee was satisfied that the army had felt the worst of Grant's attacks, and the slow firing which went on between the armies for the next few hot days gave him renewed confidence. There were minor skirmishes as he pushed forward small units of the lines; he found Grant in an impregnable position.

For three or four days the hundreds of Federal wounded who were left between the armies croaked for water and help, in weakening voices, but Grant would not ask for the customary truce to aid them, and Lee would not grant the casual arrangement the Federal commander asked. Rescue parties went out in the nights, but many helpless men died before Grant gained a truce on June seventh.[8]

Fortunately for Confederate morale, a shipment of Nassau bacon came through the blockade at this time, and the troops feasted on bacon and onions, though some regiments voluntarily turned over food to Richmond's poor, who were near starvation.

The mood of the troops was far from gay, however, after the campaign which had cost Grant more than 60,000 men, and Lee perhaps 20,000. There was an awareness that the blue regiments would be quickly filled, and that the torn gray ranks must fight on as they were. Colonel Venable heard the men talking of it:

"What's the use of killing these Yankees? It is like killing mosquitoes—two come for every one you kill."

General Alexander described the life of the Rebel infantry-men in these few days of waiting:

"A terrible fire . . . made life in our cramped and insufficient trenches almost unsupportable. Scarcely anywhere could one stand erect without being exposed to a sharpshooter . . . all the low points on the enemy's line, where men would be exposed in moving about, soon became known. The sharpshooters would then lie with guns already aimed, ready to draw the trigger at the slightest glimpse.

"To shield themselves from the midsummer sun, our men were accustomed to invert their muskets, sticking the bayonets in the ground, and letting the hammers of four guns pinch the four cor-ners of a blanket, under which the four men might crowd and get some shelter from the direct midday blaze. To visit the guns scat-tered all along the lines, one must crouch under the blankets and step over the men, who, in the summer of 1864, were far from being free of insect pests."

The Federal troops fared no better, an officer reported:

"The men in the advance part of the lines . . . had to lie close in narrow trenches; with no water, except a little to drink, and that of the worst kind, being from surface drainage; they were exposed to the great heat during the day; they had but little sleep; their cooking was of the rudest character. For over a month the army had no vegetables. . . . Dead mules and horses and offal were scattered all over the country, and between the lines were dead bodies of both parties lying unburied in a burning sun . . . sickness of malarial character increased."

The armies lay in place, just nine miles from Richmond, for more than a week. The capital was held by a garrison of fewer than 8,000 men. Lee had about 45,000, including cavalry and artillery. The enemy strength was from 120,000 to 125,000. There was only one other Confederate force nearby, Beauregard's little army of 8,000, below the James.

Amid these troubles Lee was presented with a new problem. Davis came to him with depressing news from the Shenandoah. A Union force under General David Hunter had burst into the Valley and fallen upon General W. E. Jones and his little band of cavalry; Jones was dead and more than 1,000 troopers were Federal prisoners. Hunter had taken Staunton, and was expected to combine with two other Federal forces in the region and sweep the Valley. When Davis asked Lee's advice the commander's comment was couched in grim language:

> It is apparent that if Grant cannot be successfully resisted here we cannot hold the Valley. If he is defeated it can be recovered. But unless a sufficient force can be had in that country to restrain the movements of the enemy, he will do us great evil.

The eventual answer seemed boldness born of desperation, for Lee detached General John Breckinridge, the old Presidential candidate of 1860, whom he had withdrawn from the Shenandoah, and

sent him off with a few more than 2,000 men; he was to pick up reinforcements on the way. Nor was that all.

Lee had already sent two cavalry divisions in pursuit of Sheridan's raiders, recently sent westward by Grant. On June thirteenth,
when he had word of Hunter's occupation of Lexington, and a new
threat to Richmond from the west, he sent off General Early's 8,000
veterans, about a quarter of his infantry force, to deal with the new
peril.

While dealing with that problem at long range, he puzzled over
the probable moves of Grant. There were daily reports of Federals
moving pontoons up the James River, and plentiful rumors that
Grant would cross to the south bank and strike the vulnerable defenses of Petersburg and Richmond. Lee prepared for this possible
move by shifting his strength toward the James, but until Grant
moved, he must wait; he could not afford to uncover the approach
to the capital on the north side of the river.

At daylight on June thirteenth, Rebel skirmishers found enemy trenches empty, and Lee ordered a chase. The army poured
down across the battlefields of 1862 in the Chickahominy country,
and by nightfall was around the grim old field of Malvern Hill.
Lee was ready to fight, or, if driven to it, to cross the James on his
pontoon bridge at Drewry's Bluff.

On June fourteenth he wrote Davis:

> I think the enemy must be preparing to move South of
> James River.

He suggested a close watch on Petersburg, which he suspected
was Grant's goal, and sent General Hoke's brigade south to Beauregard on June fifteenth, when he learned that Grant had flung a
heavy cavalry screen out to cloak his movements.

Even so, Grant had stolen a march on Lee, and on June sixteenth the whole Federal force was south of the James, striking for

Petersburg; the Yankee engineers had laid a 2,100-foot pontoon bridge for the crossing, to aid ferry boats.

The first Federal thrust south of the James was a failure which probably cost Grant the chance to seize Richmond and cut short the war. The Federal commander recorded his troubles, caused chiefly by General "Baldy" Smith:

"After the crossing had commenced, I proceeded to Bermuda Hundred to give the necessary orders for the immediate capture of Petersburg. The instructions to General Butler were verbal, and were for him to send General Smith immediately, that night. . . . General Smith got off as directed, and confronted the enemy's pickets near Petersburg before daylight next morning, but for some reason that I have never been able to satisfactorily understand, did not get ready to assault his main lines until near sundown. Then, with a part of his command only, he made the assault, and carried the lines northeast of Petersburg from the Appomattox River, for a distance of over two and a half miles. . . . This was about 7 P.M. Between the lines thus captured and Petersburg there were no other works, and there was no evidence that the enemy had reinforced Petersburg with a single brigade. . . . The night was clear, the moon shining brightly, and favorable to further operations. . . . By the time I arrived the next morning the enemy was in force."[9]

Perhaps the reputation of the Army of Northern Virginia and its commander had slowed General Smith and General Butler, for there had been little else in and behind the trenches of Petersburg to halt them. In the meantime, Lee was undergoing similar trials of his own.

The excited Beauregard, who was soon to be revealed as a prophet when the Federals came upon Petersburg, saw the shadow of the enemy before it fell. He assembled a mass of papers to bolster his complaints and sent it off to Lee by an aide, Colonel Samuel B. Paul. This officer left a brief account of it at the request of Beauregard:

"General Lee declined to permit me to open the papers, stating that he knew we were weak, but that we would simply have to accomplish all we could with what we had.

"At first I feared that I would be dismissed without further attention. . . . The General seemed much preoccupied. I told him that it was but a small part of my instructions to show him your [Beauregard's] weakness, the importance of your lines to his own safety, and the possibility of disaster to you, but to show the fact that attack was imminent.

"Gradually his interest seemed to increase, and he stated that he had ordered Hoke's division to rejoin you before my arrival. He then stated that you might rest assured that you were mistaken in supposing that the enemy had thrown any troops to the South side of the James River. . . . He then said you might be assured that if you were seriously threatened he would send you aid, and, if needed, come himself."[10]

Lee's preoccupation was likely caused by his constant dwelling upon the problem posed by Grant, his nearness to the James, and the necessity for shielding Richmond on both sides of the James.

The waiting soon ended, and the question as to whether Beauregard had been more nearly right than Lee became academic indeed. The race against Grant had never been more furious.

The first of the Federals to come against Petersburg in General Smith's half-hearted attack included some Negro troops, who captured some Confederate cannon in the opening skirmishes. But the first day had ended with Smith ordering his men to cook and sleep. Beauregard's men worked through the night, digging a new line of trenches between Petersburg and the line of captured forts. Federal failure to press beyond skirmish lines saved the city.

Beauregard left an account of the long hours before Lee finally arrived with the main army:

"The Confederate forces . . . on the 15th of June [at Petersburg] consisted of a real effective for duty of 2200 only . . . and had to be so stationed as to allow but one man for every four and a half yards. From Butterworth's Bridge to the Appomattox—a distance of fully four and a half miles—the line was defenseless. . . .

"At ten o'clock A.M., the skirmishing had assumed very alarming proportions. . . . Then all along the line . . . the order was given 'to hold on at all hazards!' . . .

"The enemy, continuing to mass his columns toward the center of our line, pressed it more and more. . . . Shortly after 7 P.M. the enemy entered a ravine between Batteries 6 and 7. . . .

"Strange to say, General Smith contented himself with breaking into our lines, and attempted nothing further that night. . . . Although the result of the fighting of the 15th had demonstrated that 2,200 Confederates successfully withheld nearly a whole day the repeated assaults of nearly 18,000 Federals, it followed, none the less, that Hancock's corps, now being in our front, with fully 28,000 men—which raised the enemy's force against Petersburg to a grand total of 46,000—our chance of resistance . . . was by far too uncertain to be counted on, unless strong additional reinforcements could reach us in time."

Until June eighteenth, Beauregard held Petersburg with no more than 10,000 men. He lost part of the vast lines of fortifications, but the city was safe. Just after midnight of June seventeenth he sent Lee a message:

> All quiet at present. I expect renewal of attack in morning. My troops are becoming much exhausted. Without immediate and strong reinforcements, results may be unfavorable. Prisoners report Grant on the field with his whole army.[11]

At his distance from this scene, Lee could only now determine the true danger to Petersburg, for in all the flurries of telegrams, Beauregard had not made clear just what Federal force he faced, nor its true strength. In fact, the imminent danger to Petersburg was not brought home to Lee until late on June fifteenth, when

Beauregard advised him, without warning, that he had fallen back from his advanced lines at Bermuda Neck to those of Petersburg. At this word, Lee sent him Pickett's division. By now, Lee held the north of the James with 20,000 infantrymen, which would be but a token force in case a drive on Richmond developed in that sector.

On June sixteenth, still unable to predict the final intentions of the enemy, Lee had moved his headquarters to the south, at Drewry's Bluff. Here he received a telegram from Beauregard asking more reinforcements, and mentioning dispatches Lee had never received. Lee's reply revealed his ignorance of the enemy, his lack of intelligence reports, and the crux of his problem:

> Your dispatch of 9:45 received. It is the first that has come to hand. I do not know the position of Grant's army, and cannot strip north bank of the James. Have you not force sufficient?

Events did not allow Lee to wait for further news from Beauregard, and he continued to shift his strength southward. By now about half of his army was south of the James.

In the afternoon the commander was still seeking information, and in a telegram asked of Beauregard:

> Have you heard of Grant's crossing James River?

He got no answer, despite more telegrams from Beauregard, and at night he wrote President Davis:

> I have not learned from General Beauregard what force is opposed to him in Petersburg, or received any definite account of operations there, nor have I been able to learn whether any portion of Grant's army is opposed to him.

Even the next day, when he had good word of Pickett's men recapturing some of the lost lines at Bermuda Hundred, Lee knew almost nothing of Grant, and asked Beauregard by telegraph:

Can you ascertain anything of Grant's movements? I am cut off now from all information.[12]

On June seventeenth Lee moved nearer the new scene of fighting, at the Clay House, on the Bermuda Hundred line. Even now, Lee had not been told of Grant crossing the river. He got the final word he had been seeking at ten P.M., of June seventeenth, in a telegram from Beauregard speaking of increased enemy forces, adding: "I may have to evacuate the city very shortly."

Lee waited no longer. He sent Kershaw's brigade to Petersburg, and ordered A. P. Hill to cross the James and halt within easy marching distance of Petersburg.

At the end of the days of maddening uncertainty and bootless fencing with Beauregard, Lee seemed relieved. When an officer came from the Creole's headquarters to cry: "Unless reinforcements are sent before forty-eight hours, God Almighty alone can save Petersburg and Richmond," Lee replied quietly, "I hope God Almighty will."[13]

On June eighteenth, just a few hours after the situation had cleared for Lee, the weary men of Beauregard saw the vanguard of Kershaw's troops coming into the big lines, with others pressing behind at a rapid pace.

Robert Stiles marched in the front ranks of the relief troops:

"We made a rapid all-night march . . . a very trying one, on account of the heat and the heavy dust which covered everything and rendered breathing all but impossible. We stopped an hour or so to rest the horses—we did not so much regard the men—and arrived in Petersburg in the early morning. . . . We were just in time to prevent Burnside from making an assault, which would probably have given him the city. . . .

"The whole population of the city appeared to be in the streets and thoroughly alive to the narrow escape. . . . Ladies, old and young, met us at their front gates with . . . cool water and delicious viands, and did not at all shrink from grasping our rough and dirty hands."

Lee rode into Petersburg at about noon of June eighteenth and lost no time in finding Beauregard, with whom he rode on an inspection of the lines. Even as the tired troops were moving into the position he had so lately given up for lost, Beauregard was enthusiastically pointing out to Lee a means to launch an attack against the enemy. Lee pointed out that the exhausted, outnumbered men could not be thrown forward.

The army settled into a new phase of its life. Lee had predicted the coming of the day two weeks earlier, when he had told General Early: "We must destroy this army of Grant's before he gets to James River. If he gets there, it will become a seige, and then it will be a mere question of time."[14]

As the troops from Lee's army went into the lines, where vast trenches stretched out of sight, they caught a glimpse of their future. Robert Stiles wrote:

"We thought we had before seen men with the marks of hard service upon them, but the appearance of this division of Mahone's . . . made us realize for the first time what our comrades in the hottest Petersburg lines were undergoing. We were shocked at the condition, the complexion, the expression of the men . . . even the field officers; indeed we could scarcely realize that the unwashed, uncombed, unfed and almost unclad creatures were officers of rank and reputation in the army."

14 *THE TRENCHES*

It WAS an ugly landscape, a bare valley lying between eroded hillocks, scarred by the burrowings of the armies. On its fringe was Petersburg, well within range of Federal cannon, already becoming the shell of a city, like an ancient ruin across the dusty plain.

Lee's line ran for about thirty-six miles north and south of the James, shielding both Richmond and Petersburg. Behind the lines, which could be held only by daily miracles, was a little network of four railroads, which alone could feed the hungry army and the twin cities. Famine was coming to Richmond; there was no longer a question of its countryside feeding the capital.

Confederate currency was all but worthless. There was no sugar; sorghum, becoming rarer, was the only sweetening. The poor ate a treat known as "Benjamin," in honor of a less-popular member of the Davis cabinet; it was only hardtack, soaked in hot water and lightly salted. A bushel of potatoes brought $160; a peck of corn meal $20.[1]

Some places on the railroad lines were within enemy range, and were soon blasted by the big guns; Lee's wagoners were forced to carry loads around the breaks, and supply became slower. Men in the trenches were soon rationed to eighteen rounds per day for their muskets, though they were showered with plentiful ammunition by their enemies.

The trenches were occasionally within a hundred yards of each other, and the Federal sharpshooters had telescopic sights; life became a matter of animal caution in the pits of pallid clay.

Lee's letters to Mary in the last days of June reflected the changed times:

> I hope it is not as hot in Richmond as here. The men suffer a great deal in the trenches; and this . . . with the heat of the sun, nearly puts an end to military operations.

On June thirtieth he duly remembered their wedding anniversary:

> I was very glad to hear that you were better. I trust you will continue to improve. . . . God grant that you may be entirely restored in his own good time! Do you recollect what a happy day thirty-three years ago this was? How many hopes and pleasures it gave birth to! God has been very merciful and kind to us, and how thankless and sinful I have been. I pray that he may continue his mercies and blessings to us and give us a little peace and rest together in this world, and finally gather us and all he has given us around his throne in the world to come.
>
> The President has just arrived, and I must bring my letter to a close.

There were others:

> The ladies of Petersburg have sent me a nice set of shirts. . . . In fact, they have given away everything—which I fear they cannot spare—vegetables, bread, milk, ice cream. Today one of them sent me a nice peach—the first one I think I have seen for two years. I sent it to Mrs. Shippen.
>
> Mr. Platt held services again today under the trees near

my camp. We had quite a large congregation. . . . During the services I constantly heard the shells crashing among the houses of Petersburg.

Once more:

> The shells have scattered the poor inhabitants in Petersburg, so that many of the churches are closed.

Lee had pitched his tent in the yard of Violet Bank, a comfortable home on the main road from Richmond to Petersburg. The Mrs. Shippen of whom he wrote Mary was the mistress of the house, a large building set in a shady grove. For the first time during the war he had a new tent, since his old one, which had been with him since the long-ago foray into the Virginia mountains, was leaking. He seemed to have recovered from his recent illness. Long pictured him:

"He had aged somewhat in appearance . . . but had rather gained than lost in physical vigor, from the severe life he had led. His hair had grown gray, but his face had the ruddy hue of health, and his eyes were as clear and bright as ever. . . . Though always abstemious in diet, he seemed able to bear any amount of fatigue."

One day Lee, inspecting an exposed battery on the line below Richmond, was surrounded by soldiers from nearby positions. The crowd attracted enemy gunfire.

"Men, you had better go farther to the rear," Lee said. "They are firing up there, and you are exposing yourselves to unnecessary danger."

The men fell back, but Lee, as if unaware of danger to himself, went across the open, picked some object from the ground, and placed it in a tree overhead. The curious soldiers soon discovered that he had rescued an unfledged sparrow from the ground, and returned it to its nest.[2]

Lee was able to see two of his sons with some frequency in the

first weeks, since Custis had been removed from the staff of Davis
for active field duty (he confessed to some embarrassment over his
brigadier's stars in the presence of the "fighting colonels" of his father's staff); and Rooney was leading his cavalry in flank actions.
Rob was in the line, but saw his father only once over a period of
months.

Life settled into a painful routine, with tension ever present,
lest the line part somewhere. There was good news from Wade
Hampton shortly after the army crawled into its trenches, for he
had overtaken the raiding Sheridan across the state, and defeated
him at Trevillians Station on June eleventh and twelfth. Hampton
came to the army in late June. He was just in time to team with
Rooney's men in trapping a bold Federal raid led by General James
H. Wilson. The cavalry and an infantry brigade under Mahone
trapped the enemy at Reams Station on the Petersburg and Weldon
Railroad and took 1,000 prisoners and a whole train of supplies and
loot.

With so many of his veteran general officers gone (Ewell now
commanded the Richmond garrison, and there was no immediate
prospect of the wounded Longstreet's return), Lee came into intimate contact with other men. One of these who proved valuable in
the trench warfare was General Mahone—Fighting Billy—the profane, poker-playing, cock-fighting president of a peacetime railroad,
a son of a tavern keeper who had become a man of means.

Mahone had a tiny, grumbling, voice. He was sketched by a
young soldier about this time:

"The sauciest-looking little manikin imaginable . . . a perfect
tin soldier . . . not over five feet seven inches tall, and as attenuated
as an Italian greyhound . . . his face was covered with a drooping
mustache and full beard of rich chestnut color . . . he wore a large
sombrero hat, without plume . . . a hunting shirt of gray . . . plaited
about the waistband . . . boots as small as a woman's . . . and when
he ungloved one little hand, it was almost as diminutive and frail

as the foot of a song-bird; he had no sword ... in his hand he carried a slender wand of a stick ... his voice was almost a falsetto tenor."[3]

It was Mahone who led the first adventure from the new lines. On the south of Petersburg, near the Jerusalem Plank Road, the Federals were advancing in Grant's favorite fashion: One line, near to the Confederates, was supported by a new line to the rear, a longer one, with a rapidly extended flank. The second line poured out toward the Confederate forts on June twenty-second, and Mahone noted a careless gap between the two forces. He asked permission to counterattack, flung his force at the gap, and won a handsome little victory, routing two Federal divisions. He had 1,700 prisoners to prove it, an embarrassing number of new mouths to feed.

Two days later Lee struck again, this time a stab at the Federal right near the Appomattox River. This attack was manned by the divisions of Hoke and Field, there was no co-ordination, and the enemy broke the charges and many men were lost. Squabbles broke out between Hoke and Field, but Lee commented only, "There seems to have been some misunderstanding."

These were almost the only diversions of the first month of this warfare. The men became hardened to life in the tunnels. The boy soldier John Wise, son of the General and ex-Governor of Virginia, was a part of it:

"The men ... learned to burrow like conies. Into the sides of the trenches and traverses they went with bayonet and tin cups ... at sultry midday or during a rainfall, one might look up or down the trenches without seeing anybody but the sentinel. At the sound of the drum, the heads of the soldiers would pop up as if they had been gophers. Still, many lives were lost by indifference to danger. ...

"They became careless about clothes, food, ammunition, cleanliness, even personal safety. . . . For a long time they had been shot at, night and day. A man, because he had not been hit, would soon come to regard himself as invulnerable. . . . Past immunity made him so confident that he would walk coolly over the same exposed ground where somebody else had been shot the day before. . . . Mayhap he would take his short pipe out of his mouth and yell defiantly, 'Ahh—Yank—yer—cain't—shoot.' "

There were informal truces when men talked across the trenches; sometimes women came from the city to visit the Rebs, and the enemy honored their presence with a suspension of fire. Before opening fire, men would yell that officers were coming, a warning to all to take cover. Sharpshooters at their posts used mirrors to watch the enemy, for safety and comfort; they played cards and told interminable tales.

Within a few days, however, the miseries of both armies increased. A Federal artillery regiment arrived with a variety of mortars, and the exploding shells, dropping straight down into the trenches, took a few lives and drove men deeper into their burrows. General Alexander of Lee's artillery had ordered mortars of his own, and though they were light 12-pounders, and no match for the heavy Federal siege guns, they were easy to handle and effective at the short range.

Always the maze of trenches grew. The Confederate line became a vast bristling of forts on the rolling plain, connected with networks of infantry parapets, and zigzags of trenches in all directions.

General Alexander told of a night at Petersburg which remained in memory:

"Of all the moonlight nights I can remember, I recall that . . . as the most brilliant and beautiful. . . . The dust rose with every movement and hung in the air. The whole landscape was bathed in silver, and sounds were unusually distinct. . . .

"The drawing out of old guns and approach of new was attended with sounds which wandered far and with luminous clouds of dust. Then the enemy would know we were moving and there would come crashes of musketry at random and volleys of artillery from their lines. Then our infantry would imagine themselves attacked, and would respond . . . and the fire would run along the parapet to right and left, and gradually subside."

Even the mortars, however, were soon accepted as a minor irritation. John Wise noted:

"They learned to fear more danger from minié balls than from mortar shells. There was little chance of a shell's falling upon the men, for they could see it and get out of the way. . . . Iron was becoming scarce. As inducement to collecting scrap iron for our cannon foundries, furloughs were offered, a day for so many pounds collected. Thus, gathering fragments of shell became an active industry among the troops. So keen was their quest that sometimes they would start toward the point where a mortar shell fell, even before it exploded."

Men in the trenches briefly forgot their own plight in early July, with stirring news from the North. General Early, sent by Lee to check the Federal invasion of the Shenandoah Valley, had not only forced General Hunter to retreat; he had crossed the Potomac. On July ninth he defeated a Federal force under General Lew Wallace on the Monocacy River, in Maryland, and turned on Washington. He was outside the virtually undefended capital on July eleventh, but his 10,000 did not enter, for reinforcements soon came to the city from Grant's army. It seemed a sign that the war was not yet over, despite the aura of despair which hung above the trenches with the dust cloud.

In early July there was a new peril.

Somewhere along the lines one quiet night, Confederate pickets heard a muffled sound in the earth far beneath them. The news went through the army: The enemy was mining their lines. Several deep shafts were sunk, seeking the enemy miners. It was to no avail. The sounds continued through the heat of July, but headquarters had concluded that there was nothing more to be done. The men waited.

In the Federal line, commanding the 48th Pennsylvania, a regiment of coal miners, was a mining engineer, Colonel Henry Pleasants. He was intrigued by the sight of a looming Confederate work which rose some 130 yards from a railroad cut in the Federal lines, behind which was a deep ravine. He proposed a mine to blow up the enemy position with a great powder charge, and break the Confederate line; he expected an end to the stalemate at Petersburg. General Burnside approved, but few others did. Pleasants wrote:

"I found it impossible to get any assistance from anybody; I had to do all the work myself. I had to remove all the earth in old cracker boxes."

Pleasants had no way to measure the distance from the entrance of his mine to the Confederate fort, and could get no instruments, because the chief engineers thought the plan "all clap-trap and nonsense"; General Burnside finally got him an old theodolite from Washington, though the engineers protested: "Such a length of mine had never been evacuated in military operations, and could not be . . . it would either get the men smothered . . . or crushed by the falling of the earth, or the enemy would find it out and it would amount to nothing."

Pleasants kept his 400 miners hard at it, and the tunnel grew. He had to get his own lumber for framing as he went, and sent men behind the lines to operate an old Rebel sawmill. Chains of men toiled in and out with the earth. Every night brush was cut to hide the mouth of the mine. The tools were poor, for Pleasants had to take ordinary picks and straighten them, since engineers would provide no mining picks. He estimated that the work took four times as long as it should have. But on July twenty-third he was ready.

His tunnel was 510 feet long, with a 75-foot cross gallery beneath the Rebel fort where the gunpowder was to be placed. An attack was prepared for launching after the explosion; a division of Negro troops under General Edward Ferrero had been drilled for weeks for this assault. The explosion was set for July thirtieth.

But now headquarters began to change the plan. The charge of powder was reduced from 14,000 to 8,000 pounds. And one day before the deadline the plan to use Negro troops as a vanguard was changed, and a white division, unfamiliar with the operation, was substituted. They got quick instructions: Charge through the hole made by the explosion and seize a commanding eminence, Cemetery Hill, some 400 yards to the right and rear of the target fort.

Colonel Regis de Trobriand, commander of a French regiment of New York volunteers, held his men in readiness as the time neared, watching:

"The hour set for the mine explosion was half past three in the morning. . . . So from three o'clock everyone was up, the officers watch in hand, eyes fixed . . . in that direction.

"There were about 200 men in that work, sleeping tranquilly a sleep from which they would awake in eternity . . . at the instant when, beneath them, Colonel Pleasants was applying the fire to the match. . . . Upon the parapet the motionless sentinels were watching the pale light which began to brighten the horizon in the east. . . .

"From half after three the minutes were counted. It is still too dark, it was said. At four o'clock it was daylight; nothing stirred as yet; at a quarter past four a murmur of impatience ran through the ranks. What has happened? Has there been a counter-order? Or an accident? Has the assault been deferred?"

No one knew for a time, and Pleasants sent two fearless volunteers into the long tunnel to see what had gone wrong. Lieutenant Jacob Douty and Sergeant Henry Rees crawled into the hole, and about halfway found the trouble: the fuse had burned out. They relit the fuse, and scurried back to safety. There was a spectacle for de Trobriand's journal:

"Suddenly the earth trembled beneath our feet. An enormous mass sprang into the air. A mass without form or shape, full of red flames, and carried on a bed of lightning flashes. . . . It spread out like a sheaf, like an immense mushroom. . . . Then everything appeared to break up and fall back in a rain of earth mixed with rocks, with beams, timbers, and mangled human bodies, leaving floating in the air a cloud of white smoke, which rose up in the heavens, and a cloud of gray dust, which fell slowly toward the earth. The redan [fort] had disappeared. In its place had opened a gaping gulf more than two hundred feet long by fifty wide, and twenty-five to thirty feet deep.

"Immediately, as though the eruption of a volcano had poured out a torrent of lava upon our lines, they were on fire from one end to the other. All our batteries opened at once on the enemy's intrenchments. The projectiles whistled, roared, burst. Through the deafening noise . . . was heard a cry, and the first division advanced to the assault."

There was an incredible sound now in the dawn: The Negro division, climbing over the works and moving out as part of the attack, were singing their curious battle hymn:

> "We-e looks like men a-marchin' on,
> We looks like men-er-war."

Many Confederates were dead in the explosion, and for hundreds of yards on either side of the crater, the lines were undefended, open to Federal assault. Still, it was more than ten minutes before the first bluecoats went forward.[4]

John Wise, watching from the Confederate lines, saw the Federals come at last: "When they finally advanced it was . . . with rushes and pauses of uncertainty . . . they halted, peeped, and gaped into the pit, and then, with the stupidity of sheep, followed their bell-wethers into the crater itself, where, huddled together, all semblance of organization vanished. . . .

"From our ten-inch and eight-inch mortars . . . a most accurate fire was opened . . . and our batteries . . . began to pour a deadly storm of shell and canister upon the crowded masses."

A handful of artillerymen and a few infantry held the Federals at bay.

Lee did not learn of the affair until six o'clock, when he was at breakfast. Long before, Federal headquarters had taken prisoners from the crater and learned that Cemetery Hill was unprotected, and that the moment for breaking Lee's lines had come.

Lee ordered General Mahone to take two brigades to the cemetery. Mahone, sly as ever, pulled his men out of the main line without arousing Federal suspicions and made the transfer.

When Mahone's men arrived near the crater, Wise saw:

"There was no cheering, and no gaudy flaunting of uniforms or standards . . . in weather-worn and ragged clothes . . . Agile as cats, they sprang across the road and entered the covered way . . . For the first time during the day, a line of infantry was between our guns and the enemy. . . .

"At the command 'Forward!' the men . . . advanced at a run; absolutely refrained from firing until within a few feet of the enemy; then delivered a deadly fire, and, rushing upon them with bayonets and clubbed muskets, drove them pell-mell back into the intrenchments which they had just left.

"General Lee, when advised of this brilliant assault, remarked, 'That must have been Mahone's old brigade.' "

At about one o'clock, when Confederate support was brought up, the Federals raised a white flag in the crater and the great experiment was over. More than 1,100 Federals were made prisoners, the Rebels had taken several thousand small arms, and about 1,000 enemy dead were strewn about the yawning pit. Lee's line was left about as it was, and the Confederate loss was no more than 1,500, including fewer than 300 lost at the explosion.

The last glimpse of fighting at this place seemed to one witness "the most brutal" of the war:

"It was the first time Lee's army had encountered Negroes, and their presence excited in the troops indignant malice. . . . To the credit of the blacks be it said that they advanced in better order and pushed forward farther than the whites . . . but when our men, in frenzy, rushed upon and drove the cold steel into them, they did not show the stubborn power of endurance . . . our men, inflamed to relentless vengeance by their presence, disregarded the rules of warfare which restrained them in battle with their own race, and brained and butchered the blacks until the slaughter was sickening."[5]

The siege went on. Lines grew to the south and west of Petersburg, but somehow, as Grant's big columns fanned out, Lee managed to have works dug in front of them, and the thin line held. There was gossip of a permanent stalemate, for it was inconceivable that even this enemy would charge over fields checkerboarded with mines every five feet, and torpedoes on all the roads into the cities.

Lee wrote his youngest daughter four days after the crater explosion, with his thoughts on Mary's illness:

> Am very glad to hear your mother is better. I sent out immediately to try and find some lemons, but could procure only two—sent to me by a kind lady, Mrs. Kirkland, in Petersburg. These were gathered from her own trees; there are none to be purchased. I found one in my valise, dried up, which I also send, as it may be of some value. I also put up some early apples, which you can roast for your mother, and one pear. This is all the fruit I can get.
>
> You must go to the market every morning and see if you cannot find some fresh fruit for her. . . . I wish I could be with her to nurse her and care for her. . . . I think of you, long for you, pray for you: it is all I can do.

There was an almost daily weakening of his line. In early August, after conferring with Davis in Richmond, Lee detached General Anderson with a division of infantry and Fitz Lee's cavalry— this in answer to Grant's having sent a strong force from his lines to aid in the Federal chase of General Early in the Shenandoah. Almost as these troops moved Lee was called to the James, where the enemy was complicating matters by digging a great canal at Dutch Gap, whose completion would flank the Confederate lines crossing Bermuda Neck, erasing the advantage of the looping river. The enemy mounted an attack in that neighborhood on August fourteenth and Lee was forced to bring reinforcements from Petersburg, and to recall some cavalry he had sent westward. The result was a minor victory over the enemy in the vicinity of White Oak Swamp. But even this was hardly ended when there was an insistent call from Beauregard; trouble had developed on the south.

Three Federal divisions had struck the Weldon Railroad, and though Lee hurried reinforcements of infantry, and A. P. Hill managed to capture almost 3,000 prisoners, the Federals held the vital road along its northern line, and Lee concluded, after several efforts to dislodge them, that he could not shake them loose. The cities and the army, already in dire straits, must now depend on the two rickety lines to the westward which Lee could still give protection.

While these skirmishes were being fought, and the Federals pecked at various points of the line, Richmond seemed to be losing hope. Girls on city porches were singing "When This Cruel War Is Over," and most families were becoming hungry. Domestic labor was almost a thing of the past; linen was selling at $22 a yard; cotton thread at $5 a spool; cabbage at $10 a head; milk at $2.50 a quart. Yet there was a theatre season, and blockade speculators gambled in five or six figures nightly in the hotels. The hospitals were always filled now, and plagues swept the city.[6]

News from the far frontiers of the Confederacy was increasingly bad. In August, Admiral Farragut closed Mobile. On September third there was frantic cheering from the Federal lines, leading some to believe the enemy was celebrating the nomination of General McClellan as Democratic candidate for President, and that there was hope of peace at last. But it turned out that this was only joy at the announcement of the fall of Atlanta, and the opening of Sherman's march through the heart of the Confederacy.

Lee's spirits did not seem to flag, though he must have seen the growing signs of the end he had predicted.

One day, when a civilian pressed him to name the Confederacy's best friend, Lee replied:

"The only unfailing friend the Confederacy ever had was cornfield peas."

His headquarters rations were short, like those of the soldiers, and he once entertained General Hampton at Petersburg when there was a small bowl of soup on the table, placed before half a dozen or more hungry men of the staff. Lee quickly divided the soup with Hampton, and looking around the table said slyly:

"I am credibly informed that the young men of my staff never eat soup."[7]

Lee sent Beauregard to North Carolina to inspect the defenses of Wilmington, now the only important port open to blockade runners, on whom the army must depend. Since Mobile was gone, Lee reasoned, Wilmington and its shield, Fort Fisher, would next get attention from the all-powerful Federal fleet.

On September nineteenth, even worse news came in: Early had been attacked by Sheridan at Winchester, defeated, driven back, and defeated again. General Rodes was dead, and Fitz Lee was wounded.

Such news seemed to hasten the decline of the army in the trenches, and desertion became steadily worse. Late in September, Lee officially complained that he could not replace the losses caused by veterans slipping from their posts and going away home. The 50,000 with whom he had first faced Grant in the long line were becoming rapidly less. He wrote: "If things continue, the most serious consequences must result."

Young Wise, on leave in Richmond, stood in Capitol Square,

where he saw on parade a battalion of Confederate Negro troops, and he wrote: "Ah! This is but the beginning of the end."

Desertions averaged at least 100 a day, caused by terrible conditions in the homes of soldiers.

A staff officer wrote:

"Hundred of letters addressed to soldiers were intercepted and sent to headquarters, in which mothers, wives, and sisters told of their inability to respond to the appeals of hungry children for bread, or to provide proper care and remedies for the sick; and, in the name of all that was dear, appealed to the men to come home and rescue them from the ills which they suffered and the starvation which threatened them."[8]

It was thus no mystery to Lee that the regiments dwindled nightly. He was determined as ever to share the suffering of the men in every reasonable particular. Colonel Walter Taylor was only a boy, but he understood Lee, and often saw him with clarity, as on an occasion in early November, when Lee ordered a move of headquarters:

"I took possession of a vacant house and had his room prepared, with a cheerful fire, and everything made as cozy as possible. It was entirely too pleasant for him, for he is never so uncomfortable as when comfortable. A day or two after our arrival he informed me that he . . . thought it best to move our camp."

Late in the month headquarters moved to a large house of the Turnbull family, called Edge Hill, where Lee lived in a bedroom, and others of the staff had small back rooms, while Taylor was enjoying life in the big parlor, with a piano and fine furniture and paintings. When Lee found Taylor there he was amazed:

"Ah! You are finely fixed. Couldn't you find any other room?"

"No," replied the joking Taylor. "But this will do. I can make myself tolerably comfortable here."

Lee left with a shocked expression after Taylor's "impudence."

The enemy left headquarters little time to enjoy life. There were numerous raids on the Weldon Railroad, each of which had to be met with major supports, and each of which cut off a little more of the track and forced longer hauls with the wagons.

Then Grant struck north of the James, where Lee had lately reinforced the line with General Anderson, recalled from upstate. By a surprise attack on September twenty-ninth, the enemy had swarmed into a strong point of the northern line, called Fort Harrison. Lee hurried up all the brigades he could spare and went to direct the counterattack himself. After a bloody day's work of piecemeal charges, with Hoke and Field in command, and Lee going into the fire himself to urge on the men, he had to accept failure. He ordered a rebuilding of the defense line there and gave up the fort to the enemy.

On the same day a dangerous extension of the southern line was forced upon him by Federal cavalry who advanced almost to a stream called Hatchers Run and entrenched; when reinforced, they made the advance into a permanent part of the line. This so stretched Lee's lower flank as to make one division's front about three times as wide as before.

Lee wrote the Secretary of War:

> The enemy's numerical superiority enables him to hold his lines with an adequate force, and extend on each flank with numbers so much greater than ours. . . . We cannot fight to advantage with such odds, and there is the gravest reason to apprehend the result of every encounter. . . .
>
> If we can get out our entire arms bearing population in Virginia and North Carolina . . . we may be able, with the blessing of God, to keep the enemy in check to the beginning of winter. If we fail to do this the result must be calamitous. The discouragement of our people and the great material loss that would follow the fall of Richmond . . . outweigh, in my judgment, any sacrifice and hardship.[9]

He added privately to General Cooper at the War Department:

I fear it will be impossible to keep him out of Richmond.

Longstreet had returned on October nineteenth, his right arm crippled, but vigorous and anxious for service. He was shocked by his first look at Lee after his long absence:

"The general seemed worn by past labor, besides suffering at seasons from severe sciatica, while his work was accumulating and his troubles multiplying to proportions that should have employed half a dozen able men."

During this period two of the staff, Marshall and Venable, were ill, and most of the work fell upon young Taylor, the twenty-six-year-old veteran who was in fact chief of staff.

With an air of relief Lee placed Longstreet in charge north of the James. He was more confident in the direction of the troops than when Anderson had handled them on this sector, and the first brush with the enemy was comforting. Longstreet might have faults which Lee could not bring himself to correct, but he was a workman in the field when aroused. On October twenty-seventh, when the enemy flung a loud, long attack against the northern line, and pounded at Petersburg as well, Longstreet, with the aplomb of a veteran, reasoned that a turning movement was planned on his northernmost tip where support was weak. He rushed troops there and knocked out the Federal attack before it could form, capturing many prisoners.

Cold weather came, and life was more miserable in the trenches. Desertion increased, and thousands of men on both sides must have been thinking as Lieutenant R. M. Collins had, in Lee's line:

"As we lay there watching the bright stars . . . many a soldier asked himself the questions: What is all this about? Why is it that 200,000 men of one blood and one tongue, believing as one man in the fatherhood of God and the universal brotherhood of man, should in the nineteenth century of the Christian era be thus armed with all the improved appliances of modern warfare and seeking one another's lives? We could settle our differences by compromising and all be at home in ten days."

Casualties were light in these days, but were not unimportant. General John Gregg was dead, and now General Gracie of the Alabamians, another young officer of promise, was shot.

The diary entries of Colonel Taylor were an accurate guide to the times:

Dec. 4

Since the affair at Stony Creek we have had perfect quiet on our lines. General Gracie, who showed such tact in getting General Lee to descend from a dangerous position, was killed near the lines a day or so ago . . . killed while quietly viewing the enemy from a point where no one dreamed of danger.

Dec. 12

We have had much excitement during the past week. . . . Couriers were arriving during the whole of last night—and what a bitter cold night it was! So far the enemy have accomplished but little. The whole movement seems to have been a grand raid on the Weldon Railroad, and, though the bridge was saved by the valor of our troops, the enemy succeeded in destroying about ten miles of the road.

In mid-December Lee called in another division from Early's force in the western part of the state, and strength in the besieged line rose to about 60,000. This was soon reduced by calls for help from the south.

Beauregard, now in Savannah, telegraphed that Sherman was at the gates of that city. And a vast Federal fleet appeared off Wilmington, North Carolina. More bad news came from Tennessee, where General Hood had been defeated at Nashville. Davis asked Lee to spare some troops for the south.

One division was sent to aid Wilmington, where the enemy ships soon departed. Savannah fell, however, and by Christmas the Confederacy seemed wide open to attack in all directions.

Colonel Taylor wrote in his diary:

> Truly matters are becoming serious and exciting. If somebody doesn't arrest Sherman's march, where will he stop? They are trying to corner this old army, but like a brave lion brought to bay at last it is determined to resist to the death, and if die it must to die game.
>
> We are to have some hard knocks, we are to experience much that is dispiriting, but if our men are true (and I really believe that most of them are) we will make our way successfully through the dark clouds that now surround us. Our people must make up their minds to see Richmond go, but must not lose spirit, must not give up.[10]

No indication of despair was given by Lee, whose men never tired of inspecting him at close range. Robert Graham, a North Carolina captain, noted in November:

"He is neatly attired in regulation gray, but without the general's white buff coat collar and cuffs . . . there is no gold wreath, nor a particle of gold lace. . . . He might have been mistaken for a colonel in his best fatigue suit. . . .

"His hat is a soft black felt. . . . Hair and full beard are both short. Complexion is of a healthy, ruddy hue, indicating a temperate life. . . . There is a fearless look of self-possession without a trace of arrogance."

In her letters Mary pleaded with him to take better care of himself, he replied: "But what care can a man give to himself in the time of war?" He added that he lived in a tent most of the time because it was essential, and not for pleasure. But he was determined, he said, that he would not disturb families in their homes simply to acquire more comfortable quarters.

He wrote Mary often in the depths of winter:

I received . . . the box with hat, gloves, and socks; also
the barrel of apples. You had better kept the latter, as it would
have been more useful to you than to me, and I should have
enjoyed its consumption by yourself and the girls more than
by me.

Again:

The Lyons furs and fur robe have also arrived safely, but
I can learn nothing of the saddle of mutton. Bryan . . . is greatly
alarmed lest it has been sent to the soldiers' dinner. If the
soldiers get it I shall be content. I can do very well without it.

And again, drawing a picture of unconscious charm, he wrote:

Yesterday afternoon three little girls walked into my room,
each with a small basket. The eldest carried some fresh eggs
laid by her own hens; the second, some pickles made by her
mother; the third, some pop corn which had grown in her
garden. . . . The eldest, whose age did not exceed eight years,
had a small wheel on which she had spun for her two
brothers. . . .
I have not had so pleasant a visit for a long time. I fortunately was able to fill their baskets with apples, which dis-
tressed poor Bryan, and begged them to bring me nothing but
kisses and to keep the eggs, corn, etc. for themselves.
I pray daily, and almost hourly, to our heavenly Father
to come to the relief of you and our afflicted country. I know
He will order all things for our good, and we must be content.

Lee could still laugh. About this time he had a visit from a Ne-
gro cook of an army mess which provided an anecdote for the gen-
eral's store, one he would often recall.
The Negro came into headquarters, hat in hand.
"General Lee," he said, "I been wanting to see you a long time.
I'm a soldier."
"Ah. To what army do you belong?"

"Oh, General, I belong to your army."

"Well, have you been shot?"

"No, sir. I ain't been shot yet."

"How's that? Nearly all our men get shot."

"Why, General, I ain't been shot 'cause I stays back where the generals stay."[11]

In January Lee wrote the new Secretary of War, General Breckinridge, that the army had but two days' rations on hand. A special plea was sent to Virginia farmers, asking them to help save the hungry regiments. The response was meager, but somehow the army clung to life.

Lee wrote a Confederate Congressman, Representative Barksdale, that the time had come to enlist Negroes in the ranks.

On January fifteenth, the Federals had finally closed Wilmington. General Joseph Johnston was trying to get together a command to put into the path of Sherman in the south.

The country briefly expected an end to the war, when peace commissioners met in Hampton Roads with President Lincoln, but they soon returned to Richmond with nothing accomplished, and the fighting dragged on.

Lee was appointed General-in-Chief, with full power in the field, as of February sixth. But this came only after Davis had been forced to it after a wrangle with Congress. Lee had powers many had sought for him in 1861, but which Davis had denied him. The new position came when hope was all but gone, and when his relations with Davis were unusually strained.

But Lee wrote Davis:

> I know I am indebted entirely to your indulgence and kind consideration for this honorable position. . . . If I can relieve you from a portion of the constant labor and anxiety which now presses upon you . . . I shall be more than compensated for the addition to my present burdens. I must,

however, rely upon the several commanders . . . and hold
them responsible. In the event of their neglect or failure I
must ask for their removal.

As the food supply dwindled and signs of the approaching end
multiplied, Lee became firmer in dealing with Richmond. He
wrote Breckinridge:

If some change is not made and the commissary department reorganized, I apprehend dire results.

In the same dispatch he told a brief story of soldiers who were
forced to stay in line of battle three days and nights, almost without
food.

President Davis scratched on the back of the document: "This
is too sad to be patiently considered, and cannot have occurred without criminal neglect or gross incapacity."

That, at last, had effect. Davis ousted his old friend Northrop
as Commissary General. Not even this seemed to help. Lee, becoming desperate, proposed that Virginia's Congressmen find some new
means of supply. If someone did not act, he said, the army would be
forced to disband. This crisis led to a call from Richmond.

Lee rode into the capital to meet with the Virginia delegation
in Congress, and after an inconclusive conversation, left them and
went to Davis. He made a candid report. The President wrote of
their talk:

"He stated that circumstances had forced on him the conclu-
sion that the evacuation of Petersburg was but a question of time.
He appreciated the embarrassment which would result from losing
. . . Richmond."

"Wouldn't it be better to pull out of the lines immediately?"
Davis asked.

"The artillery and draft horses are too weak for the soft roads,"
Lee said. "We will have to wait until they become firmer."

At the end of this discouraging day in early March, Lee went to his family in its Richmond home. Mary was unable to eat with the rest of them, but Custis and two of the girls were with the General for dinner, as well as his young nephew, George Taylor Lee, son of Charles Carter. George was now a beardless soldier, a Virginia Military Institute cadet.

When the girls had retired Custis sat smoking a cigar and reading a newspaper. The observant George recorded:

"The General was walking the floor, up and down, up and down. He was so much engrossed in his own thoughts, with his eyes fixed on the floor, that he seemed to be oblivious of the presence of a third person."

George saw that Lee was "deeply troubled," and thought he had never seen his uncle so grave.

Lee faced Custis.

"Well, Mr. Custis," he said. "I have been up to see the Congress and they don't seem to be able to do anything except eat peanuts and chew tobacco, while my army is starving.

"I told them the condition we were in, and that something must be done at once, but I can't get them to do anything, or they are unable to do anything."

There seemed to be no reply. Lee did not describe the meeting in detail. He soon continued:

"Mr. Custis, when this war began I was opposed to it, bitterly opposed to it, and I told these people that unless every man should do his whole duty, they would repent it; and now . . . " Lee paused.

"And now they will repent."

He said no more. Young George thought to himself that affairs must be hopeless indeed for the General to speak so.[12]

The boy was right. Lee had obtained permission from Davis to write Grant, asking for an interview between the commanding generals to talk of an armistice.

This request went to Grant on March second, the day the Shenandoah Valley was lost, as Sheridan swept down on Early and crushed his weakened force. Grant replied in firm, uncompromising tones:

> I have no authority to accede to your proposition for a conference on the subject proposed. Such authority is vested in the President of the United States alone.[13]

15 *FLIGHT*

THERE WAS a moment in Richmond near the end when the stench and despair of the trenches seemed only a bad dream. Miss Emily Rutherford, a belle of the city, was married to Colonel William Tabb, 59th Virginia, a superbly eligible young bachelor. President and Mrs. Davis were guests.

Blockade runners had done their best with silks and ribbons and fine gowns, but they could not work miracles. Some men had come in from the ragged regiments of the trenches, and these wore misfits of many makes and sorts. Many were frankly patched. The ladies' gowns, one soldier said, looked as if they had been dragged from ransacked Richmond garrets. One girl confessed that she was wearing the gown her grandmother had worn in 1824, when Lafayette visited Richmond.

But gaiety was unrestrained. Army tents had been hung to screen a large porch of the home, and there an army band blared away amid banks of holly and mistletoe. Tabb's regiment had made a huge wedding bell of greens to hang overhead.

Jeff Davis took his tribute of a kiss from the bride and smiled to Tabb, "For a bribe like that, Colonel, you may demand a week's extension of your leave."

John Wise was there to sketch Davis:

"A very clean-looking man; his manners were those of a dignified, gracious gentleman accustomed to good society . . . looked thin and careworn . . . his hair and beard were bleaching rapidly; and his bloodless cheeks and slender nose, with its clear-cut, flat nostril, gave him almost the appearance of emaciation. Yet his eye was bright, his smile was winning. . . .

"On his arm was Mrs. Davis . . . looking as if . . . 'the gray mare was the better horse' . . . she was large and looked well-fed."[1]

There was a whole gallery of notables for the throng to see:

Secretary of War Breckinridge, with an aura of bourbon about him; the "keg-like" Benjamin, smiling through his curly beard, "over-deferential" to all; Secretary of the Navy Mallory, outspoken and bluff; Postmaster General Reagan, ". . . ill at ease and looking as if he might have left his carry-log and yoke of oxen at the door."

There was the "fashion-plate," Burton Harrison, secretary to Davis.

There was John M. Daniel of the *Examiner,* the bitter and fearless critic of the Davis administration; Heros von Borcke, the huge Prussian lieutenant who had ridden with Stuart, now whistling through a wound in his throat with every word he spoke; two large women in white, sisters of Mrs. Davis; "a Burmese elephant," waddling through the throng, was General Humphrey Marshall, a Congressman from Kentucky of whom the gossips whispered: "The most inveterate gambler and *bon vivant* in Richmond! Stakes thousands on the turn of a card, and while waiting, lights his $10 cigars with $5 Confederate bills."

There were hosts of others, among them the celebrated Canadian blockade runner, big John Carvell, who had sent the champagne for this party; there was Major Robert Ould, commissioner of prisoner exchange. There were scores of soldiers on leave, adventurers and politicians.

Only Lee seemed to be absent—Lee and the tattered generals of his command.

There was a feast:

Pyramids of butter balls, turkeys, hams, apples, hot breads, stuffed eggs, sausages and pickles. One wedding gift was a treasure: Genuine coffee, which the guests drank delightedly, though without sugar. There were big bowls of hot and cold apple toddy, with apples afloat in them.

The President, the ladies, and the Cabinet, going to their homes, and the soldiers, going back to the muddy burrows, went off as did the diarist John Wise: "In the gray of a winter morning, the cold bright stars twinkling above us," thinking: "eat, drink and be merry, for tomorrow. . . ."

For more than a week after he had conferred with Davis and the Virginia Congressmen, Lee was in a strange mood; he was restless, desperate, fully aware of the increasing helplessness of his army, yet as defiant and bold as ever.

Before he approached Davis again he talked out his troubles with General Gordon, the thirty-three-year-old Georgian. There were few others on whom Lee could lean. Longstreet and Ewell were both more than twenty miles away, and A. P. Hill was on furlough because of poor health.

Gordon reached headquarters at two A.M. one bitter day and found Lee alone, "standing at the fireplace, his arm on the mantel and his head resting on his arm as he gazed into the coal fire. . . . He had evidently been up all night. For the first time . . . I saw a look of painful depression on his face."

Lee waved a hand toward a long table covered with army reports. He asked Gordon to look them over. Gordon leafed through dozens of them:

"Each report was bad enough, and all . . . were sufficient to destroy all cohesive power and lead to the inevitable disintegration of any army. . . . I was not prepared for the picture of the lack of shoes, hats, overcoats, blankets, food."

Some of the officers had not been content with formal reports, and wrote pitiable stories of the emaciation of the few men left for duty in their commands. When Gordon had seen enough, Lee began a slow analysis: Against the 35,000 Confederates in line, Grant had within reach 150,000 men, and General Thomas was coming in from Tennessee with 30,000 more Federal veterans. Grant could bring in 20,000 from the Valley—a total of about 200,000 men would soon face them, exclusive of the forces of Sherman.

Lee paced the room. Gordon noticed that it was four o'clock. "What should I do under these circumstances, General Gordon? Tell me frankly."

"General, there are but three courses, it seems to me.

"First, make terms with the enemy, the best we can get.

"Second, retreat, abandon Richmond and Petersburg, unite with Johnston in North Carolina and strike Sherman before Grant can join him.

"Lastly, fight, and without delay."

After a long wait Lee said, "I agree with you fully."

Gordon asked if he had presented the problem to Davis in this way.

"No, I have not. I scarcely feel authorized to suggest the advisability of making terms with the United States.

"The best course would be to retreat and join Johnston, but I doubt the President will consent to that. . . .

"But if both Davis and General Grant gave me permission, there would still be the pitiable plight of the men."

He talked of the condition of the men and animals. Gordon saw that he had not yet come to the final decision, and that armistice, retreat and fight to the death were all in his mind.

The commander threw off the mood of depression for a moment, smiling at Gordon.

"By the way, I had a verbal message from General Grant to-day."

"What was it?"

"An officer who came in with a flag of truce brought it to me from Grant: 'Give General Lee my personal compliments, and say to him that I keep in such close touch with him that I know what he eats for breakfast every morning.' "

"What did you reply?"

"I told him there must be some mistake . . . for unless he had fallen from grace since I saw him last, he would not permit me to eat such breakfasts as mine without dividing his with me.

"I also asked the officer to present my compliments to General Grant and to say to him that I knew perhaps as much about his dinners as he knew about my breakfasts."

Lee then agreed to go to Davis with his presentation of the army's plight. He promised:

"I will go, and will send for you again on my return from Richmond."[2]

It was near sunrise when Gordon left him. Lee soon departed for Richmond.

On this visit he made his nearest approach to taking matters into his own hands. Before he went to Davis he talked with Senator R. M. T. Hunter, the learned Secessionist who was once Secretary of State, and had lately been one of the peace commissioners on the futile visit to President Lincoln at Hampton Roads.

Lee went directly to the point:

"If you think there is a chance for a peace that would get us better terms than they will give after surrender, it is your duty to make the effort now," he said.

Hunter explained the failure in their talk with Lincoln, who had declared "he would not treat with us with arms in our hands." Hunter also said it would be foolish for him to try peace-making again, since confidential matters of his first effort had spread through Richmond and were now the subject of gossip. Hunter suspected that President Davis had betrayed the secrets.

Lee mused. "If I recommend peace negotiations publicly, it will be almost equivalent to surrender."

"I am aware of that, "Hunter said. "But if you think the chance for success is desperate, I think you should say so to the President."

Lee did not reply. In the whole of the long, rambling all-night talk, Hunter remembered, Lee did not ever say "the chances were over," but he left that impression on Hunter's mind.

Lee told the story of a recent Federal attack which had been gallantly beaten off by his men.

"As I rode along the line next morning," Lee said, "a soldier stuck his bare foot out and said, 'General Lee, I have no shoes.'

"Another would say as I passed, 'I am hungry. I haven't enough to eat.' "

Hunter listened to the brief tale in dismay: "These and other circumstances betraying the utmost destitution he repeated with a melancholy air and tone which I never shall forget."[3]

Lee went next to Davis. He did not ask for an attempt at an armistice, nor even retreat to the south. Instead, he made one of his characteristically audacious proposals: He would attack!

If Davis was astounded, he had recovered when he wrote of the proposal:

"General Lee presented to me the idea of a sortie. If entirely successful, it would threaten Grant's line of communication with his base, City Point, and might compel him to move his forces around ours to protect it . . . it would relieve our right and delay the impending disaster until the more convenient season for retreat."[4]

Lee went back to the army from these two conferences and called in Gordon. He was brief in his report of accomplishments:

"Nothing could be done. The Congress doesn't seem to appreciate the situation."

He gave Gordon hardly a hint that he found Davis difficult.

"The nearest approach to complaint or criticism," Gordon wrote, "were the words which I can never forget: 'You know that the President is very pertinacious in opinion and purpose.' "

"Then what is to be done?" Gordon asked.

"There is but one thing to do—fight. To stand still means death."

Lee gave Gordon instructions for his incredible plan. He had determined to hit the Federals from the northern end of his line:

"Move your troops into the works around the city as I withdraw one of the other commands. . . . Make your headquarters in the city. Study General Grant's works at all points, consider carefully . . . then tell me what you can do, if anything, to help us."

It was an assignment to Gordon's liking. He moved his men to the front of Richmond, where he took several Federal deserters into his lines and, after questioning them, began to choose his target for attack.

He fixed on Fort Stedman, a work on a hill not quite a mile southeast of the Appomattox River. Gordon saw what he took to be three other Federal forts to the rear of this one, facing in the opposite direction. If he took Stedman, he could then seize the other three from the rear. He took the plan to Lee:

Gordon would send picked men out of the lines just at dark, to remove obstructions between the lines. At the foot of the enemy fort, where sharp poles were lashed together, he would have fifty volunteers chop away the points with axes, under fire. This should carry the work, even if the men in advance had to fight with axes rather than bayonets.

It had a desperate sound, even from the impetuous Gordon, but he seemed to have overlooked no details of his melodramatic plan. When Lee asked how he would save his troops once he got into the Federal lines, Gordon explained:

"I have learned the name of every enemy officer of rank in my front. I propose to select three officers from my corps, who are to command each a body of 100 men. These officers are to assume the names of three Union officers . . . each is to rush in the darkness to the rear with his 100 men, shouting: 'The Rebels have carried Fort Stedman and our front lines! . . . I am ordered by General Mc-Laughlin to rush back to the fort in rear and hold it at all hazards!' "

The 300 men would overpower guards in the rear forts and capture the works. Lee debated the scheme with Gordon at length before he agreed to find guides for the parties. He also improved on the daring of the plan: He would draw other troops from the thin line and make the attack in great strength, once Gordon had opened the way. He promised more than four divisions, and agreed to send Pickett's division as well, if it could reach the scene in time. March twenty-fifth, at four A.M. was set for the attack.

Lee wrote Gordon on the afternoon of March twenty-fourth, giving him free rein and offering all possible support, adding:

> I pray that a merciful God may grant us success and deliver us from our enemies.

He was sitting Traveller on a knoll behind the lines in the darkness as he waited for Gordon's attack. He betrayed his anxiety over the plan only by his presence. If he felt himself forced to this forlorn attempt by Jefferson Davis, he gave no hint of it.

While Lee sat in the rear, Gordon stood on his breastworks with only a private at his side. The men beneath them in the darkness made noises as they cleared debris. A voice called from the Federal line, "What'cha doin' there, Johnny? Quick, or I'll shoot."

The soldier at Gordon's side yelled back, "Never mind, Yank. Go to sleep. Just gettin' a little corn. Rations short over here."

The relieved Gordon heard the Federal call assurances that he would not fire while the Confederates were foraging, but just at four, when the private at his side was to fire his rifle as a signal, the soldier was evidently overcome by his conscience, and yelled, "Wake up, Yank! We're goin' to shell the woods. Look out, we're comin'!"

The rifle shot rang out, and in the darkness troops scrambled over the works and through the passage to the enemy fort. Axemen chopped at the logs, and scattered firing broke out. Only yells and the popping of muskets marked the attack's progress. First of the men to crowd behind the axemen were Gordon's chosen 300, with white rags tied around their arms for identification. They were quickly over the Federal parapet and the startled enemy troops were overcome. Fort Stedman was captured, almost instantly. Gordon was in Stedman himself, sending word to Lee:

The fort was taken, with long lines of breastworks on either side. More than 1,000 prisoners, including General McLaughlin; there were but half a dozen casualties. But after that word was slow in coming. The storming parties of 300 were stumbling about in the rear, seeking the three forts assigned to them, but no progress was reported. Word came at last that the guides could not find their objectives.

The fight spread down the Federal front, and though Lee could make out little of it from his hill, the growing danger to Gordon's attackers was plain enough. The enemy was closing on their flanks. Daylight revealed Gordon's lines in a sprawl of confusion. At eight o'clock they were ordered back, for Lee feared to risk them longer.

As the men came back over the exposed route casualties became higher, and at the same moment the enemy struck at the far end of the line. For a time Lee thought a general engagement had opened. News from other sectors was bad. Lower on the line the enemy had overpowered the light outer works where pickets had lain, and could not be driven out. From there, they would constantly threaten the main line.

Gordon reported the capture of almost 3,000 Federals, but

Lee's loss for the day had been about 5,000, and the attack was a failure.

In explanation, it could only be said that the three forts Gordon had seen, and made so vital in his battle plan, were old Confederate works, long since abandoned by the enemy. And so one more hope was lost.[5]

On his way to the rear Lee met two of his sons, Rooney and Robert, coming up with cavalry support. Robert noted the sad careworn expression of his father's face, which became a smile as he saw the boys. Lee explained that the horsemen would not be needed, since the morning's thrust had been in vain.

Colonel Taylor's diary had recently been increasingly gloomy:

March 5

I do not, cannot yet despair; but it is evident that there has been a rapid, radical change in the tone of public sentiment. . . . I do not think our military situation hopeless by any means; but I confess matters are far worse than I ever expected to see them.

March 23

The dread contingency of which some intimation has been given is near at hand. . . . Now is the hour when we must show of what stuff we are made.

March 27

There appears to be an unaccountable apathy and listlessness in high places. . . . There seems to be no preparation for the removal . . . of the government.

On March twenty-seventh, too, Lee saw that the end was near. Sheridan's powerful cavalry had not only joined Grant, but was crossing the James, and would be hacking at the flank. Petersburg must be evacuated. He turned to maps of the country in his rear. The day of which he had so lately written Mary had come:

I think General Grant will move against us soon ... and no man can tell what may be the result; but, trusting to a merciful God, who does not always give the battle to the strong, I pray we may not be overwhelmed. I shall, however, endeavor to do my duty and fight to the last. Should it be necessary to abandon our position to prevent being surrounded, what will you do? Will you remain, or leave the city? You must consider the question and make up your mind.

For two days, March twenty-seventh and twenty-eighth, reports of the enemy's movement to the south and southwest came to Lee. He concluded that Grant was crossing Hatcher's Run not far from the Weldon Railroad, moving west to Dinwiddie Court House, turning north to strike at the right flank of the Confederate line, where the Southside Railroad was not far in the rear. From the evidence, the movement was being made in considerable force.

Lee's line held by infantry, almost twenty-eight miles in length, was so thin that to strip men from it anywhere would invite its breaking; there were few more than 1,000 men for every mile. He extemporized by ordering Pickett with his division, now shrunken to 5,000 by desertion, to the far right of the line; he gathered just over 4,000 cavalry to aid them.

Fitz Lee had brought word of ominous Federal concentration at Dinwiddie, and said he thought the goal was just north of that point, at Five Forks. Lee watched things carefully through the rainy night. The situation looked more grim with news that the entrenched Federal line had been stretched to Dinwiddie; Lee could not match that move, and must prepare to meet Sheridan's flank thrust with the small mobile force he was gathering. He added the 20 guns of Colonel William Pegram's artillery to his right and warned Longstreet, far to the north, on the upper side of the James, that he might have to send help.

On March thirtieth Lee stretched the thin line even farther, giving Gordon two more miles to cover on the southern flank. Late that afternoon fighting broke out near Five Forks, when Fitz Lee drove some Federals back toward Dinwiddie, and Pickett fought his way into Five Forks, barely escaping destruction of his wagon train. The small force, waiting for the arrival of more cavalry, had scarcely room to camp among the swarming enemy. Pickett and Fitz Lee combined had no more than 10,000 men. About 50,000 Federals opposed them. And Pickett went to camp with his unprotected flank some four miles from the end of the Confederate works.

Before dawn of March thirty-first a bold Confederate attack rolled back the enemy in the front of General Anderson, who manned the southern end of Lee's main line. Lee helped direct this attack himself, and was not noticeably discouraged in the evening, even when his men were forced back almost to their original positions. The action at Five Forks, to his right, had been promising during the day. Fitz Lee and Pickett had pushed some six miles, almost to Dinwiddie Court House. Still, April first dawned with Lee aware of increasing danger, since the Federal lines began to lap the positions of the right; several main roads were already closed. The two railroads nearby were certain to be cut, he felt, and he wrote to Davis that the position around Richmond must be abandoned.

Pickett sent in a surprising message: He must fall back under increased pressure. Lee replied that Five Forks must be held at all costs, for that was the shield to the Southside Railroad, and the key to the whole flank. In the afternoon at Five Forks, while Lee was busy five or six miles to the left, disaster fell.

There had been heavy fighting in the morning, but Federal attacks slowed, and it seemed that the 6,000 weary Confederates at Five Forks would hold the ground. General Rosser arranged a shad-bake for the chief officers, and Fitz Lee and Pickett, persuaded that the day's action was over, went to enjoy the fresh fish from nearby rivers.[6]

The Five Forks position was by no means impregnable, but whatever it had been, it could hardly have stood under the flood of bluecoats which poured upon it. The crucial moments were sketched by the veteran reporter who rode with Sheridan, George Alfred Townsend:

"A colonel with a shattered regiment came down upon us in a charge . . . the men came on with a yell . . . swept all the while by scathing volleys . . . a group of horsemen took them in the flank. It was an awful instant, the horses recoiled, the charging columns trembled like a single thing, but at once the Rebels, with rare organization, fell into a hollow square, and with solid sheets of steel defied our centaurs. The horsemen rode around them in vain . . . until our dismounted carbineers poured in their volleys afresh, making gaps in the spent ranks, and then . . . the cavalry thundered down. The Rebels could stand no more; they reeled and swayed, and fell back broken and beaten. . . .

"Through wood and brake and swamp, across field and trench, we pushed the fighting defenders steadily. For a part of the time, Sheridan himself was there, short and broad, and active, waving his hat, giving orders, seldom out of fire . . . and close by fell the long yellow locks of Custer. . . . At four o'clock the Rebels were behind their wooden walls at Five Forks, and still the cavalry pressed them hard . . . while a battalion dismounted, charged squarely upon the face of their breastworks. . . . Then, while the cavalry worked round toward the rear . . . the concealed infantry, many thousand strong, sprang up and advanced. . . .

"Mounted on his black pony . . . Sheridan galloped everywhere, his flushed face all the redder. . . . The fight . . . was singularly free from great losses on our side, though as desperate as any contest ever fought on the continent. One prolonged roar of rifle shook the afternoon. The birds of the forest fled afar. . . . Imagine along a full mile, thirty thousand men struggling for life. . . .

"At seven o'clock the Rebels came to the conclusion that they were outflanked and whipped . . . horsemen charged them . . . and in the rear . . . slant fire, cross fire, and direct fire . . . rolled in perpetually, cutting down their bravest officers and strewing the fields with bleeding men. . . . They had no commanders, at least no orders, and looked in vain for some guiding hand. . . . A few more volleys, a new and irresistible charge . . . and with a sullen and tearful impulse, five thousand muskets are flung upon the ground."

Townsend was not far wrong; more than 3,200 Confederates had been taken at Five Forks. But even worse than this drain on the dwindling army, the position had fallen apart, the railroads were open to attack, and the besieged line itself was little more than a tissue. Colonel Pegram had been seriously wounded, and early on the morning of Sunday, April second, he died.

Lee prepared for the day by shifting strength to the right end of the line, strength he did not have to spare, and along great reaches of the line, behind the imposing fortifications, men were twenty feet apart. Lee sent an urgent message to Longstreet to come to the scene with Field's division. That stripped the defenses around Richmond north of the James to little more than a token.

Longstreet came down the line in a night march. Old Pete described his arrival:

"Before the first rays of morning we found the general headquarters. Some members of the staff were up and dressed, but the general was yet on his couch. When told of my presence, he called me to a seat at his bedside, and gave orders for our march to support the broken forces about Five Forks. He had no censure for any one, but mentioned the great numbers of the enemy and the superior repeating rifles of his cavalry. He was ill, suffering from the rheumatic ailment that he had been afflicted with for years, but keener trouble of mind made him in a measure superior to the shooting pains. . . .

"General Lee was not through with his instructions for our march when a staff officer came in and reported that the lines in front of his headquarters were broken.

"Drawing his wrapper about him, he walked with me to the

front door and saw, as far as the eye could cover the field, a line of skirmishers in quiet march towards us. It was hardly light enough to distinguish the blue from the gray."

Wagons tore wildly in the roads, and enemy skirmishers were less than half a mile from headquarters. The lines were open, and the Federals poured through almost at will.

Some two miles nearer Petersburg, where the ailing A. P. Hill made his headquarters, firing was so heavy that Hill went out to investigate.

Lee soon saw that the skirmishers in front of him were Federals. He sent Colonel Venable and another officer through the melee to warn Hill. The commander quickly dressed in full uniform, and emerged with a sword buckled at his waist. He saw a group of riders approaching. One of them rode A. P. Hill's gray horse.

When they came near Lee recognized the rider as Sergeant G. W. Tucker, Hill's favorite courier. He had a brief story to tell: Hill and Tucker had come upon two Federal soldiers and shouted to them to surrender. The enemy replied with gunfire, and Hill had dropped to the ground. Tucker had taken his horse and dashed away.

"He is at rest now," Lee said. "And we who are left are the ones to suffer."

He sent Tucker with one of Hill's staff to advise the dead general's widow.[7]

Lee soon found that he was cut off from his line to the right, and that he was under heavy attack on the whole length of the earthworks. Beyond him Gordon's men were making a savage defense, and were actually driving the enemy in a counterattack; but the Federal tide, though now slowed, had broken through in two huge gaps. Lee determined to try to hold Petersburg until nightfall, and then pull out. He sent a telegram to the President, which was delivered to Davis in church at Richmond's Saint Pauls:

I advise that all preparation be made for leaving Richmond tonight. I will advise you later, according to circumstances.

He stayed near headquarters in the Turnbull house until the telegrapher and Taylor and all others were out, and shells were falling about it. One shell tore through the building. Lee galloped off. Colonel Long heard him say calmly as they rode, "This is a bad business, Colonel."

After a pause he said, "Well, Colonel, it has happened as I told them at Richmond it would. The line has been stretched until it has broken."[8]

Lee gave several hours to issuing orders for a general withdrawal, including all troops still in the lines, and the Richmond garrison under Ewell. He gave close attention to routes and bridges, and ordered the latter destroyed after crossings. The army, in five trains, was to march southwest in the triangle formed by the Appomattox River, the Richmond and Danville Railroad, and the James River. The objective for the army's concentration was Amelia Court House where supplies and food would be waiting.

He was interrupted by a rather querulous reply from President Davis, saying that the move out of Richmond that night would mean "the loss of many valuables, both for the want of time to pack and of transportation."

As late as three P.M., Lee was writing a long, full, leisurely dispatch to Davis, filled with details of plans for raising Negro troops, but warning that he must withdraw from Petersburg during the night. He lost Colonel Taylor after dark, when he was giving his staff their orders. Taylor begged leave to go to Richmond, for the astonishing purpose of being married, so that his bride would not be left in enemy lines. Lee sent him off promptly.

When night had fallen, the army began to pour out of the city across the Appomattox toward the west. A short distance from the river Lee reined and sat at the fork of a road, listening to the steady passage of his regiments in the darkness. The guns hammering away at the lines beyond were not now so ominous. He followed the last of the perhaps 12,000 infantrymen who left Petersburg; there were fewer than 30,000 in all.

April third passed with the army struggling to the west in good order, though commands had shrunk terribly and the wagon teams were poor. The enemy was pushing in the same direction on the south side of the river, and had the shorter route to Burkeville, but there was no sign of pursuers during the day. In the route of retreat, however, the world seemed in a state of turmoil. Young John Wise, who found himself at Clover Station, saw train after train come past, fleeing from Richmond, all loaded to capacity, with men hanging on the cars. He wrote:

"A train passed Clover bearing the President, his Cabinet and chief advisers. . . . They had left Richmond after midnight. . . . Mr. Davis sat at a car window. The crowd at the station cheered. He smiled and acknowledged their compliment, but his expression showed physical and mental exhaustion. Near him sat General Bragg, whose shaggy eyebrows and piercing eyes make him look like a much greater man than ever he proved himself to be. . . . The Presidential train was followed by many others. One bore the archives and employees of the Treasury Department, another those of the Post Office Department, another those of the War Department. . . .

"I saw a government on wheels. . . . There were very few women on these trains. . . . In one car was a cage with an African parrot, and a box of tame squirrels and a hunchback! . . . The last arrivals brought the sad news that Richmond was in flames."[9]

It was near Clover that Lee made his only pause during the day, a leisurely meal amid the retreat. Judge James H. Cox, master of the nearby plantation house, Clover Hill, invited Lee, Longstreet and their staffs for luncheon.

The home was already swarming with guests, and Lee and Longstreet were soon surrounded by dozens of people, who hung on their every word. Kate Cox, the young daughter of the house, sat by Lee.

"General Lee," the girl said, "we shall still gain our cause, you will join General Johnston and together you will be victorious."

"What ever happens," Lee said, "no men ever fought better than those who have stood by me."

The family butler interrupted, serving a large tray of mint juleps. Kate wrote:

"General Lee took his glass and, according to the universal custom, asked me to taste it. He scarcely touched it himself, but took a goblet of ice water, saying, as he looked around at the men who were enjoying the juleps:

"'Do you know that this glass of cold water is, I believe, far more refreshing than the drinks they are enjoying so much?'"

"After this we went into the dining room, and the general insisted on my going with him, although I protested and told him that we had decided in that house that every morsel prepared that day should be eaten by his men. He continued to insist. . . .

"General Longstreet was on the opposite side of the table, and as he had [use of] only one arm, the butler was told to bring his plate to me that I might cut up his food."

The luncheon was good and plentiful. Near the end of it coffee was passed. Lee poured cream into his cup.

"Why, General Lee," Kate said, "do you take cream in your after-dinner coffee?"

Lee smiled. "I have not taken coffee for so long that I would not dare to take it in its original strength."

A staff officer told the girl as they left, "You know the general sends all his coffee to the hospital."

The child watched the procession ride down the mile-long lane of the house through clover fields, Lee with his red-lined cape thrown back over his shoulders, and Traveller disappearing at a hurried pace.[10]

The officers left the place for scenes of incongruous contrast, where men waded rutted roads, around bogged wagons, and horses fell of exhaustion. The columns were beginning to snarl, too; the road leading to Bevill's Bridge over the Appomattox was flooded, and the men of Longstreet and Gordon were routed to the next highest bridge at Goode's. This snarled traffic, and men and wagons were forced to wait for hours to cross the crowded bridge. It was late in the day before Lee found that one bridge of pontoons had not been laid by engineers, and in the end, Ewell's troops, too, had to be marched into another road. Still, the army had made more than twenty miles by night of April third, and had not been in touch with the enemy. During the night the last of the straggling commands came in, including the remnants of Pickett's division, almost destroyed by casualties and captures at Five Forks.

Longstreet met the first of the enemy, some cavalry just south of the crossing at Goode's bridge. Lee crossed the river here at seven thirty A.M., April fourth, and realized that the hurrying Federals would soon know where he was, and would not be long in closing in.

He hurried into Amelia Court House, where a huge supply of stores was awaiting the army, but found only ammunition and other supplies. There was no food, and the army was near starvation. From that moment, some officers thought, defeat showed itself in his face. Lee halted the columns and sent wagons into the country to find food. He published an appeal to the farmers of the county, pleading for help in feeding "the brave soldiers who have battled for your liberty for four years." The day dragged slowly while the wagons were out, and the columns poured into Amelia. It was clear that the loss of the day's march would bring the enemy on their heels, and Lee ordered much of the wagon train sent off on a southward route, and had General Pendleton put surplus guns on a train.

Lee saw more Federals during the day, and had a close brush

while scouting an enemy cavalry party, one of whose members dashed through heavy fire directly at Lee. As officers drew their guns on the lone rider, Lee shouted, "Don't shoot!" He soon showed them that the rider was wounded, and had him cared for.

April fifth dawned in a steady rain, and the foraging wagons came home with virtually no food. The ravaged countryside had none to offer, and the remaining men fell into line, going off once more in the sound of firing. Just seven miles from the court house village there was firing. The enemy was in front, digging in.

Lee studied the scene with as much caution as ever. He could find no means of prying the enemy loose with the weakened force at hand, and though he called up a number of farmers from the neighborhood, none seemed to know much about the country lying behind the Federals. Lee used his glasses for a long time, but in the end put them away. Only a march by night could shake off the enemy. He put Longstreet in the van, and slowly, stumbling, the army left the railroad, turning to the northwest in the direction of Amelia Springs. Lee's objective now was to reach the railroad nearer Lynchburg, where he could get supplies by rail from the west. Then, perhaps, he could make one more stand.

There were soon new obstacles in the night. The wagon train had been attacked and much of it burned; after a long halt, some of the wagons had been put into other roads. Wagons and troops mingled in darkness, and progress was painfully slow. Then, somewhere near the van, a bridge broke under the weight, and the guns and wagons could not pass. It was a long night.

16 *DISASTER*

GENERAL GORDON was halted as the army streamed ahead in the dark. His men said they had caught two spies.

Gordon was patient, but could find no flaw in the story told by the two young captives in gray, who said they belonged to Fitz Lee's cavalry and told a plausible tale. Gordon questioned them with care, but was at first satisfied by their self-possessed air. They rattled off the names of Lee's commanders, down to the companies. They told him to which mess they belonged, and gave names of members without hesitation.

But one of Gordon's men was adamant.

"No, General, they are not all right. I saw them by the starlight counting your files."

One of the prisoners spoke up:

"Yes. We were trying to get some idea of your force. We have been at home on sick leave for a long time, and wanted to know if we had any army left." This aroused Gordon's suspicions, and he asked to see their furlough papers. The party rode to a nearby fire, where the prisoners displayed papers. But when light fell on their faces, one of Gordon's scouts recognized them as two men who had captured him months before, near Grant's headquarters. The prisoners scoffed, and again showed their papers, properly signed by General Lee.

"The signatures are forged, General," the scout insisted. "Or they captured some of our men. Make them dismount, and I'll search them."

At last, in a boot, he found a paper which Gordon sent to Lee after one quick glance.

It was an order from General Grant to General Ord, directing a move which would cut Lee's line of retreat at Appomattox Court House.

The order was fresh, and bore the ominous heading: "April 5, 10:10 P.M., Jetersville." It was addressed to Ord, at Burkeville. By four in the morning Lee had read it and acknowledged its receipt.[1]

The news was much worse than Lee had been prepared for. Two armies now lay almost in his path, either of which could overwhelm him. Further, Sheridan's cavalry was now hanging off the left flank. There was no alternative but to push ahead.

As daylight came the army wound over worsening roads through country as drab as it had seen in its four years. Ragged folds of the pine barrens ran across their path, hunching into endless hills, and vaulting downward to the wandering Appomattox. In the morning the troops dragged into the watershed of Sayler's Creek, a small stream with a network of branches among the ravines. Longstreet was in front, his fragment the army's strongest corps. Behind him, with no more than 3,000 of the exhausted and frightened Richmond clerks, was the one-legged Ewell.

The first heavy blow fell at eleven A.M. when Sheridan's cavalry stormed down the roads of the flank to strike the vulnerable wagon train. Ewell fought back, though he was already worn and in despair. He forced back the enemy and sent the wagon train forward toward Gordon's command, so as to shorten the length of road the rear guard must protect. The passage of the wagons forced the troops of Ewell and Anderson out of the roadway, where they lay to watch the bony teams struggle past.

To the front, where the wagons went, there seemed to be no orders. Veteran commanders lost their grasp in the endless thrusts of swift Federal cavalry raiders. Sheridan kept three divisions at work, until the Confederate wagons and infantry commands were hopelessly entangled. In the midst of it a decisive error developed. The wagoners pushed between the commands of Mahone and Anderson, where they were isolated, an alluring target. The nearest of Sheridan's men—Custer's troopers—were not long in finding it.

They fell upon the wagons on the hills, hacked a gap in the line, shunted aside the gray infantry, and fell to the slaughter. They cut traces, felled horses, fired wagons, and blocked the roadway so completely as to doom the men at the rear. The VI Corps of the enemy was at hand, too, and before Ewell and Anderson realized what had befallen them a tide of bluecoats spilled over the hill.

While the wagons burned, the little band of Confederate infantry fell into ranks and prepared for the end. Blue cavalry struck the flanks, and while bugles were crowing the charge, the infantry came on irresistibly. Confederates here and there struggled furiously, hand to hand, but most of them threw down their muskets. Ewell's entire force was gone in a few moments, and the general himself was captured.

Lee was far ahead when this blow fell, and it was some time before he could make out what had happened in the rear. He had been apprehensive, and rode back to see for himself. Colonel Garnet Wolseley, the future commander of the British Army, had a brief meeting with him here:

"He was looking across the country at a large collection of white objects, which appeared like a flock of sheep."

Lee spoke to the Englishman. "Are those sheep or not?"

"No, General, they are Yankee wagons."

Lee peered through the glasses for a time. "You're right. But what are they doing there?"[2]

He could not bring himself to believe his lines were broken and that the enemy was swarming forward at will.

He soon found General Mahone at his side, grumbling something about the interference of Colonel Marshall in his command, but still in a fighting mood. As Mahone and Lee talked, Colonel Venable came up.

"Did you get my message?" Venable asked.

"No. What message?"

"The enemy has captured the wagon trains."

They rode to the central scene of the disaster.

Lee shouted. "Where is Anderson? Where is Ewell? It is strange I can't hear from them."

He turned to Mahone. "I have no other troops," he said. "Will you take your division to Sayler's Creek?"

Mahone's men were soon on the run. Lee and Venable rode with Mahone to a hill overlooking the scene of Ewell's defeat.

Here was the explanation of the easy advance of Federal wagons. It was one of the most stunning sights of Lee's military career. Mahone said:

"The scene beggars description—hurrying teamsters with their teams and dangling traces, retreating infantry without guns, many without hats, a harmless mob, with the massive column of the enemy moving orderly on.

"At this spectacle General Lee straightened himself in his saddle, and, looking more the soldier than ever, exclaimed, as if talking to himself:

"'My God! Has the army been dissolved?'

"As quickly as I could control my own voice I replied, 'No, General, here are troops ready to do their duty. . . . In a mellow voice he replied, 'Yes, General, there are some true men left. Will you please keep those people back?'   .

"As I was placing my division in position to 'keep those people back,' the retiring herd just referred to had crowded around General Lee while he sat on his horse with a Confederate battle flag in his hand. I rode up and requested him to give me the flag, which he did."[3]

Lee's voice had a stricken sound. "That half of the army has been destroyed," he said.

Soon afterward he learned of a more personal loss. Custis had been captured and his division wiped out; his fate was unknown.

But one admiring staff officer saw Lee about this time as he rode out to lead one of the stands against the closing enemy—"Sweeping on upon his large iron-gray . . . carrying his field glass half raised in his right hand, with head erect, gestures animated and in the whole face and form the expression of hunter close upon game. . . . He rode in the twilight among the disordered groups of men, and the sight of him aroused a tumult.

"Fierce cries resounded on all sides, and, with hands clinched violently and raised aloft, the men called on him to lead against the enemy:

" 'It's General Lee! Uncle Robert! Where's the man who won't follow Uncle Robert!'

"On all sides swarthy faces full of dirt and courage, lit up every instant by the glare of burning wagons."[4]

By the same red light Mahone and Lee made plans to elude the enemy. Mahone was asked how the escape might be made.

"Let Longstreet move by the river road," Mahone said, "into Farmville and cross the river there, and I will go through the woods to High Bridge—the railroad bridge—and cross there."

Lee agreed, and Mahone asked for orders, once he had crossed the bridge.

"Exercise your judgment," Lee said.

"What shall I do with the bridge once I have crossed?"

"Burn it."

At the rear General Gordon could see the inevitable end:

"On and on, hour after hour, from hilltop to hilltop, the lines were alternately forming, fighting and retreating, making one almost continuous shifting battle.

"Here . . . a battery of artillery became involved; there . . . a blocked ammunition train required rescue: and thus came short but sharp little battles which made up the side shows of the main performance, while the different divisions of Lee's lion-hearted army were being broken or scattered or captured. . . .

"Every portion of our marching column was being assailed. The roads and fields and woods swarmed with eager pursuers, and Lee was now and then forced to halt his whole army, reduced to less than 10,000 fighters, in order to meet these . . . attacks."

But Gordon saw Lee "riding everywhere" through the flame-lit scene, herding the advance toward the west in hope of saving at least this remnant.

Lee sat Traveller under fire near Farmville as the army struggled past. A young officer rode across the open with a message for the general, and Lee upbraided him for risking his life.

"Why didn't you ride on the side of the hill where you'd be hidden from the fire?"

"I'd be ashamed to, General, while you were exposing yourself out here."

Lee shouted, "It is my duty to be here. Go back the way I told you, sir!"[5]

Lee now began to develop a last desperate plan to save the army. He would use the Appomattox as a shield, since it was impassable to infantry in this sector, and he might be able to deal with cavalry which crossed from the north bank. There were two bridges nearby: High Bridge on the railroad, and its twin, a wagon bridge. If he could destroy them and outrace the enemy into the small town of Farmville he might yet escape.

He was soon near High Bridge himself, at a lonely station on the Southside Railroad. Here he was met by John Wise:

"It was past midnight when I found General Lee. He was in an open field north of Rice's Station and east of the High Bridge. A camp fire was burning low. Colonel Charles Marshall was in an ambulance, with a lantern and a lap-desk. He was preparing orders at the dictation of General Lee, who stood near, with one hand resting on a wheel and one foot upon the end of a log, watching intently the dying embers as he spoke in a low tone."

Wise said that President Davis had sent him for word of the army's situation, and Lee replied: "I hardly think it is necessary to prepare written dispatches in reply. They may be captured. . . . You may say to Mr. Davis that, as he knows, my original purpose was to adhere to the line of the Danville road. I have been unable to do so, and am now trying to hold the Southside road as I retire in the direction of Lynchburg."

Wise asked if Lee had chosen a site where he might make a stand.

"No," the general said, "I shall have to be governed by each day's developments. . . . A few more Sayler's Creeks and it will be all over—ended—just as I have expected it would end from the first."

Lee sent the boy to rest for the night in Farmville. Wise discovered his father's remaining troops in the village at daybreak, sprawled asleep without a sentinel posted. General Wise, a spectacle in a blanket pinned about his neck, bareheaded and afoot, furiously chewing tobacco and cursing his commanders, had fought through the night near High Bridge.

Just at sunrise Lee found General Wise in Farmville. The old general, without a water supply, had washed in a roadside puddle and his face was brick-red with mud. Lee gave him a salute and an amused smile.

"Good morning, General Wise," he said. "I see that you, at any rate, have not given up, since you're in your war paint this morning."

A few minutes later Wise met Lee on the back porch of a house in the town, where the commander had gone to get some rest.

Lee had been washing his face in a tin basin, and was drying his beard with a towel.

Wise broke in abruptly: "General Lee, my poor men are lying on the hill yonder more dead than alive. They have fought for more than a week without food, and by God, sir, they shall not move another step until somebody gives them something to eat!"

"Come in, General," Lee said. "They deserve something to eat, and shall have it; and meanwhile you shall share my breakfast." This was little more than a cup of tea, miraculously produced from the family cupboard of this home as a particular favor to Lee. Wise's troops were soon being fed from a wagon train.

Wise began shouting a bitter denunciation of General Bushrod Johnson, his superior, who had left his men to their fate yesterday while he sought safety.

Lee replied with feigned sternness, "General, are you aware that you are liable to court-martial and execution for insubordination and disrespect toward your commanding officer?"

"Shot!" Wise yelled. "You can't afford to shoot the men who fight for cussing those who run away. Shot! I wish you would shoot me. If you don't, some Yankee probably will in the next twenty-four hours."

Lee tried to halt the governor's runaway excitement: "What do you think of the situation?"

"Situation?" Wise said. "There is no situation. Nothing remains, General, but to put your poor men on your poor mules and send them home in time for spring ploughing. The army is hopelessly whipped . . . these men have already endured more than I believed flesh and blood could stand, and I say to you, sir, emphatically, that to prolong the struggle is murder, and the blood of every man who is killed from this time forth is on your head, General Lee."

"Oh, General," Lee said, "don't talk so wildly. My burdens are heavy enough. What would the country think of me, if I did what you suggest?"

"Country be damned," Wise said. "There is no country. There has been no country, General, for a year or more. You are the country to these men. They have fought for you. . . . there are still thousands left who will die for you."

Lee did not reply. He looked out the window at passing troops for a moment, then turned to young John and sent him off with a message for the President.[6]

He then went north of the river to see Longstreet's men coming in. These troops were unaware of the catastrophe at Sayler's Creek, and thought themselves safe, with High Bridge burned behind them. They were ready for a few hours of rest.

Longstreet watched them served with two days' rations, their first since leaving Richmond. As the men made fires for breakfast, Lee rode up and told Old Pete that the bridges had been fired before some of the cavalry units had crossed, and that part of the command was cut off. Longstreet should hurry his troops ahead to Cumberland Church.

Old Pete recorded the reaction to this alarming news:

"Everything except the food was ordered back to the wagons and dumped in . . . and our teamsters, frightened by reports of cavalry trouble . . . joined in the panic, put whips to their teams as quick as the camp kettles were tumbled over the tailboards of the wagons, and rushed through the woods to find a road somewhere in front of them. The command was ordered under arms and put in quick march, but General Lee urged double-quick."[7]

Longstreet's corps went toward Cumberland Church, where the confusing fight soon concentrated.

Lee turned from him to a surprise meeting with George Taylor Lee, the nephew he had last seen in Mrs. Lee's Richmond home.

The commander was making a meager breakfast at the moment, and walked toward young George holding a chicken leg in a slice of bread.

"My son," Lee said, "why did you come here?"

"I thought it was my duty to come."

"You ought not to have come," Lee said. "You can't do any good here."

"I thought they would make me a prisoner, if I had stayed at home."

"No. I don't think they would do that."

George asked about Custis.

"I fear he has been captured," Lee said.

A group of officers approached them.

"Have you had any breakfast?" Lee asked the boy.

George said he had not eaten, and Lee handed him the bread and chicken. "Go somewhere and eat it," he said, and turned to meet the oncoming officers.[8]

Now came word of a fateful error at the rear—more serious by far than the isolation of some cavalrymen: Federal infantry was south of the Appomattox, and was still pouring across by thousands at High Bridge. It had been going on since nine o'clock the night before. It was the end of Lee's hope of fending off the enemy by sliding westward along the south bank of the river.

No one knew quite what had happened at the crossing. Mahone had burned the railroad bridge and its flaming timbers had plunged into the water long before the enemy appeared. The lower wagon bridge, however, had been set afire just before the enemy arrived on the opposite bank, and the bluecoats quickly extinguished the flames and trotted across.

Lee's anger impressed General Long, who recorded the moment:

"Only once during the retreat was he perceived to lose the most complete self control. On inquiring at Farmville why a certain bridge had not been burned, he spoke of the blunder with a warmth and impatience which served to show how great a repression he ordinarily exercised over his feelings."

Lee regained control and called up Alexander in an effort to mend things. Alexander's men had marched only six miles, attempting to thread the maze of mire and burning wagons. Lee showed Alexander his problem with the aid of a map, and ordered him to guard the bridges at Farmville, burning these when the army had crossed. Alexander hurried off to his task.

Federal cavalry had crossed the river by now, and new fighting flared. Lee came upon the end of a skirmish with the bluecoat horsemen, in which a number of the bold enemy were captured, including General J. Irvin Gregg. Lee saw Rooney at this place and told him, "Keep your command together and in good spirits, General—don't let them think of surrender—I will get you out of this."[9]

The army, now so weary that its commanders seemed unable to move it, settled down about Cumberland Church, and on every hand the enemy pecked away; artillery fire crashed throughout the night. The vague situation was becoming darker.

Alexander was at last overcome by exhaustion:

"It was the third consecutive night of marching, and I was at last scarcely able to keep from falling off my horse for sleep, so with my staff, I left the column and went a quarter of a mile or more, off to our right through old broom grass and second growth pines, by cloudy moonlight, until we found a secluded nook by an old worm fence and there we all laid down and slept for three or four hours.

"It was necessary to hide out, or our horses would have been stolen from us while we slept. Cases occurred where officers, seated by the roadside, holding their horses by the bridles, had them stolen while they dozed, the thief cutting the bridle and leaving a piece in the officer's hand."[10]

Earlier in the night a new note was sounded in the history of the Army of Northern Virginia—the first official talk of surrender. It was Colonel Herman Perry of General Sorrel's staff who brought it in to the army.

At five in the afternoon a Federal flag of truce had been waved, and Perry was sent to answer it. As he climbed over the trenches a hail of enemy bullets fell about him, two of them cutting his coat; men behind him were wounded. The attempt to bring in the flag of truce came to an end, but at about nine o'clock, just as the moon rose, a Federal voice again called that a flag of truce was out. Perry went about fifty yards beyond the pickets, halted and called for the truce flag. He waited in a field scattered with enemy dead and wounded. He remembered:

"I . . . met a very handsomely dressed officer . . . he spoke first, introducing himself as General Seth Williams of General Grant's staff. He felt in his side pocket for . . . a nice-looking silver flask . . . he offered me some very fine brandy. I wanted that drink awfully, but I raised myself about an inch higher, bowed, and refused politely, trying to produce the ridiculous appearance of having feasted on champagne and pound cake not ten minutes before. . . . The truth is, I had not eaten two ounces in two days, and I had my coat-tail then full of corn, waiting to parch it as soon as an opportunity might present itself.

"He then handed me a letter, which he said was from General Grant to General Lee, and asked that General Lee should get it immediately, if possible. . . .

"We bowed very profoundly to each other and turned away. . . . In twenty minutes after I got back in our lines a Confederate courier, riding a swift horse, had placed in General Lee's hands the letter. . . . In an hour's time we were silently pursuing our way toward the now-famous field of Appomattox."[11]

Lee got the dispatch at a cottage near Mahone's headquarters:

Headquarters Armies of The United States
April 7, 1865—5 P.M.

General R. E. Lee
Commanding C.S. Army:

General: The results of the last week must convince you of the hopelessness of further resistance on the part of the Army of Northern Virginia in this struggle. I feel that it is so, and regard it as my duty to shift from myself the responsibility of any further effusion of blood, by asking of you the surrender of the C.S. Army known as the Army of Northern Virginia.

Very respectfully, your obedient servant,
U. S. Grant,
Lieutenant-General,
Commanding Armies of the United States

Longstreet was with Lee at this moment. He was handed the note, read it quickly, and passed it back to Lee.

"Not yet," Longstreet said.

Lee did not show Old Pete the reply he sent to Grant:

7th Apl '65

Genl

I have recvd your note of this date. Though not entertaining the opinion you express of the hopelessness of further resistance on the part of the Army of N. Va.—I reciprocate your desire to avoid useless effusion of blood, and, therefore before considering your proposition, ask the terms you will offer on condition of this surrender.

Very respy your obt. Servt.
R. E. Lee
Genl

Lt. Genl U. S. Grant
Commd Armies of the U. States

Longstreet did not need to be told that Lee had rejected the offer, for the orders of the night meant continued fight. Longstreet's corps was passed to the rear to guard the tail of the column and by midnight the army was in motion.

A number of the general officers held a private council of war during the night; they debated whether the army should disband, abandon the wagons and attempt to cut through, or surrender at once. The council unanimously agreed on surrender as the logical course. General Pendleton was selected to tell Lee of this decision; to bolster his courage the others assured him that the agreement would be a relief to Lee, offering moral support in the making of a painful decision.

The men dragged through the night and halted at the village of New Store, some twenty miles west of Farmville, but were soon aroused and pushed into the road once more. They left a nightmare memory with Longstreet:

"Broken down caissons and wagons abandoned and sometimes not even pulled out of the road before they were fired. . . . One of my battery commanders reported his horses too weak to haul his guns. He was ordered to bury the guns and cover their burial-place with old leaves and brushwood."

A British correspondent who traveled this road, Francis Lawley of the *London Times,* was struck by signs of the army's misery:

"Behind . . . every mud hole and every rise in the road choked with blazing wagons, the air filled with deafening reports of . . . shells bursting when touched by flames, dense columns of smoke ascending . . . exhausted men, worn-out horses, dead mules, dead men everywhere—death many times welcomed as God's blessing in disguise."

The army pushed on through the sunshine of Saturday morning, April eighth, trying, as Alexander put it, to creep out of the "jug-shaped peninsula between the James River and the Appomattox—and there was but one outlet, the neck of the jug at Appomattox Court House, and to that General Grant had the shortest road."

Hours passed without sign of the enemy; hope grew with some that the race had been won. There was no way to know, with only the ghost of a cavalry, that five of the big Federal corps were closing in on them, two of these north of the Appomattox and the rest driving toward Appomattox Station on the south.

Pendleton sought out Longstreet and told him of last night's council, as if he were hesitant to take the report directly to Lee. He asked Longstreet to advise Lee of the council's decision. Old Pete was indignant.

"Don't you know that the Articles of War provide that men asking commanders to surrender should be shot?"

Pendleton insisted.

"If General Lee doesn't know when to surrender until I tell him," Longstreet said, "he will never know."[12]

Pendleton found Lee at rest beside the passing column and told him of the council's conclusion. He was struck by Lee's cold manner and disdainful reply:

"Surrender! I trust it has not come to that! We have too many brave men to think of laying down our arms. They still fight with great spirit; the enemy does not. If I were to intimate to General Grant that I would listen to terms, he would take it as such an evidence of weakness that he would demand unconditional surrender—and sooner than that I am resolved to die. We must all determine to die at our posts."[13]

Lee behaved as if the possibility of surrender had not crossed his mind. He rose and helped to herd the men forward. He handled a few dispatches, one a chilling message from the rear. Fitz Lee reported the enemy cavalry only twenty miles from Appomattox, and estimated that it would arrive in the village by ten the next morning. It was doubtful that the maimed column could clear the place before the enemy was upon it again.

The commander attended to an unpleasant duty during the

day. He relieved three generals from command: Bushrod Johnson, Dick Anderson and George Pickett, whose ranks had been torn
apart in the retreat. The orders went out into the confusion.

There was a second dispatch from Grant after dark, which Lee
read with Venable holding a candle over his shoulder:

April 8, 1865

General R. E. Lee,
Commanding C.S.A.

Your note of last evening in reply to mine of same date,
asking the condition on which I will accept the surrender
of the Army of Northern Virginia is just received. In reply
I would say that, peace being my great desire, there is but one
condition I would insist upon, namely: that the men and officers surrendered shall be disqualified for taking up arms again
against the Government of the United States until properly
exchanged. I will meet you, or will designate officers to meet
any officers you may name for the same purpose, at any point
agreeable to you, for the purpose of arranging definitely the
terms upon which the surrender of the Army of Northern Virginia will be received.

U. S. Grant
Lieutenant General.

Lee spoke to Venable after a moment of silence. "How would
you answer that?"

"I would answer no such letter."

"Ah, but it must be answered."[14]

Lee wrote another reply to Grant:

8th Apl '65

Genl

I recd at a late hour your note of today. In mine of yesterday I did not intend to propose the surrender of the Army

of N. Va.—but to ask the terms of your proposition. To be frank, I do not think the emergency has arisen to call for the surrender of this army, but as the restoration of peace should be the sole object of all, I desired to know whether your proposals would lead to that and I cannot therefore meet you with a view to surrender the Army of N. Va—but as far as your proposal may affect the C.S. forces under my command & tend to the restoration of peace, I shall be pleased to meet you at 10 A.M. tomorrow on the old stage road to Richmond between the picket lines of the two armies.

Very respy your Obt sevt.
R. E. Lee
Genl.

Lt. Genl U. S. Grant
Commg Armies of the U.S.

The dispatch went out the rear of the army and was taken by Federal pickets.

The army crawled among low hills and at midafternoon the vanguard already lay at Appomattox Court House. There had been no sight of the enemy all day.

The men stumbled to camp in fields of sedge and scrubby thickets. Many a company made its supper on roots and swollen twigs; but most of the surviving horses ate nothing, for grass was scant, and the only striking sign of the season was the pale catkins of oaks in flower.

As men made camp there was a ludicrous air of cheerfulness in their ranks. Captain James C. Gorman of a Carolina regiment wrote:

"The bands of the divisions enlivened the departing hours of day with martial music, and were applauded with the usual cheers of the troops. The old spirit seemed to be returning."

Many of the men were asleep before dark, exhausted by their forty-eight-hour march. But to those who were awake and saw the solemn faces of general officers in conference at Lee's headquarters, things seemed in serious disorder.

Lee had called them there: Longstreet, Gordon, Fitz Lee, and General Pendleton. They sat around a low fire in the woods without a tent, table, chair or camp stool in sight. The generals sat or lay on blankets as they listened to Lee's slow voice.

Gordon remembered that: "It would be impossible to give the words that were spoken. . . . The letters of General Grant asking surrender, and the replies, evoked a discussion as to the fate of the Southern people. . . . There was also some discussion as to the possibility of forcing a passage through Grant's lines and saving a small portion of the army, and continuing a desultory warfare until the government at Washington should grow weary."

The decision was reached late in the night: Fitz Lee's cavalry, Gordon's infantry, backed by Long's artillery, would strike at sunrise in an effort to break through the Federal line at Appomattox. Longstreet was to follow in support.

"The utmost that could be hoped for," Gordon said, "was that we might reach the mountains of Virginia and Tennessee with a remnant of the army, and ultimately join Joe Johnston."

The generals were clinging to a forlorn hope. Gordon's corps was reduced to 2,000 armed infantrymen; the cavalry had no more than 2,100 horsemen. In all, there were about 28,000 men, but most of them were without arms, and no more than 8,000 were in fighting condition.

As the council ended and the officers went to their beds, Gordon sent a staff officer back to ask for instructions as to where his corps should halt for the next night—as if it were inevitable that he would brush aside the enemy.

Lee could still smile. "Yes," he said, "tell General Gordon that

I should be glad for him to halt just beyond the Tennessee line."
That was some two hundred miles to the west.[15]

Lee went to his bed under the trees.

In the woods nearby, bending over a writing board with his
greased ringlets glinting about his shoulders, George Pickett wrote
a melodramatic letter to his young bride in fallen Richmond.

A few hours earlier Lee had caught sight of Pickett in the
swarming retreat, and in strange musing tones had said, "I thought
that man was no longer with this army."

It was evident that Pickett had not received the orders remov-
ing him from command. As if unaware of the blow from his commander he wrote:

Midnight, April 8-9

. . . I would have our life, my darling, all sunshine, all
brightness. I would have no sorrow, no pain, no fear come to
you. . . .

And yet . . . tomorrow may see our flag furled forever.

Jackerie, our faithful old mail-carrier, sobs behind me as
I write. He bears tonight this—his last—message from me to
you. . . .

Lee's surrender is imminent. It is finished.

From now, forever only your soldier.

17 *PALM SUNDAY*
(*April 9, 1865*)

HORSES KEPT Colonel Marshall awake. He burrowed into his coat against the cold, but still he heard the hungry animals gnawing bark from trees in the dark grove.

The other staff officers slept around him, and not far away was Lee, wrapped in a blanket, his head on a saddle. Longstreet lay a hundred feet beyond. A full moon had hung in the sky since afternoon, but was now behind the unseen clouds and there was a feel of rain in the air.

Just after one o'clock, when he had dozed off, Marshall started awake. Troops were marching. Perhaps headquarters was already surrounded, he thought. He sat, listening, and then fell back to the saddle as the steady slogging of ranks went by in the road. The colonel soon identified the troops.

A few lines of doggerel were drawled in the darkness:

> Oh, the race is not to them that's got
> The longest legs to run,
> Nor the battle to them people,
> That shoots the biggest gun.

Texas troops, the colonel knew; it was one of their favorite marching chants. Their passage stirred men in the grove and headquarters awoke for the day. There was little to be done. Marshall completed his toilet, "consisting mainly of putting on our caps and saddling our horses."

Someone found a double handful of corn meal and from nowhere came a shaving can, a small tin in which water was soon boiling atop a fire. The staff ate in turn, by age and seniority. Each heated his can of water, sifted in some meal, and held the tin until the gruel was cool enough to be gulped down.[1]

Lee had nothing to eat, Marshall recalled, and the enemy raid on the wagon train had left him but one uniform. The general put on the new uniform and buckled his best sword about him. At about three o'clock, when they heard gunfire and knew that Gordon had begun, Lee rode to the front.

On Confederate outskirts his commanders handled the troops as if unaware of the paralysis creeping through the ranks. Gordon took his 2,000 survivors through the village of Appomattox, past the cavalry, whose troopers were asleep in the saddles. The army was dissolving into a mob behind them, and hundreds threw aside muskets or thrust them into the ground by bayonets and wandered aimlessly, searching for food. Many thronged around the remaining wagons.

To the west of Appomattox was Gordon's thirty-six-year-old North Carolina fire-eater, Bryan Grimes, impatient with the weight of his new rank. He had been a major general just six weeks. He rode out to reconnoiter before daylight and came within two hundred yards of the enemy. He returned, drew a battle line, and awaited orders from Gordon. It was almost sunup when Gordon came, and Fitz Lee rode with him. The two superior officers fell into an argument.

Gordon thought that the enemy troops were cavalry and that Fitz Lee should attack. Fitz Lee thought they were infantry, and that Gordon should attack.

Grimes broke in:

"It's somebody's duty to attack, and that immediately. We can drive them from the crossroads, if you want the wagon train to go through there. I'll try it, if you'll let me."

"Well, drive them off," Gordon said.

"I can't do it with my division. I'll need help."

"You can take the other two divisions," Gordon said.

It was becoming light, and now the group could see the earth-works thrown up by the Federals. They did not look formidable. Fitz Lee trailed off to take the enemy in the flank with his cavalry.

As the horsemen scrambled into the open the ragged men of Grimes surged over the field and with one of their last quavering Rebel Yells leapt the Union trenches and ran after the retreating enemy. The bluecoats fell back for almost a mile to their waiting infantry support; Grimes saw that he had faced only dismounted cavalry.

The young general learned from prisoners that the 10,000 men of the Army of the James, under General Ord, were on the right, in position to crush him. Grimes halted the troops and ordered the brigade of Cox to lie in hiding. He turned his flank and began to pull back most of his force. When the enemy followed, Cox's men waited until the range was point-blank, and rose with a blazing volley to break the attack. Grimes sent word to Gordon that the front was static for the moment, and that an escape route to Lynch-burg was open for the wagons.

An incredible order came back to him: Retreat. Withdraw to the original position. Grimes refused and held his place through a series of insistent orders from Gordon until finally there was word from Lee. Grimes pulled back his men and sought Gordon.

That corps commander was in trouble, and in no mood for academic debate. A heavy Union column was moving on him, and he was trying to hold it off with the aid of his headquarters marks-men. At this moment a body of enemy cavalry appeared in the gap between Gordon and Longstreet. Gordon saw that in a few minutes the cavalry "would not only have seized the trains but cut off all communication between the two wings of Lee's army and rendered its capture inevitable."

About the time he sent a brigade to meet the newest threat, Grimes arrived, breathing fire. Grimes was forced to wait, for Lee had sent up Colonel Venable to find out what was happening in the fog.

Venable pressed Gordon for information and got a quick reply, blunt and hopeless. Venable spurred off to the rear.

"Where shall I form my line?" Grimes asked Gordon.

"Anywhere you choose," was the laconic reply.

Grimes was puzzled, and asked Gordon to explain.

"We're going to be surrendered," Gordon said.

Grimes turned to him in blazing wrath, scolding his superior for not having warned him, so that he could escape with his command.

"I'm going to tell my men," Grimes shouted, "and if they want to go, I'll take them with me."

He galloped away, but Gordon overtook him and put a hand on the young man's shoulder: "Are you going to desert the army and tarnish your honor as a soldier? It will be a reflection on General Lee and an indelible disgrace."

Grimes at last agreed to say nothing to his men, but when he rode among them:

"One of the soldiers asked me if General Lee had surrendered, and upon my answering that I feared it was a fact . . . he cast away his musket, and holding his hands aloft, cried in an agonized voice: 'Blow, Gabriel, blow! My God, let him blow! I am ready to die!'"

The news spread, though there was as yet no surrender. Young Tom Devereux of Gordon's staff watched as "some burst into tears, some threw down their guns, others broke them against trees, and I saw one man thrust his musket between a forked sapling, bend the barrel and say, 'No Yankee will ever shoot at us with you.'"[2]

The day of travail had only begun for Lee. Not long after five o'clock, he was on the knoll behind Gordon's tiny battle, peering through fog and smoke. Venable soon returned to him with word from Gordon:

"Tell General Lee I have fought my corps to a frazzle, and I fear I can do nothing unless I am heavily supported by Longstreet."

After a brief silence Lee spoke:

"Then there is nothing left for me to do but go and see General Grant, and I would rather die a thousand deaths."

One of the officers blurted, "Oh, General, what will history say of the surrender of this army in the field?"

"Yes," Lee said. "Yes. I know they will say hard things of us. They will not understand how we were overwhelmed by numbers. But that is not the question, Colonel: The question is, is it right to surrender this army. If it is right, then I will take all the responsibility."[3]

The officers saw him in one of the rare moments in which he seemed to lose control of himself:

"How easily I could be rid of this, and be at rest!" Lee said. His voice was higher than usual. "I have only to ride along the line and all will be over." He sighed. "But it is our duty to live. What will become of the women and children of the South if we are not here to protect them?"

Lee sent orders for Longstreet and Mahone to come. Longstreet arrived, himself a future reporter of the scene:

"He [Lee] was dressed in a new uniform . . . and a pair of gold spurs. At first approach his compact figure appeared as a man in the flush vigor of forty summers, but as I drew near, the handsome apparel and brave bearing failed to conceal his profound depression."

The two stood by the embers of a rail fire, talking slowly. Lee talked of the loss of the stores in wagons, and the enormous force surrounding them.

Longstreet asked if the bloody sacrifice of the army "could in any way help the cause in other quarters."

"I think not," Lee said.

"Then," Longstreet said, "your situation speaks for itself."

Lee turned to Mahone, who stood, shivering, poking at the coals of the fire.

"I don't want you to think I'm scared," Mahone said. "I'm only chilled."

When Lee asked his opinion, the loquacious Mahone asked numerous questions, and Longstreet listened with only half an ear. "But I heard enough of it," he wrote, "to know General Mahone thought it time to see General Grant."

When Lee turned to ask Longstreet's opinion once more, Old Pete nodded his head.[4]

Lee seemed yet unable to bring himself to the move while fighting sputtered in front of him. The morning was still shaken by gunfire when General Alexander came up.

Troops shouted after Alexander, "Don't you go surrender no ammunition, Ginral! You been tellin' us all this war to save ammunition!"

Lee took the gunner of the First Corps to an oak log, stripped clean of its bark, and they sat there.

Lee began in his customary musing fashion:

"Well, here we are at Appomattox, and there seems to be a considerable force in front of us. Now what shall we have to do today?"

"If there's any chance to cut our way through, I'll answer for the artillery making a good fight."

Lee explained the chief trouble, a lack of armed infantry. Surrender was inevitable, he said.

"Well, sir," Alexander said, "then we have only two alternatives. . . . We must either surrender, or, the army may be ordered to scatter in the woods and bushes."

"Well, what would you hope to accomplish by that?"

"If there is any hope for the Confederacy, it is in delay. If this army surrenders, every other army will give up as fast as the news reaches it."

Alexander spoke rapidly, carried away with emotion:

"You don't care for military fame or glory, but we are proud of your name and the record of this army. We want to leave it to our children . . . a little blood more or less now makes no difference.

"The men who have fought under you for four years have got the right to ask you to spare us the mortification of having to ask Grant for terms and have him say, 'Unconditional Surrender.' They call him that. . . . General, spare us the mortification of having you get that reply."

Lee was as patient as if he intended to spend the day in consultation with young Alexander:

"If I do as you say, and order the army to disperse, how many do you suppose would get away?"

"Two thirds of us. We would scatter like rabbits and partridges in the woods, and they could not scatter to catch us."

Lee finished the long talk:

"As Christian men, General Alexander, you and I have no right to think for one moment of our personal feelings. . . . And as for myself, while you young men might afford to go bushwhacking, the only . . . course for me would be to surrender and take the consequences.

"I expect to meet General Grant this morning in the rear of the army and to surrender this army to him."

Alexander's eyes filled with tears.

"But," Lee said, with a faint smile, "I can tell you for your comfort that General Grant will not demand Unconditional Surrender. He will give us as honorable terms as we have a right to ask or expect."

Alexander turned away, and went toward Gordon, who was still hard-pressed by the enemy.[5]

Lee was preparing to mount when Colonel Taylor approached. The general told him he had decided to surrender.

"Well, sir," Taylor said, "I can only speak for myself; to me any other fate is preferable."

"Such is my individual way of thinking," Lee said, but added, ". . . it would be useless and cruel to shed more blood, and I have arranged to meet General Grant with a view to surrender, and I want you to accompany me."

The general mounted Traveller and with Taylor and Marshall rode behind Sergeant G. W. Tucker, who carried the flag of truce. Tucker was the courier who had been with A. P. Hill at his death; the truce flag he carried today was nothing more than a handkerchief on a stick.

As they passed, Marshall recalled, troops "cheered General Lee to the echo, as they had cheered him many a time before. He waved his hand to suppress the cheering, because he was afraid the sound might attract the fire of the enemy."

They rode between the lines and Tucker went ahead with his flag until halted by a Federal outpost. Lee sent Marshall after him. A Union officer emerged and introduced himself to Marshall; he was Lieutenant Colonel Charles Whittier, from the staff of General Humphreys. He had heard nothing of a meeting between Lee and Grant, at the rear or anywhere else, but surprised Marshall by handing him a letter. He would wait, Whittier said, in case Lee wished to reply.[6]

Marshall walked back between the staring pickets of the armies. He opened the letter and read it to Lee:

> Headquarters Armies of the United States
> April 9, 1865

General R. E. Lee,
Commanding C.S. Armies:

General: Your note of yesterday is received. As I have no authority to treat on the subject of peace the meeting proposed for 10 A.M. today could lead to no good. I will state, however, General, that I am equally desirous for peace with yourself, and the whole North entertain the same feeling. The terms upon which peace can be had are well understood. By the South laying down their arms they will hasten that most desirable event, save thousands of human lives, and hundreds of millions of property not yet destroyed. Sincerely hoping that all our difficulties may be settled without the loss of another life, I subscribe myself,

> very respectfully your obedient servant,
> U. S. Grant,
> Lieutenant General U.S. Army.

Lee was silent for a moment. "All right," he said to Marshall. "Write a letter to General Grant and ask him to meet me to deal with the question of surrender of my army, in reply to the letter he wrote me at Farmville."

Marshall sat and began to write:

> April 9th, 1865

General:
   I received your note this morning on the picket line, whither I had come to meet you and ascertain definitely what terms were embraced in your proposition of yesterday with reference to the surrender of this army.

Marshall was bent over his board, his busy pencil scratching on the heavy paper, when a horseman tore past them. The speeding man was Colonel Jack Haskell, a one-armed staff officer from Longstreet. Lee recognized his mare. Haskell reined, in obvious excitement.

"What is it?" Lee said. "What is it? Oh, why did you do it? You have killed your beautiful horse."

Haskell shouted his message. Fitz Lee had found an escape route. With haste the army could slip away.

Lee asked Haskell a couple of quiet, almost casual questions about the situation at the front, and then turned from him, as if satisfied that nothing had changed since he left the scene. He continued working with Marshall on the message to Grant, which ended:

> I now request an interview in accordance with the offer contained in your letter of yesterday for that purpose.
>   Very respectfully,
>   Your obt. servt
>   R. E. Lee

Marshall handed the paper to Lee, who traced his signature across it, the letters so much larger than usual that generations later the most industrious student of his life would conclude that the giant signature resulted from Lee having written without his spectacles.[7]

Marshall went into the Federal lines; Whittier took the dispatch and was gone for five minutes. He returned with disturbing news:

"I have been directed to say that an attack has been ordered, and that the commander here has no discretion. General Grant left General Meade some time ago, and the letter cannot reach him in time to stop the attack."

Marshall asked Whittier to try once more. "Ask him to read General Lee's letter. Perhaps under the circumstances, he can stop it."

Whittier went again into the thickets. This time he was gone much longer. In his absence Federal pickets advanced and a picket with a flag of truce came into the Confederate lines to warn them to withdraw, or face the coming attack.

Lee seemed momentarily in danger, for he remained in his

place as if determined to hold the ground. At last when the head of the enemy column was just one hundred yards away, he mounted Traveller and went back past Longstreet's breastworks into the center of his forces.

He had another message from Fitz Lee: The route was blocked. Lee gave no sign of emotion.

It was an hour before Whittier returned. He said that General Meade had suspended firing until noon. That gave the truce-makers an hour and a half. Grant was far around on the right, and Lee's letter was still following him. Meade suggested that Lee write a duplicate of his letter and have it carried through the lines as a safeguard.

The general dictated to Marshall, and yet another note went off to the Federal commander.

About this time Lee had a bit of cheering news. The Federal General Seth Williams sent a note saying that Custis was alive and unharmed, despite the report that he had been missing at Sayler's Creek. Lee brightened only momentarily.

The commander's party had gone into a valley below the village, at the side of a creek bridge, and here at the roadside under a scrubby apple tree, Alexander and others had dragged together for him a bed of rails, over which blankets were thrown.

Lee lay down, Marshall noted, "much fatigued," and went to sleep.

Officers crowded about the place, and at times throngs threatened to disturb Lee, or to crowd too closely about him. Taylor had them herded back by a cordon of soldiers. They waited more than an hour in the bottom.[8]

On the front Federals were becoming persistent, and Gordon soon had a colorful visitor. Gordon told Colonel Green Peyton of his staff to ride out with a white flag, advising the enemy that firing had been suspended. Peyton said there was no truce flag.

"Well, take your handkerchief and tie it on a stick, and go!"

"I have no handkerchief."

"Then tear your shirt, sir."

"General, I have on a flannel shirt, and I see you have. I don't believe there's a white shirt in the army."

"Get something, sir, and go."

Peyton found a rag of some description and rode away.

He was soon back with an apparition: George A. Custer, Major General. That much could be seen from afar, engraved on an enormous gold pin at his throat, clasped in a scarlet neckerchief. The young officer, Gordon saw, was "slender and graceful, and a superb rider. He wore his hair very long, falling almost to his shoulders."

Custer saluted with his saber and said courteously, "I am General Custer, and bear a message from General Sheridan . . . to demand the immediate and unconditional surrender of all the troops under your command."

"You will please, General, return my compliments to General Sheridan," Gordon said, "and say to him that I shall not surrender my command."

"He directs me to say to you, General, that if there is any hesitation about your surrender, that he has you surrounded, and can annihilate you in an hour."

Gordon replied that he knew his position well enough, and that Sheridan would move at his own risk. Sheridan himself soon galloped up, Gordon noted a bit scornfully, "accompanied by a mounted escort almost as large as one of Fitz Lee's regiments . . . mounted on an enormous horse."

Sheridan argued briefly with Gordon, his snapping black eyes looking everywhere about them. The Federal said he had no word from Grant about a truce. Gordon showed him the note from Lee, which seemed to satisfy Sheridan, for he dismounted, and the two generals sat on the gound.[9]

There was a crash of musketry to the left. Gordon remembered: "Sheridan sprang to his feet and fiercely asked, 'What does this mean, sir?' I replied, 'It's my fault, General. I had forgotten that brigade.' "

Gordon sent Colonel William Blackford of the engineers with Lieutenant Vanderbilt Allen of Sheridan's staff to halt the firing. The two came upon one of the last killings of the war, a macabre scene.

"I dashed off through the pines," Blackford wrote, ". . . found a line of infantry reloading . . . and a few paces in front a Yankee officer splendidly mounted, his uniform buttoned up to his chin, displaying a fine, manly figure. But from the closely fitting coat sprouted a dozen streams of blood, and his horse was tottering with his hide riddled with bullets . . . the dying rider rolled at the feet of the men, exclaiming, 'My God, boys, you have killed me!' "

The Rebels explained that the Federal major, more than half drunk, had galloped on them, waving his sword and demanding their surrender. This was too much for the regiment, which shot the Federal down.

Blackford's companion, Lieutenant Allen, had by now disappeared. Blackford found him in the hands of a South Carolina regiment whose commander, General John Geary, was shouting furiously in the Federal's face, "And you expect me to believe any such damned story as that! Where is the officer who brought you? No, sir, damn you, you shall go to the rear with the other prisoners."

Blackford explained to the stunned general.

"General, the army is surrendered."

Blackford could not forget Geary's face:

"He quivered as if he had been shot, and sat still in his saddle a moment, and then, returning his sabre, which he held still drawn in his hand, he said, 'Then I'll be damned if I'll surrender.' And that night he passed out of the lines to join Johnston's army."[10]

It was soon the turn of Longstreet, who saw in his front a Federal party:

"Down they came in fast gallop, General Custer's flaxen locks flowing over his shoulders, and in brusque excited manner, he said, 'In the name of General Sheridan I demand the unconditional surrender of this army.'

"He was reminded that I was not the commander . . . that he was within the lines of the enemy without authority addressing a superior officer, and in disrespect to General Grant as well as myself . . ."

The eruption of the defeated Confederate seemed to stun Custer, who replied mildly, ending: "It would be a pity to spill more blood today."

"As you are now more reasonable," Longstreet said, "I will say that General Lee has gone to meet General Grant, and it is for them to determine the future of the armies."

Custer rode back to his lines, puzzled by the strange behavior of Old Pete, who acted so much the conqueror. Longstreet turned back to seek Lee.[11]

Old Pete found his commander had stirred from the crude bed in the apple orchard. Lee was in a somber mood.

The chief described to Longstreet the note from Grant and pointed out anxiously its absence of specific terms. He was apprehensive that his refusal to meet Grant's first proposal might "cause him to demand harsh terms."

Longstreet assured him: "I know Grant well enough to say that the terms will be about what you would demand under the circumstances."

Lee was still skeptical, and was silent as he rather morosely eyed an oncoming Federal officer under a white flag. Longstreet sought once more to bolster him.

"If he won't give you honorable terms," he said, "break it off, and tell him to do his worst."

Lee straightened, Longstreet noticed: "The thought of another round seemed to brace him."

The Federal rider came up and was introduced by his Confederate escort as Colonel Orville Babcock of Grant's staff. Babcock saluted and held forth a letter. Lee read:

> Headquarters, Armies of the U.S.
> April 9, 1865
>
> General R. E. Lee,
> Commanding C.S. Army:
>
> Your note of this date is but this moment (11:50 A.M.) received. In consequence of my having passed from the Richmond and Lynchburg road to the Farmville and Lynchburg road I am writing this about four miles west of Walker's church and will push forward to the front for the purpose of meeting you. Notice sent on this road where you wish the interview to take place will meet me.
>
> Very respectfully, your obedient servant
> U. S. Grant,
> Lieutenant-General.

Lee called Marshall to ride with him, but the aide, "in a very dilapidated state," had to dress for the occasion. He borrowed a dress sword, leaving behind the plain one Jeb Stuart had given him long ago. He also begged from a friend a dress shirt and collar. Lee asked Taylor to go, but the colonel made an excuse: "I have ridden twice through the lines this morning." Lee did not press him.

Lee handed a map to Venable, the map of photographic linen Lee had carried in his breast pocket for months, and had fought with since coming into the Richmond-Petersburg trenches. Venable was to burn it—but Alexander first snatched it and cut off a corner with the legend: "South side James River, R. E. Lee."

The group mounted.

Five of them left the army: Lee, Marshall, Babcock, a Union orderly, and Sergeant Tucker.

They "struck up the hill towards Appomattox Court House,"

in Marshall's words, but there was a pause. Traveller was thirsty, and Lee halted at the stream until he had his fill. As the party mounted the hill more men of the army caught sight of it and there were bursts of cheering, ending as the troops took in the significance of the commander trailing the white flag. Silence fell.

Marshall was sent in front to find a place of meeting, and as he entered the village he met a man named Wilmer McLean, who had once lived on the battlefield of Bull Run, but had moved his family to this quiet village to escape the war. Marshall was startled: "Of all people, whom should I meet but McLean."

"Can you show me a house where General Lee and General Grant can meet together?"

McLean led him to a vacant house, a littered place bare of furniture.

"It won't do." Marshall said.

"Maybe my house will do," McLean said.

He led the colonel to a roomy and comfortable two-story brick house at the roadside in the village.

"I think this will suit," Marshall said. He sent Tucker back for Lee and Babcock. They soon arrived.

Marshall recorded some of it: "So General Lee, Babcock and myself sat down in McLean's parlour and talked in the most friendly and affable way."

Lee faced the younger officers from the side of a small table with spool legs, near the front window, in the corner opposite the door. For half an hour they waited, and pale light fell through the south window into the eyes of Lee, who sat with his legs crossed, his hat and gloves on the table. In the lengthening silences there was the creaking of his new boots, which were embroidered in red silk.

On the back roads, out of touch with headquarters, riding without baggage or even his sword, Grant circled toward the village of Appomattox. He would not forget the night just past:

"I was suffering very severely with a sick headache and stopped at a farmhouse. . . . I spent the night bathing my feet in hot water and mustard, and putting mustard plasters on my wrists and the back part of my neck, hoping to be cured by morning."[12]

Grant had slept little, lying on a sofa in the farmhouse. At midnight he got Lee's noncommittal letter offering to talk peace, but refusing to surrender his army. General Horace Porter of his staff kept watch over him in the night:

"About 4 o'clock . . . I found his room empty and . . . saw him pacing up and down in the yard holding both hands to his head . . . he said he had had very little sleep, and was still suffering the most excruciating pain."

"Well," Porter said, "there is one consolation in all this, General; I never knew you to be ill that you did not get some good news."

Grant gave him a weary smile: "The best thing that can happen to me today is to get rid of this pain in my head."[13]

He went back into the house, replied to Lee, and rode off, refusing to lie in an ambulance. He was on the road when a courier overtook him with Lee's message, offering to give up the Army of Northern Virginia. Grant dismounted and sat at the roadside to scribble his reply to Lee. He recalled of the moment:

"When the officer reached me I was still suffering with the sick headache; but the instant I saw the contents of the note I was cured."

They lost no time on the road into Appomattox. At the edge of the village Grant met Sheridan. He reined his horse, Cincinnati.

"Good morning, Sheridan, how are you?"

"First rate, thank you, General. How are you?"

Grant only nodded. "Is General Lee up there?" He looked toward the court house.

"Yes. In the brick house."

Sheridan and his officers began to talk excitedly. "This is a trick. We will whip them now in five minutes, if only you will let us go in."

Grant "had no doubt about the good faith of Lee."

He broke into their chattering. "Very well, then, let's go up."

Grant rode to the yard of McLean's house, followed by a dozen or more officers. Colonel Babcock appeared on the porch, and led in Grant and a few others. Babcock shortly reappeared and signalled two more: Robert Lincoln, the President's son, and Grant's loyal aide, Adam Badeau, who went into the house. A growing crowd waited outside. There were subdued sounds from within, but the waiting men could make out nothing. Blue-clad figures shut the view at the window of the room to the left.[14]

Marshall thought they had been in the room about half an hour when he heard horses, but he was surprised to see Grant walk in. Behind the Federal commander others crowded—Sheridan, Ord, Badeau, Porter, and Colonel Parker among them. Marshall missed little:

"General Lee was standing at the end of the room opposite the door when General Grant walked in. Grant had on a sack coat, a loose fatigue coat, but he had no side arms. He looked as though he had had a pretty hard time. He had been riding and his clothes were somewhat dusty and a little soiled."

The Federals walked in quietly and stood around the sides of the room, "very much as people enter a sick chamber when they expect to find the patient dangerously ill," Porter wrote.

Some sat on the sofa and the few chairs, but most of them stood. Porter sketched Grant's appearance with care:

"Nearly 43 years of age, five feet eight inches in height, with shoulders slightly stooped. His hair and full beard were a nut-brown, without a trace of gray in them. He had on a single-breasted blouse, made of dark blue flannel, unbuttoned in front. . . . The boots and portions of his clothes were spattered with mud . . . a pair of thread gloves, of a dark yellow color, which he had taken off on entering the room. His felt 'sugar-loaf' stiff-brimmed hat was thrown on the table beside him. He had no sword, and a pair of shoulder straps was all there was about him to designate his rank. In fact, aside from these, his uniform was that of a private."

Grant walked to Lee—much embarrassed, he later confessed.

"I met you once before, General Lee," Grant began. "In Mexico, when you came over from Scott's headquarters to visit Garland's Brigade." Lee nodded.

"I have always remembered your appearance," Grant said. "And I think I'd have recognized you anywhere."

"Yes," Lee said. "I know I met you then, and I have often thought of it and tried to recollect how you looked, but I have never been able to recall a single feature."

There was a brief silence. The generals talked pleasantly of the weather, and of Mexico. Lee at last had to draw Grant's attention to the surrender, as if the Federal were reluctant to open the subject.

Porter's version of the story had the ring of careful accuracy:

"I suppose, General Grant," Lee said, "that the object of our meeting is fully understood. I asked to see you to ascertain upon what terms you would receive the surrender of my army."

"The terms I propose," Grant said, "are those stated substantially in my letter of yesterday—that is, the officers and men surrendered to be paroled and disqualified from taking up arms again until properly exchanged, and all arms, ammunition, and supplies to be delivered up as captured property."

Lee nodded. "Those are about the conditions I expected."

"Yes," Grant said, "I think our correspondence indicated pretty clearly the action that would be taken . . . and I hope it will lead to a general suspension of hostilities . . . preventing any further loss of life."

"I presume, General Grant, we have both carefully considered the proper steps to be taken, and I suggest that you commit to writing the terms you have proposed, so that they may be formally acted upon."

"Very well," Grant said, "I will write them out."

He motioned to one of his huge officers, a dark-skinned colonel, Ely Parker, a full-blooded Indian, the actual Chief of the Six Nations. Parker, the secretary whose penmanship was the finest on Grant's staff, carried a small table to his commander's side.

"The order-book," Grant said, and a pad was brought to him.

"He wrote very rapidly," Porter recorded, "and did not pause until he had finished the sentence ending with 'officers appointed by me to receive them.' Then he looked toward Lee, and his eyes seemed to be resting on the handsome sword that hung at that officer's side . . . after a short pause he wrote the sentence: 'This will not embrace the side arms of officers, nor their private horses or baggage.'

"When he had finished the letter he called Colonel Parker . . . to his side and looked it over with him and directed him as they went along to interline six or seven words and to strike the word 'their' which had been repeated . . . he handed the book to General Lee and asked him to read over the letter.

"Lee took it and laid it on the table beside him, while he drew from his pocket a pair of steel-rimmed spectacles and wiped the glasses carefully with his handkerchief.

"Then he crossed his legs, adjusted the spectacles very slowly and deliberately, took up the draft of the letter, and proceeded to read it attentively."

Colonel Babcock slipped out of the room and eased open the front door. On the porch he removed his hat and twirled it around on one finger, as a signal to those in the yard. General George Forsyth, who was watching, interpreted the sign to mean: "It's all settled." Babcock took Sheridan and General Ord back into the house with him.

Lee read the letter slowly:

General R. E. Lee, Commanding C.S.A.
Appomattox Ct.H., Va., April 9, 1865

General: In accordance with the substance of my letter to you of the 8th inst., I propose to receive the surrender of the Army of Northern Virginia on the following terms, to wit: Rolls of all the officers and men to be made in duplicate, one copy to be given to an officer designated by me, the other to be retained by such officer or officers as you may designate. The officers to give their individual paroles not to take up arms against the Government of the United States until properly, and each company or regimental commander to sign a like parole for the men of their commands. The arms, artillery, and public property to be parked, and stacked, and turned over to the officers appointed by me to receive them. This will not embrace the side arms of the officers, nor their private horses or baggage. This done, each officer and man will be allowed to return to his home, not to be disturbed by the United States authorities so long as they observe their paroles, and the laws in force where they may reside. Very respectfully,

U. S. Grant, Lieutenant-General.

Lee looked up when he had finished the first of the two pages. "After the words, 'until properly,' the word 'exchanged' seems to be omitted. You doubtless intended to use that word."

"Why, yes," Grant said. "I thought I had put it in."

"With your permission I will mark where it should be inserted."

"Certainly," Grant said.

Porter watched as if aware that this was a climactic moment of history:

"Lee felt in his pocket as if searching for a pencil, but did not seem to be able to find one. Seeing this and happening to be standing close to him, I handed him my pencil . . . he noted the interlineation.

"During the rest of the interview he kept twirling this pencil in his fingers and occasionally tapping the top of the table with it. When he handed it back it was carefully treasured by me as a memento of the occasion."

When Lee reached Grant's sentence concerning the side arms of officers, and their horses and private baggage, Porter noticed for the first time "a slight change of countenance . . . evidently touched by this act of generosity."

Lee looked up to Grant, and spoke warmly: "This will have a very happy effect upon my army."

"Unless you have some suggestions to make in regard to the form," Grant said, "I will have a copy of the letter made in ink and sign it."

Lee paused. "There is one thing I would like to mention," he said. "The cavalrymen and artillerymen in our army own their own horses. Our organization differs from yours. I would like to understand whether these men will be permitted to retain their horses."

"You will find that the terms as written do not allow this," Grant said. "Only the officers are allowed to take their private property."

Lee read over the second page of the letter. "No, I see the terms do not allow it. That is clear."

Porter saw: "His face showed plainly that he was quite anxious to have this concession made."

Grant spoke quickly, giving Lee no time to make a second request: "Well, the subject is quite new to me. Of course I did not know that any private soldiers owned their animals, but I think this will be the last battle of the war—I sincerely hope so—and . . . I take it that most of the men in the ranks are small farmers, and it is doubtful whether they will be able to put in a crop and carry themselves and their families through next winter without their horses.

"I will arrange it in this way: I will not change the terms as they are written, but I will instruct the officers to let all the men who claim to own a horse or mule take the animals home with them to work their little farms."

"This will have the best possible effect upon my men," Lee said. "It will be very gratifying and will do much toward conciliating our people."

Lee passed the copy book to Grant, who called Colonel Bowers of his staff to copy the terms. Bowers said that he was "a little nervous," and asked to be excused. The papers were passed to Parker, who carried his table to the wall at the rear of the room. He discovered that McLean's inkwell held no ink, and there was a brief search for ink.

Colonel Marshall saved the day with a small boxwood inkwell which he always carried with him.

Lee and Grant talked as Marshall began to write a letter accepting Grant's terms. Marshall wrote in a florid, formal style, beginning: "I have the honor to reply to your communication."

Lee took it, reading swiftly. "Don't say, 'I have the honor,' he told Marshall. "He is here. Just say, 'I accept the terms.' "

Marshall turned to make a final copy in ink, and discovered that he had no paper. The enemy officers passed him a few sheets. He wrote:

> Headquarters, Army of Northern Virginia
> April 9th, 1865
>
> General: I have received your letter of this date containing the terms of the surrender of the Army of Northern Virginia as proposed by you. As they are substantially the same as those expressed in your letter of the 8th inst., they are accepted. I will proceed to designate proper officers to carry the stipulations into effect.
>
> R. E. Lee, General
>
> Lieutenant General U. S. Grant

Grant and Lee turned to other officers in the room. There were introductions. Porter once saw Lee pause:

"He did not exhibit the slightest change of features during this ceremony until Parker was introduced to him. . . . When Lee saw Parker's swarthy features he looked at him with evident surprise, and his eyes rested on him for several seconds. What was passing in his mind probably no one ever knew, but the natural surmise was that at first he mistook Parker for a Negro, and was struck with astonishment to find that the commander of the Union armies had one of that race on his personal staff."

Lee did not speak during introductions, nodding to one officer after another, until he faced Seth Williams, who had sent him the word of Custis that morning. The two exchanged remarks and Williams, who had been Lee's adjutant in his days as commandant at West Point, recalled a joke of the old days. Lee did not smile, Porter said: "He did not unbend, or even relax the sternness of his features."

Sheridan sat on the sofa next to Colonel Marshall, who had now completed his letter.

"This is very pretty country," Sheridan said.

"General," Marshall said, "I haven't seen it by daylight. All my observations have been made at night, and I haven't seen the country at all myself."

Sheridan laughed.

Grant interrupted them. "Sheridan, how many rations do you have?"

"How many do you want?"

"General Lee has about a thousand or 1500 of our people prisoners and they are faring the same as his men, but he tells me his haven't anything. Can you send them some rations?"

The amused Federal officers craned to see the generals, for they knew Sheridan had seized Lee's missing rations on the rails at Appomattox Station the night before.

"Yes," Sheridan said.

"How many can you send?"

"Twenty five thousand."

Grant asked Lee if that would be enough.

"Plenty, plenty. An abundance," Lee said.

Grant asked his commissary chief, Colonel Morgan, to send the food. The Federal commander once more glanced at Lee's exquisitely worked sword. The sight of it seemed to disturb Grant.

"I started out from my camp several days ago without my sword," Grant said, "and I have not seen my headquarters baggage since. I have been riding without side arms. I have generally worn a sword as little as possible."

Grant soon returned to the subject.

"I was about four miles from the wagons where my arms and uniforms were, and I thought you would rather receive me as I was, than be detained."

"I'm much obliged to you," Lee said. "I'm very glad you did it in that way."

Some of the older officers were probably thinking back to the Mexican War, perhaps remembering the incident when Grant had reported, dusty from the field, to Scott's headquarters, and because of the commander's orders against untidy dress, Lee was forced to send him back to change his uniform. Colonel Marshall wondered if the memory crossed Grant's mind today.

Sheridan approached Lee. He had sent Lee notes during the morning in protest of Confederate movements during the truce, and in his haste had not made copies.

"Will you let me have them long enough to have copies made?" Sheridan asked.

Lee murmured his regrets. "I'm sure it must have been some misunderstanding," he said. He gave Sheridan the papers from his breast pocket.

There was a little general conversation. Lee asked Grant to notify Meade of the surrender, to avoid an outburst of fighting, and Grant sent men to carry out the order.

It was just before four o'clock. Lee shook hands with Grant bowed slightly to the others and left the room. Marshall followed.[15]

The crowd waiting outside had been growing more tense. Custer had arrived, and sat on the porch with other ranking officers. A tableau in the yard drew the eyes of watching Federals: "A soldierly-looking orderly"—that was Sergeant Tucker—neat in his ragged gray uniform, held the reins of three horses. One of these was Traveller, who appeared to the enemy as "a fairly well-bred looking grey in good heart though thin in flesh."

Tucker sensibly loosed the reins so the horses could crop the tender grass. Traveller ate at the base of McLean's porch pillars, and thus was hidden from view of those above.

There was a scraping of chairs inside. General Forsyth of the Federals squeezed as near the door as possible:

"As I did so . . . General Lee stood before me. As he paused for a few seconds . . . I took my first and last look at the great Confederate chieftain. . . . A clear, ruddy complexion—just then suffused by a crimson flush, that rising from his neck overspread his face and even tinged his broad forehead, which, bronzed where it had been exposed to the weather, was clear and beautifully white where it had been shielded by his hat—deep brown eyes, a firm but well-shaped Roman nose."

A Northern newspaper correspondent saw more:

"He is growing quite bald, and wears one of the side locks of his hair thrown across the upper portion of his forehead . . . his demeanor was that of a thoroughly possessed gentleman."

Lee took a few deliberate steps onto the porch. His scabbard banged on the floor as he went to the head of the stairs; he carried his hat and gloves in his hands. He put on the hat and gave a perfunctory return salute to the salutes of the Federals on the porch. He gazed out over the yard, where Federals had risen to stare at him, looking beyond the village and into the valley where his army waited for him.

Forsyth could not take his eyes from him: "He paused, and slowly drew on his gauntlets, smiting his gloved hands into each other several times after doing so, evidently utterly oblivious of his surroundings. Then, apparently recalling his thoughts, he glanced deliberately right and left, and not seeing his horse, he called in a hoarse, half-choked voice:

" 'Orderly! Orderly!' "

Tucker appeared. "Here, General, here." Tucker tried to replace the bit in Traveller's mouth. The horse fought for a few more strands of grass.

Lee stood in front of Traveller's head as Tucker worked to buckle the bridle; Lee slipped the dark forelock over its brow-band, smoothed it, and absently patted the gray's forehead. He caught the reins and with a slow, tired motion swung into the saddle with his old-fashioned dragoon mount.

"He settled into his seat," Forsyth wrote, "and as he did so there broke unguardedly from his lips a long, low deep sigh, almost a groan in its intensity, while the flush on his neck and face seemed, if possible, to take on a still deeper hue."

When Marshall had mounted Lee pulled up the reins and they moved toward the gate.[16]

Grant came into the yard, and looked up as Lee crossed his path. In unison, as if by signal, the generals exchanged salutes and raised their hats. Lee rode off. Grant mounted Cincinnati. Forsyth saw nothing in the Federal commander's face: "If he felt any elation, neither his voice, features nor his eyes betrayed it."

Grant turned to his officers under the locust trees. "Sheridan, where will you have headquarters tonight?"

"Here, or near here. Right here in this yard, probably."

"Very well, then. I'll know where to find you . . . Good day."

"Good day, General." Grant went out of the gate at a fast trot.

Peals of cannon fire rolled into the village from the Federal lines, but soon ceased. In the distance was a great outburst of cheering. The Federal troops went mad with joy, and sprang into each other's arms, flung hats into the air, howling deliriously. In the midst of one mad scene was the usually solemn General Meade, yipping high-pitched yells, twirling his horse about in circles, waving his hat over his head. Grant soon brought this to an end: "The Confederates were now our prisoners, and we did not want to exult over their downfall."

The vigil of Major Wilmer McLean, the peace-loving host to the surrender party, had only begun. McLean "had been charging about in a manner which indicated that the excitement was shaking his system to its nervous center," Porter wrote.

And it was now that Federal officers as "relic hunters, charged down upon the manor-house and made various attempts to jump Mr. McLean's claims to his own furniture."

The mob might have torn the house apart but for the example of Sheridan, who offered McLean twenty dollars in gold for the table Lee had used. McLean agreed—and Sheridan passed the table to Custer, who rode off with it on his shoulder, as a gift for his wife.

The auction became brisk. Ord gave McLean forty dollars for the table Grant had used, as a souvenir for Mrs. Grant.

Porter watched the end of it: "Bargains were struck at once for all the articles in the room and it is even said that some mementoes were carried off for which no coin of the realm was ever exchanged."

The room was left bare to McLean, who had once, so long ago, lost a house to Beauregard as battle headquarters.

Lee, unseeing, passed many regiments like the 75th North Carolina, one of whose officers wrote: "We drove our guns into the hard earth to tie our horses to, made a fire, burned our flag to keep the Yankees from getting it, and waited for further orders and something to eat."

The old man rode down the steep slope, across the bridge, and into his apple orchard. Colonel Talcott threw a picket around the place to hold off the swarming Federals, who came to chatter with the Rebels and hunt souvenirs.

Among the guard was Colonel Blackford, who watched Lee at bay in the shade of an apple tree, while Taylor and Venable, a little in advance, tried to discourage visitors:

"Lee paced backwards and forwards . . . like a caged lion . . . he seemed to be in one of his savage moods and when these moods were on him it was safer to keep out of his way; so his staff kept to their trees except when it was necessary to introduce the visitors.

"Quite a number came; they were mostly in groups of four or five and some of high rank. It was evident that they came from curiosity, or to see General Lee as friends in the old army.

"But General Lee shook hands with none of them. It was rather amusing to see the extreme deference shown by them to General Lee. When he would see Colonel Taylor coming with a party towards his tree he would halt in his pacing and stand 'at attention' and glare at them with a look which few men but he could assume.

"They would remove their hats entirely and stand bareheaded during the interview while General Lee sometimes gave a scant touch to his hat in return and sometimes did not even do that . . . the interviews were short."

Near sunset, after he had seen to the handling of Federal rations for the men, Lee mounted Traveller and went through the army to his headquarters about a mile to the rear.

Colonel Blackford rode behind him, down two solid walls of men who rushed to the roadside to greet Lee. Most of the army was there. The men broke into wild cheering. Blackford wrote:

"Tears filled his eyes and trickled down his cheeks . . . cheers changed to choking sobs as with streaming eyes and many cries of affection they waved their hats. . . . Each group began in the same way with cheers and ended in the same way with sobs, all the way to his quarters.

"Grim-hearted men threw themselves on the ground, covered their faces with their hands and wept like children. Officers of all ranks made no attempt to hide their feelings, but sat on their horses and cried aloud."

Traveller seemed to think the applause was for him, for he tossed his head all down the line.

One man held his arms wide above the crowd and shouted, "I love you just as well as ever, General Lee!"

Longstreet saw it, too:

"Those who could speak said goodbye, those who could not speak, and were near, passed their hands gently over the sides of Traveller. Lee had sufficient control to fix his eyes on a line between the ears of Traveller and look neither to right nor left until he reached a large white oak tree, where he dismounted to make his last headquarters, and finally talked a little."

Blackford was not near enough to hear what he said, but Lee's son Robert recorded the words: "Men, we have fought through the war together; I have done my best for you; my heart is too full to say more."

Other soldiers heard more, among them Lieutenant George Mills of the 16th North Carolina:

"General Lee . . . took off his hat and made a little speech:

" 'Boys, I have done the best I could for you. Go home now, and if you make as good citizens as you have soldiers, you will do well, and I shall always be proud of you. Goodbye, and God bless you all.'

"He seemed so full that he could say no more."

Lee went into the tent, and after a time the men left. There was still work to be done, Marshall remembered:

"Lee sat with several of us at a fire in front of his tent, and after some conversation about the army and the events of the day . . . he told me to prepare an order to the troops."

In the early darkness Lee left the staff and disappeared into the tent, alone. It rained in the night.

18 REQUIEM

A COLD RAIN fell through Monday, April tenth, but there was much visiting between the armies.

Federal quartermaster wagons entered Lee's lines with fresh-killed beef, but there was not enough for all the regiments and many ate only parched corn.

A guest at Lee's headquarters was an old friend and classmate of Colonel Marshall's, Captain Fred Colston. The two talked of plans to return home and reminisced until Marshall recalled that Lee had set him to a chore he had not begun.

"Fred," he said, "General Lee has told me to write a farewell address. What can I say to those people?"

Colston "took this for a hint" and left Marshall alone, so that he could write Lee's farewell to his troops.[1]

At about nine o'clock in the morning Lee was called to the picket lines where his troops had embarrassed him by halting General Grant and his party, who had come visiting.

Grant was forced to wait with his officers until a messenger had been sent to headquarters. Within a few minutes Lee arrived "at a gallop."

Grant and Lee met on a knoll between the armies, lifting their hats to each other in salute; the officers surrounding them moved off in a semicircle, beyond earshot. Only Grant left a first-hand account of this quiet talk with Lee:

". . . A very pleasant conversation of little over half an hour, in the course of which Lee said to me that the South was a big country, and that we might have to march over it three or four times before the war entirely ended, but that we would now be able to do it, as they could no longer resist us.

"He expressed it as his most earnest hope . . . that we would not be called upon to cause more loss and sacrifice of life; but he could not foretell the result.

"I then suggested to General Lee that there was not a man in the Confederacy whose influence with the soldiery and the whole people was as great as his, and that if he would now advise the surrender of all the armies I had no doubt his advice would be followed.

"But Lee said, that he could not do that without consulting the President first. I knew there was no use to urge him to do anything against his ideas of what was right."[2]

At last Lee asked Grant to have his officers see to the final details of surrender, and the ceremony of giving up Confederate arms was set for the next day.

Lee gave permission for Grant's officers to visit in his camps, and parties rode to noisy reunions with companions from old army days. Many Rebel officers returned with the Federals to the McLean house, where Grant had made headquarters: Longstreet, who had been at Grant's wedding many years before; Wilcox, who had been Grant's groomsman; Heth, Gordon and Pickett all trooped to the house.

Longstreet, on his way to meet Federal commissioners to discuss the surrender, had a glimpse of the Union commander:

"Grant looked up, recognized me, rose, and with his old-time cheerful greeting gave me his hand, and after passing a few remarks offered a cigar, which was gratefully received."[3]

Grant, after "an hour pleasantly passed" with officers of both armies, rode off to the nearest rail junction, at Burkeville, on his way to Washington.

Lee had left Grant and gone back toward his headquarters, where he found that Marshall had not yet completed the address to the troops. Marshall had an excuse:

"Many persons were coming and going, so that I was unable to write without interruption until about 10 o'clock, when General Lee, finding that the order had not been prepared, directed me to get into his ambulance, which stood near his tent, and placed an orderly to prevent anyone from approaching me. I made a draft in pencil and took it to General Lee."

Lee struck out one paragraph of Marshall's address, which he said "would tend to keep alive the feeling existing between North and South," and made a couple of minor changes. Marshall then went back into the wagon, copied the order, and handed it to Norman Bell, a twenty-year-old clerk in the Adjutant General's office, for a copy in ink.[4] It was the final document addressed to the troops, and was destined for fame:

Headquarters, Army of Northern Virginia,
April 10th, 1865

After four years of arduous service, marked by unsurpass-ed courage and fortitude, the Army of Northern Virginia had been compelled to yield to overwhelming numbers and resources. I need not tell the survivors of so many hard-fought battles, who have remained steadfast to the last, that I have consented to this result from no distrust of them, but, feeling that valor and devotion could accomplish nothing that could compensate for the loss that would have attended the continua-

tion of the contest, I have determined to avoid the useless
sacrifice of those whose past services have endeared them to
their countrymen.

By the terms of the agreement, officers and men can return to their homes, and remain there until exchanged. You
will take with you the satisfaction that proceeds from the con-
sciousness of duty faithfully performed; and I earnestly pray
that a merciful God will extend to you his blessing and protection.

With an increasing admiration of your constancy and devotion to your country, and a grateful remembrance of your
kind and generous consideration of myself, I bid you an affectionate farewell.

R. E. Lee, General.

General Meade, the stout adversary of Gettysburg, came to
visit Lee. He went as far as the Confederate pickets and sent Colonel Theodore Lyman of his staff to find some general officer to
lead them to headquarters.

Lyman saw Rebels at camp "looking tired and indifferent. . . .
I judged they had nothing to eat, for there was no cooking going
on."⁵

General Field came out from Longstreet's corps to meet
Meade. Field's men came to the roadside to see "the first Yankees"
as they passed. Meade pointed to the ragged troops.

"Those men are complimentary to me," he said.

"What was that?" Field asked.

"Just now they said I looked like a Rebel."

"I didn't suppose people on your side of the question thought
that a compliment," Field said.

Meade laughed. "Oh, yes, we do. Any people who have made
such a defense as you have, we can but respect and admire."

"Our men have, or think they have, cause for a different feeling," Field said. "And while their arms are in their hands, and our

defeat is fresh, it might be better to keep them from any general intercourse."[6]

Meade met Lee, who was riding with three or four staff officers. Meade took off his hat. "Good morning, General."

Lee did not at first recognize him, and when he saw the rider was Meade exclaimed, "But what are you doing with all that gray in your beard?"

"You have to answer for most of it," Meade said.

As they met, Colonel Lyman was staring at Lee:

"In manner he is exceedingly grave and dignified—this, I believe, he always has; but there was evidently added an extreme depression, which gave him the air of a man who kept up his pride to the last, but who was entirely overwhelmed. From his speech I judge he was inclined to wander in his thoughts.

"You would not have recognized a Confederate officer from his dress, which was a blue military overcoat, a high gray hat, and well-brushed riding boots."

Lee shook hands with Meade's officers, Lyman noticed, "with all the air of the oldest blood in the world. I did not think . . . that I should ever shake the hand of Robert E. Lee, prisoner of war!"

As the party went back toward Confederate headquarters it passed a South Carolina regiment, which began to cheer at sight of the officers.

Meade turned to his color bearer, who had the headquarters flag rolled up, and ordered him to unfurl the American flag. But a ragged man shouted:

"Damn your old rag! We're cheering General Lee!"[7]

The group dismounted at headquarters in a light rain. Lee and Meade disappeared into the single small fly tent; other officers gathered about a campfire. Inside, Lee and Meade fell to talking of the war, and of old times. At last Meade asked, "How many men did you have at Petersburg, at the time of our last assault?"

"At no time more than 35,000 men. Often it was less."

"General, you amaze me. You mean you had that many men just around Petersburg?"

"No. I had no more than that from my left on the Chickahominy to the right at Dinwiddie Courthouse."

Meade seemed genuinely surprised. "I had more than 50,000 men in my wing of the army, south of the James," he said.

Lee called in Taylor for confirmation. "Is my memory correct on our returns? Thirty-five thousand?"

Taylor nodded.[8]

General Wise appeared; he was Meade's brother-in-law, and had been called. The former Governor of Virginia had come in his only clothing, "an old wet gray blanket." He was happy to have the gift of a biscuit and coffee from the Federals.

Captain Colston went in to Lee while other visitors were crowding around. Colston remembered:

"At my request he wrote his name and the date in a pocket testament. . . . General Longstreet also wrote his name, with his left hand, as his right was still disabled from his wound at the Wilderness."

There were many paroles to be signed. Lee signed only one, for Colonel Taylor, who signed all the rest for headquarters.

Among other visitors was General Henry Hunt, the Federal artillerist. He asked to be taken to General Long, who had been in Hunt's battery before the war. Lee sent him off with a guide:

"Long will be very glad to see you. But you will find him much changed in appearance; he has suffered much from neuralgia of the face. He is now with General Longstreet's corps."

In the evening, though there was little to eat except what the Federals had brought, Lee made a meal with his staff. Major Giles B. Cooke entered the occasion briefly in his diary:

"Raining all day. Did not leave camp except to dine with the general and staff. Had no heart for conversation with anybody."[9]

Lee busied himself with the final dreary reports of the army's death on Tuesday. His generals brought in their reports, and from these, with a stern exertion of will, he composed a lengthy statement for President Davis, describing in plain language the details of the army's disaster. He was seen by few soldiers during the day.

A number of men came seeking Lee after dark. They filed into the woods of his headquarters, where they could see the dim light in his tent. A band began to play in the darkness. Lee fell silent, listening. The musicians played several familiar airs, and then one of the army's favorites: "Parting Is Pain," also known as "When the Swallows Homeward Fly."

Lee stepped from the tent, and the music ended:

> Now the Battle din is o'er,
> Shot and shell and cannon roar,
> Sad hearts within us die,
> Useless now, our good swords lie. . .
> Parting, oh parting, parting is pain.

"Who is it?" Lee asked. "Who's playing such sweet music for me?"

"The Fourth North Carolina band, General," someone said.

Lee took a step forward as if about to say something, but could not speak. He raised his hands as if in benediction, and all but sobbed:

"God bless you, men. God bless you. I can say no more."[10]

Lee remained in camp Wednesday morning, as if he could not bring himself to leave, but he did not ride out among the men. He was nearby when the fragments of his regiments went out to the formal surrender, but he could not go with them, somehow.

Federal troops had been astir since the first gray light of April twelfth, and in an old field outside the village General Joshua Chamberlain, of the Maine troops, a future governor of his state, watched his men step into line. Chamberlain was distracted and emotionally disturbed as he watched the beaten Confederate army come to its final field. He watched it coming from the camps on the far hillside, where tents were being struck:

"And now they move. The dusky swarms forge forward into gray column of march. On they come, with the old swinging route step and swaying battle flags. In the van, the proud Confederate ensign, the great field of white with a canton of star-strewn cross of blue on a field of red, the regimental battle flags . . . following on, crowded so thick, by thinning out of men, that the whole column seemed crowned with red."

But not all the Rebel flags were there. A few minutes earlier General Gordon had seen many of them torn from their staffs by sobbing men, who hid them in their shirts. Officers tried to check it, but many of the banners disappeared.

Those that were left bobbed up the hill beyond the stream and through the street of Appomattox. Chamberlain was so moved that he ordered a salute to the Rebel banners:

"Before us in proud humiliation stood . . . men whom neither toils and sufferings, nor the fact of death, nor disaster could bend from their resolve; standing before us now, thin, worn and famished, but erect, and with eyes looking level into ours, waking memories that bound us together as no other bond."

As the head of each division passed, the Federal buglers called the marching salute, and there was a long rattle of arms.

When Gordon rode past the spot and heard the salute, he wheeled his horse, pulling him on hind-quarters into the air, flourishing his sword, and ordered his troops to march past at the same stiff salute.

Chamberlain remembered it:

"On our part not a sound of trumpet more, nor roll of drum; not a cheer, nor word nor whisper . . . nor motion . . . but an awed stillness rather, and breath-holding, as if it were the passing of the dead.

"As each . . . division halts, the men face inward towards us across the road, twelve feet away; then carefully dress their line . . . worn and half-starved as they were . . . they fix bayonets, stack arms; then, hesitatingly, remove cartridge boxes and lay them down. Lastly—reluctantly, with agony of expression—they tenderly fold the flags, battle-worn and torn, blood-stained, heart-holding colors, and lay them down; some frenziedly rushing from the ranks, kneeling over them, clinging to them, pressing them to their lips with burning tears."

Chamberlain watched the gray regiments pass, calling to himself the terrible names of battlefields where he had met them. He wrote: "How could we help falling on our knees, all of us together, and praying God to pity and forgive us all!"[11]

There was no such humble spirit in Confederate breasts as Chamberlain imagined. Frank Mixson, a South Carolina private, spoke for his regiment on the way to the surrender field: "Every man fully armed, cartridge boxes full and the men well rested . . . we did not lag or skulk. Had General Lee then and there ridden out and said, 'Boys, there are the enemy. Go for them,' there would have been no man to question the odds. But we marched in front of them with our heads up."

If there was fight left in the ranks of Lee's defeated army it was to be seen in the defiant, upright figure of John B. Gordon. One of his soldiers said that "it would put fight into a whipped chicken" just to see the lean general on the field.

The surrender scene had hardly closed when Gordon rode into an adjoining field and, with his men pressing about him, began to shout:

"Soldiers of the Second Army Corps! No mathematician can compute the odds against which you have contended!"

He praised their courage, and told them that, if the war

were renewed, he would be willing to lead them again.''The blood of the martyrs was the seed of the church,'' he cried.[12]

In his own recollection of the speech Gordon wrote: "I closed with the prophecy that passion would speedily die, and that the brave and magnanimous soldiers of the Union army, when disbanded and scattered among the people, would become promoters of sectional peace and fraternity."

Many Union soldiers had crowded into the field to hear him speak, and among them was Elihu Washburne, an intimate of Lincoln and Grant who had come to visit the Federal army. Afterward Washburne shook hands with Gordon, announced his pleasure at the speech and predicted that the Federal Government would be gentle with the South.

"Why do you think so?" Gordon asked.

"Because Abraham Lincoln is at its head," Washburne said.

But the display of brotherly love was not universal. As General Grimes appeared near the surrender scene his ragged veterans cried out to him, and one voice Grimes would not forget:

"A cadaverous, ragged, barefoot man grasped me by the hand, and, choking with sobs, said, 'Goodbye, General. God bless you; we will go home, make three more crops, and then try them again.' "

Most of the Johnnies, however, neither saw nor spoke with the enemy as they left the field of surrender. Nor did they catch another sight of Lee.

The commander had his tent struck, his wagon packed, and moved from camp as quietly as it could be done, as if he did not want another glimpse of the army or its conquerors.

Three of the staff officers were with him. Major Cooke, who was sick and riding in an ambulance provided by the Federals, and Taylor and Marshall. A couple of servants completed the caravan which moved out on the poor road toward Richmond.

The enemy had offered an escort of twenty-five of the hand

some blue-clad troopers, and they were on hand, despite Lee's refusal of their company. The cavalry escort walked about him until the party was a mile or more from camp, and then turned back.

It was the cavalrymen of the Army of the Potomac who had the last glimpse of the erect figure in a blue cloak, under a wide-brimmed hat, holding his dark-maned gray horse to the road, with three or four riders about him, trailed by two clumsy wagons. Some of the enemy troopers watched for a long time, until the homely procession was out of sight beyond the greening trees.

ACKNOWLEDGEMENT

Of the many people who helped with this book, I am especially indebted to:

Colonel Margaret B. Price, of the North Carolina State Library; Brig. Gen. John R. Peacock of High Point, N.C., and other Civil War Round Table commanders; Monroe Cockrell of Evanston, Ill., and Roy Bird Cook of Charleston, W. Va., who so ably pointed out past sins.

To John Ware, a learned Civil War historian of Rome, Ga.; Hubert A. Gurney, superintendent of Appomattox Court House National Military Park, who read the chapters on Appomattox, but must bear no blame for that portion of the narrative; a certain Virginia book reviewer who suggested in a charitable review of *They Called Him Stonewall,* that Robert E. Lee, often depicted, had not yet emerged as a figure of flesh and blood;

To its editor, Robert D. Loomis, who much improved it; to the staffs of Greensboro Public Library, Guilford College, University of North Carolina, Duke University and Raleigh, North Carolina.

To Marvin Case, Zeb Case, Dick Edwards, Chalmers Heath, and J. C. Troxler, artisans; Miles Wolff and Carl Jeffress of the *Greensboro News;* and to my wife and children.

439

BIBLIOGRAPHY

General Reference Works

Battles & Leaders of The Civil War, R. U. Johnson & C. C. Buel, editors, 4 vols., 1887–88.
Confederate Military History, 12 vols., 1899.
Confederate Veteran, 40 vols., 1893–1932
Histories of The Several Regiments & Battalions from North Carolina in The Great War 1861–65, Walter Clark, editor, 5 vols., 1901.
The Land We Love, D. H. Hill, editor 1866–69.
Lee's Confidential Dispatches to Davis, D. S. Freeman, editor, 1915.
The Life of Johnny Reb, Bell I. Wiley, 1943.
Military Essays & Recollections, Military Order of the Loyal Legion of the U.S., Illinois Commandery, 1907.
The Rebellion Record: A Diary of American Events, Frank Moore, editor, 12 vols., 1862–71.
Southern Historical Society Papers, 49 vols., 1876–1944.
War of The Rebellion: A Compilation of the Official Records of the Union & Confederate Armies, War Dept., 70 vols., 1880–1901.

In addition, some issues of the following magazines were consulted: *Blackwood's, Century, Harper's, Maryland Historical Society, Scribner's, South Atlantic Quarterly.*

Special help was provided by the *R. E. Lee Papers* in the Manuscript Department, Duke University Library, and by the papers of E. P. Alexander, T. P. Devereux, James W. Albright, K. K. Chapman, and Charles S. Venable, all in the Southern Historical Collection, University of North Carolina Library.

Eye-Witness Accounts

Alexander, E. P., *Military Memoirs of a Confederate*, New York, 1907.

Anderson, Chas., *Texas Before & on the Eve of the Rebellion*, Cincinnati, 1884.

Bartlett, Napier, *A Soldier's Story of The War*, New Orleans, 1874.

Blackford, W. W., *War Years with Jeb Stuart*, New York, 1945.

Boykin, E. M., *The Falling Flag*, New York, 1874.

Buell, Augustus, *The Cannoneer*, Washington, 1890.

Casler, John O., *Four Years in the Stonewall Brigade*, Guthrie, Okla., 1893.

Chamberlain, Joshua L., *The Passing of the Armies*, New York, 1915.

Chamberlaine, W. W., *Memoirs of the Civil War*, Washington, 1912.

Chamberlayne, C. G., editor, *Ham Chamberlayne, Virginian*, Richmond, 1933.

Chesnut, Mary Boykin, *A Diary from Dixie*, New York, 1906. (An expanded edition, edited by Ben Ames Williams, is of 1949 date.)

Collins, R. M., *Chapters from the Unwritten History of the War Between The States*, St. Louis, 1893.

Cooke, Giles B., *Just Before and After Lee Surrendered to Grant*, 1922.

Cooke, John Esten, *A Life of General Robert E. Lee*, New York, 1871.

Cooke, John Esten, *Wearing of the Gray*, New York, 1867.

Dabney, R. L., *Life and Campaigns of Lt. Gen. Thomas J. Jackson*, New York, 1866.

Dame, William M., *From the Rapidan to Richmond and the Spotsylvania Campaign*, Baltimore, 1920.

Davis, Jefferson, *The Rise and Fall of the Confederate Government*, New York 1881.

Davis, Varina H., *Jefferson Davis*, New York, 1890.

De Fontaine, F. G. *Marginalia (by "Personne")*, Columbia, S. C., 1864.

De Leon, T. C., *Four Years in Rebel Capitals*, Mobile, Ala., 1890.

Douglas, Henry K., *I Rode with Stonewall*, Chapel Hill, N. C., 1940.

Early, Jubal A., *A Memoir of the Last Year of the War*, Lynchburg, Va., 1867.

Eggleston, George C., *A Rebel's Recollections*, New York, 1875.

Fremantle, A. J. L., *Three Months in the Southern States*, New York, 1864.

Fletcher, W. A., *Rebel Private, Front and Rear*, Beaumont, Tex., 1908.

Gerrish, Theodore, *Army Life*, Portland, Me., 1882.

Gill, John, *Reminiscences*, Baltimore, 1904.

Goode, John, *Recollections of a Lifetime*, Washington, 1906.

Gordon, John B., *Reminiscences*, New York, 1903.

Gorman, J. C., *Lee's Last Campaign,* Raleigh, N. C., 1865.
Goss, Warren L., *Recollections,* New York 1890.
Graham, James A., *Papers,* H. M. Wagstaff, ed., Chapel Hill, N.C., 1928.
Grant, U. S., *Personal Memoirs,* New York, 1886.
Grimes, Bryan, *Extracts of Letters of . . . to His Wife,* Raleigh, N.C., 1883.
Hamlin, P. G., *Old Bald Head (Gen. R. S. Ewell); The Portrait of a Soldier,* Strasburg, Va., 1940.
Harrison, Mrs. Burton, *Recollections Grave and Gay,* Richmond, 1911.
Haskell, Frank, *The Battle of Gettysburg,* Wisconsin History Commission, 1908.
Hoke, Jacob, *The Great Invasion of 1863,* Dayton, O., 1887.
Hood, John B., *Advance & Retreat,* New Orleans, 1880.
Howard, McHenry, *Recollections,* Baltimore, 1914.
Hunter, Alexander, *Johnny Reb and Billy Yank,* Washington, 1904.
Hunton, Eppa, *Autobiography,* Richmond, 1933.
Jackson, Mary Anna, *Memoirs of Stonewall Jackson,* Louisville, 1895.
Johnston, Joseph E., *Narrative of Military Operations,* New York, 1872.
Jones, J. B., *A Rebel War Clerk's Diary,* Philadelphia, 1866.
Keyes, E. D., *Fifty Years' Observation of Men and Events,* New York, 1884.
Lee, Fitzhugh, *Chancellorsville,* Richmond, 1879.
Lee, Fitzhugh, *General Lee,* New York, 1894.
Lee, R. E., *"To Markie," The Letters of R. E. Lee to Martha Custis Williams,* Cambridge, Mass., 1935.
Lee, R. E., Jr., *Recollections and Letters of General Robert E. Lee,* New York, 1904.
Livermore, Thomas L., *Days and Events,* Boston, 1920.
Logan, Kate V. Cox, *My Confederate Girlhood,* Richmond, 1932.
Long, A. L., *Memoirs of Robert E. Lee,* New York, 1886.
Longstreet, James, *From Manassas to Appomattox,* New York, 1898.
Lyman, Theodore, *Meade's Headquarters,* Boston, 1922.
McCarthy, Carlton, *Detailed Minutiae of Soldier Life,* Richmond, 1882.
McClellan, H. B., *The Life and Campaigns of Maj.-Gen. J. E. B. Stuart,* Richmond, 1885.
McGuire, Judith W., *Diary of a Southern Refugee,* Richmond, 1889.
McKim, R. H., *A Soldier's Recollections,* New York, 1911.
Marshall, Charles, *An Aide-de-Camp of Lee, Being the Papers of Col. Charles Marshall,* Sir Frederick Maurice, editor, Boston, 1927.
Mixson, Frank M., *Reminiscences of a Private,* Columbia, S.C., 1910.
Moore, Edward A., *The Story of a Cannoneer Under Stonewall Jackson,* New York, 1907.

Morse, Charles F., *Letters Written During the Civil War*, Boston, 1898.

Mosby, John S., *War Reminiscences*, Boston, 1887.

Myers, Frank M., *The Comanches: A History of White's Battalion, Virginia Cavalry*, Baltimore, 1871.

Nicolay, John G., and Hay, John, *Abraham Lincoln, A History*, New York, 1890.

Norton, Oliver, *Army Letters*, Chicago, 1903.

Oates, William C., *The War Between the Union and the Confederacy*, Washington, 1905.

Owen, William M., *In Camp and Battle With the Washington Artillery of New Orleans*, Boston, 1885.

Peyton, John L., *The American Crisis*, London, 1867.

Pickett, George E., *The Heart of a Soldier, as Revealed in the Intimate Letters of General George E. Pickett*, New York, 1913.

Polley, J. B., *Hood's Texas Brigade*, New York, 1910; and *A Soldier's Letters to Charming Nellie*, New York, 1908.

Porter, Horace, *Campaigning with Grant*, New York, 1897.

Pryor, Mrs. Roger A., *Reminiscences of Peace and War*, New York, 1904.

Quintard, Charles T., *Dr. Quintard, Chaplain C.S.A. and Second Bishop of Tennessee*, A. H. Noll, editor, Sewanee, Tenn., 1905.

Reagan, John H., *Memoirs*, New York, 1906.

Russell, Wm. Howard, *My Diary North and South*, London, 1863.

Scales, Alfred M., *The Battle of Fredericksburg*, Washington, 1884.

Scheibert, Justus, *Der Burgerkrieg in dem Nordamerikanischen Staaten*, Berlin, 1874.

Sorrel, G. Moxley, *Recollections of a Confederate Staff Officer*, Washington, 1917.

Stiles, Robert *Four Years Under Marse Robert*, Washington, 1903.

Taylor, Richard, *Destruction and Reconstruction*, New York, 1879.

Taylor, Walter H., *Four Years with General Lee*, New York, 1877.

Townsend, E. D., *Anecdotes of the Civil War*, New York, 1884.

Townsend, G. A., *Rustics in Rebellion*, Chapel Hill, N.C., 1950.

de Trobriand, Regis, *Four Years with the Army of the Potomac*, Boston, 1889.

von Borcke, Heros, *Memoirs of The Confederate War for Independence*, London, 1866.

Welch, S. G., *A Confederate Surgeon's Letters to His Wife*, Washington, 1911.

Wise, John S., *The End of an Era*, Boston, 1899.

Worsham, John H., *One of Jackson's Foot Cavalry*, New York, 1912.

Biographies and Other Studies
R. E. Lee

Bradford, Gamaliel, *Lee The American,* Boston, 1912.
Brooks, W. E., *Lee of Virginia,* Indianapolis, 1932.
Freeman, D.S., *R. E. Lee,* New York, 1935.
Jones, J. William, *Personal Reminiscences, Anecdotes and Letters of Robert E. Lee,* New York, 1874; and, *Life and Letters of Robert Edward Lee,* Washington, 1906.
Mason, Emily V., *Popular Life of General Robert Edward Lee,* Baltimore, 1872.
Maurice, Sir Frederick, *Robert E. Lee, the Soldier,* Boston, 1925.
McCabe, James D., Jr., *Life and Campaigns of General Robert E. Lee,* New York, 1866.
Page, Thomas Nelson, *Robert E. Lee, Man and Soldier,* New York, 1911.
White, Henry A., *Robert E. Lee and the Southern Confederacy,* New York, 1897.
Winston, Robert W., *Robert E. Lee . . .* New York, 1934.
Young, James C., *Marse Robert, Knight of the Confederacy,* New York, 1929.

Other Biography

Cook, Roy Bird, *Family and Early Life of Stonewall Jackson,* Charleston, W. Va., 1948.
Davis, Burke, *They Called Him Stonewall,* New York, 1954.
Freeman, D. S., *Lee's Lieutenants,* New York, 1944.
Henderson, G. F. R., *Stonewall Jackson and the American Civil War,* London, New York, 1898.
Hughes, Robert M., *General [Joseph E.] Johnston,* New York, 1893.
Hunter, Martha T., *A Memoir of R. M. T. Hunter,* Washington, 1903.
Roman, Alfred, *Military Operations of General Beauregard,* New York, 1884.
Thomason, John W., Jr., *Jeb Stuart,* New York, 1930.
Williams, T. Harry, *Beauregard,* Baton Rouge, La., 1955.
McElroy, Robert, *Jefferson Davis: The Unreal and the Real,* New York, 1937.

Additional Sources

Catton, Bruce, *A Stillness at Appomattox,* New York, 1953.
Miller, Francis T., editor, *Photographic History of the Civil War,* New York, 1911.
Swinton, William, *Campaigns of the Army of the Potomac,* New York, 1874.
Wise, Jennings C., *The Long Arm of Lee,* Lynchburg, Va., 1915.

NOTES

Chapter One

[1] Lee, R. E., Jr. *Recollection & Letters of General R. E. Lee,* p. 4.

[2] Bryan, Thomas B., *Military Essays & Recollections,* pp. 3, 14. (Illinois Commandery, Military Order, Loyal Legion of U.S.)

[3] July 2, 1859, cited in Jones, J. Wm., *Life & Letters of General R. E. Lee,* p. 102.

[4] Lee's departure from Texas is sketched by Johnson, R. W., in *A Soldier's Recollections in Peace & War,* pp. 132–33; and Darrow, Caroline, in *Battles & Leaders of the Civil War,* Vol. 1, p. 33. Johnson's formal verbiage has here been slightly altered.

[5] Probably to Custis, Jan. 23, 1861, from Jones, J. Wm. (*Life & Letters . . .*), pp. 120–1.

[6] Cited by Freeman, D. S., in *R. E. Lee,* Vol. 1, p. 108, from the T. M. R. Talcott manuscripts.

[7] Lee's meeting of the crisis of his life comes from his letter to Reverdy Johnson cited in Lee, R. E. Jr., p. 27; Simon Cameron's statement in Jones, J. Wm., *Life and Letters,* p. 130; Mason, Emily, *Popular Life of R. E. Lee,* p. 73; Townsend, E. D., *Anecdotes of the Civil War,* p. 29; Blair, Montgomery, in *National Intelligencer,* Aug. 9, 1866.

[8] Mosby, John S., *Memoirs,* p. 379.

[9] Jones, J. Wm., *Life and Letters,* p. 133, on authority of Mrs. Lee.

[10] *South Atlantic Quarterly,* July 1905, p. 235.

Chapter Two

[1] Mosby, John S., *Memoirs,* p. 379.

[2] From the *Journal of the Virginia Convention of 1861,* pp. 186–8; both Janney's speech and Lee's reply are from this source.

[3] Stephens, A. H., *A Constitutional View of The War Between the States,* Vol. 2, p. 385.

[4] Lee's foresight in concentrating at Manassas is amply documented in the *Official Records*, especially O.R. Vol. 2, pp. 806, 817, 819, 821, 824.

[5] Russell, W. H., *My Diary North & South*, Vol. 1, p. 252.

[6] Chesnut, Mary Boykin, *A Diary from Dixie*, p. 119.

[7] *Official Records*, Vol. 2, p. 986; the *Official Records* supply myriad details on Confederate handling of the first big battle, and reveal Lee's share in the planning.

[8] Roman, Alfred, *Military Operations of General Beauregard*, Vol. 1, pp. 121–2.

Chapter Three

[1] Difficulties of the Western Virginia campaign are sketched in Taylor, *Four Years with General Lee;* and Long, *Memoirs of General Robert E. Lee.* Long, in particular, makes implicit Lee's failure to discipline the first of his defiant subordinates.

[2] Lack of defined authority was a chief reason for Lee's failure in the campaign. It is probable that President Davis did not realize the handicap imposed on Lee. In addition to Lee's evident modesty in asserting his authority, he lacked the trappings, in particular a staff; thus he made desperate efforts to perform chores in the field, such as the gathering of intelligence.

[3] Wise, John S., *End of An Era*, pp. 333–4.

[4] *Confederate Veteran*, Vol. 14, p. 521.

[5] Details of the singular battle plan involving Rust are from: Long (Memoirs), pp. 122–4; Taylor's *Four Years*, pp. 23–8; and Fitz Lee's *General Lee*, pp. 119–21.

[6] *Official Records*, Vol. 5, p. 192. This order stands as the most high-flown to appear over Lee's name; later ones, written by Col. Charles Marshall, were often rhetorical, but occasionally approached true eloquence.

[7] Worsham, John H., *One of Jackson's Foot Cavalry*, pp. 44–5.

[8] Buist, Dr. J. R., in the *National Intelligencer*, Nov. 22, 1861.

[9] *Richmond Dispatch*, Sept. 26, 1861.

[10] Biographers can only guess when the gray beard appeared on the familiar face of Lee. The only record known is Lee's letter of Nov. 15, 1861, to his daughter Mildred, mentioning that Rob commented on the beard on Oct. 30. Dr. Freeman sets the date as Oct. 20, but there is an error somewhere; Lee met Rob in Charlottesville Oct. 30.

[11] The basic accounts of Traveller's origin and Lee's first acquaintance with him are in Broun, Thomas L., *Southern Historical Society Papers*, Vol. 35, pp. 99–100; and LaBree, *Campfires of the Confederacy*, pp. 307 ff. A thorough review is in Freeman, *R. E. Lee*, Vol. 1, Appendix 1–5.

[12] Morton, Captain, in *Southern Historical Society Papers*, Vol. 11, p. 518.

[13] From an address by Davis in Richmond, Nov. 3, 1870.

[14] Davis, *The Rise & Fall of The Confederate Government*, Vol. 1, p. 309.

[15] Long, pp. 134–6, gives a full account of the Charleston fire and Lee's part in it.

Chapter Four

[1] Bill, A. H., *The Beleaguered City*, pp. 100 ff.

[2] Frequent references in *Official Records* attest to Davis' defense of his authority here. Some contemporaries took note of the struggle, as the *Richmond Whig:* "The President never for a moment relinquished his rights as commander-in-chief. . . . This earth holds not the human being more jealous of his constitutional rights than Mr. Davis."

[3] Mrs. Chesnut, who reported this gossip, while not always the most accurate reporter on the Richmond scene, was usually the brightest, and her faithful noting of sights and sounds made a valuable record. Chesnut, *A Diary from Dixie*, p. 175, 1949 edition.

[4] Johnston, Davis, Smith and Longstreet left accounts of this council of war.

[5] A documentation of this tempest of the high command is in *Official Records*, especially Vol. 11, part 3, pp. 499–503.

[6] This opening battle account by the fire-eating Gordon is one of a series by a man who was in the midst of the most severe fights of the Army of Northern Virginia; he is not always accurate, and reveals partisanship.

[7] This reconstruction is by Freeman, D. S., in *R. E. Lee*, Vol. 2, p. 74.

[8] *Lee's Confidential Dispatches to Davis*, D. S. Freeman, ed., pp. 6–7.

[9] Alexander, E. P., *Military Memoirs of a Confederate*, pp. 110–11.

[10] Davis, Vol. 2, p. 132.

[11] Longstreet, p. 119.

Chapter Five

[1] Chesnut, *A Diary* . . . p. 170.

[2] Stiles, Robert, *Four Years with Marse Robert*, pp. 80, 114. This sprightly book abounds with unexpected details of life in war.

[3] Taylor, Richard, *Destruction & Reconstruction*, p. 86.

[4] Harrison, Constance Cary, *Battles & Leaders*, Vol. 2, pp. 446–8.

[5] Cooke, J. E., *Life of General R. E. Lee*, p. 84.

[6] Hood, John B., *Advance & Retreat*, p. 28.

[7] After an account by Jones, J. William, *Southern Historical Society Papers*, Vol. 14, pp. 451–2.

[8] Alexander, E. P., *Memoirs*, 150. Full accounts of Jackson's behavior of this day are in Freeman, D. S., *R. E. Lee*, Vol. 2, Appen. 2–3; and in Davis, B., *They Called Him Stonewall*, pp. 234 ff.

[9] Hill, D. H. in *Battles & Leaders*, Vol. 2, p. 391; this is from a full account of battle action and incidents involving the general staff.

[10] Goode, John, *Recollections of a Lifetime*, p. 58.

[11] Lamb, Captain, in *Southern Historical Society Papers*, Vol. 25, p. 217; this was expanded in a later conversation with D. S. Freeman, the late Lee biographer noted.

¹² This striking scene is reconstructed from the account of Davis, Vol. 2, pp. 149–50 of his *Rise & Fall of The Confederate Government,* and from reminiscences of members of Jackson's staff, especially Dr. Hunter McGuire and Major R. L. Dabney.

Chapter Six

¹ Boteler, a unique figure of the war, told this story in detail in *Southern Historical Society Papers,* Vol. 40, pp. 180–1.

² The feud is dealt with in *Official Records,* and in Sorrel, *Recollections of A Confederate Staff Officer,* pp. 88–9.

³ *Lee's Dispatches,* p. 48; Lee gave a full, concise picture of the strategic situation in the body of this dispatch.

⁴ Longstreet, pp. 161–2.

⁵ Aug. 17, 1862; cited in Fitzhugh Lee, pp. 181–2.

⁶ Lee at the peak of his powers of observation and analysis is revealed in the myriad references to the planning and development of this campaign in *Official Records,* Vol. 12, part 3, pp. 544–965.

⁷ Dabney, R. L., *Life & Campaigns of General T. J. Jackson,* p. 517.

⁸ Chamberlayne, Ham, in Moore's *Rebellion Record,* Vol. 5, p. 404.

⁹ Lee, R. E. Jr., pp. 76–7.

¹⁰ A brief quotation from the account of D. H. Strother, in *Harper's,* Vol. 35, 1867, pp. 713 ff.

¹¹ Lee, G. T., in *South Atlantic Quarterly,* July, 1927, pp. 247–8.

¹² Longstreet, p. 192.

¹³ *Lee's Dispatches,* pp. 59–60.

¹⁴ *Marginalia,* by "Personne," pp. 86–7.

Chapter Seven

¹ Alexander, p. 223.

² Sept. 3, 1862; *Official Records,* Vol. 19, part 2, p. 391.

³ Parks, Leighton, *Century Magazine,* Vol. 70, No. 2, p. 258 ff.

⁴ *Official Records,* Vol. 19, part 2, pp. 601–2.

⁵ Longstreet, pp. 201–2; these two incidents are revealing not only of the unfolding campaign, but of Longstreet's highly partisan view of his role and that of Lee.

⁶ Walker, in *Battles & Leaders,* Vol. 2, pp. 605–6.

⁷ This incident, now a part of military legend, is related in Long, p. 264; Taylor, p. 67; D. H. Hill, Vol. 2, pp. 345–6; colorful detail is added in Longstreet, p. 213. Federal accounts are also numerous.

⁸ Polley, J. B., *Hood's Texas Brigade,* p. 114. Hood wrote of the following incident in his *Advance & Retreat,* p. 39.

⁹ Walker, *Battles & Leaders,* Vol. 2, p. 675.

¹⁰ Moore's *Rebellion Record,* Vol. 5, pp. 447–8.

11 Clark's *N.C. Regiments*, pp. 433–4; Longstreet's version is in *Battles & Leaders*, Vol. 2, pp. 669–70.

12 Thompson, David, in *Battles & Leaders*, Vol. 2, p. 661.

13 Williams, Capt. A. B., in Clark's *N.C. Regiments*, Vol. 1, p. 575.

14 This was General Stephen D. Lee, in speeches and articles during his later years. His version has often been published by historians, but was rejected by the well-informed D. S. Freeman.

Chapter Eight

1 Wolseley, Col. Garnet, future commander of the British Army, in *Blackwood's Magazine*, XCLLL, pp. 18, 20–21.

2 Taylor, Walter, p. 76.

3 Longstreet, in *Battles & Leaders*, Vol. 3, p. 70.

4 Cooke, John E., *Life of Gen. Robert E. Lee*, p. 177.

5 This Jackson-Longstreet exchange, by Smith, *Southern Historical Society Papers*, Vol. 5, p. 30, and in Sorrel, p. 138.

6 A minor controversy over Lee's companion in this conversation results from J. E. Cooke's report in *Life of Lee*, p. 184, that Lee spoke to Longstreet; and from Gen. Pendleton, who says Lee spoke to him, in an account in *Southern Magazine*, XV, 1874, pp. 620–1.

7 *Extracts of Letters of Major-General Bryan Grimes to His Wife*, p. 27.

8 The saga of Lee's headquarters hen may be found in Long, pp. 241–2.

9 A full account of this dinner and Jackson's Moss Neck headquarters is in *Southern Historical Society Papers*, Vol. 5, p. 37 ff.; see also *They Called Him Stonewall*, pp. 383 ff.

10 *Official Records*, Vol. 21, p. 550.

Chapter Nine

1 Smith, James P., *Richmond Times-Dispatch*, Jan. 20, 1907.

2 Bill, A. H., *The Beleaguered City*, pp. 151 ff., gives a full picture of Richmond at this period.

3 Swinton, Wm., *Campaigns of the Army of the Potomac*, pp. 259–60.

4 Welch, S. G., *A Confederate Surgeon's Letters to his Wife*, p. 47.

5 *Official Records*, Vol. 25, part 2, p. 687.

6 Smith, James P., in *Battles & Leaders*, Vol. 3, p. 203.

7 Stiles, pp. 168–9.

8 The major sources on this important Lee-Jackson collaboration: Talcott, T. M. R., in *Southern Historical Society Papers*, Vol. 34, pp. 12 ff.; Smith, J. P., *Battles & Leaders*, Vol. 3, pp. 204–5.

9 *Official Records*, Vol. 25, part 2, p. 765.

10 McGuire, Dr. Hunter, "Stonewall Jackson, an Address," in *The Confederate Cause and Conduct in The War Between The States*, H. H. McGuire & Geo. L. Christian.

[11] Lee, Fitz., *Chancellorsville*, p. 320.

[12] One of the best narratives by a Federal participant at Chancellorsville, richly detailed, is this by Pleasanton, in *Battles & Leaders*, Vol. 3, pp. 172 ff.

[13] Scenes of Lee talking with both Wilbourn and Hotchkiss are in Cooke's *Life of Lee*, pp. 238–9, and *Southern Historical Society Papers*, Vol. 8, pp. 230 ff.

[14] Marshall, Charles, *An Aide-de-Camp of Lee*, pp. 173–4.

[15] *Confederate Military History*, Vol. 3, p. 392.

[16] *Official Records*, Vol. 25, part 2, pp. 782–3.

[17] Dabney, p. 725.

Chapter Ten

[1] McKim, R. H., *A Soldier's Recollections*, p. 134.

[2] Maury, D. H., *Recollections of A Virginian*, p. 239.

[3] *Official Records*, Vol. 27, part 3, p. 882.

[4] Stiles, p. 192.

[5] *Official Records*, Vol. 27, part 3, p. 913, 923.

[6] *Official Records*, Vol. 27, part 3, p. 931.

[7] *Marginalia*, by "Personne," p. 21.

[8] Hoke, Jacob, *The Great Invasion of 1863*, p. 63.

[9] Hood, p. 55.

[10] Longstreet, p. 383, note.

[11] *Southern Historical Society Papers*, Vol. 4, pp. 158–9.

[12] *Battles & Leaders*, Vol. 3, pp. 339–40; also Longstreet, 358–9.

[13] The revealing arbor scene was drawn by Early, *Southern Historical Society Papers*, Vol. 4, pp. 271–4.

[14] Long, p. 281.

[15] Longstreet, p. 384.

[16] Wise, John S., *The End of an Era*, pp. 338–9.

[17] *Heart of a Soldier*, George Pickett's Letters, pp. 94–6. Pickett's whereabouts during the famed charge are still warmly debated by historians, but D. S. Freeman concluded he was in his proper place with his command. A persistent dissenter to the Freeman theory is Monroe Cockrell of Evanston, Ill., who cites 110 sources on Pickett's whereabouts this afternoon, and concludes he was well to the rear.

[18] *Rebellion Record*, Vol. 7, p. 114.

[19] *Blackwood's Edinburgh Magazine*, XCIV, pp. 380–2, has Fremantle's well-known account.

Chapter Eleven

[1] Owen, Wm., *In Camp & Battle With the Washington Artillery*, p. 256.

[2] Long, p. 242, note.

[3] Imboden's journey from Gettysburg and the story of the river crossing is in *Battles & Leaders*, Vol. 3, pp. 428–9.

4 *Official Records,* Vol. 27, part 2, p. 300.

5 Venable's story is in Long, p. 301.

6 *Official Records,* Vol. 27, part 3, p. 1075; the fading of Pickett's star may be traced from his complaint to Lee, courteously answered by the commander.

7 This famous exchange is in *Official Records,* Vol. 51, part 2, pp. 752-3; and Vol. 29, part 2, p. 640.

8 Long, pp. 309-10.

9 *N.C. Regiments,* Vol. 2, p. 440.

10 Lee, Fitz., p. 319.

11 *Marginalia,* p. 233.

12 *Southern Historical Society Papers,* Vol. 4, p. 160.

13 Taylor, Walter, p. 120.

14 *Battles & Leaders,* Vol. 4, p. 240.

15 This series of observations by Mrs. Chesnut is in the 1906 edition of her *Diary,* pp. 281, 284, 292, 299; and in the 1949 edition, edited by Ben Ames Williams, pp. 366-7.

16 This rather surprising note is in the new edition of Mrs. Chesnut's *Diary;* though, as usual, she gives it the ring of truth, Mrs. Chesnut was not infallible, and may have garbled this incident.

17 *Official Records,* Vol. 33, p. 1244.

18 *N.C. Regiments,* Vol. 2, p. 399.

Chapter Twelve

1 This glimpse of Lee is from Mixson, F. M., *Reminiscences of a Private,* p. 65.

2 Signals opening the Wilderness Campaign are described in *Confederate Veteran,* Vol. 21, p. 68, and in *Battles & Leaders,* Vol. 4, p. 118.

3 *Official Records,* Vol. 36, part 2, p. 948.

4 McClellan, H. B. manuscript, Confederate Memorial Institute; cited by D. S. Freeman, *R. E. Lee,* Vol. 3, p. 284.

5 By "R. C. —— of Hood's Texas Brigade," in *Land We Love,* Vol. 5, p. 485; other literature on the incident is plentiful.

6 Oates, Wm. C., pp. 343-4.

7 The story of Longstreet's wound is a composite, chiefly from: Longstreet, pp. 563, 566; Sorrel, p. 238; Stiles, pp. 246-7.

8 For Lee's musings on the change of command, see Sorrel, pp. 242-3.

9 Details of this impressive demonstration of Lee's military intuition are in Gordon, pp. 267-9.

10 *N.C. Regiments,* Vol. 2, p. 383, by Asst. Surgeon Geo. C. Underwood.

11 *Lee's Dispatches,* p. 176.

12 Long, p. 239.

13 *Southern Historical Society Papers,* Vol. 31, p. 200; also, Gordon, p. 278.

14 Capt. Gordon McCabe to R. E. Lee, Jr., in *R. E. Lee, Jr.,* p. 124.

15 *N.C. Regiments,* Vol. 2, p. 384.

16 *Official Records,* Vol. 36, part 3, p. 800.

Chapter Thirteen

[1] The mathematician is Bruce Catton, in *A Stillness at Appomattox*; the Wilderness casualty figures are drawn from Colonel Venable, *Battles & Leaders*, Vol. 4, pp. 243-4, and Alexander, p. 529.

[2] For a detailed analysis of this line, see D. S. Freeman, *R. E. Lee*, Vol. 3, p. 356.

[3] *Confederate Military History*, Vol. 13, p. 460, an account by Jed Hotchkiss, Jackson's former map-maker.

[4] The picture of Lee in this illness is given by Venable, *Southern Historical Society Papers*, Vol. 14, p. 535, and Cooke, p. 404. Additional details are cited by Freeman from the McClellan mss.

[5] This exchange, including a facsimile of one dispatch, is in *Battles & Leaders*, Vol. 4, pp. 244-5.

[6] Long, p. 347.

[7] Reagan, J. H., *Memoirs*, pp. 192-3.

[8] Truce details are in *Official Records*, Vol. 36, part 1, pp. 1033-4; same volume, part 2, p. 984; same volume, part 3, pp. 638-39.

[9] *Official Records*, Vol. 36, part 1, pp. 22-5.

[10] Roman, Alfred, *Military Operations of General Beauregard*, Vol. 2, pp. 579 ff.

[11] Beauregard in *Battles & Leaders*, Vol. 4, pp. 540 ff.

[12] *Official Records*, Vol. 40, part 2, p. 664.

[13] Roman, Vol. 2, pp. 576-7.

[14] Jones, J. Wm., *Personal Reminiscences*, p. 44.

Chapter Fourteen

[1] Details of Richmond life from Bill, A. H., *Beleaguered City*, pp. 220 ff.

[2] Long, p. 387.

[3] Wise, John, p. 325.

[4] Best Federal sources on the Crater are *Battles & Leaders*, Vol. 4, pp. 545 ff.; and de Trobriand, Regis, *Four Years With The Army of the Potomac*, pp. 608 ff.

[5] Slaughter of Negro troops as seen by Wise, John, p. 366.

[6] *The Beleaguered City*, pp. 236 ff.

[7] Long, p. 388.

[8] Taylor, Walter, p. 145, note.

[9] *Official Records*, Vol. 42, part 3, p. 1134.

[10] Taylor's diary is an invaluable, if sketchy, account of the siege.

[11] Gordon, p. 383.

[12] Lee, G. T., in *South Atlantic Quarterly*, July, 1927, pp. 236-7.

[13] *Official Records*, Vol. 46, part 2, p. 825.

Chapter Fifteen

[1] This and other details of this singular occasion from Wise, John, pp. 400 ff.

[2] Gordon, pp. 385 ff. General Gordon was an old man when he wrote, and had a taste for melodrama, but was probably close to fact here.

[3] *Southern Historical Society Papers,* Vol. 4, pp. 308–9.

[4] Davis, Jefferson, Vol. 2, p. 551.

[5] The story of the attack on Fort Stedman is based on Gordon, pp. 393 ff.

[6] Walker, C. Irvine, *The Life of Lt. Gen. Richard Heron Anderson,* pp. 225 ff.

[7] Details of the Hill death scene are in *Southern Historical Society Papers,* Vol. 11, pp. 564 ff.

[8] These two quotations from Long, p. 410.

[9] Wise, John, pp. 414–5.

[10] Logan, Kate Cox, *My Confederate Girlhood,* pp. 70–1.

Chapter Sixteen

[1] This spy story, often retold, is in Gordon, pp. 425–7.

[2] *Southern Historical Society Papers,* Vol. 25, pp. 110–11.

[3] Mahone's story is in Longstreet, pp. 614–5.

[4] Cooke, J. E., *Wearing of The Gray,* p. 596.

[5] Gordon, pp. 430–1; also for description of the army's march, pp. 423–4.

[6] This highly colorful account, not always accepted at full value, is in Wise, John, pp. 428 ff.

[7] Longstreet, p. 618.

[8] *South Atlantic Quarterly,* July, 1927, p. 238.

[9] Long, p. 415.

[10] *E. P. Alexander Papers,* So. Historical Col., Univ. of N.C. Library; this version, with its vivid detail, was eliminated in Alexander's published work.

[11] *Southern Historical Society Papers,* Vol. 20, pp. 58–9.

[12] Longstreet, p. 620.

[13] Lee, Susan P., *Memoirs of Wm. Nelson Pendleton,* p. 402; slight alterations here from Pendleton's rhetoric.

[14] Venable's version, derived from a letter of 1894 to Walter Taylor, cited by D. S. Freeman, *R. E. Lee,* Vol. 4, p. 112.

[15] Some evident inaccuracies in Gordon's account, chiefly in detail, are not examined here.

Chapter Seventeen

[1] Details of the narrative here are from *An Aide-de-Camp of Lee, The Papers of Charles Marshall,* pp. 259–60; time of moonrise by G. M. Clemence, Dir. Nautical Almanac, U.S. Naval Observatory.

[2] Grimes' story in *Southern Historical Society Papers,* Vol. 27, pp. 93 ff.; Devereux' in *T. P. Devereux Papers,* Univ. of N. C. Library.

[3] All this exchange, in Long, pp. 421–2, is corroborated by others, especially Gordon, p. 437.

[4] Longstreet, pp. 624–5.

[5] *E. P. Alexander Papers,* Univ. of N. C. Library.

[6] Details of Lee's movements of this morning from: Taylor, Walter, pp. 151–2; *An Aide-de-Camp of Lee,* p. 262; *E. P. Alexander Papers.*

[7] The biographer was D. S. Freeman in *R. E. Lee,* Vol. 4, p. 127.

[8] The story of these two hours is told in the memoirs of Taylor, Marshall, Longstreet.

[9] Gordon, pp. 438–41.

[10] Blackford, W. W., *War Years With Jeb Stuart,* pp. 290, 291.

[11] Longstreet, p. 627.

[12] Grant, U. S., *Memoirs,* p. 483.

[13] Porter, Horace in *Battles & Leaders,* Vol. 4, pp. 731–3.

[14] *An Aide-de-Camp of Lee,* p. 269.

[15] This account of the surrender, one of the most famous scenes of American history, rests almost entirely on accounts by Marshall and Porter, with an effort to speed narrative flow, yet make clear eye-witness testimony.

[16] This touching glimpse of Lee in the saddest moments of his life is from Forsyth, George, in *Harper's Magazine,* April, 1896, pp. 708–10.

Chapter Eighteen

[1] The account of the writing of Lee's farewell address rests on sketchy accounts by Marshall and that of Colston in *Southern Historical Society Papers,* Vol. 38, pp. 12–3.

[2] Grant, p. 497.

[3] Longstreet, p. 630.

[4] *Norfolk Virginian-Pilot,* May 21, 1951; documents seem to bear out Bell's claim.

[5] Lyman, Theodore, *Meade's Headquarters, 1863–65,* pp. 359 ff.

[6] Field's account is in *Southern Historical Society Papers,* Vol. 14, p. 562.

[7] Mixson, F. M., *Reminiscences of A Private,* p. 120.

[8] Taylor, Walter, p. 154.

[9] Cooke in *Richmond News-Leader,* Jan. 19, 1923.

[10] *T. P. Devereux Papers,* Univ. of N. C. Library.

[11] Chamberlain, Joshua, *The Passing of The Armies,* pp. 258–65.

[12] *N.C. Regiments,* Vol. 5, p. 264.

INDEX

457